Beginning Android

Fifth Edition

Grant Allen

apress®

Beginning Android

ISBN-13 (pbk): 978-1-4302-4686-2

ISBN-13 (electronic): 978-1-4302-4687-9

Managing Director: Welmoed Spahr
Lead Editor: Jonathan Gennick
Technical Reviewer: Jon Westfall
Editorial Board: Steve Anglin, Louise Corrigan, Jim DeWolf, Jonathan Gennick, Robert Hutchinson, Michelle Lowman, James Markham, Susan McDermott, Matthew Moodie, Jeffrey Pepper, Douglas Pundick, Ben Renow-Clarke, Gwenan Spearing
Coordinating Editor: Jill Balzano
Copy Editor: Rebecca Rider
Compositor: SPi Global
Indexer: SPi Global
Artist: SPi Global

Distributed to the book trade worldwide by Springer Science+Business Media New York, 233 Spring Street, 6th Floor, New York, NY 10013. Phone 1-800-SPRINGER, fax (201) 348-4505, e-mail orders-ny@springer-sbm.com, or visit www.springer.com. Apress Media, LLC is a California LLC and the sole member (owner) is Springer Science + Business Media Finance Inc (SSBM Finance Inc). SSBM Finance Inc is a Delaware corporation.

For information on translations, please e-mail rights@apress.com, or visit www.apress.com.

Apress and friends of ED books may be purchased in bulk for academic, corporate, or promotional use. eBook versions and licenses are also available for most titles. For more information, reference our Special Bulk Sales–eBook Licensing web page at www.apress.com/bulk-sales.

Any source code or other supplementary material referenced by the author in this text is available to readers at www.apress.com. For detailed information about how to locate your book's source code, go to www.apress.com/source-code/.

To all the future Android developers out there.

Contents at a Glance

Contents

About the Author

Grant Allen has worked in the information technology field for over 20 years as a chief technology officer, entrepreneur, enterprise architect, and data management expert. Grant's roles have taken him around the world, specializing in global-scale systems design, together with mentoring and coaching startups and hi-tech companies like Google on building great teams and great technology. He is a frequent speaker on topics such as big data, mobile ecosystems, Android, wearables, the Internet of Things, disruptive innovation, and more. Grant has a PhD in building innovative high-technology environments and is the author of six books on mobile development with Android and data management. You can learn more about all his work at www.grantxallen.com.

About the Technical Reviewer

Jon Westfall, PhD, is an assistant professor of psychology, researcher, programmer, and speaker. He has worked as a consultant since 1997, founding his own firm, Bug Jr. Systems. As a consultant he has developed custom software solutions (including native Windows 32 applications, Windows .NET applications, Windows Phone 7 and Android mobile applications, as well as ASP, ASP.NET, and PHP web applications). He has also served as a senior network and systems architect and administrator (on both Windows and Unix networks, and hybrids) and has also been recognized as a Microsoft Most Valuable Professional (MVP) 2008–2012. He has authored several books and presented at academic as well as technology conferences and gatherings. He can be found writing on his blog at JonWestfall.com, and on twitter @jonwestfall.

Acknowledgments

I'd like to thank all the great folks at Apress for helping get this newest edition of *Beginning Android* into the hands of you, the reader. In particular, Jonathan Gennick and Jill Balzano have been an amazing support team, encouraging, cajoling, and pushing me along the way.

I will also take this opportunity to thank all those Android developers who have encouraged me at countless conferences and events around the world. It is great to hear how books like *Beginning Android* help budding developers get started.

Introduction

Welcome to *Beginning Android, Fifth Edition*. In this fifth edition, I have completely rewritten the book and have taken stock of all the great changes that have happened to the Android platform with the releases of version 5.0 Lollipop and version 6.0 Marshmallow.

Tackling the latest and greatest aspects of Android will become second nature once you explore this book, but more importantly, you will also have a rock-solid foundation into the fundamentals of Android that span all its versions. You will explore and learn about activities, fragments, all of the user interface and user experience elements, services, data management, web services, and many, many more building blocks for your Android applications.

The best judge of this book's value is the great applications you can create from the knowledge with which it provides you. I look forward to trying all of the great applications that will flow from the knowledge you take from this book. You can explore more about the book itself at the website, `www.beginningandroid.org` (that's `.org`, not `.com`), and contact me via that site or my personal site at `www.grantxallen.com`.

All the best with your Android development!

—Grant Allen

November 2015

Get Android and Get Coding!

Welcome to Android

I would like to welcome you to this book, *Beginning Android, 5th Edition*. This is a new edition of the book, but I'm sure this is not the first time you have encountered Android—either by using one of the billion or more Android devices currently activated throughout the world, or by hearing about it from friends, colleagues, or the media. It is hard to escape Android; not only is it the world's most prevalent mobile device operating system, but it keeps growing. Google reports that it sees more than one million Android devices activated every day.

If the growth doesn't excite you, then the diversity of Android devices should. We all know Android was developed for phones, and later, for tablets. But did you know that it now powers everything from inflight entertainment systems, to TVs, headsets, glasses, watches, shoes, games consoles, and even a brand of Japanese toilet? As Android grows, so does people's need for great applications they use on their devices. And that is where this book helps. As a new Android developer, it will be natural for you to use this book in conjunction with online searches, and I encourage you to do that. Be aware, however, that because Android has rapidly changed over the last eight years, the material you find online can be of varying quality and applicability. Sites like Stack Overflow are excellent resources, but it's prudent to check for what version of Android (or in what year) their content was written.

The Fast Path to Learning Android Development

Given the plethora of devices, you might be left wondering where to start. Too many choices can lead to indecision, and I want to get you, the reader, working with Android as quickly as possible. To help you make a rapid start, this book largely focuses on the original and most common device type on which Android runs: the smartphone. I extend that to also include tablets, since they have matured to be mainstream devices and the line is blurred between phones and tablets in any case—thus the current "Phablet" trend.

This focus on phones helps you in lots of ways right from the start. You will be learning skills and approaches for the largest device market in history, so your applications will have the biggest possible audience. And you will also be learning the largest, richest, and most mature parts of Android development. Don't worry, though! I also cover the leading edge of Android later in the book, so you can also start mastering topics like Google Glass and Android Wear.

Thinking in a Smartphone Mindset

As a reader of this book, you might well be new to Android development, but your background as a developer in other areas, your technology expertise, and your know-how is harder to predict. Before we delve into your first look at Android code and the building blocks of an Android device, it is useful to start with some understanding of the fundamentals common to all Android development on smartphones and tablets.

Computing on the Go!

The first, and most obvious, point to make about thinking like an Android developer is that Android devices may have their roots in mobile phones, but today, actually making and receiving phone calls is only a minor part of their popularity and pervasiveness. You should think of the billion or more Android devices in circulation as little engines of mobile computing that just happen to be able to make phone calls as one of their many capabilities. They are literally mobile computers!

Size Matters

In developing for Android, you are dealing with screens of many sizes, but one thing in common for the vast, vast majority of mobile Android devices is that you are working with small screens or displays. Although you may develop for Android with the comfort of a full-sized desktop on a modern notebook computer, your target audience, at the extreme, will have only a square inch or so of display real estate on which to enjoy your development efforts.

The Interface Is More Than the Screen

Modern smartphones are more than just a screen for viewing text and other content. Phones make calls, play music, vibrate and provide haptic feedback for games, sense the temperature, report direction and location, and much more. When you think of the way in which your users might interact with your applications, think beyond the simple visual screen. A phone interacts with multiple senses, and you should design with all of them in mind.

You Are Not Alone

Yours will not be the only application running on someone's Android device. In fact, they may not just have other applications, but other applications that can do similar—or even the same—work as your own. Be mindful that you cannot hog all of the device and all of its features. Also keep in mind that for your users, it is two simple taps of a finger for them to switch to another application.

In later chapters, I also cover how resources and capabilities are shared and managed across an Android device, and how being aware that your application can be interrupted at any time is one of the key use cases you need to consider when developing Android applications.

Translating Developer Dreams into Android Action

Now that you know how to think about developing for Android, you might also be thinking that it sounds like a lot of compromises, and is that all there is to it? The good news is that by taking care of a bunch of heavy lifting for you and by providing you with an amazing array of support, tools, and the foundation on which to build applications of all sorts, Android lets you focus on the essentials of mobile development.

First, Android's dominant programming language is Java. That's good, because it is one of the most widely used languages on the planet. When you are developing, you get to use the vast majority of standard Java, as well as additional libraries the community has added over the years since Android's public release.

Second, you have access to a range of development tools that are totally free! Yes, free. Google provides not one, but two, free integrated development environments (IDEs) from which to choose in which you can let your developer imagination go wild. We discuss both of these in more detail in Chapter 2, but for now, you can rest easy knowing you can work with either or both—Android Developer Tools (ADT) in Eclipse, or Android Studio, which is an IntelliJ IDEA–based IDE.

Third, many additional tools—such as emulators, performance monitors, templates, design tools, runtime environments, and more—have been added to the developer's world. And that's not all: you can write an entire book on this! Joking aside, Android does ask you to adopt a different development mindset to the one you need to design traditional desktop applications, but then it makes an enormous effort to support you every step of the way.

A Look Inside Android

To finish your introduction to thinking like an Android developer, let me introduce the fundamental building blocks of Android applications. I cover each of these areas in much more detail in the coming chapters.

Activities are the fundamental "screens" or UI elements with which users interact. Because of the nature of Android and the many display sizes with which you might work, a user might see one or more activities as part of the user interface at any one time. Activities are easy for you to design and develop, and they are easy for users to launch and use. Your target Android systems love activities, so feel free to be prolific in your creation and use of them!

Intents are messages passed between applications and the Android environment and are akin to events-driven messaging in modern desktop development environments. You can write your applications so they listen out for events and respond appropriately—whether that's answering a phone call, reacting to information from onboard sensors, or responding to changes in application state. Even better, you can create and pass your own intents, expanding the capabilities of your applications *and others* on the same device.

Services are background applications that provide features, abilities, or actions on which your applications (and their activities) can rely. Much like services or daemons in other operating systems, Android services are long-lived and generally run without a visible user interface (UI). Some services do provide visual elements, and you'll learn more about services in Chapter 22.

Content providers are a convenient abstraction to the many types and sources of data you might want to use in your application. In traditional development environments, you have to worry about all the tedious logistics of working with files, databases, network sockets, protocols, and the like. Android vastly simplifies your life as a developer by supporting the content provider metaphor for any data that needs to be shared on the device (and even for off-device data). When building your own applications, you are also able to define and develop your own content providers to enable data sharing with other applications, without needing to work with low-level storage issues, proprietary query languages, odd protocol considerations, or any other baggage.

A Look Inside This Book

With your mind now surging with thoughts of Android development, here's the roadmap of how we'll explore all of the topics already mentioned, and more.

- The next three chapters complete Part I of the book; you'll code your first Android application in the very next chapter! No delays, no excuses. After you write your first Android application, we'll then pull it apart to ensure you are familiar with the real-world code that represents the concepts I've already described here. We'll also tinker with and explore what Android is doing for you, and what you need to be doing yourself as a nascent Android developer.

- Part II helps you master the world of activities and the possibilities for user interface magic with Android. I cover all the essential components at your disposal for interface design and behavior and how mobile-specific concepts like device rotation work.

- Part III expands on your new knowledge of interface design for Android and introduces you to the power and flexibility of *fragments*. Fragments allow you to work with devices of any size, from 1 inch to 100 inches! As well as displays, we also explore input devices such as the camera, the microphone, and other onboard capabilities.

- Part IV delves behind the scenes, building your knowledge of services, resource handling, and other powerful components of Android that you will want to use to make the best possible applications.

- Part V, the final part of the book, takes you the frontiers of Android and looks at a range of topics, such as Google Play services, cloud-based facilities you can incorporate into your application, and the explosive growth in wearable Android with Google Glass and Android Wear.

Now that you have had a proper introduction to Android development and know where you are going, it's time to get started actually developing your first Android application!

Chapter **2**

Ready, Set, Code!

There is no time like the present to get started with your very first Android application. That's right, you are going to start coding right now! This chapter takes you right through setting up the tools to create Android applications, and you'll have your first working Android application before this chapter is done. Ready? Let's code!

Getting the Prerequisites for Android

There are two main prerequisites to quickly consider for your forthcoming Android development journey: will you need to separately install Java, and do you know what I call "minimum viable Java" for the development you might like to do?

Determining the Right Java for You

In a moment, I discuss the two most popular ways to set up a development environment for Android applications: preconfigured Eclipse and Android Developer Tools (ADT), and Android Studio. Both of these options give you everything you need bundled together, including Java, so you can start coding straight away. But if you are like me, you want more than two options; you might also like to learn about how the tools are set up and how to use them to create Android apps.

If you want to take full control of setting up the Android developer components and not use one of the all-in-one bundles, or if you have an existing development environment in mind and don't want to use one of the options provided by Google, then you need to ensure you have Java set up and available on your machine.

Getting the JDK

The Java Development Kit (JDK) has always been readily accessible, first through Sun and now through Oracle. If you point your browser to `java.oracle.com`, Oracle redirects you to the latest-and-greatest landing page for getting the JDK. But be warned! When it comes to getting Java for Android development, you need to make sure you choose a supported version of Java. For now, this means avoiding any Java 8 release. Regardless of platform—Windows, Linux, Mac—you want to choose either Java 6 or Java 7 (also known as Java 1.6 and Java 1.7—confusing, eh?).

Before you dive straight in to picking a JDK version, it is worth noting that, over the years, Java has been a very large source of security vulnerabilities and has been notoriously difficult to keep patched. This is thanks to repeated changes of ownership, changes in approach to managing Java on operating systems of all kinds, and the tendency of various software companies to bundle versions of Java with products that they then never update. You can't escape the need to install the JDK because the Java language is the chosen development language for Android, but you should at least be aware of the added security implications of having it on your development machine.

Android has supported Java 6 since its relatively early versions and has officially supported Java 7 since the KitKat version 4.2 release (with a few very minor no-go areas, such as `try-with-resources`). If you are setting up an entirely new environment, I recommend that you choose Java 7 for your platform because doing so will future-proof your Android development environment to the greatest degree possible.

> **Note**   When Android was first released, Java 5 was supported, but that version is best left to the history books.

Because a few of the tools bundled with the Android development environments from Google still only come in 32-bit form, you should choose the 32-bit distribution of Java 7 for your system if you want to get maximum benefit. For Mac users, however, only a 64-bit JDK is available, which means a handful of tools are not available to you, though none of those feature in this book. For the purposes of this book, you only need the standard edition (SE) version of the JDK. At the time of writing, the latest security patch release for Java 7 was Java SE 7u71/72.

To download your version of the JDK, follow the links on the Oracle download page, and choose the correct JDK distribution for your platform. For Linux users, this is the file `jdk-7u71-linux-i586.rpm`; for Windows, it is `jdk-7u71-windows-i586.exe`; and for Mac, it is `jdk-7u71-macosx-x64.dmg`. Make very sure it is the JDK you are downloading, and not myriad other pieces of software that are mixed in to the Oracle download pages. You do not want just the Java Runtime Environment (JRE), nor are you after OpenOffice, Oracle database software, or the other pieces you see on the quite-confusing download page.

ALTERNATIVES TO THE OFFICIAL JAVA RELEASE

Astute Linux fans will note that Oracle only provides an RPM distribution for Java. If you are a user of Debian, Ubuntu, Mint, or some other flavor of Linux that doesn't use RPM for package management, you do have options. Although it is not officially supported by Oracle, the OpenJDK distribution of Java works well on Debian and its derivates. Using this distribution helps you avoid any complications you'll encounter if you try to convert the official RPM using a tool like `alien`.

Once you have downloaded the relevant JDK bundle, you are ready to install.

Installing the JDK

Follow the instructions included in your Java bundle to install the JDK appropriately. On some systems, you might need administrative privileges to make your Java installation available system wide.

Knowing (Enough) Java for Android

This book assumes you have a passing knowledge of coding in Java, as do most other books and resources on Android development. If you are new to Android and new to Java, then I recommend a crash course in the basics of Java—such as that offered by the book *Learn Java for Android Development* by my fellow Apress author, Jeff Friesen (Apress, 2010). Alternatively, countless online Java tutorials can get you up to speed quickly. The secret is knowing on which topics you need to focus to be productive with Android development and which you can ignore for now.

To help focus your learning, or refresh your memory if it has been a while since you last wrote Java code, the following are the key topics that will get you (re)started with Java.

General coding knowledge:

- Structure and layout of code
- Object-orientation, classes, and objects
- Methods, data members

Java-specific coding knowledge:

- Interfaces and implementations
- Threading and concurrency
- Garbage collection
- Exception handling
- File handling
- Generics
- Collections

There is plenty more to Java than these topics alone, but they provide the foundation you need to get started quickly with Android development.

Choosing a Development Environment

In the years since Android's initial release, the tools and technology available to help build applications have exploded in variety and capability. Google provides several options, which I explore shortly, and many other companies and groups also offer development tools. I cover a few of those more exotic options much later in this book. For now, I stick to the most common environments you are likely to use: Android Studio and Eclipse.

The following sections cover installing Android Studio, as well as installing and configuring Eclipse with Android Developer Tools (ADT); this coverage includes putting the ADT pieces together yourself, since this gives you an appreciation for what you are actually getting when you opt for one of the prebuilt developer bundles. Most importantly, remember you only need one development environment. Don't feel that you need to follow both the Android Studio and Eclipse approaches, although you are welcome to if you have enough disk space and curiosity.

Option 1: Choosing Android Studio

Google announced Android Developer Studio (now just Android Studio; the word *Developer* has slowly been dropped from the name over the last year) a few years back as an alternative new way to create Android applications. It is built on a foundation of the IntelliJ IDEA environment, with ADT and other tools bolted on.

Despite the years that have since passed, Android Studio is still in beta! As of this writing, the current version is 0.8.4, and although it is packed full of fantastic tools and features, it is also prone to the odd quirk, bug, and crash. That said, Android Studio is rapidly approaching maturity, and it is well worth your effort to learn to use it to develop Android applications.

Downloading Android Studio

Head to the Android developer site at developer.android.com/sdk/installing/studio.html and download Android Studio. At the time of writing, zip files for Windows, Mac OS X, and Linux are available for release number 135.1538390, in addition to an "all-in-one" installer .exe file for Windows. Choose the download appropriate for your platform, and remember where you save it.

Installing Android Studio

This process is as simple as unpacking the zip file and doing the following, depending on your platform:

- **Linux**: Simply run studio.sh from the bin subdirectory, and Android Studio completes the setup for you. It may prompt you to import settings from a previous version of Android Studio, as shown in Figure 2-1.

Figure 2-1. Android Studio prompts you to import settings from earlier versions

- **Windows**: If you are using the all-in-one installer, you now have a shiny new program group in the start menu for Android Studio and a launch icon within of the same name. If you download and extract the zip file, you can run the studio.bat batch file from the bin subdirectory, which deals with locating your JDK and determining the address width of your version of Windows in order to run the right version of Android Studio— 32-bit or 64-bit.

- **Mac OS X**: When you drag the android studio.app file from the archive into your Applications directory, Android Studio installs itself and makes itself available as a normal application on your system.

No matter which platform you are on, you are likely to see the import settings option the first time you run Android Studio, as shown in Figure 2-1. You can import any previous Android Studio settings you may have.

Downloading the Android SDK

Unless you are using the all-in-one installer for Windows, you need to download the base Android SDK for your platform from developer.android.com. On Linux and Windows, remember to ensure you select the "bit-edness" that matches your existing installations of Eclipse and Java: either 32-bit or 64-bit.

Unzip the Android SDK into a directory, and note where this is because you'll need that information shortly. For instance, this might be /home/myname/android-sdk on a Linux machine.

Configuring the Android SDK for Android Studio

If you aren't using the all-in-one installer, you need to tell Android Studio where to find the Android SDK. To do this, use the menu option Configure ➤ Project Defaults ➤ Project Structure; this opens the SDK Location setting shown in Figure 2-2.

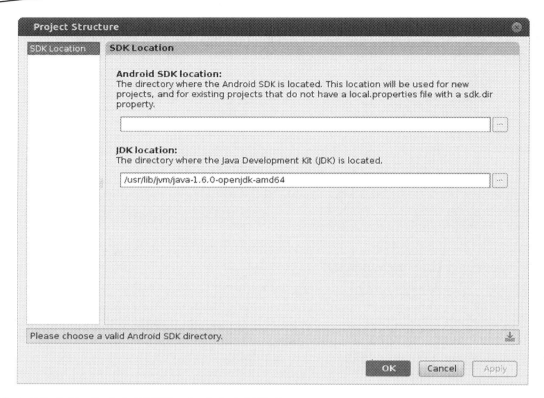

Figure 2-2. Setting the Android SDK location in Android Studio

Set the directory to the location in which you unzipped the SDK earlier, and click OK. Now you're ready to add the additional SDK components you need to make the most of Android Studio. You can now jump ahead to the "Completing Your Development Environment Setup" section of this chapter, or read on for instructions on how to set up Eclipse as your IDE.

Option 2: Choosing Eclipse the Quick Way

By far the easiest way to get the Android Developer Tools (ADT) and the Android SDK installed and configured with Eclipse is to use the preconfigured bundle available from the developer.android.com site. This bundle takes care of all the base components, leaving you with the simple task of fetching additional SDK components—just as you'd need to with Android Studio.

Options 3: Choosing Eclipse the Do-It-Yourself Way

Although the prepackaged methods of setting up an IDE are great, some people already have Eclipse installed (and set up just the way they like it), and others are curious about how all the developer tools fit together. If you are in this second camp, you want to put the pieces together yourself. Next, I step you through downloading the Android SDK and adding the ADT to your existing Eclipse installation.

> **Note**   You need to use Eclipse 3.7 or later in order to use the most recent versions of the Android SDK and ADT. On a Mac OSX machine, you are also warned that Eclipse is not signed by a valid Apple Developer ID's certificate and that it might be unsafe software. Although Apple is trying to practice good security in this regard, as long as you acquire Eclipse from the official website, it is perfectly safe to allow it to run on your Mac.

Downloading the Android SDK

First, start by downloading the base Android SDK for your platform from `developer.android.com`. On Linux and Windows, remember to ensure you select the bit-edness that matches your existing installations of Eclipse and Java: either 32-bit or 64-bit.

Unzip the Android SDK into a directory, and note where this is because you'll need this information shortly—for instance, `c:\program files\android-sdk-windows` on a Windows machine.

Adding ADT to Your Existing Eclipse IDE

Next, you need to add the ADT to Eclipse. To do this, start Eclipse, and from the Help menu, choose Install New Software. You should see the Install dialog or something very similar to it, as shown in Figure 2-3.

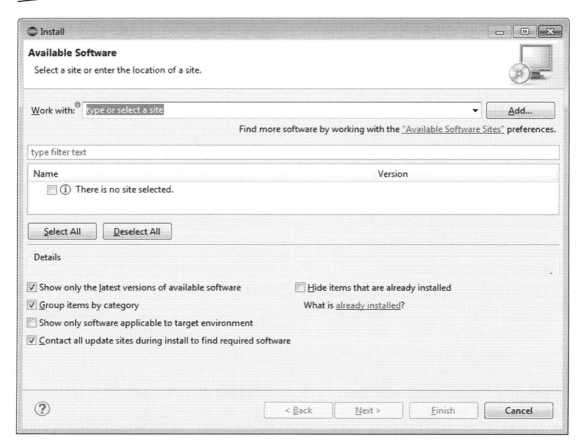

Figure 2-3. *Eclipse Install Available Software dialog*

When you click the Add button in the top right of the Install dialog the Add Repository dialog appears. Choose a memorable name for the Android repository, such as Android Repository, and for the location, enter `https://dl-ssl.google.com/android/eclipse/`, as shown in Figure 2-4.

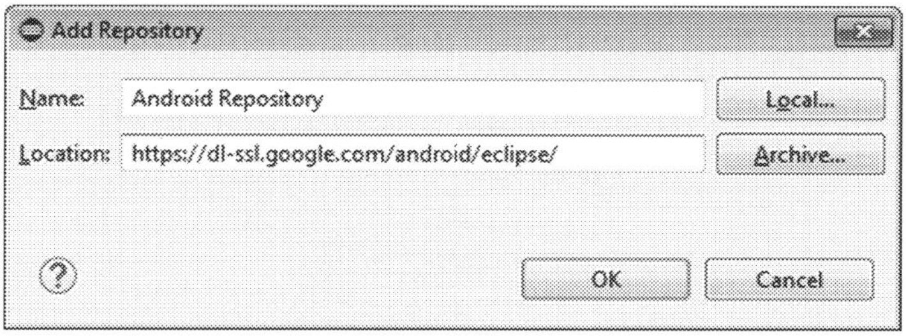

Figure 2-4. *Configuring the Android repository in Eclipse*

You might find that the Android Eclipse repository is already listed in the drop-down, in which case you do not need to repeat the setup process. But assuming it isn't already present, once you click the OK button, the main Install dialog shows the status "Pending" in the main area of the dialog briefly, until it contacts the URL shown and fetches the available packages. You should then see this change to the main entry, Developer Tools, which represents the ADT. When you click the triangular arrow to the left, the detailed components of Developer Tools appear, as shown in Figure 2-5.

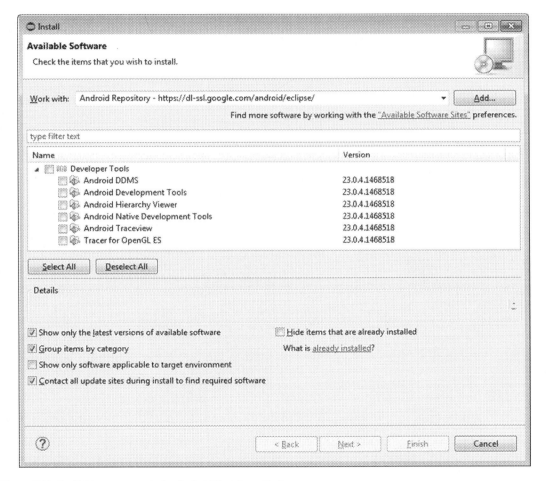

Figure 2-5. Available components for Android Developer Tools

At this stage, if disk space permits, choose all the options. If you are looking to economize, you can safely omit Native Development Tools and Tracer For OpenGL ES because I do not cover those in this book. With your selection chosen, click the Next button, at which point Eclipse presents an installation review dialog, as shown in Figure 2-6.

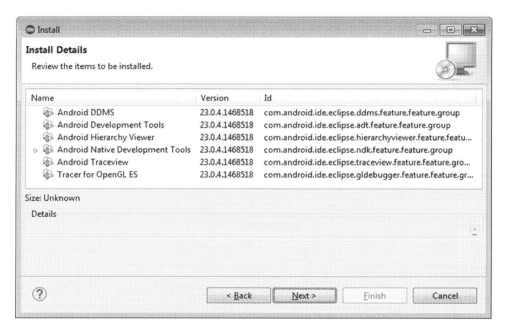

Figure 2-6. Installation review of developer tools in Eclipse

Choose the Next button, and you are presented with a license confirmation screen that contains several different open source licenses. You need to accept all of the licenses that correspond to the ADT components you have selected before you can click Finish to continue. Figure 2-7 illustrates the common licenses you see at this point.

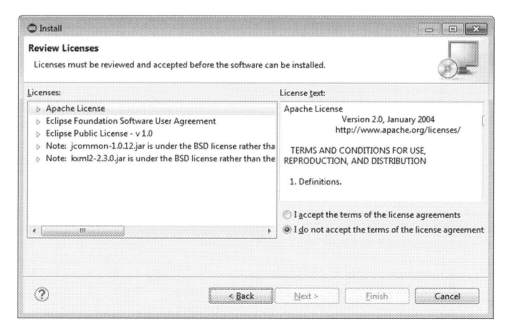

Figure 2-7. ADT installation license confirmation

Once you've digested the various license texts, you can click Finish and Eclipse commences downloading and installing the ADT components. You see the normal Eclipse progress dialog while this installation work is happening.

> **Note**   If you see any warnings about installing unsigned content, it is safe to continue.

When the ADT installation is complete, Eclipse prompts you that it requires a restart to continue. Save any other work you might have open, and allow the confirmation dialog to restart Eclipse for you.

At this point, you have the ADT installed as part of Eclipse, but it has no idea where to find the Android SDK with which to do its work. So let's fix that now.

Configuring the Android SDK for ADT in Eclipse

When Eclipse restarts, you need to inform ADT where to find the SDK. To do this, open Preferences in Eclipse; observe the new category, Android. Click Android to see a configuration section, as shown in Figure 2-8.

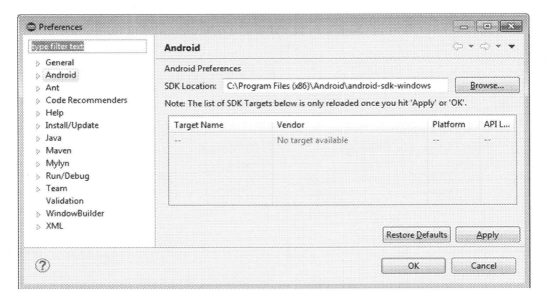

Figure 2-8. Configuring ADT with the Android SDK location

In the SDK Location field, enter the path to the location where you have extracted the Android SDK archive. Click OK. You have completed the basic ADT configuration. ADT quickly tells you if it can't find the SDK components, as it performs a check to determine whether it can see the `tools` directory within the Android SDK. If you see an error complaining that it can't find the `tools` directory, you know you need to double-check the directory setting in `Preferences for Android` or confirm where you extracted your Android SDK.

At this point, you are in a common position to all other IDE setup approaches, whether that's Android Studio, the bundled Eclipse-plus-ADT installs, or some other esoteric or manual approach. You now have the basic IDE set up and you've made Android SDK available, but you still need to add specific SDK packages for Android versions and extensions, as well as device images, in order to do anything useful. We handle that final part of set up next and get you coding in a few short pages.

Completing Your Development Environment Setup

Welcome back, readers who have taken the Android Studio or bundled Eclipse-plus-ADT approach! Regardless of your chosen IDE, you are now at the stage in which you have the basics of the development environment in place, together with the core of the Android SDK. The only things missing are the many version-specific additional packages, support libraries, and device images that let you work with all manner of APIs and Android devices. Let's get those now and get you coding!

To complete the Android SDK setup, you need to launch the Android SDK Manager and choose the additional packages you want for developing with Android. To launch the SDK Manager, choose it from the Window menu in Eclipse or from the Configure menu in Android Studio, or choose the SDK Manager binary from the directory to which you extracted the Android SDK archive (for instance, `SKD Manager.exe` on Windows). The SDK Manager appears as shown in Figure 2-9.

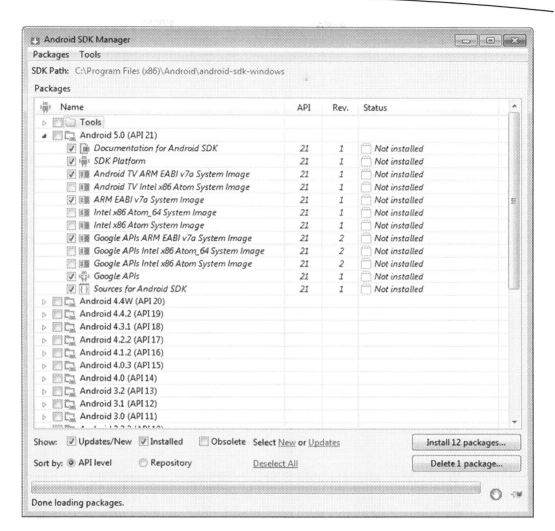

Figure 2-9. The Android SDK Manager

If you scroll up and down the packages list, you see a lot of packages from which to choose. This extensive list is a combination of the diversity and depth of Android, and its longevity. In addition to ARM and x86 system images, various support libraries, documentation, and so forth, you also see every Android SDK release library, from the early Donut and Éclair releases, through to the very latest Jelly Bean and Lollipop versions.

Although you might want to work with an older set of APIs for Android in some situations, to learn development, it's best to start with the latest and greatest. That means we are going to start with the Android Lollipop libraries, system images, and documentation, and the essential extras you need to learn Android development quickly. To that end, choose the following options to install.

From the Android 5.0 (API 21) section:

- ▨ Documentation for Android SDK

- ▨ SDK Platform

- ▨ Both the regular and TV ARM EABI system images

- ▨ Google APIs for ARM

- ▨ Base Google APIs

- ▨ Sources for Android SDK

From the Extras section:

- ▨ Android Support Library

- ▨ Google Play Services

- ▨ Google USB Driver

Click the Install 12 Packages button (or however many packages you've chosen), and another familiar license acceptance screen displays. Accept the licenses shown, and choose Install. The Android SDK Manager Log window opens to show you the progress of the download and installation of your select SDK packages. Now is the time to fetch a coffee or other refreshing beverage, because this install takes a few minutes. The Android SDK Manager Log shows a completion message when it is done in addition to advising you to restart any components that were updated during the process.

All of the components you need to start writing Android programs are now in place. The one extra piece that is very handy for your development work is somewhere to *run* your Android programs.

Creating Your First Android Virtual Device

Your Android development environment—whether it is Eclipse with ADT, or Android Studio—provides you with the ability to emulate a real Android device so that you can test and debug your Android code without needing to load it onto a real device. This is done by creating Android Virtual Devices (AVDs).

To create and manage AVDs, open the Android Virtual Device Manager. You can access this from the Window menu in Eclipse, the Tools ➤ Android menu in Android Studio, or by launching the AVD Manager binary from your SDK installation directory—this is AVD Manager.exe on Windows.

When the Android Virtual Device Manager starts for the first time, it presents an empty list of devices, as shown in Figure 2-10.

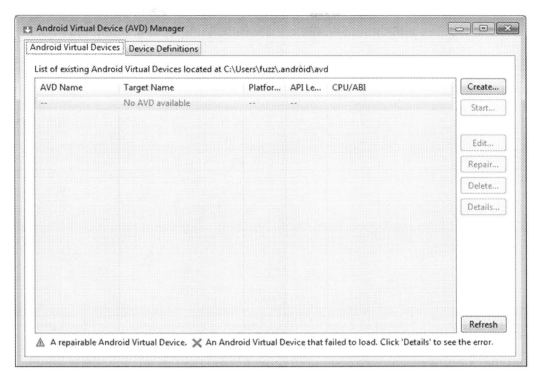

Figure 2-10. The AVD Manager

To create your first virtual device, click the Create button. A dialog of configuration options appears, as shown in Figure 2-11. I have supplied some good starting values for your first virtual device, so go ahead and copy the settings you see, and click the OK button when you're done.

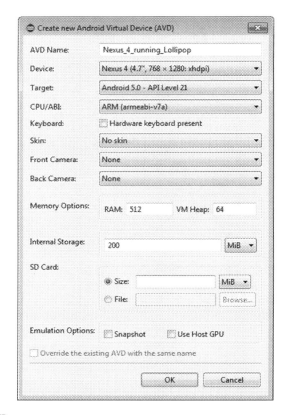

Figure 2-11. Defining an AVD

Now that your device is created, it is listed in the AVD Manager. To launch your virtual device, highlight it and click the Start button. You are prompted with launch options, as shown in Figure 2-12.

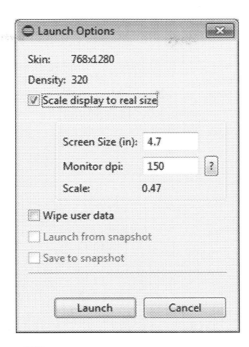

Figure 2-12. Launch options for you AVD

For the moment, the main setting to choose is Scale Display To Real Size. This attempts to draw the virtual device window to the size of the device you specified in the device configuration, which in this instance, is 4.7 inches (about 11.9cm).

Click Launch and the virtual device starts. This can take some time, even on a powerful machine. (Later in the book, you explore installing on a real device, which is normally faster.) You should now see a Starting Android Emulator status window, and then the splash screen for Android in the simulated device screen, as shown in Figure 2-13.

Figure 2-13. *The AVD splash screen that shows when you start a virtual device*

Once the virtual device has finished starting, it displays the Android home screen and unlock prompt, as shown in Figure 2-14. Feel free to unlock the screen and follow the help screens that guide you through the various screens and menus.

Figure 2-14. *The running AVD*

When you are done exploring your new virtual device, feel free to close it or leave it running in the background. It is time to code!

Creating Your First Android Application

Without further ado, it is time to create your first Android application and write your first Android code!

One of the huge benefits of setting up your IDE, whether it is Eclipse or Android Studio, is that the Android Developer Tools exist to do all kinds of heavy lifting for you, including putting all the structure and plumbing in place for a new application. You get to focus on just writing the functional code to make you application do as you wish.

To have the developer tools do their magic, simply select File ➤ New ➤ Project in Eclipse, or New ➤ Project in Android Studio, and then choose Android Application Project as your project type. Figure 2-15 shows this step in Eclipse.

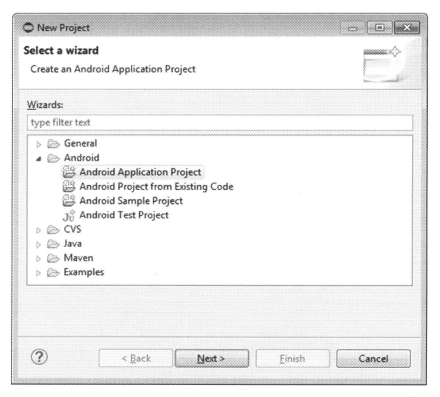

Figure 2-15. *Choosing the Android Application Project type*

Click next, and you are prompted to enter a range of details about your new Android project, as shown in Figure 2-16.

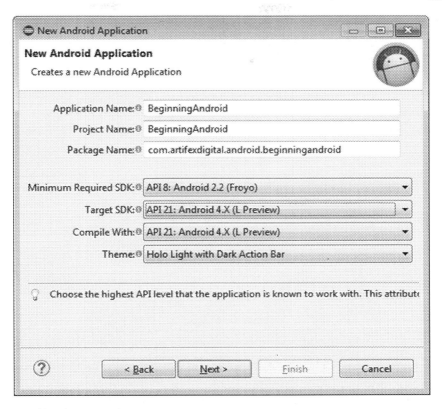

Figure 2-16. Android project properties

Here, you want to specify the following settings, leaving anything else you see at the default provided in the wizard.

- **Application Name:** This is the name you see for your application when it is installed on an Android device, and also when it appears in the Play Store.

- **Project Name:** A unique name to identify your project within your IDE. No other project in your IDE's repository or workspace can have the same name.

- **Package Name:** The Java package name that is used for packaging this project. This follows the normal globally unique requirements of Java packages. In this example, I've anchored the package name to one of my registered domains.

- **Target SDK:** For the purposes of this chapter, check to ensure this has picked up the most recent SDK version you chose to install earlier in this chapter. Later in the book, I talk more about targeting well-adopted SDK versions and how to deal with older versions you haven't catered for specifically in your project.

You can leave all the other settings at their defaults. When you're done, click Next, and you are presented with the next configuration screen, as shown in Figure 2-17. This screen deals with launchers, activities, and other Android topics I cover shortly.

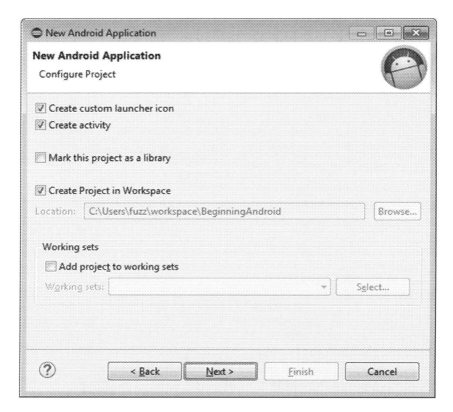

Figure 2-17. Setting Android project launcher and activity details

You should leave all of these settings at the default. We return to them in later chapters to discuss other options. Click Next to continue, and you see the Launcher Icon configuration screen, as shown in Figure 2-18.

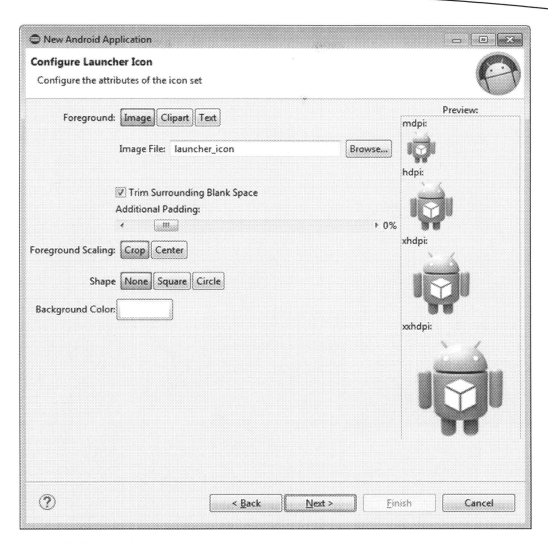

Figure 2-18. *Configuring a launcher icon for your Android project*

Icons are very much items of personal preference and artistic taste. Feel free to play around with the scaling and shape options and the trimming and color settings here. When you finish choosing your creative flourishes, click Next to move to the screen shown in Figure 2-19, in which you choose the initial activity configuration for your new project.

Figure 2-19. *Choosing the initial activity behavior for an Android project*

For the purposes of this very first application, choose the Blank Activity option, and then choose the Next button. At last, you are at the end of the project configuration, as shown in Figure 2-20.

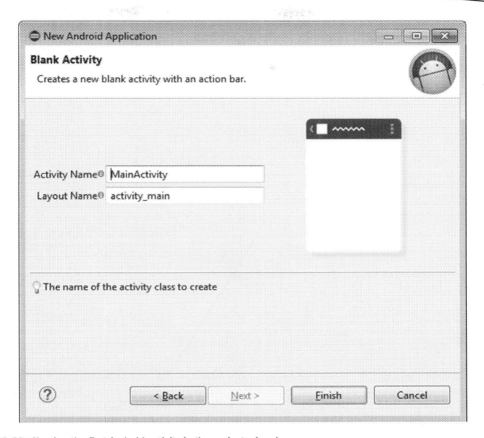

Figure 2-20. Naming the first Android activity in the project wizard

The principal thing to remember on this screen is that the Activity Name is used for the associated Java class, and so it must conform to Java class naming conventions and rules. You can leave this at the default, `MainActivity`, and then click the Finish button. We discuss exactly what an activity is in the next few chapters.

Writing Your First Android Code

When the Android project wizard finishes creating your project, you see a project structure that includes many directories such as `src`, `libs`, `res`, and so on, as shown in Eclipse in Figure 2-21. Do not worry about what all of these directories represent just yet. I cover that in Chapter 3.

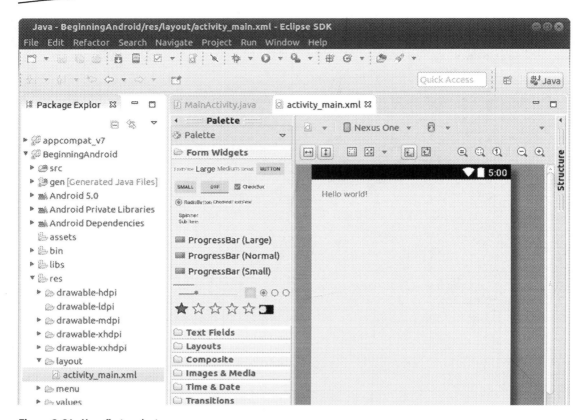

Figure 2-21. *Your first project*

For now, drill down into the values folder until you find the `strings.xml` file. Open this in your IDE or editor; you should see half a dozen lines of XML.

```
<?xml version="1.0" encoding="utf-8"?>
<resources>

    <string name="app_name">BeginningAndroid</string>
    <string name="hello_world">Hello world!</string>
    <string name="action_settings">Settings</string>

</resources>
```

Your first act of actual Android development should be to change the line, shown in bold, here:

```
<?xml version="1.0" encoding="utf-8"?>
<resources>

    <string name="app_name">BeginningAndroid</string>
    <string name="hello_world">Beginning Android!</string>
    <string name="action_settings">Settings</string>

</resources>
```

That's it! You have written your first Android application and are ready to run it. Save the `strings.xml` file, change the focus in your IDE back to the `MainActivity.java` file, and choose the Run option from the toolbar or menu.

> **Note**   When first running a new project in Eclipse, you may be prompted to configure a Run Configuration. If this happens, you can set the Target of your Run Configuration so it either prompts you every time about which AVD to use to run your application, or sets a preference to automatically run for you every time.

You should see some log messages scroll past in your IDE; these let you know that your application is being deployed to the AVD, and shortly after, if you unlock the screen on your AVD, you should see the pleasing results of all your setup work in this chapter, as shown in Figure 2-22.

Figure 2-22. Your first Android application running in the Virtual Device emulator

Congratulations! You are on your way to mastering the world of Android development.

Chapter 3

Inside Your First Android Project

In the previous chapter, I helped you get your development environment set up and then quickly created the classic default application so you could rapidly get a feel for a real Android project working in your environment. Regardless of whether you chose Android Studio or Eclipse, you now have a real Android project at your disposal, and you can use this to dissect what goes into such a project and learn the many options present. So let's get started!

Looking at Android Project Structure

The best way to understand all of what goes into a standard Android project is to start with a visual overview. Because the developer tools and SDK are doing a great deal for you, this turns out to be a pretty big picture. So big, in fact, that I have to split it into two figures to show it to you. Figures 3-1 and 3-2 show you the full project structure of your Beginning Android project; many of the key folders are open so I can refer to their contents throughout this chapter.

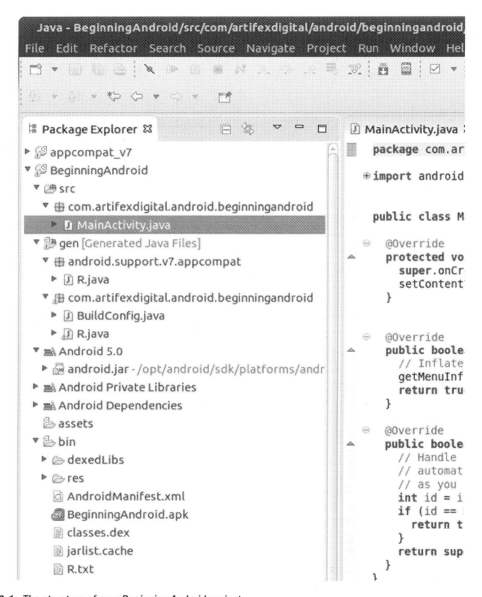

Figure 3-1. *The structure of your Beginning Android project*

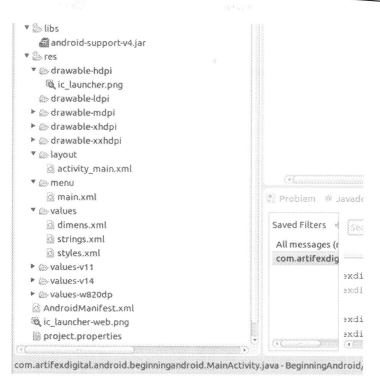

Figure 3-2. *The structure of your Beginning Android project (cont.)*

> **Note**   If your project structure looks a little (or even a lot) different, don't panic. Some of the major
> parts of the Android project structure have gradually changed over the many releases of Android,
> ADT, and SDK. The structure shown here is from the v21 SDK for Lollipop, but yours may differ.

Starting at the Source

Take a look at the first items in the project's root directory; they are dedicated to source
code. The src folder is generated for you automatically (along with the other folders I mention
throughout this chapter). Within it, you see a directory tree based on the Java class name
you specified when you used the wizard to create your new project. In my case, this part of
the tree under src is com.artifexdigital.android.beginningandroid. If you chose to use a
different fully qualified class name, you see this change reflected here. Note that although it is
conventional in the Java community to use reversed domain names to provide uniqueness, you
do not strictly need to adhere to this convention. For instance, you can pick a fully-qualified
name that is unique based on other options, such as the reverse of your email address.

The one file you see at the leaf of the src tree is the initial Java source code file that
ADT created for you. In my case, this is the file MainActivity.java, which came from
the default name suggested by the new project wizard, but you can actually call this file
anything you like. This might prompt you to ask, "How does Android know where to find

the `main()` method if I mess with the name of this file?" I talk a little more about what is in `MainActivity.java` (or its equivalent) in a moment, and I also cover the mystery of `main()` in the context of Android.

Benefitting from Generated Components

Moving on from the `src` folder, you next see a `gen` folder. The contents in this folder vary depending on what version of ADT you are using in your environment and whether or not you have successfully built your project at any point. Assuming you are using an ADT release of a similar vintage to Android Lollipop and that you have successfully built your project at least once, you find at least two fully-qualified Java package references within.

The first package reference is to the mysterious `android.support.v7.appcompat` package, though the mystery is partly solved through the truth-in-naming of the package itself. I'll come back to this package a little later in the chapter. You also see the fully-qualified Java package reference based on your chosen name during project creation.

Within both of these package references is a file named `R.java`. This is an automatically compiled representation of the layout of your application, and it is created (or re-created, depending on the circumstances) during project build events. I'll talk more about how this is used later in this chapter, as well as in Chapter 5, when we discuss layouts.

Using Libraries and JARs

I've already talked about Android's use of Java as the foundational programming language for Android development. As you would expect with any Java development, much of the heavy lifting is done by other libraries and classes that are already built for you, typically packaged as Java Archive (JAR) files.

Our Beginning Android application currently has these notable libraries:

- `android.jar`—Listed in Figure 3-1 under Android 5.0, this is the JAR file for the Android SDK. Note that it is specific to the version of Android you told the new application wizard to use for your application.

- Android Private Libraries—`android-support-v7-appcompat.jar` and `android-support-v4.jar` are recent and more historic examples of Android's support and compatibility libraries. These exist to back-port new platform features to old devices and the applications that target them. I'll talk more about this when we discuss relevant parts of UI design and application behavior in Parts II and III.

As you build more and more complex applications, other libraries you import also show up here and are also referenced further down in the `libs` directory.

Counting Your Assets

Next up, you should see an `assets` folder. Within it, you will likely find…nothing! Well, at least initially—there is no default content in the `assets` folder. As you build more and more complex projects, this is the location in which a variety of custom components and datasources reside. Examples include video and audio files, SQLite databases, and any other file-based resource that doesn't fit within the predefined project structure provided by the ADT.

Putting Things in the Bin

The `bin` directory continues the fine UNIX tradition of abbreviating binary to bin. Here you find your compiled Android application. Look for the `.apk` file—this is the actual package file that is installed on a phone or emulator for your application. It uses the ZIP format to hold the application's executable, resources, and the `AndroidManifest.xml` file (which we discuss shortly).

Within the `bin` directory, you'll also find a range of other compilation artifacts, such as the dex file, which is the compiled Java application file itself, in addition to optimized code objects, compressed images, and other compilation objects with which you ordinarily don't need to interact.

You can ignore anything else within the `bin` directory for now.

Using Resources

A great deal of the tooling and support with which Android, the ADT, and the SDK provide you deals with using resources in extensive and clever ways to cut the amount of coding you actually need to do. The files in `res` and its subdirectories are all static files that are typically packaged with your application in the `.apk` file for deployment. The main types of resources are covered next.

Picturing What Drawables Can Do For You

The first set of subdirectories in the `res` folder are the `drawable-*` folders. Projects created with Android Jelly Bean, KitKat, Lollipop, or later start with five `drawable-*` folders:

- `drawable-ldpi`: The location for low-density artwork, typically 120dpi or worse. This was more important historically; because of the continuous improvement in screen quality, storage size, bandwidth, and so on over the years, you may never need to concern yourself with low-density drawables.

- `drawable-mdpi`: Meant for medium-density drawables, for resolutions up to 160dpi.

- `drawable-hdpi`: High-density images are those with resolution approaching 240dpi.

- ▓ drawable-xhdpi: The first of the "extra" high-density targets, xhdpi is considered anything up to 320dpi.

- ▓ drawable-xxhdpi: Believe it or not, this isn't the highest possible resolution for which Android caters. xxhdpi is considered resolutions up to 480dpi. Want more? xxxhdpi has been defined for resolutions reaching 640dpi, but you won't see a default folder for it in your project structure.

Android is smart enough to deal with missing drawables for a given size by scaling images from another size. The results aren't always pixel-perfect, but for the user of your application, it means they get an application that works rather than a mysterious missing image in the middle of their activity.

SELECTIVE RESOURCE USE AND SUFFIXES

You will notice many more examples of resource directories like the drawables folders that have names and somewhat-cryptic suffixes. In the drawables case, the suffix relates to the apparent resolution or pixel-density of the image being used.

Other forms of selective resource control through directory name suffixes for other resources include version-based suffixes like v8, v11, and v14 relating to SDK versions, and w820dp, w1280dp, and similar suffixes that target exact device-independent pixel dimensions.

User Interface Layouts

In later chapters, I explore layouts and the many options and techniques for designing Android user interfaces (UIs). For now, you can focus on the one file you see in the layout folder, which is used for the default layout for the initial activity: activity_main.xml. If you think of an activity as a screen or dialog in your Android application with which your user interacts, then the XML in the layout provides a consistent language for describing those user interfaces. There's a lot more to know on this topic, but for now, you know where layout XML files reside.

What's on the Menu?

The design and use of menus within Android applications has evolved over the many versions of Android. From a developer perspective, menus are treated as first-class UI citizens, enjoying similar descriptive support through XML files as seen about with layouts in general. As of yet, I don't have any menus separately defined for the Beginning Android application, so for now, the menu folder is empty.

Valuable Values

Using values in a separate XML file should already be familiar to you, since you edited the onscreen text in the `strings.xml` file for the working example in Chapter 2. More broadly, the contents of the values directory are strings, dimensions, styles, and other reference data that is best handled through abstraction away from the code. Rather than embed my "Beginning Android" string in my Java code, I can easily reference it, and other values.

You can already see how the abstraction supported by the XML approach to values makes tasks such as internationalization and localization much easier. We'll explore other uses for this approach in later chapters too.

Working with Other Key Files in Your Project

Within the root folder of your project reside a few more critical files that either glue all the disparate parts together or enable various project-level smarts within an IDE or other environment to help manage the project.

Controlling Applications with Android Manifests

At the heart of every Android application is the manifest, represented in the file `AndroidManifest.xml` within your project's root folder. The manifest acts as the central point of declaration for the project, enumerating everything from activities and services, to permissions and SDK compatibility, and more.

The manifest is also used as the blueprint for bolting together the constituent parts of your application, for instance, by specifying what activity will act as the launcher activity the user first sees when the application starts.

The ADT aids your work here (and with any new project) by automatically creating a skeleton manifest file for any new project. Listing 3-1 shows the manifest from the Beginning Android example in Chapter 2.

Listing 3-1. The AndroidManifest.xml File

```xml
<?xml version="1.0" encoding="utf-8"?>
<manifest xmlns:android="http://schemas.android.com/apk/res/android"
    package="com.artifexdigital.android.beginningandroid"
    android:versionCode="1"
    android:versionName="1.0" >

    <uses-sdk
        android:minSdkVersion="8"
        android:targetSdkVersion="21" />

    <application
        android:allowBackup="true"
        android:icon="@drawable/ic_launcher"
        android:label="@string/app_name"
        android:theme="@style/AppTheme" >
```

```
        <activity
            android:name=".MainActivity"
            android:label="@string/app_name" >
            <intent-filter>
                <action android:name="android.intent.action.MAIN" />
                <category android:name="android.intent.category.LAUNCHER" />
            </intent-filter>
        </activity>
    </application>

</manifest>
```

As with any XML schema, element names are arbitrary, and so the Android designers chose the not-unreasonable `manifest` element as the root element name. The namespace provided here is a little quirky if you are used to vanilla namespace conventions in other uses of XML. In Android, the convention is to assume the namespace only for attributes, not for elements as well. This is strange, but workable, once you become familiar with it.

The first and most important following attribute is the `package` attribute. The `package` refers to the name of the Java package that you wish to use as the core package for your application. In the example, this is `com.artifexdigital.android.beginningandroid`. In addition to acting as the base for your application, this sets up a nice short hand for other references to this package throughout the manifest. Instead of having to type the full package name (and they can be much longer than the one I've used here), you can refer to the package with a leading dot, ".", notation instead. You can see this in action if you look further down in the `activity` element, where the first attribute `android:name` refers to ".MainActivity" instead of `com.artifexdigital.android.beginningandroid.MainActivity`. I don't know about you, but I'm all in favor of not have to type all that. Your package name acts as the unique identifier for your application, both on devices such as phones and tablets, and also on Google Play and other application market places. This means your should choose wisely, since there is no way to change the package name, but have the application appear as the same unchanged application in those locations!

The other key attributes of the `manifest` element are your `android:versionName` and `android:versionCode`. The `versionName` value is designed to be a human-friendly representation of what version of your application is in use. This can be any string value you like, such as `1.0` shown in the example, or anything else you care to use. This is the value that people see on their devices, on Google Play, and so on, so you might like to help them out by sticking to something understandable.

`android:versionCode` has a different purpose. This is strictly an integer value, and successive generations of your application must use higher values than previous generations. This is, in effect, the true (internal) version number. By convention, developers usually start `versionCode` at 1 and go from there, but you can start with any positive number you like.

Caution   Only one version of your application (typically, the one with the highest known `versionCode` value) appears in Google Play at any one time. There are ways to make older versions available, such as by using `.apk` side-loading, but the vast bulk of your audience probably won't do this.

The first child element of the manifest is the uses-sdk element. In the example manifest file, you see two attributes: one for minSdkVersion and one for targetSdkVersion. The minSdkversion controls the age/vintage of devices, emulators, and the like that you will support with your application. In practice, this also governs which SDK features you should use. If you stick to developing with Eclipse and the ADT, or Android Studio, then you get helpful warnings if you try to use features introduced after your minSdkVersion level. The targetSdkVersion is a short-hand way of indicating which SDK was used to develop and test the application. It has some compatibility implications that we will discuss in later chapters. If you are interested in real-time data on what SDK versions Google knows are in use, and in what proportion, some data is made available in the Android Developer dashboards at https://developer.android.com/about/dashboards/index.html.

The remaining elements within the manifest govern the initial behavior of your application. You see one application element, and within that, one activity element. Even with the very short coverage of drawables and strings earlier in this chapter, you can probably guess at what the attributes android:icon, android:label, and android:theme are doing. They're referencing resources and values to provide an onscreen icon and name for your application, and so on.

The activity element is given a label and defines which Java class is implementing the activity's logic. It usually also includes an intent-filter child attribute that specifies under which conditions this activity can be invoked. I talk more about intents in Part II of the book, but for now, simply note that in this example, I have an action and a category, and my category flags that my application should appear in the device's launcher so a user can run it by choosing its icon.

You can (and will) place a great deal more in a manifest file; we'll discover more about these options throughout the rest of the book.

Permutating Projects with Properties

From a developer perspective, you build and maintain your Android application as a project. Depending on which IDE you have chosen, you may see one or more of project. properties, gradle.properties, ant.properties, or local.properties files. Each of these controls project-specific configuration settings, such as cross-project references, key material location for project signing, and so forth. Some are particular to a given build environment or IDE, so for instance, you typically only see ant.properties if you're using ant to build your projects from the command line.

"R" You Forgetting Something?

I promised earlier in the chapter to explain more about the R.java files you see within your project. The R.java file acts as an index to all of the resources identified in your project. Any time you change, add, or remove a resource, ADT takes responsibility for regenerating the R class and its contents. This happens automatically, so you should never manually edit the R.java source files.

You can see how I already used this automatic referencing support in the Beginning Android application in Chapter 2. If you open the MainActivity.java file in your IDE or editor, you see a call to the setContentView() method within the onCreate() method. I return to this in much more detail in the coming chapters, but in this example, I pass R.layout.activity_main as the parameter to the method. This is my way of telling Android I want to use the layout specified in the activity_main.xml file in my layout resource directory. The R class takes care of all the plumbing to make the necessary link back to my layout definition. You will see this approach again and again with layouts, drawables, and other UI components.

Solving the Appcompat Mystery

If you pay attention to everything that is created for you when you use Android Studio or Eclipse to create your new Android project, you will notice a second project that is created automatically. The project is named appcompat_v7, and it is one of the elements of the Android Support Library for older versions of Android and the devices that run them. You can safely ignore this project for now; rest assured it's doing some heavy lifting for you in order to make your Android applications support a huge range of legacy devices.

Chapter 4

Changing and Enhancing Your Project

Now that you know your way around your Android project's structure, it is time to get your hands dirty, change things, and see what breaks! OK, perhaps you won't break things immediately, but in this chapter, I show you more of the capabilities of your project and how to quickly leverage more of the developer tools. You also start to add more user interface elements and program logic to your application. Let's get to it.

Extending Your Application with the Android Manifest

Whether you use the New Project wizard in Eclipse, Android Studio, or another IDE that supports Android Developer Tools (ADT), the job of creating your initial `AndroidManifest.xml` file is done for you. The file itself is a little spartan, with just enough to get the job done. You can control many of a project's key additional features and optional settings by just adding elements and attributes to `AndroidManifest.xml`.

Right now, you probably find this to be useful information in an abstract way, but it will become increasing practical as your Android knowledge grows—in fact, many of you should eventually feel happy to flick back to this chapter when you need to.

Editing the Android Manifest

The `AndroidManifest.xml` file comprises XML, and therefore is only text, as you saw in Listing 3-1 in the preceding chapter. Editing XML/text is certainly doable, and many of the early examples in this book ask you to do just that. But as the file becomes larger and more complex, it can become cumbersome to perform clean edits and not inadvertently upset opening and closing tags, disturb nesting levels, and make other mistakes. To help overcome this annoyance, ADT includes a graphically-enhanced editor that displays the elements and their attributes as selectable items with text fields in which to make edits. This XML editor is shown in Figure 4-1.

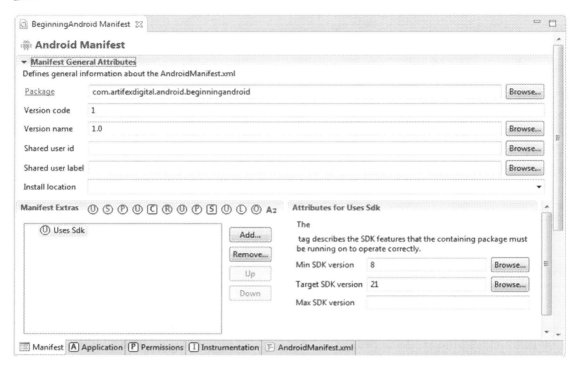

Figure 4-1. *The graphical XML editor provided by the Android Developer Tools*

Note the tabs at the bottom of the figure. You can switch between graphical and text modes by simply selecting the desired tab.

Specifying Target Screen Sizes

The range of screen sizes for Android devices is now truly mind-blowing. From the miniature wearable watches with 1-inch (2.54cm) screens, to Android-driven 50-inch and larger TVs, you may find your applications running on a vast array of screen sizes and densities. To make them easier to manage and customize, Android divides these devices into multiple categories based on diagonal screen size and the distance at which users normally view them:

- **Small**—Under 7.5cm/3in, at least 426dp×320dp resolution

- **Normal**—7.5cm to around 11.5cm/3in to around 4.5in, at least 470dp×320dp resolution

- **Large**—11.5cm to around 25cm/4.5in to around 10in, at least 640dp×480dp resolution

- **Extra-large**—Over 25cm/10in, at least 960dp×720dp resolution

If you, as a developer, do nothing to change the default screen support in your manifest file, your application will support normal screens and will attempt (and usually succeed) to support large and extra-large screens via some automated conversion by scaling and resizing code built into Android. It will also attempt to support small screens, but on older devices and SDK levels it will encounter historic issues and may not work.

As a developer, you might immediately ask the question, "Which screens sizes should I explicitly support, and how many of these different sizes are in use throughout the world?" The Android developer site at https://developer.android.com/about/dashboards/index.html attempts to provide some guidance, giving you a partial breakdown of which screen sizes are active in the wild. Figure 4-2 shows a snapshot of the screen sizes listed during the early writing of this book. If you take a look at the Android developer site dashboard as you read this book after publication, you should get an interesting idea of how screen sizes and densities are evolving with Android over time.

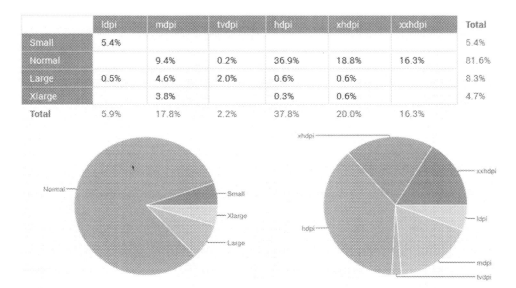

	ldpi	mdpi	tvdpi	hdpi	xhdpi	xxhdpi	Total
Small	5.4%						5.4%
Normal		9.4%	0.2%	36.9%	18.8%	16.3%	81.6%
Large	0.5%	4.6%	2.0%	0.6%	0.6%		8.3%
Xlarge		3.8%		0.3%	0.6%		4.7%
Total	5.9%	17.8%	2.2%	37.8%	20.0%	16.3%	

Figure 4-2. Partial data provided by Google on screen sizes being used throughout the world

Note that this is not an entirely accurate picture, since it only deals with devices that report data back to Google. However, it's useful as a rough estimate.

MYSTERIOUS GOOGLE TV SIZE

As part of the original release of Google TV—and later, the Nexus 7 tablet—Google targeted some specific screen sizes and densities "in between" the standard sizes shown in Figure 4-2. You don't need to worry about these now or even really consider them at all. For those of you who are curious, however, I'll talk more about screen sizes in Chapter 11.

To add support for all the screen sizes you want to target, you add a `<supports-screens>` element in your manifest file. This lists the screen sizes for which you have explicit support. For example, if you want to support large screens, you need to include the `<supports-screens android:largeScreens="true" >` element and attribute. The pattern for small and extra-large screens is similar; you can simply specify both by including

additional attributes, for example, `<supports-screens android:smallScreens="true"`
`android:xlargeScreens="true" >`. It is fine to use the default setting of `AndroidManifest.xml`
to "just work," however, if you plan on tailoring your user interface and artwork for larger
screens, be sure to add the relevant support for these screen sizes.

From Android 3.2 on, you can employ an alternative method to more accurately specify
the space requirements of your screen layouts. These attributes specify the smallest width,
`sw<N>dp`, available width, `w<N>dp`, and available height, `h<N>dp` (where N is the pixel count). At
first, using these prescriptive options may seem more complicated, but for many designers,
it is more natural to design a layout and a set of features, and then determine the minimum
and optimum sizes to the nearest pixel for presentation requirements.

Go ahead and edit your existing `AndroidManifest.xml` file to include broad screen support
using this addition:

```
<supports-screens android:smallScreens="true" android:normalScreens="true"
        android:largeScreens="true" android:xlargeScreens="true" >
```

Save your changes, and you should see a warning reported immediately. Because support
for extra-large screens was not introduced until a later version of Android and its SDK, you
will see a message similar to the following:

```
Attribute "xlargeScreens" is only used in API level 9 and higher (current min is 8)
```

Is this a problem? Not at all. You could take the easy way out and remove support for
extra-large screens. But where's the fun in that? Instead, you can learn how to adjust and
control API-level support and the SDK versions with which you build Android applications.
Let's do that instead!

Controlling Support for Different Android Versions

Android provides you with some control over the behavior of your application when it comes
to writing and running it across different devices with different versions of Android. The
principal method for controlling this is via the `<uses-sdk>` element in the Android Manifest,
as I briefly mentioned in Chapter 3. If you examine your manifest for the Beginning Android
example, you'll see that it already specifies a minimum supported Android version and a
target version using the `minSdkVersion` and `targetSdkVersion` attributes I described earlier.
This covers enough to get you app working in the device emulator and even on a range of
real devices. However, thanks to the variety and age range of the more than 1 billion Android
devices active throughout the world, you probably want to add specific details about what
versions of Android your application can support. Table 4-1 lists API levels for the Android
SDK and the equivalent Android version release.

Table 4-1. *Android SDK Official API Levels and Equivalent Android Version*

API Level	Android Version
1	Android 1.0
2	Android 1.1
3	Android 1.5
4	Android 1.6
5	Android 2.0
6	Android 2.0.1
7	Android 2.1
8	Android 2.2
9	Android 2.3
10	Android 2.3.3
11	Android 3.0
12	Android 3.1
13	Android 3.2
14	Android 4.0
15	Android 4.0.3
16	Android 4.1
17	Android 4.2
18	Android 4.3
19	Android 4.4
(unnumbered)	Google Glass extensions for Android 4.4
20	Android 4.4 for Wearables
21	Android 5.0
22	Android 5.1
23	Android 6.0

Why list all of those versions and API levels here? The gotcha with all of the attributes for `<uses-sdk>` is that they expect the integer matching the API level to be specified, not the SDK version or Android version. Keep that in mind when you're setting any of these values.

Keep the following considerations in mind when you are choosing a `minSdkVersion` attribute. First and foremost, on what APIs will your application rely and are any of them specific to newer versions of Android? A very simple example of this is the switch user interface element (it looks just like a light switch). This was only introduced in API level 14 with the release of Android 4.0. The action bar is another excellent example, although you don't need to worry about what this is for the moment. Google has gone to some significant effort to provide you with the ability to use or mimic features released in later versions of the API with devices that predate them. The most notable of these are the `appcompat` project you already saw in Chapter 2 and the Android Support Library.

Another consideration for minSdkVersion is how broadly you want to support older devices. Because of the control telecom carriers exert over the availability and timeliness of updates to Android devices, the vast majority of phones, tablets, and other devices in the wild are running something other than the latest Lollipop 5.0 release with API 21. The Android website tracks a breakdown of devices activated and their current Android release at https://developer.android.com/about/dashboards/index.html (the same URL that tracks screens, discussed earlier), and Figure 4-3 shows the state of device activations at the time of writing.

Version	Codename	API	Distribution
2.2	Froyo	8	0.5%
2.3.3 - 2.3.7	Gingerbread	10	9.1%
4.0.3 - 4.0.4	Ice Cream Sandwich	15	7.8%
4.1.x	Jelly Bean	16	21.3%
4.2.x		17	20.4%
4.3		18	7.0%
4.4	KitKat	19	33.9%

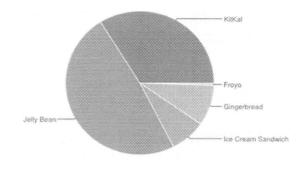

Figure 4-3. Partial data on Android releases in use and related API level for SDK settings

From this figure, you can see that you can target the vast majority of devices using a minSdkVersion of 8 (from Android release 2.2, the first truly widespread release). In practice, you also might think about the geographic spread of devices—what markets you might want to sell or release into, and how that changes the distribution of Android versions. The demographics and economic situations of those users will also come in to play—investment bankers in New York will have very different ideas about purchasing apps compared to backpackers in Vietnam.

The second and more subtle manifest value controlling Android versions is the targetSdkVersion setting. With developers in mind, Android offers this value so you can indicate which version you are writing your code against. The main benefit from this setting comes behind the scenes, on devices running newer versions of Android. Knowing that your code was written for version X, successive versions of Android implement a range of optimizations and enhancements that can actually improve the behavior and responsiveness of your code long after you've written it. One example of this is where Android allows your application to adopt new system-default themes if the targetSdkVersion is high enough.

The targetSdkVersion setting is entirely optional, but if you do decide to use it, you must have that release of the SDK installed on the system on which you are developing your application. If you don't have that particular version present, the ADT detects this and displays errors in the logging area for your IDE. For instance, Figure 4-4 shows the error you see in the Eclipse console output when it loads a project referencing a targetSdkVersion with no matching SDK installed.

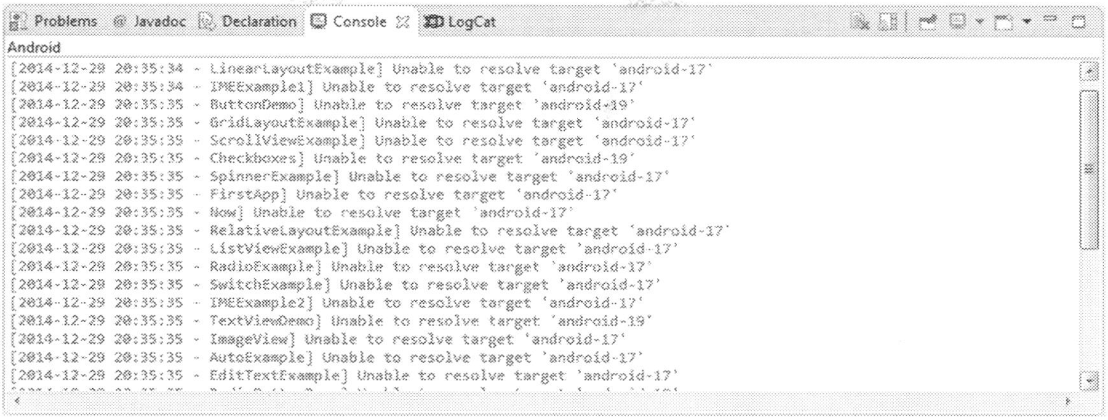

Figure 4-4. Example errors from missing targetSdkVersion versions

> **Note**   You can have as many different versions of the SDK installed as you like. The only practical limitation is disk space.

The last of the three version-related manifest settings is `maxSdkVersion`. Ordinarily you should never need to set this value; in fact, Google strongly recommends that you not do so. However, it exists for very old versions prior to 2.0.2, where Android would perform a running version instead of a declared `maxSdkVersion` check and refuse to install an application if the device was running a higher (later) version.

When I examined screen sizes earlier in this chapter, I left you with an unresolved warning about extra-large screen sizes needing at least API level 9 for support. Go ahead and edit your `AndroidManifest.xml` to change the `android:minSdkVersion` to 9. The `<uses-sdk>` element in your manifest should look like this:

```
<uses-sdk
    android:minSdkVersion="9"
    android:targetSdkVersion="21" />
```

Writing Actual Android Code

Up to this point, I have been taking things slowly to familiarize you with your new environment and the framework Android and its build tools provide. But editing XML isn't exactly ground breaking. If you are itching to get at the heart of coding for Android, then the wait is over.

Using the Beginning Android example I introduced in Chapters 2 and 3 as the basis, you will step through the code for you project and modify it to perform some application logic and present the user (that's you, for now) with some real interaction. Along the way, you can start to build your knowledge of the basic Java building blocks of all Android applications, starting with an Android activity.

> **Note**   This chapter assumes you are following the naming conventions of the project and files I used in the original instructions in Chapter 2. If you are using different names, just adjust the instructions provided here so that the names match yours.

Introducing the Activity

I covered the overall project structure and file layout in Chapter 3, and if you look within your project's `src/` directory, you can see that the tree of folders I discussed all derive from the Java package name I used when I created the project. For example, `com.artifexdigital.android.beginningandroid` results in the directory structure `src/com/artifexdigital/android/beginningandroid`. At the lowest directory, the ADT generates the file named `MainActivity.java`, which is where you create your first activity.

If the `MainActivity.java` file isn't already open in your IDE—Android Studio, Eclipse, or whatever you've chosen to use—open it now and paste in the following code, overwriting the existing content. You can find the example code for the book on the Apress website—look for `Ch04/BeginningAndroid` for this example, shown in Listing 4-1.

Listing 4-1. The Java Code for BeginningAndroid

```
package com.artifexdigital.android.beginningandroid;

import android.os.Bundle;
import android.app.Activity;
import android.view.View;
import android.widget.Button;

public class MainActivity extends Activity implements View.OnClickListener{
    Button myButton;
    Integer myInt;

    @Override
    public void onCreate(Bundle savedInstanceState) {
        super.onCreate(savedInstanceState);
        myButton = new Button(this);
        myButton.setOnClickListener(this);
        myInt = 0;
        updateClickCounter();
        setContentView(myButton);
    }

    public void onClick(View view) {
        updateClickCounter();
    }

    private void updateClickCounter() {
        myInt++;
        myButton.setText(myInt.toString());
    }
}
```

Looking Inside Your First Activity

Let's examine the Java code in Listing 4-1 piece by piece. We'll start with the package declaration and imported classes; they are as follows:

```
package com.artifexdigital.android.beginningandroid;

import android.app.Activity;
import android.os.Bundle;
import android.view.View;
import android.widget.Button;
import android.widget.Button;
```

Your package declaration has to match the one you used at project creation time. From there, as with any sort of Java project, you need to import any classes you reference. Most of the Android-specific classes are in the android package. You also have a wide range of Java SE and Java ME classes from which to choose for incorporating into any Android program, such as java.util.Date and others. Not every Java SE or ME class is available— Google doesn't provide an exhaustive list of differences, instead it just documents what is supported, which is largely derived from the Apache Harmony Java implementation.

Activities are the fundamental building blocks of user interaction in Android. You can think of an activity as roughly analogous to a screen or device interface that the user sees and the (initial) logic to control interaction with the user. An application is typically made up of multiple activities that work together to present your application's overall experience, even though each activity is an independent object in its own right. An activity is a public class in the Java sense, and it inherits from the android.app.Activity base class. In this case, the activity holds a button (myButton):

```
public class MainActivity extends Activity implements View.OnClickListener {
  Button myButton;
```

Anyone familiar with any other UI toolkit, like Swing, immediately recognizes a button as a typical UI widget. (I cover all available UI widgets and elements in Part II of the book.) In this example, for the sake of simplicity, I have made the button the only UI widget of the activity, and therefore, because I want all button clicks trapped just within the activity itself, I also have the activity class implement OnClickListener.

The onCreate() method is invoked when the activity is started. This is one of the four fundamental methods that control the lifecycle of an Android application. I cover more on the lifecycle in the next chapter, but for now, you can rely on the fact that onCreate() is invoked once and only once in the life of your activity.

From here, we first chain up to the superclass, calling its onCreate() method. This ensures that our activity invokes the base Android activity initialization on instantiation:

```
@Override
public void onCreate(Bundle savedInstanceState) {
    super.onCreate(savedInstanceState);
    myButton = new Button(this);
    myButton.setOnClickListener(this);
```

```
    myInt = 0;
    updateClickCounter();
    setContentView(myButton);
}
```

In our implementation, we then perform the following set up work:

- Create the button instance myButton (via new Button(this)).

- Instruct the button to send all button clicks to the activity instance itself (via setOnClickListener()).

- Initialize the myInt counter that we'll use to track the number of button clicks.

- Call the private updateClickCounter() method as a shorthand way to populate the text of the button so it can be drawn successfully.

- And finally, set the activity's content view to be the button itself (via setContentView()).

In later chapters, I examine more closely the purpose of the curious Bundle savedInstanceState. For the moment, consider it a handle to a blob of useful state information that all activities receive upon creation.

As an activity that implements the OnClickListener interface, this activity is responsible for providing the necessary plumbing for the onClick() method, shown next.

```
public void onClick(View view) {
  updateClickCounter();
}
```

In Android, clicking a button invokes onClick() in the OnClickListener instance configured for that button. The View object that triggered the click (in this case, the button) is then passed to the listener. All we do here is call that private updateClickCounter() method:

```
private void updateClickCounter() {
    myInt++;
    myButton.setText(myInt.toString());
}
```

When we initially start the activity (onCreate()) or whenever the button is clicked (onClick()), the text label of the button refreshes to be the current count of the number of clicks on myButton via the setText() method.

Building and Running Your Enhanced Application

You can (re)build your application at any time using your IDE's built-in Android packaging tool. For example, Project->Build All in Eclipse. Then run the application. Android Studio or Eclipse should launch your device emulator automatically if it is not already running, install the apk file for your application, and launch the activity. If, for any reason, the activity doesn't appear to launch, try finding the activity in the home screen of your emulated device, and click on it to start it. You should see an activity very much like the one in Figure 4-5, which shows what our app looks like after we click on the button several times.

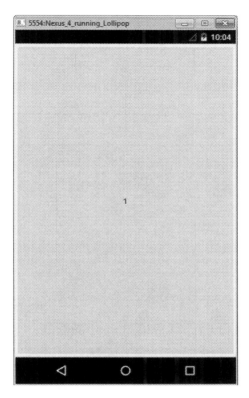

Figure 4-5. Your enhanced application displaying the click counter feature

Because the button consumes pretty much the entire device screen, you can press just about anywhere to update the click counter shown in the button's label.

You will note some UI effects, such as the pale border that surrounds the button and the centering of the label text. These result from defaults in your layout and other styling defaults, which I'll explore in the coming chapters.

Congratulations, you have enhanced your Beginning Android application, turning it into a piece of push-button wizardry. When you are done playing with your new creation, press the Back triangle on the emulator, and return to the home screen.

Part II

Activities and the User Interface

Chapter 5

Working with Android Widgets

In Chapters 2 and 3 you briefly walked through the process of creating a new project and saw the files and project structure generated by the Android build tools. You also delved into modifying and enhancing your first project in Chapter 4, adding a button to the user interface and some program logic behind it. As you have probably guessed, there is much, much more to the world of creating Android user interfaces and the logic that drives them.

In this chapter I introduce the many different kinds of user interface elements and how you can used them to create a huge variety of applications. You will master not only how to use these UI widgets in their own right, but you will also start to learn how they can control, influence, and interact with your activities and the other program logic of your application. Let's get to it.

Understanding Activity Fundamentals

In Chapter 4, I introduced the activity as the basic building block for the screens or windows with which your users interact with your Android application. Your application probably has many different screens for showing data, capturing user input, displaying results of actions, and more.

Android has developed a design philosophy that promotes less visually crowded or cluttered screens that have plenty of space around screen elements or widgets. In its current form, this design approach is known as Material Design, and you can find out much more about it at `http://developer.android.com/design/material/index.html`. By no means do you need to become an expert in all the suggestions on that site. As a new Android developer, the one point to take on board right now is that if your application has activity user interfaces (UIs) that are less cluttered and with fewer widgets, you will almost certainly end up with more screens to cover all of your desired functionality. In Android terms, that means more activities. In fact, the many-activity approach predates Material Design and its predecessors (and will probably outlive its successors, too). With the knowledge of UI widgets you gain in this chapter, let your activities flourish! Consider them cheap, easily used, and easily discarded, and always feel at liberty to add more activities whenever it suits your design needs.

Naming with Labels

Labels are the most fundamental and straightforward of all user interface widgets. Almost every UI toolkit ever devised has the notion of a label—a simple piece of (hopefully descriptive) text that sits next to some other UI element or widget to add explanation, a caption, detail, or notes. In Android, the label is known as a TextView. It is designed to be a static string, though there are ways in which TextView values can be changed at runtime.

As with all widgets, you are totally at liberty to define a TextView in Java within your application. Those of you familiar with designing nontrivial user interfaces solely in code will realize that this gets very tedious very quickly. The faster, easier, and more elegant way of adding labels is by inserting the TextView XML element into your XML layout through the graphical layout editor, which will make the XML layout file changes for you.

Whether you code directly in Java or use the layout editor, setting the android:text property is key to making your text appear as the label text. Even though you have used the XML layout approach to use the TextView label, you can still control its value (the text seen on screen) by referring to a string resource. I cover this later in the chapter, but examples of when you might want to do this include when you want to localize your UI into different languages, or when you want to adopt a user's chosen preference.

Over 70 different properties can control the appearance and behavior of TextView labels. These are some of the most commonly used properties:

- android:hint: A hint to display.

- android:typeface: Sets the typeface to use for the label (e.g., monospace).

- android:textStyle: Indicates what combination of bold (bold), italic (italic), or both (bold_italic) should be applied to the text.

- android.textAppearance: An omnibus property that lets you combine text color, typeface, size, and style in one go!

- android:textColor: Uses the common RGB notation in hexadecimal to choose the text color for the label. For example, #0000FF is blue.

When you open the ch5/LabelExample project, you see the contents for the layout.xml resource, as shown in Listing 5-1.

Listing 5-1. Using a TextView in Your XML Layout

```
<RelativeLayout xmlns:android="http://schemas.android.com/apk/res/android"
    xmlns:tools="http://schemas.android.com/tools"
    android:layout_width="match_parent"
    android:layout_height="match_parent"
    tools:context=".LabelExample" >

    <TextView
        android:layout_width="wrap_content"
        android:layout_height="wrap_content"
        android:text="A label by any other name is still a label" />

</RelativeLayout>
```

With only this layout, along with the bare-bones Java inserted for you by using the new project option in either Android Studio or Eclipse, you get the result shown in Figure 5-1.

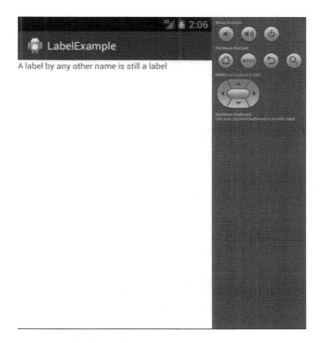

Figure 5-1. *The label example showing TextView in action*

Pressing Buttons (redux)

We return to the topic of buttons, and in particular, the widget that you first employed in the race to get coding in Chapter 2. Let me provide you with a little more detail to arm you with all the useful knowledge you need for adding Buttons to your UIs. First, as with all other widgets, Button is derived from the View object, and in particular, it is a subclass of the TextView. This means everything mentioned in the previous section on labels applies to the Button.

Android allows you two approaches when dealing with the on-click listener for a Button. The first option is the "classic" way of defining an object and explicitly stating in the definition that it implements View.OnClickListener. Even better than the classic method is the contemporary Android way of simplifying things. This simple option has two steps:

1. Create a public method on your activity that returns void. Have this method accept a View parameter.

2. Modify your Button element in the XML to include the android:OnClick attribute. Set the string value of the attribute to the method name defined in step one.

Here is an example of how this looks in the Java code:

```
...
public void methodOnMyActivity(View myButton) {
    // method logic
}
...
```

And here is the matching XML layout to wire the Button widget to the method:

```
...
<Button android:onClick=" methodOnMyActivity " />
...
```

At first you may not feel this is any simpler than the traditional approach. But consider the ease with which this method opens up options to change the Activity for a given Button through simple dent of differing options in your XML specification—for instance, under different language locales, screen sizes, and so on. I talk more about these options in coming chapters.

Handling Images with ImageView and ImageButton

There's an old saying that a picture is worth a thousand words. In that vein, as a developer, you often want to let an image or picture speak for you, rather than attempt to deploy a long text description. Android offers a number of image-based UI widgets. The two most commonly used are parallels to the TextView and Button you have already seen; the ImageView and ImageButton are their graphical equivalents.

Like the text-based widgets, you will most often define these in your XML layout rather than build them laboriously in Java. The key XML attribute that both ImageView and ImageButton share is android:src, which indicates the image to be used. If you remember back to the overview of the typical project layout in Chapter 3, you can likely guess that the default approach for specifying android:src values is to refer to graphics resources you have placed in your project's res/drawables directory (and/or density-specific variants thereof).

As the name suggest, ImageButton adds button-like behaviors, meaning onClickListener() and other behaviors and semantics you use with a Button can also be used. Listing 5-2 shows an example of an ImageView configured to use a picture from res/drawables.

Listing 5-2. ImageView in Action

```
<RelativeLayout xmlns:android="http://schemas.android.com/apk/res/android"
    xmlns:tools="http://schemas.android.com/tools"
    android:layout_width="match_parent"
    android:layout_height="match_parent"
    tools:context=".MainActivity" >

    <ImageView
        android:id="@+id/icon"
        android:layout_width="fill_parent"
        android:layout_height="fill_parent"
```

```
        android:adjustViewBounds="true"
        android:src="@drawable/chair"
        android:contentDescription="A Chair" />
</RelativeLayout>
```

You can find the code for this example in the ch05/ImageViewExample project, and it includes a picture of my favorite chair. You can see the results in Figure 5-2.

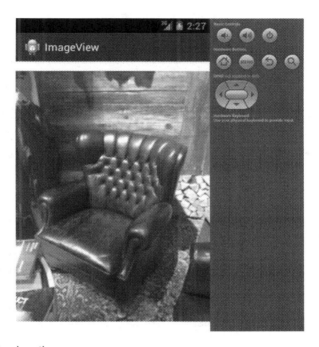

Figure 5-2. *The ImageView in action*

Fielding Text with EditText

Static strings of text and interesting images are vital parts of many user interfaces, but a time comes when you need the user to act, and that can mean asking them to input text. As with almost every other widget toolkit ever invented, Android provides a UI widget for soliciting text input: the EditText widget.

EditText is subclassed from TextView, and therefore inherits many of the same characteristics available to TextView such as textAppearance. Also, a number of specific properties ensure you can craft exactly the input field you want. These include the following:

- android:autoText: Manages the use of the built-in spelling correction feature.

- android:digits: Limits the field to only accept digits as input.

* android:password: Configures the field to display password dots as characters are typed into the field, hiding the typed characters.

* android:singleLine: Manages the behavior of the enter key to determine if this should create a new line within the text field or more focus to the next widget.

An alternative approach exists for specifying field characteristics for EditText, which is the use of the inputType property instead. I cover this in much more detail along with keyboards and input methods in Chapter 8. For now, Listing 5-3 shows inputType in action with other options.

Listing 5-3. Using android:inputType to Control EditText Field Behavior

```
<RelativeLayout xmlns:android="http://schemas.android.com/apk/res/android"
    xmlns:tools="http://schemas.android.com/tools"
    android:layout_width="match_parent"
    android:layout_height="match_parent"
    tools:context=".EditTextExample" >

    <EditText
        android:id="@+id/myfield"
        android:layout_width="fill_parent"
        android:layout_height="fill_parent"
        android:inputType="textCapSentences"
        android:singleLine="false" />
</RelativeLayout>
```

In this example, I set the android:inputType attribute to flag that the user's text should have the first word automatically capitalized, and android:singleLine is false, enabling multiple lines of text within the one widget. Listing 5-4 shows the accompanying Java package. You will find this example in ch05/EditTextExample.

Listing 5-4. The EditText Widget in Action

```
package com.artifexdigital.android.edittextexample;

import android.os.Bundle;
import android.app.Activity;
import android.widget.EditText;;

public class EditTextExample extends Activity {

    @Override
    protected void onCreate(Bundle savedInstanceState) {
        super.onCreate(savedInstanceState);
        setContentView(R.layout.activity_edit_text_example);

        EditText myfield=(EditText)findViewById(R.id.myfield);
        myfield.setText("Veni, Vidi, Vici");
    }

}
```

You can see the results from this example in Figure 5-3.

Figure 5-3. *Text input example showing EditView in action*

If you look closely at Figure 5-3, you can see some telltale signs that this is an editable field. Android's built-in dictionary and spell-check features have flagged words with red underlining that they think are misspelled. We'll have to forgive the stock dictionary for not including famous Latin phrases. You can also see the cursor at the end of the text; it's ready for you to actually edit, as the name EditText implies. If you think your users will tire of doing all the typing themselves, you can employ Android's AutoCompleteTextView variant (again subclassed), which prompts the users with auto-completed suggested words as they enter text.

CheckBox? Got It.

Let's continue with the familiar theme of UI widgets you have certainly seen before—Android includes the classic CheckBox, which provides a binary yes/no or checked/unchecked widget. As with the other widgets we have discussed, this is a subclass of View and TextView, which means a range of useful properties are inherited.

The CheckBox object provides you with some Java helper methods to do useful things with your check boxes:

- isChecked(): A method to examine if the CheckBox is checked.
- setChecked(): Checks (sets) the CheckBox regardless of the current state.
- toggle(): Toggles the state of the CheckBox.

Listing 5-5 is an example check box layout with simple logic, which you can find in the ch05/CheckboxExample project:

Listing 5-5. Layout for a CheckBox Widget

```
<RelativeLayout xmlns:android="http://schemas.android.com/apk/res/android"
    xmlns:tools="http://schemas.android.com/tools"
    android:layout_width="match_parent"
    android:layout_height="match_parent"
    tools:context=".CheckboxExample" >

    <CheckBox
        android:id="@+id/check"
        android:layout_width="wrap_content"
        android:layout_height="wrap_content"
        android:text="The checkbox is unchecked" />

</RelativeLayout>
```

To have the check box actually do something useful, you can add Java logic to partner your layout. Listing 5-6 is the Java package that demonstrates the check box.

Listing 5-6. The CheckBox Java Code

```
package com.artifexdigital.android.checkboxexample;

import android.os.Bundle;
import android.app.Activity;
import android.widget.CheckBox;
import android.widget.CompoundButton;
import android.widget.CompoundButton.OnCheckedChangeListener;

public class CheckboxExample extends Activity {

    CheckBox myCheckbox;

    @Override
    protected void onCreate(Bundle savedInstanceState) {
        super.onCreate(savedInstanceState);
        setContentView(R.layout.activity_checkbox_example);

        myCheckbox = (CheckBox)findViewById(R.id.check);
        myCheckbox.setOnCheckedChangeListener(new OnCheckedChangeListener() {
            @Override
            public void onCheckedChanged(CompoundButton buttonView, boolean isChecked) {
                if (buttonView.isChecked()) {
                    myCheckbox.setText("The checkbox is checked");
                }
```

```
            else
            {
                myCheckbox.setText("The checkbox is unchecked");
            }
        }
    });
    }
}
```

Surprise! Obviously much more is going on in that code than just the auto-generated skeleton from Android Studio or Eclipse with ADT. The fifth import in the Java code alludes to what is happening. By importing OnCheckedChangeListener and providing the implementation for the onCheckedChanged() callback method, we've set up our check box to be its own listener for state change actions. When the check box is toggled, the callback fires, and the code updates the text of the check box with a written description of its new state. This not only acts to nicely parcel all the behavior of the widget in one place, but it means you can do things like form validation during entry, without needing to pass all of the data and widget attributes to some other function for checking. Using this method, you avoid lots of delays, and your code and its own sanity checks are nicely side by side.

You can see the results of this immediate update to the text along with the check box in Figures 5-4 and 5-5.

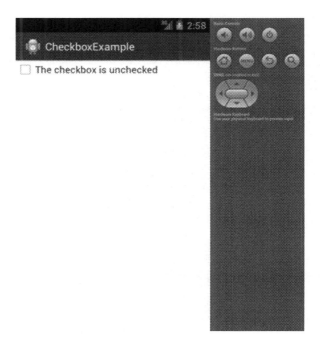

Figure 5-4. An unchecked check box

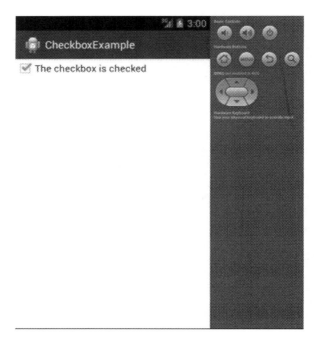

Figure 5-5. The check box is now checked

Switching to the Switch

New to Android 4.0 and later releases (Ice Cream Sandwich, Jelly Bean, KitKat, Lollipop, and Marshmallow) is a variant on the Checkbox. This is a two-state toggle Switch that provides users with the ability to swipe or drag with their finger as if they were toggling a light switch. They can also tap the Switch widget as if it were a Checkbox to change its state.

The Switch provides an android:text property to display associated text with the Switch state, which is controlled via the setTextOn() and setTextOff() methods of the Switch.

Other useful methods available for a Switch include these:

- getTextOn(): Returns the text used when the Switch is on
- getTextOff(): Returns the text used when the Switch is off
- setChecked(): Changes the current Switch state to on (just like Checkbox)

For example, Listing 5-7, an excerpt from the ch05/SwitchExample project, shows a simple switch layout:

Listing 5-7. Layout for the SwitchExample

```
<RelativeLayout xmlns:android="http://schemas.android.com/apk/res/android"
    xmlns:tools="http://schemas.android.com/tools"
    android:layout_width="match_parent"
    android:layout_height="match_parent"
    tools:context=".SwitchExample" >
```

```
<Switch
    android:id="@+id/switchdemo"
    android:layout_width="wrap_content"
    android:layout_height="wrap_content"
    android:text="The switch is off" />

</RelativeLayout>
```

Note that we can't call the widget "switch," due to reserved word conventions in Java. The corresponding SwitchExample.java shown in Listing 5-8 retrieves and configures the behavior of the switch:

Listing 5-8. The SwitchExample Java Code

```java
package com.artifiexdigital.android.switchexample;

import android.os.Bundle;
import android.app.Activity;
import android.widget.Switch;
import android.widget.CompoundButton;
import android.widget.CompoundButton.OnCheckedChangeListener;

public class SwitchExample extends Activity {

    Switch mySwitch;

    @Override
    protected void onCreate(Bundle savedInstanceState) {
        super.onCreate(savedInstanceState);
        setContentView(R.layout.activity_switch_example);

        mySwitch = (Switch)findViewById(R.id.switchdemo);
        mySwitch.setOnCheckedChangeListener(new OnCheckedChangeListener() {
            @Override
            public void onCheckedChanged(CompoundButton buttonView, boolean isChecked) {
                if (buttonView.isChecked()) {
                    mySwitch.setText("The switch is on");
                }
                else
                {
                    mySwitch.setText("The switch is off");
                }
            }
        });
    }
}
```

You can see from the general structure, use of methods, and behavior that the Switch operates in very similar ways to the Checkbox. In fact, if you line up the layout and the code side by side for both check box and switch examples, you can see a one-for-one equivalence in both the layout and logic. You can see the results in Figures 5-6 and 5-7 with the switch in each possible state.

Figure 5-6. *The switch in the off position*

Figure 5-7. *The switch is now on*

Working with Radio Buttons

With the previous widget examples, I have mentioned how common they are across lots of other UI toolkits. This trend continues with the RadioButton widget. The RadioButton shares the two-state operation that you see with CheckBox and Switch widgets, and it gains many of the same features by also being a subclass of CompoundButton. This means you can set colors, fonts, and so on, just as you can with the other widgets; you can also diagnose and set state through methods like toggle() and isChecked().

RadioButton takes these capabilities further by adding an extra layer of functionality to allow multiple radio buttons to be grouped into a logical set, and then allowing only one of the buttons to be set at any time. That should sound familiar if you have used a web page or other Android application any time in the last decade or so. The grouping is achieved through adding each RadioButton to a RadioGroup container element in the XML layout.

You can assign the RadioGroup a reference ID in the layout via the android:id attribute (just like you can with all other widgets), and by doing this, you can then access additional methods available on the entire group of RadioButtons. These methods include the following:

- check(): Checks/sets a specific radio button via its ID, regardless of its current state.
- clearCheck(): Clears all radio buttons in the RadioGroup.
- getCheckedRadioButtonId(): Returns the ID of the currently checked RadioButton (this will return -1 if no RadioButton is checked).

Listing 5-9 is taken from the ch05/RadioExample application as an example of the XML layout for RadioButtons inside a RadioGroup.

Listing 5-9. The XML Layout Showing RadioButton Grouping

```
<RelativeLayout xmlns:android="http://schemas.android.com/apk/res/android"
    xmlns:tools="http://schemas.android.com/tools"
    android:layout_width="match_parent"
    android:layout_height="match_parent"
    tools:context=".RadioExample" >

    <RadioGroup
        android:orientation="vertical"
        android:layout_width="fill_parent"
        android:layout_height="fill_parent" >

        <RadioButton android:id="@+id/radio1"
            android:layout_width="wrap_content"
            android:layout_height="wrap_content"
            android:text="Rock" />

        <RadioButton android:id="@+id/radio2"
            android:layout_width="wrap_content"
            android:layout_height="wrap_content"
            android:text="Paper" />
```

```
    <RadioButton android:id="@+id/radio3"
        android:layout_width="wrap_content"
        android:layout_height="wrap_content"
        android:text="Scissors" />

    <RadioButton android:id="@+id/radio4"
        android:layout_width="wrap_content"
        android:layout_height="wrap_content"
        android:text="Lizard" />

    <RadioButton android:id="@+id/radio5"
        android:layout_width="wrap_content"
        android:layout_height="wrap_content"
        android:text="Spock" />

</RadioGroup>

</RelativeLayout>
```

You can add other widgets such as a TextView within the RadioGroup too, and these render
within the group structure. You don't need to add any custom code to the skeleton of a
newly generated project—you can see the RadioButton behavior just fine, as shown in
Figure 5-8.

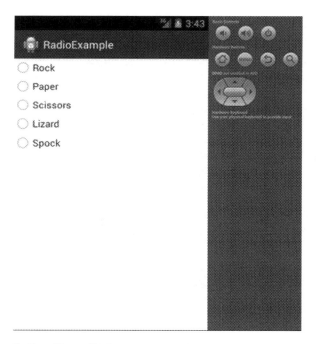

Figure 5-8. Fresh from the Big Bang Theory TV show, everyone's favorite game in RadioButtons

> **Note** I've taken liberties with the traditional Rock-Paper-Scissors game, using the new rules
> popularized in a certain comedy TV show. I think it's for the best.

You can observe the behavior described above for a freshly instantiated RadioGroup. None of
the RadioButtons is set by default. If you wish to have a default set at rendering time, you
can use setChecked() on the RadioButton from your onCreate() callback in your activity.

Timing All Manner of Things with Clocks

A pair of simple widgets are available to display the current time on an Android device;
which you choose to use depends on your preference for analog or digital readouts. Both
the DigitalClock widget and AnalogClock widget do all the work for you by refreshing
themselves based on the system clock.

You do not need Java code to use either widget. Simply place the relevant widget XML into
your layout file, as shown in Listings 5-10 and 5-11.

Listing 5-10. XML Layout for an AnalogClock

```
<RelativeLayout xmlns:android="http://schemas.android.com/apk/res/android"
    xmlns:tools="http://schemas.android.com/tools"
    android:layout_width="match_parent"
    android:layout_height="match_parent"
    tools:context="com.artifexdigital.android.analogclockexample.AnalogClock" >

    <AnalogClock android:id="@+id/analog"
        android:layout_width="fill_parent"
        android:layout_height="wrap_content"
        android:layout_centerHorizontal="true"
    />

</RelativeLayout>
```

Listing 5-11. XML Layout for a DigitalClock

```
<RelativeLayout xmlns:android="http://schemas.android.com/apk/res/android"
    xmlns:tools="http://schemas.android.com/tools"
    android:layout_width="match_parent"
    android:layout_height="match_parent"
    tools:context="com.artifexdigital.android.digitalclockexample.DigitalClock" >

    <DigitalClock android:id="@+id/digital"
        android:layout_width="wrap_content"
        android:layout_height="wrap_content"
        android:layout_centerHorizontal="true"
    />

</RelativeLayout>
```

You can use either of these layouts with a stock new Android project from Android Studio or Eclipse to display the running clocks shown in Figures 5-9 and 5-10.

Figure 5-9. The AnalogClock in action

Figure 5-10. The DigitalClock in action

These examples are available in the ch05/ folder. I cover some other examples of clocklike views, such as timers and other time counters, in later chapters.

Easing Input with SeekBar

When we looked at EditView earlier, I mentioned one of the attributes available to you was android:digits, for limiting the field so it only accepts numeric input. This can be very useful for the input of data such as telephone numbers, but sometimes you want people to provide numeric or pseudo-numeric input in places where typing digits is awkward or tedious.

Enter the SeekBar widget, which can be used to gather user input. The user simply slides the selector on the SeekBar to a visual point of the user's liking. Classic examples of where this type of user interface appears include volume controls (though we cover Android's dedicated volume control widgets in Chapter 12), color mix selection, answers to survey questions on a disagree-to-agree scale, and so forth.

By default, positioning the selector determines the numeric property of the SeekBar somewhere between 0 and 100. You can override the default range by using the setMax() method. The getProgress() method, while it has a slightly misleading name, is used to determine the current position and associated numeric value of the selector. You can also register a listener for the SeekBar using the setOnSeekBarChangeListener() method to capture activity and values whenever a user changes the selector position. You can find the code for the example in ch05/SeekBarExample.

Views: The Base of All UI Widgets

All of the UI widgets described in this chapter inherit from the same base class: View. Because this is true, you are provided with benefits, some of which you have already seen, such as font settings, colors, and so forth.

In addition to these, you have a range of attributes and methods available that are inherited from View, and these are fully covered in the Android documentation. Here are just a few of the most commonly used ones.

Useful Common Inherited Properties

Properties available to all View-descended widgets that you will commonly use include these:

* android:contentDescription: This is a text value associated with any widget that accessibility tools can use, where the visual aspect of the widget is of little or no help to the user.

* android: visibility: Determines if the widget should be visible or invisible at first instantiation.

* android:padding: Expands the size of the overall widget beyond the minimum size required to fit its content. For example, this can increase the size of a button beyond what is required for its text or image. Dimensions are in pixels, device-independent pixels, or millimeters.

* android:paddingLeft, android:paddingRight, android:paddingTop, android:padding Bottom: A fine-grained alternative to android:padding, which allows different pad values on all sides of the widget.

Note that for padding, you may also use the setPadding() method in Java to achieve padded layout at runtime.

Useful Common Inherited Methods

As you might already have guessed, the commonly used methods inherited from View for all widgets mostly revolve around basic state management, and navigating what widgets exist, their groupings, their parent and child objects in the layout, and so forth. The most commonly used include the following:

* getParent(): Finds the parent object, whether its a widget or container.

* findViewById(): Finds the widget with a given ID.

* getRootView(): Gets the root of the tree provided from the activities original call to setContentView().

* setEnabled(), isEnabled(): Sets and checks the enabled state of any widget, commonly used when you wish to deactivate other widgets on screen based on checked items, switched options, or radio button options.

Even More UI Widgets

We have covered many of the UI building blocks in this chapter, and you should now know how to start building the activity interfaces you might want to use for your application. Note that this coverage is not exhaustive. In particular, I return to cover some of the media-focused widgets in the audio and video chapters.

I cover an additional widget, `TabView`, in the next chapter on layouts, because its use and features rely on some understanding of `FrameLayout`, which is also covered in that chapter.

And lastly, there are more complex widgets for dealing with dynamically generated content, choice of data, and so forth, which I cover in Chapter 7.

Chapter 6

Layouts and UI Design

In this chapter, I explore how to expand your knowledge of simple widgets so it covers the full canvas of controlling your overall application and activity layout and design. I use Android layouts as the definition-based way of describing how to organize and display all of the widgets and other UI artifacts that comprise your user interface. In order to understand how layouts work, you need to think of layouts as containers. A layout stores all of the widgets and their attributes so that they are ready to be used, just like ingredients in kitchen containers. The widgets I introduced in Chapter 5 are fine, but as soon as you want two or more widgets on a screen, it becomes increasingly cumbersome to manage each one—each has its own position, spacing, and inter-widget relationships—if you attempt to manage each individually. You have already seen a hint of how managing groups of widgets makes your life easier—through the `RadioGroup` element, which allows the aggregate control of multiple `RadioButton` widgets.

This is where Android's concept of containers for UI layout comes to the forefront. As you will see during the introduction to each of the layout styles Android supports, one of the key features provided by layouts is inheriting implicit layout specifications for the various widgets you wish to display. This lets you focus on the key parts of your UI design that add the functionality, flair, or behavior you seek and spend less time laboriously specifying repetitious drawing instructions. This approach is also flexible enough to cover any given screen that is "inflated" from a container, or multiple containers that are nested, stacked, or otherwise combined together.

In this chapter, I walk through the four major layout containers provided by Android:

- `RelativeLayout`—Now the default in Android for new projects, the `RelativeLayout` is a rules-governed approach to having UI elements self-arrange.

- `LinearLayout`—Historically the most commonly used Android layout (and the default for new projects until Android 4.0 and later). Following a traditional box model, `LinearLayout` imagines all widgets as boxes to fit within and around each other.

- ▓ TableLayout—A model that considers the screen area a grid, to be filled in a similar way to how an HTML table gets filled.

- ▓ GridLayout—Not to be confused with the grid approach for TableLayout, the GridLayout uses an infinite fine-line approach to splitting screen space into successively more specific areas.

Following on from there, I explore, in more depth, the process of building layouts with the layout editor introduced earlier, and the fundamentals of manipulating your XML layouts from Java code. Lastly, I show you how to rewrite your click-counting button application so it uses layouts. This is a big chapter, so let's get started.

Working with Relative Layouts

The RelativeLayout, as you would assume, given its name, places your widgets on the screen based on their relationships with other widgets and the parent container itself. If you look back at the examples I used in the first chapters of the book, you'll see that they all used RelativeLayout by default, and in fact, this is the default for a new layout.xml file if you use ADT in Eclipse or Android Studio. For example, you can place a given widget below another, have top edges align, or ensure all widgets align to the right edge of the container or a parent widget, and so forth.

Relative referencing relies on a set of standard attributes that describe the desired relationships, which you include within your widgets' element definitions in the XML specification.

Positioning Relative to the Activity Container

The most fundamental of relationships is covered by specifying how a UI widget relates to its parent container. A range of true/false attributes are used to specify these relationships, including the following:

- ▓ android:layout_alignParentTop: Aligns the widget's top edge with the top of the container.

- ▓ android:layout_alignParentBottom: Aligns the widget's bottom edge with the bottom of the container.

- ▓ android:layout_alignParentStart: Aligns the widget's start side with the left side of the container; used when taking account of right-to-left and left-to-right written scripts. For instance, in an English language left-to-right layout, this positioning would control the widget's left side.

- ▓ android:layout_alignParentEnd: Aligns the widget's end side with the left side of the container; used when taking account of right-to-left and left-to-right written scripts.

- ▓ android:layout_centerHorizontal: Positions the widget horizontally at the center of the container.

- ▓ android:layout_centerVertical: Positions the widget vertically at the center of the container. If you'd like both horizontal and vertical centering, you can use the combined layout_centerInParent.

Note that other layout modifiers like padding are taken into account when determining edges, so you should think of any edge-aligning attributes as applying to the absolute outer boundary of you widget.

Identifiying Properties for Relative Layout

To further control the layout of widgets and to describe their relative position to other widgets in the layout, you need to provide the identity of the widget in the layout container. Do this by using the android:id identifier attribute on any widget that you want to refer to.

The first time you reference an android:id value, ensure you use the plus modifier (i.e., @+id/button1). Subsequent references to the same widget do not need to use the plus sign. Using the plus notation helps the ADT linting tools spot instances in which you start referring to an id that has not been properly introduced. Think of this as equivalent to declaring variables before using them. Note that if you are using a version of the SDK older than level 16, no linter support is available, but runtime checks are still performed for missing plus notation on first use of an id.

With the id in place, another widget, such as another button like button2, can now reference our example @+id/button1, introduced earlier,by nominating that id string in its own layout-related properties. Note that names like button1 and button2 are OK for this example, but in reality, you want to choose meaningful names for your widgets; you should consider thinking up a naming scheme that will help you manage your layouts when they become more complex.

Relative Positioning Properties

With the id semantics in place, you can use these six properties to control the position of widgets relative to each other:

- android:layout_above: Used to place a UI widget above the widget referenced in the property

- android:layout_below: Used to place a UI widget below the widget referenced in the property

- android:layout_toStartOf: Used to indicate that the end edge of this widget should be placed at the start edge of the widget referenced in the property

- android:layout_toEndOf: Used to indicate that the start edge of this widget should be placed at the end edge of the widget referenced in the property

- android:layout_toLeftOf: Used to place a UI widget to the left of the widget referenced in the property

- android:layout_toRightOf: Used to place a UI widget to the right of the widget referenced in the property

More subtly, you can also use one of numerous other properties to control the alignment of a widget when compared to another. Some of these properties include the following:

- android:layout_alignStart: Flags that the widget's starting edge should be aligned with the start of the widget referenced in the property
- android:layout_alignEnd: Flags that the widget's ending edge should be aligned with the end of the widget referenced in the property
- android:layout_alignBaseline: Flags that the baseline of any text, regardless of borders or padding, of the two widgets should be aligned (see below)
- android:layout_alignTop: Flags that the top of the widget should be aligned with the top of the widget referenced in the property
- android:layout_alignBottom: Flags that the bottom of the widget should be aligned with the bottom of the referenced widget in the property

> **Tip**   If you have ever tried to exactly position text in a label to line up with text in an editable field in any UI design system, you know it can be a pain nudging each widget so that the text alignment of the characters entered by your user looks "right," especially when you consider different fonts, labels with no borders versus EditView with borders, and so on. RelativeLayout provides a great attribute called android:layout_alignBaseline that does all the hard work of this for you automatically. It's a great one to use for TextView and EditView combinations.

In your two-button example, if you want button2 to be positioned to the right of button1, then in the XML element for button2, include the attribute android:layout_toRightOf="@id/button1".

Determining the Order of Layout Relationships

Since way back in Android 1.6, Android has used a two-pass approach to process the evaluation of relative layout rules; this means that it is safe to have forward references to as-yet-undefined widgets. Prior to version 1.6, only a single-pass method was used, meaning you couldn't reference a widget until it had been declared in the layout XML. This complicated some layouts, making developers take awkward workarounds. Thankfully, it's unlikely you'll have to develop for a pre-version-1.6 envionment, so you can safely use forward-referencing without further thought.

A RelativeLayout Example

Before you get lost in too much theory surrounding relative layouts, it is time to actually see an example. Listing 6-1 shows the RelativeLayout from the ch06/RelativeExample project.

Listing 6-1. Using a RelativeLayout

```xml
<RelativeLayout xmlns:android="http://schemas.android.com/apk/res/android"
    xmlns:tools="http://schemas.android.com/tools"
    android:layout_width="match_parent"
    android:layout_height="wrap_content"
    tools:context=".RelativeLayoutExample" >

    <TextView android:id="@+id/label"
        android:layout_width="wrap_content"
        android:layout_height="wrap_content"
        android:text="URL:"
        android:layout_alignBaseline="@+id/entry"
        android:layout_alignParentLeft="true"/>
    <EditText
        android:id="@id/entry"
        android:layout_width="match_parent"
        android:layout_height="wrap_content"
        android:layout_toRightOf="@id/label"
        android:layout_alignParentTop="true"/>
    <Button
        android:id="@+id/ok"
        android:layout_width="wrap_content"
        android:layout_height="wrap_content"
        android:layout_below="@id/entry"
        android:layout_alignRight="@id/entry"
        android:text="OK" />
    <Button
        android:id="@+id/cancel"
        android:layout_width="wrap_content"
        android:layout_height="wrap_content"
        android:layout_toLeftOf="@id/ok"
        android:layout_alignTop="@id/ok"
        android:text="Cancel" />

</RelativeLayout>
```

Let's examine the various elements in this RelativeLayout. First and foremost is the RelativeLayout root element. In addition to the XML namespace attributes, I specify three other attributes for the layout itself. I want the RelativeLayout to span the entire available width on whatever sized screen is being used, so I choose android:layout_width="match_parent". I could do the same for the height, but instead, I tell the RelativeLayout to only use as much vertical space as is required to enclose the contained widgets. That's the purpose of android:layout_height="wrap_content".

When you examine the remaining code, you also see four widgets as child elements. These are the TextView of my label, the EditView for my editable field, and the buttons, Button1 and Button2.

For the TextView label, my layout instructs Android to align its left edge with the left edge of the parent RelativeLayout, using android:layout_alignParentLeft="true". I also want the TextView to have its baseline automatically managed once I've introduced the adjacent EditView, so I invoke the pixel-nudging perfection using android:layout_alignBaseline="@+id/entry". Note that I introduce the id with a plus sign because I haven't yet described the EditView, so I need to forewarn of its impending existence.

For the EditView, I want it to be to the right of the label so that baseline magic can work, and I want to have the EditView itself sit at the top of the layout, consuming all the remaining space to the right of the TextView. I instruct it to lay out to the right using android:layout_toRightOf="@id/label" (which was already introduced, so I do not need to add the plus notation). I then force the EditView to sit as high as possible in the remaining space of the RelativeLayout using android:layout_alignParentTop="true" and take the remaining space on the canvas to the right of the TextView by using android:layout_width="match_parent". This works because I know I also asked the parent to use the maximum available remaining space for width.

The daisy-chaining of relative rules continues with the two buttons. I want Button1 placed below the EditView and aligned with its right side, so I give it the attributes android:layout_below="@id/entry" and android:layout_alignRight="@id/entry". I then tell Android to place Button2 to the right of Button1 so the tops of the buttons are aligned using android:layout_toLeft="@id/Button1" and android:layout_alignTop="@id/Button1".

By using the stock skeleton of a new Android project in Android Studio or Eclipse, you can see the resulting layout, rendered in Figure 6-1.

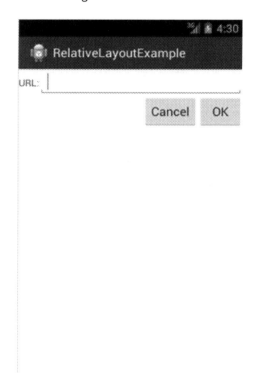

Figure 6-1. The RelativeLayoutExample sample application

Overlapping Widgets in Relative Layouts

One feature unique to the RelativeLayout is its ability to have widgets overlap each other so that when they are rendered in the Android UI, they appear to sit on top or under one another. Android achieves this by keeping track of the child elements from the XML definition, and it successively adds new "layers" for each new child element in the RelativeLayout. This means that items defined later in the layout sit on top of older/earlier items if they use the same space within the UI.

Let me show you how this works in a very straightforward example. Listing 6-2 shows the layout definition from ch06/RelativeOverlapExample. The layout has two buttons declared.

Listing 6-2. Drawing Overlapping Widgets in RelativeLayout

```
<RelativeLayout xmlns:android="http://schemas.android.com/apk/res/android"
    xmlns:tools="http://schemas.android.com/tools"
    android:layout_width="match_parent"
    android:layout_height="match_parent"
    tools:context=".RelativeOverlapExample" >

    <Button
        android:text="BIG BUTTON AT BACK"
        android:textSize="72dip"
        android:layout_width="match_parent"
        android:layout_height="match_parent" />
    <Button
        android:text="Small overlapping button"
        android:layout_width="wrap_content"
        android:layout_height="wrap_content"
        android:layout_alignBottom="true"
        android:layout_alignLeft="true" />

</RelativeLayout>
```

The first button is set to fill all available screen real estate in the activity using the match_parent options for width and height. Because I used such a large button, you can immediately tell that the next widget defined—in this case, the second button—will overlap this one to some degree. I've chosen the wrap_content option for Button2 so that it takes only as much space as is needed to display the text. You can see the resulting effect of Button2 sitting on top of (or if you prefer, in front of) Button1 in Figure 6-2.

Figure 6-2. Overlapping widgets in action

You can overlay any combination of widgets like this, and they can be of any type. All of the widgets are still responsive in the normal way, except where they overlap. In the region of overlap, any taps or clicks are handled by the top-most widget. As to why you would want to overlap widgets, there are numerous reasons, from artistic desires for slight overlaps, to tricks you might want to practice with widgets "hidden" behind others but still contributing in some way to activity functionality, among others.

Working with Linear Layouts

If you have every worked with other widget toolkits, such as Swing, or the graphic design world, you have probably heard of the box model, which at heart, asks you (the UI designer) to think of the interface as a set of widgets that are added in rows and columns. Because it was the original default layout for earlier versions of Android (now superseded by RelativeLayout), you can use LinearLayout for pretty much all your layout container needs, and then spend time tweaking how your widgets are boxed, nested, and so on. You don't get some of the fancy features of other layouts—such as the overlap capabilities of RelativeLayout I described earlier—but it works, after a fashion.

Controlling the Five Key Qualifiers for LinearLayout

For any given `LinearLayout`, you configure a core set of attributes to control the positioning and appearance of the container and its widgets.

Orientation

The most basic attribute of a `LinearLayout` is to control whether the widgets fill the layout in order horizontally, or vertically. For instance, in the box-model metaphor, are the boxes stacked from the top down, or from one side to the other? You control orientation in your XML Layout by using the `android:orientation` attribute of the `LinearLayout` element, or at runtime, by using the `setOrientation()` method, passing either `HORIZONTAL` or `VERTICAL` as the parameter.

Margins

In a `LinearLayout` container, when widgets are placed by default, no extra space is allocated as a buffer between the widgets. You can alter this behavior using the margin-based attributes, `android:layout_margin`, which affects all sides of a widget, or the various one-sided attributes such as `android:layout_marginTop`. The value for the margin attributes is a margin size, such as `10dip`.

Specifying a margin in this way has a similar effect to the padding attributes I discussed with relative layouts. The key difference is that margin attributes are only relevant where the widget has a nontransparent background, such as is the case with a button. In these cases, padding is considered to be within the boundary of the background, so in the button example, the edges of the button are pushed further away from the text that is written on it. Margin, on the other hand, affects the space outside the boundary of the widget, creating a metaphorical moat that makes it so no other widgets can encroach. For any widget without nontransparent backgrounds, margin and padding have identical effects.

Fill Method

Recall the discussion in the `RelativeLayout` example on using `wrap_content` or `match_parent` as a way to specify how much space should be filled by a given widget. To recap, `wrap_content` instructs the widget to dynamically size itself so it is only as large as it needs to be to contain its content (whether that's button text, an image, text in a `TextView`, etc.). In contrast, `match_parent` instructs the widget to take as much of the parent's available layout space as possible (that's simplifying things a little, but I'll return to this topic in more depth).

In `LinearLayout` containers, all contained widgets must specify a fill method, passing values to the attributes `android:layout_width` and `android:layout_height`. Three options for specifying fill method are available: `wrap_content`, `match_parent`, and lastly, the least common method of specifying an exact device-independent pixel value, such as `256dip`.

Weight

There is an obvious issue with using the fill method of `match_parent` with more than one widget in the `LinearLayout` container. If two (or more) widgets are demanding all the available free space, which one gets what? Weight is the answer!

In order to allocate the space across multiple widgets demanding the `match_parent` behavior, the `android:layout_weight` attribute is added to those widgets to assign the proportion of free space each one should receive. This attribute takes a simple number, such as 1 or 7. Android then parses all of the widgets with an `android:layout_weight` attribute in the layout, sums the weights, and gives a given widget its fraction of the total.

As an example, if you have two buttons, both configured to `match_parent`, and you set one to `android:layout_weight=1` and the other to `android:layout_weight=7`, then the first button takes up one-eighth of the available space, 1/(1+7); and the other button takes up the remaining seven eighths, 7/(1+7).

Other methods are available to set the weight as well, but this proportional method is the most intuitive.

Gravity

The default behavior for a `LinearLayout` is to align all widgets—from the top if you are using `VERTICAL` orientation, or from the left if you are using `HORIZONTAL` orientation. There are situations in which this is not what you want, such as for fancy display effects, or when you are manually overriding Android's built-in regional and language settings to force right-to-left layout. The XML attribute `android:layout_gravity` allows you to override the default behavior, as does the method `setGravity()` at runtime.

Acceptable values for `VERTICAL` orientation for `android:layout_gravity` are `left`, `center_horizontal`, and `right`. For `HORIZONTAL` orientation, Android defaults to aligning with respect to the invisible base of the text of your widgets. Use the value `center_vertical` to have Android use the notional center of the widget instead.

An Example LinearLayout

All the `LinearLayout` options can be daunting when you are thinking in purely theoretical terms. The dynamic example in Listing 6-3 shows you how many of these options work.

Listing 6-3. Exploring Options for LinearLayout

```
package com.artifiexdigital.android.LinearLayoutexample;

import android.os.Bundle;
import android.app.Activity;
import android.view.Gravity;
import android.widget.LinearLayout;
import android.widget.RadioGroup;
```

```
public class LinearLayoutExample extends Activity implements RadioGroup.
OnCheckedChangeListener {
    RadioGroup orientation;
    RadioGroup gravity;

    @Override
    protected void onCreate(Bundle savedInstanceState) {
        super.onCreate(savedInstanceState);
        setContentView(R.layout.activity_linear_layout_example);

        orientation=(RadioGroup)findViewById(R.id.orientation);
        orientation.setOnCheckedChangeListener(this);
        gravity=(RadioGroup)findViewById(R.id.gravity);
        gravity.setOnCheckedChangeListener(this);
    }

    public void onCheckedChanged(RadioGroup group, int checkedId) {
        switch (checkedId) {
            case R.id.horizontal:
                orientation.setOrientation(LinearLayout.HORIZONTAL);
            break;

            case R.id.vertical:
                orientation.setOrientation(LinearLayout.VERTICAL);
            break;

            case R.id.left:
                gravity.setGravity(Gravity.LEFT);
            break;

            case R.id.center:
                gravity.setGravity(Gravity.CENTER_HORIZONTAL);
            break;

            case R.id.right:
                gravity.setGravity(Gravity.RIGHT);
            break;
        }
    }
}
```

This example is very simple to begin with. I have defined two separate RadioGroup widgets—one containing RadioButtons to control orientation, the other to contol gravity. I start with the XML definition including the android:orientation="vertical" orientation, which stacks the RadioGroups one above the other, and the RadioButtons within them in vertical fashion as well. Rather than leaving this as is, I override this vertical stacking of the two radio buttons in the first RadioGroup, giving them a horizontal layout by specifying android:orie ntation="horizontal". This shows another useful feature that is available to you—nested elements can inherit defaults but can also override them. To finish the initial definition, I set some padding around all of my widgets—5dip—and opt for the wrap_content option.

If I run a default Android project with just this layout definition and no supporting Java code, you will still see the layout take effect, even if the radio buttons do nothing for now. The layout is shown in Figure 6-3.

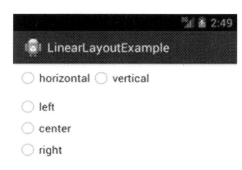

Figure 6-3. The starting point for the LinearLayoutExample application

Obviously, to show the working options changing your layout's orientation and gravity, I need to add some Java code to make the relevant runtime calls. Listing 6-4 covers the code that brings each `RadioButton` to life.

Listing 6-4. LinearLayout Java Code to Enable RadioButton Logic

```
package com.artifiexdigital.android.LinearLayoutexample;

import android.os.Bundle;
import android.app.Activity;
import android.view.Gravity;
import android.widget.LinearLayout;
import android.widget.RadioGroup;

public class LinearLayoutExample extends Activity implements
RadioGroup.OnCheckedChangeListener {
    RadioGroup orientation;
    RadioGroup gravity;
```

```
    @Override
    protected void onCreate(Bundle savedInstanceState) {
        super.onCreate(savedInstanceState);
        setContentView(R.layout.activity_linear_layout_example);

        orientation=(RadioGroup)findViewById(R.id.orientation);
        orientation.setOnCheckedChangeListener(this);
        gravity=(RadioGroup)findViewById(R.id.gravity);
        gravity.setOnCheckedChangeListener(this);
    }

    public void onCheckedChanged(RadioGroup group, int checkedId) {
        switch (checkedId) {
            case R.id.horizontal:
                orientation.setOrientation(LinearLayout.HORIZONTAL);
            break;

            case R.id.vertical:
                orientation.setOrientation(LinearLayout.VERTICAL);
            break;

            case R.id.left:
                gravity.setGravity(Gravity.LEFT);
            break;

            case R.id.center:
                gravity.setGravity(Gravity.CENTER_HORIZONTAL);
            break;

            case R.id.right:
                gravity.setGravity(Gravity.RIGHT);
            break;
        }
    }
}
```

The setup for my code is straightforward. During the applications onCreate() call, I use setOnCheckedChangedListener() to register two listeners for clicks on the RadioGroup widgets. As I implement OnCheckedChangeListener in the activity, it becomes the listener.

When a click occurs, the listener invokes the callback onCheckChanged(). The first thing I determine in the callback method is which RadioButton was clicked. Based on that, I call either setOrientation() to toggle from vertical to horizontal layout flow, or setGravity() to the relevant left, right, or center value. Some examples of how the layout changes are shown in Figures 6-4 and 6-5.

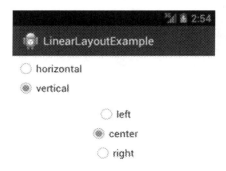

Figure 6-4. *Example changes in the LinearLayout*

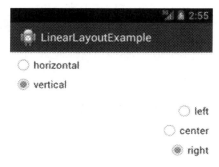

Figure 6-5. *Example changes in the LinearLayout*

Working with Table Layouts

If you remember the early days of the World Wide Web, you probably have memories of page design of the times. I am not just talking about the gratuitous use of the `blink` tag, but more specifically, about the tendency to use HTML tables as layout containers for everything people wanted to see on a web page. Whether it was for the title bar, menus, pictures, or text, the table could do a passable job of managing layout.

In the Android world, this approach is also supported, thanks to the `TableLayout` container. `TableLayout` has many of the same quick-to-use, hard-to-perfect characteristics of the HTML use of tables, but it is certainly useful in many layout situations. The key to `TableLayout` is its use of `TableRow` child elements to control the size of the table (its number of columns and rows). This should remind you even more of HTML if you have ever used it, with its `<table>` and `<tr>` tags for table and rows.

Understanding Widget Behavior within TableLayout

Before using `TableLayout`, it is helpful to understand what you can control directy using XML layout attributes or Java at runtime and what Android will implicitly manage for you.

You Count the Rows, Android Counts the Columns

Adding rows to your `TableLayout` is as simple as you would expect. Within your `TableLayout` XML definition, you simply add one or more `TableRow` child elements to act as subcontainers for widgets. When it comes to adding columns, on the other hand, you don't explicitly specify a number of columns in advance. Instead, when detailing the widgets in your rows, Android pays attention to the row with the highest widget count. This implicitly becomes the number of columns used to render your `TableLayout`.

Obviously leaving column counting to Android is great from a simplicity perspective, but you may find yourself wanting a more fine-grained control over widget and column behavior. You can achieve this, at least partially, by providing an `android:layout_span` attribute to any widget, where you would like that widget to span more than one column.

As an example, this layout fragment uses a `TextView` that spans five columns and an `EditView` that only uses one implicit column. Android then renders this as if it is effectively six columns.

```
<TableRow>
  <TextView android:text="How old were you at your last birthday?:"
    android:layout_span="5" />
  <EditText
    android:id="@+id/age" />
</TableRow>
```

By default, Android fills widgets into columns starting with the first avaliable column. You can override this behavior by specifying an explicit `android:layout_column` attribute for your UI widget.

> **Caution**   Android uses zero-based column numbering! As much as this seems sensible to the hard-core computer science major, it will inevitably cause you—as a keen new Android developer—to stumble into column numbering purgatory at least once. Zero-based indexing of columns will eventually become second nature to you.

We can amend the above fragment to "push" our `TextView` and `EditView` to later columns as follows:

```
<TableRow>
  <TextView android:text="How old were you at your last birthday?:"
    android:layout_column="3"
    android:layout_span="5" />
  <EditText
    android:id="@+id/age" />
</TableRow>
```

When I use this approach, my `TextView` starts in column 4 (remember, zero-based column indexes!) and continues until it has consumed through to column 8. The `EditText` field is then automatically placed in column 9 since I have done nothing to alter Android's built-in column handling at that point.

Widgets without TableRows in a TableLayout

It is possible to intersperse UI widgets in your table outside of a `TableRow` child element. In this case, any widgets so defined implicitly behave as if they were placed in a `LinearLayout` with `VERTICAL` stacking, and their fill method implicitly defaults to `match_parent`. Effectively, any widget in your `TableLayout` but outside a `TableRow` stacks downward from the last `TableRow`, filling the full width of the row determined to be the widest of all your `TableRows`.

You might wonder why you would ever want to use this approach. To continue my earlier HTML analogy, if you have ever used the `<hr>` element in HTML, you know that it creates a horizontal rule (line) across the entire screen area. You can use the widget-outside-`TableRow` approach to do the same thing, without needing to worry about how many columns Android determines your layout has at runtime.

Controlling the Size of Columns in a TableLayout

Controlling the width of a given column is left to Android by default. It follows a scheme similar to `wrap_content`, wherein Android sizes the column to fit the natural width of the widest widget within it. This often works well, but at times, you want to have more control over column width, particularly when you're dealing with very wide or very narrow widgets whose default width causes an undesirable look to your UI.

Android offers three attributes to provide hints on final sizing of columns. I should say that again for emphasis. Column sizing is not precise, and you, as the developer, can only do so much to influence the final size of a column. This might sound like a restriction, but as you experience more of the UI feature set of Android, and the plethora of device sizes and resolutions, you will appreciate that this is actually a benefit. Here are the three attributes to guide column sizing:

* `android:stretchColumns`: The column(s) specified stretch to consume any extra space available on the `TableRow`.

* `android:shrinkColumns`: Any of the column(s) specified that contain text have their horizontal space reduced and the text word-wrapped to reduce the space they consume.

* `android:collapseColumns`: The column(s) specified are initially included in the logical layout, but are hidden from display when the UI is initially rendered. You can reveal them at runtime using the `setColumnsCollapsed()` method.

Each of these attributes takes a comma-delimited set of column numbers. You can shrink and stretch columns at runtime by using the `setColumnsShrinkable()` and `setColumnsStretchable()` methods.

An Example TableLayout

Now that you have the theory of `TableLayout` under your belt, let's look at a working example that demonstrates a variety of the attributes I discussed earlier. Listing 6-5 shows an example `TableLayout`, which mimics the earlier layout you saw for `RelativeLayout`. You can also find the code in `ch06/TableLayoutExample`.

Listing 6-5. A TableLayout to Mimic the Earlier RelativeLayout

```
<TableLayout xmlns:android="http://schemas.android.com/apk/res/android"
    xmlns:tools="http://schemas.android.com/tools"
    android:layout_width="match_parent"
    android:layout_height="match_parent"
    android:stretchColumns="1"
    tools:context=".TableLayoutExample" >

    <TableRow>
        <TextView
            android:text="URL:" />
        <EditText android:id="@+id/entry"
            android:layout_span="3"/>
    </TableRow>
    <View
        android:layout_height="2dip"
        android:background="#0000FF" />
```

```
    <TableRow>
        <Button android:id="@+id/cancel"
            android:layout_column="2"
            android:text="Cancel" />
        <Button android:id="@+id/ok"
            android:text="OK" />
    </TableRow>

</TableLayout>
<TableLayout xmlns:android="http://schemas.android.com/apk/res/android"
    xmlns:tools="http://schemas.android.com/tools"
    android:layout_width="match_parent"
    android:layout_height="match_parent"
    android:stretchColumns="1"
    tools:context=".TableLayoutExample" >

    <TableRow>
        <TextView
            android:text="URL:" />
        <EditText android:id="@+id/entry"
            android:layout_span="3"/>
    </TableRow>
    <View
        android:layout_height="2dip"
        android:background="#0000FF" />
    <TableRow>
        <Button android:id="@+id/cancel"
            android:layout_column="2"
            android:text="Cancel" />
        <Button android:id="@+id/ok"
            android:text="OK" />
    </TableRow>

</TableLayout>
```

If you include this layout with a stock project from Android Studio or Eclipse, you see the output as shown in Figure 6-6.

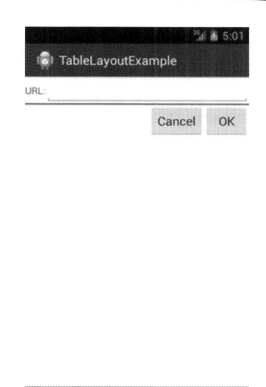

Figure 6-6. *Using TableLayout to mimic the earlier RelativeLayout*

Working with Grid Layouts

A TableLayout appeals to those who yearn for HTML-style or CSS-style pixel precision (or lack thereof). Often you'll find yourself knowing how you'd like the elements of your layout to appear relative to one another, or needing more finess when it comes to specifying the placement of widgets in your layout. Enter the all-new GridLayout, released with Android 4, Ice Cream Sandwich.

GridLayout is a layout that places its children onto a grid of infinitely detailed lines that separate the area into cells. The key to GridLayout's fine control is that the number of cells, or more accurately the grid lines used to describe the cells, has no limit or threshold—you specify how many or how few grid lines your GridLayout should have using rowSpec and columnSpec properties. This means you can create a layout that mimics a simple table with a few cells (that is, rows and columns), or for those demanding situations in which you need fantastically fine precision, you can go crazy specifying thousands or even millions of cells.

> **Note**   To complement GridLayout's different view of the UI world, it uses android:layout_gravity in place of android:layout_weight.

As an example, here in Listing 6-6 is a GridLayout used in an XML layout file
(from ch06/GridLayoutExample):

Listing 6-6. GridLayoutExample XML Definition

```
<GridLayout xmlns:android="http://schemas.android.com/apk/res/android"
    xmlns:tools="http://schemas.android.com/tools"
    android:layout_width="match_parent"
    android:layout_height="match_parent"
    android:orientation="vertical"
    tools:context=".GridLayoutExample" >

    <Button
        android:text="Defying gravity!"
        android:layout_gravity="top" />
    <Button
        android:text="Falling like an apple"
        android:layout_gravity="bottom" />

</GridLayout>
```

In an Ice Cream Sandwich Android emulator, you can see the activity using the GridLayout
as shown in Figure 6-7.

Figure 6-7. The GridLayoutExample sample application

The buttons have followed their various gravity directions to place themselves on the GridLayout, using the defaults for rowSpec and columnSpec counts. You can observe the utility of the GridLayout not needing the somewhat tedious static layout directives of the TableLayout by adding another button to your declarations in activity_grid_layout_example.xml.

```
...
    <Button
        android:text="Defying gravity!"
        android:layout_gravity="top" />
    <Button
        android:text="Floating middle right"
        android:layout_gravity="right|center_vertical" />
    <Button
        android:text="Falling like an apple"
        android:layout_gravity="bottom" />
...
```

Figure 6-8 shows how your GridLayout adapts to display its children:

Figure 6-8. *The GridDemo revised*

Layout Manipulation with the Layout Editor

So far in this chapter I have used a write-your-own-XML approach to adding widgets to your user interface. Although it's certainly possible to do this for more and more complex interface designs, you probably want an easier and more elegant way to design the look and feel of your applications. That's exactly what Android offers you by allowing you to edit the XML-based layout files with developer tools like the graphical layout editor in Android Studio and Eclipse.

Recap of the Layout Editor UI

Like any developer, you will face the age-old user interface development tug-of-war: should user interfaces be coded logically and clinically, or laid out with flair and fashion on some design canvas in graphical form?

The good news is that the Android developer tools cater to both approaches, even simultaneously! You already saw the layout editor introduced briefly in Chapter 2. Let's now take a longer look to be sure you know its key capabilities, and then you can decide for yourself when to lay out on a canvas, when to handcraft XML, and when to code Java to deal with layout at runtime (which I cover next in this chapter). You can access the editor by opening any layout XML file in your res/layout directory. So far in the example applications you have typically only had one layout file, such as the FirstApp example using the res/layout/activity_first_app.xml layout specification. Click on it, and when it opens, you'll see the graphical layout editor's default view, shown in Figure 6-9.

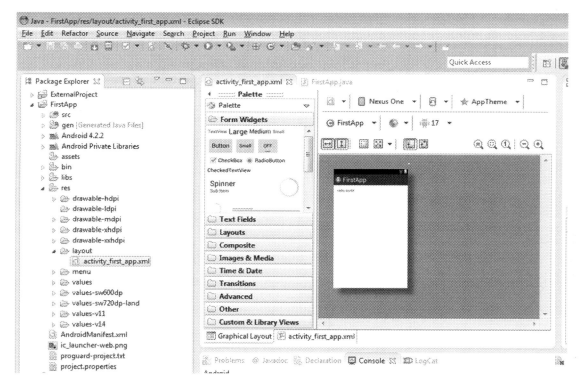

Figure 6-9. *Graphical Layout of the FirstApp activity*

This actually works on any layout file. You might have many activities in your application, each with a layout. You can also have layouts and layout XML files for only part of a view. For instance, in the next chapter, we explore adapters and lists, and you can have a layout for an individual row in a list.

Note the two tabs at the bottom of the layout: Graphical Layout and `activity_first_app.xml`. These are two presentations of the same thing. The `activity_first_app.xml` tab contains the actual textual content of that file, which is the XML specification that describes your layout. The Graphical Layout tab is the notional user interface that your XML file describes. This tab shows the results of the developer toolset parsing the XML and layout out the visual interface your users would see for the given layout file.

On the left side of the graphical layout editor, you see categories for all of the widgets—or layout elements—that are provided in stock form with Android. This includes text fields, check boxes, buttons, and more that I introduced in Chapter 5. You also see a Layouts category, which includes all of the layout containers I've already discussed in this chapter.

Android's SDK ships with the Android Asset Packaging Tool (AAPT), which is designed to take all of the various XML resource files, including layouts, and package/process them into their final usable state. For layouts, your toolset (Eclipse, Android Studio, Ant, Beacon Mountain, etc.) invokes AAPTand its principle job in this instance it to generate the `R.java` source files within your project's gen directory. The mystery of the R file is solved! As you've already seen, this allows you to access your layouts and their widgets directly from within your Java code.

Even More Reasons for XML Layouts

We have already explored how using XML layouts lets you describe each aspect and interface element of your Android application, without you needing to use Java. We return to the Java story shortly, but there is another very compelling reason to use XML for layout definitions, even though many people consider it a little cumbersome and text-heavy.

One of the best reasons to use XML layouts is so you can enable the creation of tools, like the graphical layout editor I just recapped, that, in turn, greatly assist in creating new layouts, but more importantly, in rereading the definition into a design tool to support edits and extensions. This kind of programmatic parsing and rendering is a huge challenge, but it is made so much more tractable when the data is in a structured format like XML.

If you have experienced other development environments, you know that this principle of separating layout definitions and application logic is a very popular architectural choice— equivalents such as XUL, GWT, and XAML from Microsoft, Google, and Mozilla are all examples of this technique.

Converting to XML-based Layouts with Java Logic

The good news about Java-driven layouts, and XML layouts, is that you can change your mind. You might like to prototype in XML and use the graphical layout editor, or you might like to try really fancy runtime layout choices using Java. At any point, you can change your mind with a little recoding or rewriting of XML. As an example, Listing 6-7 shows the counting `Button` from Chapter 2's first application, converted into an XML layout file. You can find this code in the `ch06/FirstAgain` sample project.

Listing 6-7. Redefining Layouts in XML

```
<RelativeLayout xmlns:android="http://schemas.android.com/apk/res/android"
    xmlns:tools="http://schemas.android.com/tools"
    android:layout_width="match_parent"
    android:layout_height="match_parent"
    tools:context=".FirstAgainActivity" >

    <Button
        android:id="@+id/button"
        android:layout_width="fill_parent"
        android:layout_height="fill_parent"
        android:layout_alignParentBottom="true"
        android:layout_alignParentLeft="true"
        android:layout_alignParentRight="true"
        android:layout_alignParentTop="true"
        android:text="" />

</RelativeLayout>
```

You can see the XML equivalents of the pieces we put together for the sample application, including these:

- Establishing the root element and namespace for the layout, and deciding to use `RelativeLayout`.

- Defining the `Button` child element and giving it an `android:id` so we can reference it from Java (where our counter keeps track of the number of button clicks).

- `androind:layout_alignParentBottom`, `androind:layout_alignParentTop`, `androind:layout_alignParentLeft`, and `android:layout_ alignParentRight`: Each of these four layout attributes controls how this widget aligns with its parent. In the current example, these are a little redundant, because our button and its parent consume the whole activity space, so you won't notice any effect. You can try editing the layout to remove these to demonstrate this for yourself.

- `android:layout_width` and `android:layout_height`: As I did in the original example, here I have the button's width and height match the parent (the entire screen).

- `android:text`: Indicates the initial text to be displayed on the button, which, in this case, is an empty string.

This is admittedly a simple example converted to XML. More complex examples need more that just the one child `Button` element: they are likely to end up with multiple branches of XML hierarchies. You get to see more and more complex examples from here on, because I favor XML layouts over Java-defined ones for the rest of the book, unless I am demonstrating a particular runtime effect or behavior.

Attaching Layout Definitions to Java

Let us assume you have become a convert to the XML layout approach and have sweated over the definitions for the widgets and containers for your activity's view in an XML layout file. How do you tell your Java logic which layout to use (even if you only have one)? I'm glad you asked. When it is invoked in your activity's onCreate() callback, one simple method joins up the parts. This is the setContentView() method. In order for your example application to use the newly-minted XML layout in res/layout/activity_first_again.xml, simply invoke it like this:

```
setContentView(R.layout.activity_first_again);
```

If you look back to the original version of our first example app, you can see that setContentView() was called there as well. What differs here is that you are passing a reference to the XML-based view you've defined, based on the aapt utility having parsed your XML, and you've generated the R class so that you can reference it in this way. No matter how many layout files you have, AAPT packages them all and makes them available in the R.layout namespace, using the format R.layout.<your_layout_file_name_without_the_XML_extention>.

In order to then access the various widgets in your layout, you invoke the findViewById() method and pass it the numeric reference for your widget. Wait! What numeric reference? I'm glad you asked. At packaging time, AAPT also assigns each widget in your layouts an ID number and includes it as member data in the R.java file. You can open the file at any time to see this, but tracking and using explicit numbers would be cumbersome and error prone. Instead, you can have Android resolve the ID number for you using the R.id.<widget_android:id_value> parameter. You can use this to resolve the ID for any widget subclassed from the base View class (which is pretty much everything).

You can already see some of the possibilities this approach enables. Different activities can be passed different instances of a View, and more intriguingly, you can change the View based on some program logic, enabling you to, for instance, use a different layout when you detect a different style of device.

Completing Your Revised App

In the original FirstApp demo, the button's face showed the number of times the button had been clicked, starting with 1 for when the button was loaded via onCreate(). The majority of your existing logic, like counting clicks, still works in your modified (FirstAgain) application. The key change is shown in Listing 6-8, substituting the previous Java calls in your activity's onCreate() callback with a definition from the XML layout.

Listing 6-8. FirstAgain Application Java Code

```java
package com.artifexdigital.android.firstagain;

import android.os.Bundle;
import android.app.Activity;
import android.view.View;
import android.widget.Button;

public class FirstAgainActivity extends Activity implements View.OnClickListener {
        Button myButton;
        Integer myInt;

    @Override
    protected void onCreate(Bundle savedInstanceState) {
        super.onCreate(savedInstanceState);
        setContentView(R.layout.activity_first_again);
        myButton=(Button)findViewById(R.id.button);
        myButton.setOnClickListener(this);
        myInt = 0;
        updateClickCounter();
    }

    public void onClick(View view) {
        updateClickCounter();
    }

    private void updateClickCounter() {
        myInt++;
        myButton.setText(myInt.toString());
    }
}
```

The twin changes I described earlier are visible in the onCreate() method. First, use setContentView() to load the AAPT-created R Java class for your desired XML layout. Then find the button to use with the rest of your logic by invoking the findViewById() method, asking it to find the widget that has the android:id value of "button". This gives you the reference you need in order to track and update the value of your click counter.

The results look strikingly similar to the original FirstApp demo, as shown in Figure 6-10.

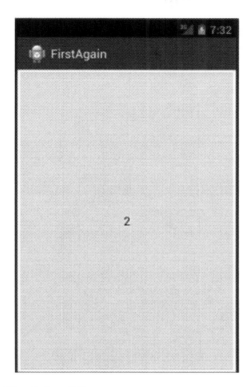

Figure 6-10. *The revised FirstAgain sample activity*

By now, you can probably imagine where you might start using some of the containers and layout styles I have described, and you might also make some educated guesses about what kinds of layouts and containers some of your favorite applications use. You've come to the end of this chapter, but read on for some more advanced layout and widget use.

7

Building Layouts with Lists and Adapters

The previous two chapters focused on widgets that convey single pieces of information or provide basic interaction, and different ways to implement the layout of those widgets in your activities. In this chapter, I cover some of the more advanced data-driven UI elements. With these UI elements, not only do definitions in your layout XML files govern the content and even the size and shape of the interface, but the interface adapts and changes based on the data populating it.

A very common design goal for application developers is to want to present users with a constrained list of choices from which they can choose. Think of applications like music players, or phone dialers working from a contact list. What the developer desires is for the user to pick the one entry they want, and then have some action performed with that entry.

That all sounds simple, right? Well, in Android, it is actually quite straightforward to show a dynamic set of content and trigger a follow-on action, which allows you to avoid the need to traverse to and fro across networks leveraging databases and remote services. All you need to do is specify two complementary parts of the solution. First, from where should the options or values originate? Second, what should the UI—our activity in this case—look like in order to present these options? Android provides adapters for sourcing data and several more advanced views that are all derived from the base View object for presenting data. Let us dive in and see how these work in tandem.

Using Adapters to Populate Options

Adapters are one of Android's fundamental building blocks; they enable you as a developer to build data-driven applications. By letting a user drive behavior by selecting choices, such as contacts, songs, to-do list entries, and similar tasks, you create applications that tailor themselves to each of your users by basing application behavior on *their* individual data.

Why Adapters?

In the previous paragraph, I mentioned many possible uses for data-driven applications. Songs, contacts, and other classes of data are all rich sources from which to shape an application. But imagine if every time you want to work with a type of data—say, videos—you have to completely rewrite the code that controls how to find those videos on your device or on the Internet, come up with the way of describing and updating data about those videos, and put rules in place for important constraints like format, length, and so on. And just to make the scenario even more burdensome, imagine you can reuse this work for songs, or ebooks, or photos, or phone numbers.

Wanting to avoid the need to reinvent the wheel in this way is the reason Android built adapters into the development framework. Adapters provide a common interface into a myriad of different kinds and sources of data. Android adapters are purpose-built to feed data from all sorts of inputs into one of Android's list-style UI elements; a user then selects one or more of the items presented. In practice, this can mean the user chooses songs for a playlist, dials a person's phone number, or checks off a to-do list item.

In order to provide you, the developer, with maximum flexibility, Android's adapter design gives you control over not only the source data for the widget that will host the data, but also optional control over the way an item of data in the widget is laid out and presented. This blurring of logic and presentation may sound a little crazy, but you are going to see some examples where it makes perfect sense.

Starting with ArrayAdapter

The most basic of adapters in your Android toolkit is the `ArrayAdapter`. As its name implies, an `ArrayAdapter` takes a Java array or array-like object, such as `java.util.List`, along with your desired layout for a row of data, and returns an `ArrayAdapter` object, ready to use.

Listing 7-1 shows a very simple code fragment with all the steps you need to create your first `ArrayAdapter`.

Listing 7-1. The Basic Form of ArrayAdapter

```
String[] sampleAA={"your","very","first","Array","Adapter"};
new ArrayAdapter<String>(this, android.R.layout.simple_list_item_1, sampleAA);
```

That is all there is to it. After instantiating the array, you can call the constructor and pass these parameters:

- The desired context for this adapter

- A layout suitable for rendering the data (which, in this case, is an Android default, android.R.layout.simple_list_item_1, but you can and will want to design your own)

- The source data array or List

When invoked over an array or List, by default, ArrayAdapter assumes the source information is text in nature and cast to string as necessary. (In later chapters, I show you how you can control this to deal with nontext data.) Once the raw data is consumed, the layout you provide is applied to generate the rendered widgets so they display in the final container—whether that is a list, a checklist, a spinner, or something else.

To get an idea of how Listing 7-1 is going to render your array, you can open the Android-provided layout android.R.layout.simple_list_item_1 by searching for the simple_list_item_1.xml file in your SDK installation path. Depending on the version of the Android SDK and developer tools you are using, it should look something like Listing 7-2.

Listing 7-2. The simple_list_item_1.xml Android-provided Layout

```
<TextView xmlns:android="http://schemas.android.com/apk/res/android"
    android:id="@android:id/text1"
    android:layout_width="match_parent"
    android:layout_height="wrap_content"
    android:textAppearance="?android:attr/textAppearanceListItemSmall"
    android:gravity="center_vertical"
    android:paddingStart="?android:attr/listPreferredItemPaddingStart"
    android:paddingEnd="?android:attr/listPreferredItemPaddingEnd"
    android:minHeight="?android:attr/listPreferredItemHeightSmall" />
```

I have omitted the multiline licensing boilerplate from the listing so you can concentrate on the actual XML. First, you can see that the resulting rows will be rendered as TextView items. That's great, because you learned all about TextView layouts in Chapter 5. You can also see that, by default, the items will stretch horizontally to match the parent width; this means they will stretch to fit the spinner, list, or other type of container I will shortly introduce. Height is set to wrap_content and therefore only consume as much space in the rendered layout as is needed to show the relevant text, and you can set some other padding and appearance characteristics to give a pleasing UI.

In the next chapter, I explore more advanced approaches that let you control how rows are created and rendered even further, but for now, you should feel comfortable with what the ArrayAdapter is doing to the data in your array.

Making Lists

Android, like many other UI toolkits, includes a basic list widget for presenting sets of data. This is the ListView, which, as the name suggests, is derived from the base View object, just as all the other widgets we have discussed have been derived. You can link a ListView to the adapter providing the source data and layout view by invoking the setAdapter() method. Finally, you can configure a ListView for user interaction by registering a listener with setOnItemSelectedListener() so that you can add your logic to react to the user's choice.

A complete example that links an ArrayAdapter to a ListView is available in the ch07/ListViewExample project, which is a simple list with a label on top that shows the current selection. Listing 7-3 shows the XML layout including the specification for the ListView:

Listing 7-3. ListViewExample Project's Layout Specification

```
<RelativeLayout xmlns:android="http://schemas.android.com/apk/res/android"
    xmlns:tools="http://schemas.android.com/tools"
    android:layout_width="match_parent"
    android:layout_height="match_parent"
    tools:context=".ListViewExample" >

    <TextView
        android:id="@+id/mySelection"
        android:layout_width="match_parent"
        android:layout_height="wrap_content" />
    <ListView
        android:id="@android:id/list"
        android:layout_width="match_parent"
        android:layout_height="match_parent"
        android:drawSelectorOnTop="false" />

</RelativeLayout>
```

The Java code to control the list's logic and connect it with its ArrayAdapter is shown in Listing 7-4:

Listing 7-4. ListViewExample Project's Java Implementation

```
package com.artifexdigital.android.listviewexample;

import android.os.Bundle;
import android.app.ListActivity;
import android.view.View;
import android.widget.ArrayAdapter;
import android.widget.ListView;
import android.widget.TextView;

public class ListViewExample extends ListActivity {
    private TextView mySelection;
    private static final String[] myListItems={"To", "be",
        "or", "not", "to", "be",
        "that", "is", "the", "question"};
```

```java
@Override
protected void onCreate(Bundle savedInstanceState) {
    super.onCreate(savedInstanceState);
    setContentView(R.layout.activity_list_view_example);

    setListAdapter(new ArrayAdapter<String>(this,
        android.R.layout.simple_list_item_1, myListItems));
    mySelection=(TextView)findViewById(R.id.mySelection);
}

public void onListItemClick(ListView parent, View v, int position,
    long id) {
mySelection.setText(myListItems[position]);
}

}
```

One of the first things you should note about this Java class is my choice of base class for the activity. I have derived from the ListActivity, which I haven't previously introduced. The name ListActivity probably helps you understand the purpose here, but just to be clear, if you are creating an activity in which the only child UI widget (or at least far-and-away the most prominent and important) is a ListView, then you can use the ListActivity subclass to shortcut many of the housekeeping steps a list-based activity warrants.

With that mystery solved, you can focus on where the list is configured to the adapter via setListAdapter()—in this case, the method call provides an ArrayAdapter wrapping an array quoting a soliloquy from a somewhat-famous play. Your application can listen in using an override for onListItemClick() to find out when the selected items in the list change, and you can invoke whatever logic you want for your application based on such a change. The running application is shown in Figure 7-1.

Figure 7-1. *ListView with data from an ArrayAdapter*

When you look at the way each row of the list has been rendered, you should be able to spot the effects of the "free" default layout XML I mentioned at the start of the chapter. The overall look is sourced both because we correctly configured the ArrayAdapter to use this layout, and because our ListActivity is our base class and only activity, which means we get things like the overall padding, font choice, Material Design or Holo theme, and more. I'll return to themes at a later point, but you can start to see what they offer and how you can easily capture their defaults with choices like ListActivity and other more tightly-focused subclasses.

Making More Sophisticated Lists

If you have used other widget toolkits like Swing, AWT, .Net and so on, you are familiar with some of the more advanced list interfaces that are very common across desktops, the Web, and even mobile devices. One very common extension of the list approach is to provide a pick list or multi–pick list from which a user can select one or more options in one pass.

You can modify the ListView example I introduced earlier to support the ability to pick one or more entries. In making these changes, you also see how the basic constructs stay the same, and all you need to do is make one configuration choice and pass an appropriate layout for your row data to have everything work as intended.

You can control whether your `ListView` accepts one selection or multiple selections by invoking its `setChoiceMode()` method or by configuring the `android:choiceMode` attribute in the corresponding XML element for the `ListView` layout. There are only two options from which to choose with `setChoiceMode()`:

- `CHOICE_MODE_SINGLE`, which as the name suggests, configures the `ListView` to only allow one selection at a time

- `CHOICE_MODE_MULTIPLE`, which allows any or all of the options in the `ListView` to be simultaneously selected

Having told Android what behavior your `ListView` will have, you now need to make sure it can render an appropriate onscreen widget to allow for your selection options. The following are the relevant defaults packaged with the Android SDK from which you can freely choose:

- `android.R.layout.simple_list_item_single_choice`: To be used in conjunction with single-choice lists

- `android.R.layout.simple_list_item_multiple_choice`: To be used when multiple choice is desired

You can also create your own, tweaking layout options if you wish.

The overall XML layout for the activity changes very little—note the additional bold lines in Listing 7-5 as compared to Listing 7-3.

Listing 7-5. ListView Layout with Multiple-Choice Behavior Configured

```
<RelativeLayout xmlns:android="http://schemas.android.com/apk/res/android"
    xmlns:tools="http://schemas.android.com/tools"
    android:layout_width="match_parent"
    android:layout_height="match_parent"
    tools:context=".CheckListExample" >

    <ListView
        android:id="@android:id/list"
        android:choiceMode="multipleChoice"
        android:drawSelectorOnTop="false"
        android:layout_width="wrap_content"
        android:layout_height="wrap_content" />

</RelativeLayout>
```

The key change in the layout is to set `android:choiceMode` to `multipleChoice`. That instructs Android to allow your user to select more than one entry (without it automatically deselecting other entries). The only other change you need to make is in your Java code to ensure you pass an appropriate layout to the `ArrayAdapter` constructor that helps the user understand and use the new multi-choice capability. In this case, Listing 7-6 shows the code using Android's default `android.R.layout.simple_list_item_multiple_choice` layout.

Listing 7-6. Adding the Relevant Multiple-Choice Java Configuration to the Multiple-Choice ListViewExample

```
package com.artifexdigital.android.checklistexample;

import android.os.Bundle;
import android.app.ListActivity;
import android.widget.ArrayAdapter;
//import android.widget.ListView;

public class CheckListExample extends ListActivity {
    private static final String[] myListItems={"To", "be",
        "or", "not", "to", "be",
        "that", "is", "the", "question"};

    @Override
    protected void onCreate(Bundle savedInstanceState) {
        super.onCreate(savedInstanceState);
        setContentView(R.layout.activity_check_list_example);

        setListAdapter(new ArrayAdapter<String>(this,
                android.R.layout.simple_list_item_multiple_choice,
                myListItems));
    }

}
```

It will not surprise you that you have now immortalized Shakespeare, and Hamlet, in a much more functional multi-choice ListView, complete with checkboxes for the users to pick out their favorite words from that part of the play. Figure 7-2 shows the multiple-choice ListView in action.

Figure 7-2. Multiple choice ListView with data from an ArrayAdapter

Adapting to the GridView

It is no coincidence that all of the words in the preceding ListView examples are short. Really, really short, in fact. You might be thinking we are wasting a huge amount of screen real estate by putting each word on its own row in a ListView. Android provides a solution to situations like this; you want situations in which a View makes the most of the available real estate, while still supporting single- or multiple-selection.

The GridView provides a row-and-column grid of items you can use in presenting "lists" of data to your users. In true Android style, GridView tries to do some of the heavy lifting for you, which means, in practice, you can control some of the aspects of the layout—the number and size of columns—while Android takes care of automatically managing the rest, in particular, the number of rows. This is similar in concept to the TableLayout we explored in Chapter 6.

You control the number and size of columns using the following attributes:

■ android:numColumns: A well-named attribute that specifies how many columns to render. You can also use the value auto_fit to have Android compute how many columns will fit the available space based on the other properties listed here and the size of the activity or screen.

■ android:columnWidth: Specifies the width of each column in pixels.

- ▓ android:verticalSpacing: Indicates spacing between rows.

- ▓ android:horizontalSpacing: Indicates spacing across one row between items in the GridView.

- ▓ android:stretchMode: Where you choose to use auto_fit for android:numColumns, this controls the behavior of unused space when laying out columns. Choices are columnWidth or spacingWidth, which gives the spare space to either the columns or the whitespace between them, respectively.

In all other respects, GridView operates in much the same way as the already-introduced list selection widgets; it takes an adapter with an associated layout that is able to be registered with a listener via the override for setOnItemSelectedListener()

To see a GridView in action, examine the example project in ch07/GridViewExample, which you can see in Listing 7-7.

Listing 7-7. The Layout XML for Use of GridView

```
<RelativeLayout xmlns:android="http://schemas.android.com/apk/res/android"
    xmlns:tools="http://schemas.android.com/tools"
    android:layout_width="match_parent"
    android:layout_height="match_parent"
    tools:context=".GridViewExample" >

    <TextView
        android:id="@+id/mySelection"
        android:layout_width="wrap_content"
        android:layout_height="wrap_content" />
    <GridView
        android:id="@+id/grid"
        android:layout_width="match_parent"
        android:layout_height="wrap_content"
        android:columnWidth="75dip"
        android:gravity="center"
        android:horizontalSpacing="5dip"
        android:numColumns="auto_fit"
        android:stretchMode="columnWidth"
        android:verticalSpacing="75dip" />

</RelativeLayout>
```

The key visual attributes for our grid are that we have elected to consume the entire screen/activity space, except for the allowance for the label at the top. We further choose to let Android decide on the optimal number of columns using the auto_fit value for android:numColumns, and we specify horizontal spacing and column width to our desired pixel sizes of 5dip and 75dip, respectively.

The structure of the supporting Java code is very similar to the earlier ListView examples, with the only material changes being that I substituted in our GridView widget in the appropriate places and selected a suitable layout file for binding to the adapter, as shown in Listing 7-8.

Listing 7-8. Java Code for the GridView

```java
package com.artifexdigital.android.gridviewexample;

import android.os.Bundle;
import android.app.Activity;
import android.view.View;
import android.widget.AdapterView;
import android.widget.ArrayAdapter;
import android.widget.GridView;
import android.widget.TextView;

public class GridViewExample extends Activity
    implements AdapterView.OnItemSelectedListener  {
    private TextView mySelection;
    private static final String[] myListItems={"To", "be",
        "or", "not", "to", "be",
        "that", "is", "the", "question"};

    @Override
    protected void onCreate(Bundle savedInstanceState) {
        super.onCreate(savedInstanceState);
        setContentView(R.layout.activity_grid_view_example);

        GridView myGrid=(GridView) findViewById(R.id.grid);
        myGrid.setAdapter(new ArrayAdapter<String>(this,
                          R.layout.cell,
                          myListItems));
        myGrid.setOnItemSelectedListener(this);
    }

  public void onItemSelected(AdapterView<?> parent, View v,
                             int position, long id) {
    mySelection.setText(myListItems[position]);
  }

  public void onNothingSelected(AdapterView<?> parent) {
    //no-op
  }

}
```

For the curious, Listing 7-9 shows the cell.xml file from the res/layouts folder used by the adapter (as R.layout.cell) to define the rendering of each cell in the grid.

Listing 7-9. Layout XML for Each Cell of the GridView

```xml
<TextView xmlns:android="http://schemas.android.com/apk/res/android"
    xmlns:tools="http://schemas.android.com/tools"
    android:layout_width="wrap_content"
    android:layout_height="wrap_content"
    android:textSize="14sp" />
```

By choosing large `verticalSpacing` and `columnWidth` values in our layout (both `75dip`), I am attempting to create large box-like cells in the resulting application. In fact, such large cells are almost like implied buttons. This effect is useful, and you can even go so far as to have widgets like `Buttons` or `ImageViews` as the content of your cells (remember, you are in complete control of the layout the adapter uses). Figure 7-3 shows our grid as it first appears.

Remember that your emulator or device might have a different screen size, and so our `android:numColumns="auto_fit"` value can result in a layout of differing numbers of rows/columns than the one you see in Figure 7-3.

Figure 7-3. GridView with data from an ArrayAdapter

Taking Options for a Spin

There are times when you want to provide your users with a full list of items from which to choose, but for other design reasons or constraints, you simply don't have the space to show them the entire list in one go. Other widget toolkits address this with the notion of a drop-down or pick list. In Android, the same approach to saving space is achieved with the spinner.

Even without code of your own, you can see how a spinner works by simply playing with the time and date settings of any Android device. In these cases, the source data is taken from the system clock. When designing your own spinners, the general approach is the same as the one you took with `ListView` or `GridView`: create an adapter to provide the data you want displayed, pick an appropriate view layout for your spinner "rows," and hook up a listener object with `setOnItemSelectedListener()` to carry out your desired logic when a user makes their choice.

Unlike other selection widgets, a spinner has two visual forms: the collapsed version and the dropped-down version that appears while selection is in progress. If you want to also customize the look and feel of your spinner in its dropped-down state, you still configure the adapter (just as you do for the regular state of all selection widgets) and not the `Spinner` widget itself. You do this with a call to the `setDropDownViewResource()` method, where you provide the necessary resource ID of your desired view for the dropped-down state.

Listing 7-10 shows our ongoing Hamlet example converted to use a spinner.

Listing 7-10. Layout XML for the Spinner Widget

```
<RelativeLayout xmlns:android="http://schemas.android.com/apk/res/android"
    xmlns:tools="http://schemas.android.com/tools"
    android:layout_width="match_parent"
    android:layout_height="match_parent"
    tools:context=".SpinnerExample" >

    <TextView
        android:id="@+id/mySelection"
        android:layout_width="match_parent"
        android:layout_height="wrap_content" />
    <Spinner android:id="@+id/spinner"
        android:layout_width="match_parent"
        android:layout_height="wrap_content"
        android:drawSelectorOnTop="true" />

</RelativeLayout>
```

The attribute `android:drawSelectorOnTop` controls whether the arrow that provides the hint that this is a `Spinner` widget is drawn on the side of the spinner UI.

You can now pour in the Java code that should look mostly familiar to you by now, with the necessary substitutions to populate and use the spinner, as shown in Listing 7-11:

Listing 7-11. Java Code to Support the Spinner Widget

```
package com.artifexdigital.android.spinnerexample;

import android.os.Bundle;
import android.view.View;
import android.widget.AdapterView;
import android.widget.ArrayAdapter;
import android.widget.Spinner;
import android.widget.TextView;
import android.app.Activity;
```

```java
public class SpinnerExample extends Activity
    implements AdapterView.OnItemSelectedListener {
    private TextView mySelection;
    private static final String[] myListItems={"To", "be",
        "or", "not", "to", "be",
        "that", "is", "the", "question"};

    @Override
    protected void onCreate(Bundle savedInstanceState) {
        super.onCreate(savedInstanceState);
        setContentView(R.layout.activity_spinner_example);

        mySelection=(TextView)findViewById(R.id.mySelection);

        Spinner spin=(Spinner)findViewById(R.id.spinner);
        spin.setOnItemSelectedListener(this);

        ArrayAdapter<String> myAdapter=new ArrayAdapter<String>(this,
                            android.R.layout.simple_spinner_item,
                            myListItems);

        myAdapter.setDropDownViewResource(
            android.R.layout.simple_spinner_dropdown_item);
        spin.setAdapter(myAdapter);
    }

    public void onItemSelected(AdapterView<?> parent,
        View v, int position, long id) {
        mySelection.setText(myListItems[position]);
    }

    public void onNothingSelected(AdapterView<?> parent) {
        mySelection.setText("");
    }
}
```

In the Java implementation, when you use spin.setOnItemSelectedListener(this), the activity itself is designated as the selection listener. You can do this because the activity implements the OnItemSelectedListener interface. As I described earlier, it is possible to have a custom View for both the collapsed and dropped-down states of a spinner, and the call to aa.setDropDownViewResource() achieves this. I have used android.R.layout. simple_spinner_item as the View for each row on the spinner—this is another of the defaults shipped with the SDK. OnItemSelectedListener() updates the other label widget with the chosen selection just as we did with the ListView and GridView examples.

Figures 7-4 and 7-5 show the spinner in action.

Figure 7-4. Spinner showing initial state/collapsed state

Figure 7-5. Spinner in dropped-down state

In Figure 7-4 you can see one of the questionable design philosophies at play in Google/Android's contemporary widgets from recent editions like Lollipop, KitKat, and so on. Although there are strong theoretical underpinnings in the minimalist look of the spinner and the little arrow showing its capability (from cognitive neuroscience, if you must know), to the uninitiated, the spinner doesn't exactly announce its purpose with great fanfare to the user. You might want to keep this in mind when opting between selection widgets in your applications. One thing you can do to help your user in the case of using a spinner is to add a TextView label providing a hint or suggestion as to its purpose.

Automatic Field Population

Lists of data can be long. Really, really long. Think for a moment about how many songs you have as MP3 or other formats, or how many people you know on social media. If you had to run through an entire list of hundreds or thousands of entries, you would probably give up. What would help is some kind of quick filtering mechanism built right into the list. That is exactly what the AutoCompleteTextView offers you.

You can think of the AutoCompleteTextView as a hybrid of the EditText and Spinner views. The autocomplete part of its name should help you understand what it offers. As users type into the widget, their text is taken and used as a search-stub to find any matching items from a provided adapter prefixed with that text. Any matching candidates are shown in a successively more refined drop-down view, just like a spinner. It is up to the users to continue typing, all the way up to the full entry they want, or they can choose an item from the suggested list at any time.

> **Caution**   Be careful with really, really long lists. It takes some time to load the data into the view when a list has hundreds or thousands of entries, and browsing that list, or typing for matches, is also a slow experience. In Chapters 17, 18, and 19, I explore other ways, like databases, files, and preferences, to feed data to your applications that are better at dealing with much larger sets.

The AutoCompleteTextView is a subclass of EditText, which means all of the properties and attributes I described for EditText views in Chapter 5 are available for use. There are also properties specific to AutoCompleteTextView, including the attribute android:completionTh reshold, which indicates the minimum number of characters a user must type to trigger the list-filtering behavior.

Adapters for the source data to your AutoCompleteTextView are set using the same setAdapter() call you are now familiar with for other list objects. Because the user is allowed to enter a value not provided by the adapter instead of registering listeners to determine what choice was made, you use a TextWatcher instead to be notified when the text changes. This is available on all TextView derived classes.

Listing 7-12 switches the running example to use the AutoCompleteTextView in the layout.

Listing 7-12. Layout for the AutoCompleteTextView

```
<RelativeLayout xmlns:android="http://schemas.android.com/apk/res/android"
    xmlns:tools="http://schemas.android.com/tools"
    android:layout_width="match_parent"
    android:layout_height="match_parent"
    android:orientation="vertical"
    tools:context=".AutoExample" >

    <TextView
        android:id="@+id/mySelection"
        android:layout_width="wrap_content"
        android:layout_height="wrap_content" />
    <AutoCompleteTextView android:id="@+id/edit"
        android:layout_width="match_parent"
        android:layout_height="wrap_content"
        android:completionThreshold="1" />

</RelativeLayout>
```

The Java code to support the layout and register the TextWatcher is shown in Listing 7-13.

Listing 7-13. Java Code for the AutoCompleteTextView

```java
package com.artifexdigital.android.autoexample;

import android.os.Bundle;
import android.text.Editable;
import android.text.TextWatcher;
import android.widget.ArrayAdapter;
import android.widget.AutoCompleteTextView;
import android.widget.TextView;
import android.app.Activity;

public class AutoExample extends Activity implements TextWatcher {
    private TextView mySelection;
    private AutoCompleteTextView myEdit;
    private static final String[] myListItems={"To", "be",
        "or", "not", "to", "be",
        "that", "is", "the", "question"};

    @Override
    protected void onCreate(Bundle savedInstanceState) {
        super.onCreate(savedInstanceState);
        setContentView(R.layout.activity_auto_example);
        mySelection=(TextView)findViewById(R.id.mySelection);
        myEdit=(AutoCompleteTextView)findViewById(R.id.edit);
        myEdit.addTextChangedListener(this);

        myEdit.setAdapter(new ArrayAdapter<String>(this,
                          android.R.layout.simple_dropdown_item_1line,
                          myListItems));
    }

    public void onTextChanged(CharSequence s, int start, int before,
                              int count) {
      mySelection.setText(myEdit.getText());
    }

    public void beforeTextChanged(CharSequence s, int start,
                                  int count, int after) {
      // no-op
    }

    public void afterTextChanged(Editable s) {
      // no-op
    }

}
```

When you implement the TextWatcher, a new set of callbacks becomes available; it is worth familiarizing yourself with these:

- beforeTextChanged(): Where you can specify logic to invoke before the selected or typed item takes effect

- onTextChanged(): Logic to invoke at the point text changes, such as when the user types the next character or deletes the previous one

- afterTextChanged(): Logic to invoke after the selection of text entry is resolved

Our example uses onTextChanged() to set the value of the label in the activity. You can see the AutoCompleteTextView and its behavior in Figures 7-6 and 7-7.

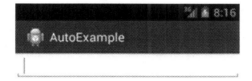

Figure 7-6. The AutoCompleteTextView waiting to show its capabilities

Figure 7-7. AutoCompleteTextView in action

Summary

That completes the introduction to lists and adapters, contributing to your growing toolset for application design. I come back to this topic later in the book when we explore databases, files, content providers, and other sources of information with which to populate your widgets.

Working with Input Methods, Menus and Dialogs

There is far more to designing great Android application activities than placing widgets on a screen. Those widgets are good for many different kinds of interaction with your user, but there are times when you need more. Whether it's dealing with more sophisticated approaches to input, offering options via menus, or providing important alerts and prompts for action via dialogs, Android has you covered.

In this chapter we will cover a number of key components that expand your user interface possibilities to all manner of things that "pop up" in the interface: keyboards, menus, and dialogs. I will cover Android's Input Method framework, which controls the use and behavior of virtual keyboards. I will also introduce you to the different approaches to menu design in Android, and explore the traditional menu approach. I will also investigate using dialogs and some of the related design ideas that apply to all of these areas.

Using The Input Method Framework

Shortly after releasing Android, Google reoganized the ways in which users can enter data on-screen into the Input Method Framework (IMF). This framework groups the ways in which users can actually input text data on-screen into three categories: The very familiar soft keyboard; hardware keyboards (either integral to the device, or as separate accessories), and handwriting recognition.

Real and Virtual Keyboards

While the very first Android device (the G1, or Dream) came with a physical keyboard, the majority of the tens of thousands of Android devices since released do not. There are still models released with physical keyboards today though, and Android's IMF means support for either type - physical or virtual - is seamlessly handled.

Android's internals include the necessary capabilities to detect the presence of a physical keyboard. If none is detected, Android makes available an input method editor (IME) for any EditText view which a user might select. By default, the stock IME will pick up a range of sensible settings from the user's locale and language settings, providing a useful and usable soft keyboard straight away, as well as other locale-specific prefernences such as whether the period or comma is used as the decimal "point", and so on. Many developers are happy with such defaults, and you can test for yourself what these look like with any of your applications. A significant majority of Android applications need no customizing code for their IMEs.

Where you do decide customizing IMEs is necessary for your application, the work is very straight-forward. If you examine the example `EditTextExample` application shown in Figure 8-1, you can probably think of a number of useful tweaks to the default soft keyboard, as well as some changes to the behavior of the text the user inputs. (The code for this example is available in `ch06/EditTextExample`. If you test this code, be sure to use a virtual device that does not have a hardware keyboard enabled).

Figure 8-1. *The input method editor showing as a soft keyboard in the EditTextExample application*

Customizing IMEs

From the introduction of Android 1.5, customizing your IME has been addressed through the bundle of attributes you can assign to a given View (e.g. an EditText) via the android:inputType attribute. This allows you to control all manner of style customizations for your field, by providing class options in a pipe-delimited "stacked" list. The combination of options chosen instructs Android what kinds of input to allow for the field. Android in turn uses that information to disable or remove from the soft keyboard any keys that can't be used with the resulting field. For instance, a phone number field would have no need for currency symbols, so these wouldn't be available from the resulting soft keyboard the input method framework generates.

The available classes of inputType are:

* text (set by default)
* number
* phone
* date
* time
* datetime

Within each of these inputType classes, there are potentially additional modifiers available to allow even more customization. Listing 8-1 demonstrates some of the inputType classes in action, and you can find the code in the activity_imeexample1.xml layout file from the ch08/IMEExample1 project.

Listing 8-1. inputType classes in action

```
<TableLayout xmlns:android="http://schemas.android.com/apk/res/android"
    xmlns:tools="http://schemas.android.com/tools"
    android:layout_width="match_parent"
    android:layout_height="match_parent"
    android:stretchColumns="1"
    tools:context=".IMEExample1" >

    <TableRow>
        <TextView
            android:text="No inputType:" />
        <EditText />
    </TableRow>
    <TableRow>
        <TextView
            android:text="Date:" />
        <EditText
            android:inputType="date" />
    </TableRow>
```

```
    <TableRow>
        <TextView
            android:text="Email address:" />
        <EditText
            android:inputType="text|textEmailAddress" />
    </TableRow>
    <TableRow>
        <TextView
            android:text="Decimal number:" />
        <EditText
            android:inputType="number|numberDecimal" />
    </TableRow>
    <TableRow>
        <TextView
            android:text="Multiline text:" />
        <EditText
            android:inputType="text|textMultiLine|textAutoCorrect"
            android:minLines="4"
            android:gravity="top" />
    </TableRow>
</TableLayout>
```

The layout from Listing 8-1 uses a TableLayout to host five variants EditText, each with different uses of inputType to demonstrate the customizations from the IMF.

■   The first row impicitly is an absolutely plain text field, as the inputType attributes on the EditText is not set, meaning you get the default behavior.

■   By using the android:inputType = "date" for the second field, we instruct the IMF to generate and IME that specifically allows only (valid) dates.

■   The third row allows for email addresses to be input, via android:inputType = "text|textEmailAddress".

■   The fourth row is configured to allow for decimal numeric input, using android:inputType = "number|numberDecimal".

■   Finally, the last EditText caters to multiline input, and uses autocorrection for any spelling mistakes.

You can see all of these classes and collections of modifiers customizing the keyboard when you run the example code. For example, a plain text-entry field results in a plain soft keyboard, as shown in Figure 8-2.

Figure 8-2. *A default soft-keyboard IME*

Remember that the default soft keyboard IME can differ between devices, particularly when user locale and language settings are considered by the IMF. Exploring our inputType results further, we can see the email customization with the @ symbol present, in Figure 8-3.

Figure 8-3. The soft-keyboard IME for email inputType in stock Android

Even here, you cannot always assume that different IMEs will necessarily present the
@ symbol on the keyboard with an inputType of email. The stock Android Lollipop and
earlier builds will do this, but you can both develop your own custom IMEs, and buy or
license them from other developers. In both cases, the @ symbol could be behind the
?123 option button, or indeed hidden further.

A more dramatic difference in the soft keyboard IME can be seen when we select a decimal
field. You can see the resulting soft keyboard in Figure 8-4.

Figure 8-4. *The soft keyboard IME for a decimal number*

The numeric keyboard shown is deliberately restricted to only providing digits and associated decimal points and commas for entering valid numbers. These ancillary soft keys will change depending on locale settings. For instance, in Europe where the comma is the decimal separator, that comma will appear on the bottom row to the right of the zero.

This kind of point-of-entry validation and filtering is one of the key additional benefits of the IMF and the various soft keyboards at your disposal. With a well-chosen android:inputType you can provide users of your application an intuitive soft keyboard for the data entry your application needs.

Accessorizing with Soft Keyboards

Look more closely at the preceeding Figure 8-1 through Figure 8-4. You should notice some other subtle differences. In Figure 8-1, the key in the lower right corner of the soft keyboard is a blue Done button. In Figure 8-2 it is a return arrow. In Figures 8-3 and 8-4, the lower right key is a blue Next button. This lower-right button is known as the *accessory button*, and its label and behavior changes depending on other inputType values.

There are two broad implicit behaviours. If you have an EditText widget with no modifiers for android:inputType, then the accessory button will take the blue-colored Next label, and when pressed will move the focus to the next EditText in the activity. The exception here is for the last EditText on a given screen. In this case, the accessory button will have the Done label.

You can control the labeling and behavior of the accessory button using the android:imeOptions attribute. For example, in the imeexample2.xml layout file from the ch08/IMEExmple2 project, I have modified the previous example to enhance the accessory buttons, as shown in Llisting 8-2:

Listing 8-2. Augmenting the look of the accessory button

```xml
<ScrollView xmlns:android="http://schemas.android.com/apk/res/android"
    xmlns:tools="http://schemas.android.com/tools"
    android:layout_width="match_parent"
    android:layout_height="match_parent"
    tools:context=".IMEExample2" >

    <TableLayout
        android:layout_width="fill_parent"
        android:layout_height="fill_parent"
        android:stretchColumns="1" >
        <TableRow>
            <TextView
                android:text="No inputType:" />
            <EditText />
        </TableRow>
        <TableRow>
            <TextView
                android:text="Date:" />
            <EditText
                android:inputType="date" />
        </TableRow>
        <TableRow>
            <TextView
                android:text="Email address:" />
            <EditText
                android:inputType="text|textEmailAddress"
                android:imeOptions="actionSend" />
        </TableRow>
        <TableRow>
            <TextView
                android:text="Decimal number:" />
            <EditText
                android:inputType="number|numberDecimal"
                android:imeOptions="actionGo" />
        </TableRow>
        <TableRow>
            <TextView
                android:text="Multiline text:" />
            <EditText
                android:inputType="text|textMultiLine|textAutoCorrect"
                android:minLines="4"
                android:gravity="top" />
        </TableRow>
    </TableLayout>
</ScrollView>
```

In Listing 8-2 I have plugged in the Send action for the accessory button, so that when pressed we trigger the actionSend action using the e-mail address. Similarly with the the middle field, we have a Go label and action, with android:imeOptions="actionGo". Pressing Next moves the focus to the following EditText, and Go attempts to take the user to the "target" of the text that has been typed. For example, Android might attempt to infer that a number is a phone number or other numeric identifier.

You can also attempt more complex or sophisticated actions with the accessory button by using the setOnEditorActionListener() on the EditText. Part of the payload you receive will be the relevant flag indicating the action specified, such as IME_ACTION_SEND.

Scrolling in to View

The sharp-sighted amongst readers will have noticed another aspect of the code in Listing 8-3 for the IMEExample2 application. The example introduces the ScrollView container to wrap the layout.

While there has been a proliferation in different Android devices, the vast majority of them are still phones, and those phones have small displays. You should also be aware of "developer bias", where as a developer you are more likely to skew towards a power user, and own and use devices with larger screens and more features. There are many approaches you as a developer can use to maximize information display, and deal with small screens. Scrolling is a well-known metaphor on the desktop, and works in a broadly similar way on Android. In principle, you can take any layout that you might otherwise describe for your Android activities, and wrap it in a ScrollView. In doing so, the user will be presented with the part of your contained layout that fits the screen, and automatic scrolling logic and scrollbars will be added to enable the user to move to the parts of your layout that don't fit on screen.

> **Note**   there are two Views that govern explicitly enabled scrolling in this fashion: ScrollView for vertical scrolling, and HorizontalScrollView for horizontal scrolling. You cannot stack these to get both forms of scrolling, so you will need to decide which suits your layout.

In addition to the implicit layout changes that scrolling introduces, use of the IME triggers other changes in your layout. When the user interacts with a widget that demands Android present the IME, screen real estate is needed to show the actual resulting soft keyboard. Where does this screen space come from, and how do you control the behavior? I'm glad you asked.

There are multiple possibilities that depend on device type and your application development choices. Amongst the options Android can take to rearrange the on-screen layout to fit your soft keyboard are:

- Activity panning can be used to slide your entire as-is layout off the "edge" of your screen, in effect moving the screen up or to the side such that only part of it is rendered and visible, but the user has the illusion that the rest still exists. The IME is then shown in the resulting, freed up space.

- Your activity can be resized, scaling the rendered layout to a smaller-than-specified scale so that the IME can fit below the activity layout, and both be visible at the same time. This approachworks well for some of the list-based layouts we explored in Chapter 7, but less well for layouts that are graphics-intensive.

- Android can choose to completely obscure your activity, and allow the IME to occupy the entire screen.

- If your activity exists within a Fragment (covered in Chapter 11), Android can reflow and rearrange all of the activities within the Fragment, and use one or more of the above techniques in combination to have the IME and original activity layouts present side-by-side as far as is feasible. This works best on larger screens and with applications written to use the fragments model.

If you choose to do nothing and let Android take the default approach, then it will bias toward the first two options of panning and resizing. When you want to take control of the IME presentation behavior, use the `android:windowSoftInputMode` attribute on the `activity` element in your manifest file for your project. Listing 8-3 shows the `AndroidManifest.xml` file for `IMEExample2`:

Listing 8-3. Controlling IME reflow and resizing behavior

```
<?xml version="1.0" encoding="utf-8"?>
<manifest xmlns:android="http://schemas.android.com/apk/res/android"
    package="com.artifexdigital.android.imeexample2"
    android:versionCode="1"
    android:versionName="1.0" >

    <uses-sdk
        android:minSdkVersion="11"
        android:targetSdkVersion="17" />

    <application
        android:allowBackup="true"
        android:icon="@drawable/ic_launcher"
        android:label="@string/app_name"
        android:theme="@style/AppTheme"
        android:windowSoftInputMode="adjustResize">
        <activity
            android:name="com.artifexdigital.android.imeexample2.IMEExample2"
            android:label="@string/app_name" >
            <intent-filter>
                <action android:name="android.intent.action.MAIN" />
```

```
            <category android:name="android.intent.category.LAUNCHER" />
        </intent-filter>
      </activity>
    </application>

</manifest>
```

Looking at the manifest, you can see the `android:windowSoftInputMode="adjustResize"` entry which instructs Android to ignore its implicit preferences and attempt to shrink the activity's layout to accommodate the IME when it needs to be presented. You can see this in action in Figure 8-5.

Figure 8-5. *Scaling the IME with explicit control*

Because we have defined our layout within a `ScrollView`, when the scaling occurs we also gain the benefit of the `ScrollView`'s scroll bars being triggered for use. This is even though the Material Design excesses of Android Lollipop make those scroll bars hard to see.

You can control Android's behavior to maximize screen real-estate using the additional methods introduced in Honeycomb, and refined in Icecream Sandwich and Jelly Bean. Use the Java methods `setSystemUiVisibility()` with the `STATUS_BAR_HIDDEN` option to hide the System Bar and allow even larger full screen modes, or `setDimAmount()` to tweak the brightness of the home buttons to remove distractions from your regularly resized full-screen layout.

Forcing the IME out of Existence

There are times when the automatic triggering of the IME would be counter-productive or interfere with the user's experience of your application. Android uses a background system service, `InputMethodManager`, to govern appearance, disappearance, and other behaviors of IMEs. Listing 8-4 shows a code snippet that invokes the `hideSoftInputFromWindow()` method, which is available to you to forcibly override the appearance of an IME.

Listing 8-4. Forcing the IME out of existance

```
InputMethodManager myIMM =
  (InputMethodManager)getSystemService(INPUT_METHOD_SERVICE);

myIMM.hideSoftInputFromWindow(myEditTextforIMEHiding.getWindowToken(), 0);
```

Here I've used the verbose but hopefully instructive name `myEditTextforIMEHiding` as the `EditText` field for which I wish to hide the IME. This will always ensure that the IME is hidden in the first instance.

But be warned, your user can always force the IME to reappear. If they explicitly tap the `EditText` field on a device with no physical keyboard, the IME will appear. It will also appear for both `EditText`-style fields and those widgets that don't normally trigger a soft keyboard if the user hits the menu (soft) button. In the case of tapping the `EditText`, you can alter the call to the `hideSoftInputFromWindow()` method as follows:

```
myIMM.hideSoftInputFromWindow(myEditTextforIMEHiding.getWindowToken(),
InputMethodManager.HIDE_IMPLICIT_ONLY);
```

In changing the second parameter to the method call, you instruct the `InputMethodManager` to surpress the IME even on an explicit tap. Take care when using this approach and test it thoroughly, lest you accidentally trigger IME supression and prevent the user from entering text when you most want them to.

Working with Menus

Menus are a way in which your users will interact with your application outside of the widgets you present in your UI layout. Just like the IME, menus appear near or over your layout, and understanding their behavior will help you create useful additional interaction modes for your application.

You and your users will almost certainly be familiar with the menu metaphor from using desktop or notebook computers, and even TV sets. As well as application level menus, Android provides the ability to create context menus for various UI elements, meaning you can create a context menu for an `EditText` or similar field. In a traditional operating system, users would normally have a mouse with which they could right-click or command-click to make a context menu appear. In the Android world, gestures such as the "long press" can be used to invoke a context menu.

> **Note**   Historically Android devices came with a fixed "menu" button or soft button equivalent. With Google's release of Honeycomb, and especially since the advent of JellyBean, KitKat and Lollipop, interface standards have shifted to heavily discourage the existence of any permanent menu button. Interface standards instead promote use of the Action Bar, which we will cover in Chapter 10. You may still find users deploying applications on devices with dedicated menu buttons, so knowing the overall picture of menus remains useful.

Android offers two broad types of menus for use in your applications. The first is the Activity or Options menu, and then there is the Context menu mentioned. Activity menus, since the advent of Android Honeycomb, have migrated to the Action Bar, but they are still available as Options menus on older devices. We'll return to talk more about menus in the Action Bar context in Chapter 10.

Creating Menus for your Application

Traditional menus are created using the dedicated callback method `onOptionsMenuCreate()`. This method is triggered at the time a menu would come in to existence, and it is passed an instance of a `Menu` object. If you want to keep updating or modifying what your menu can do in response to further user actions, for instance making an option unavailable once a one-time activity has occured, you should preserve the `Menu` object so you can reference it after the callback has gone out of scope.

Android will have its own notions of the various system features and other options that should be injected in to your menus, and you can take advantage of what Android can do by making the first line of you `onOptionsMenuCreate()` implementation a call to the `super.onCreateOptionsMenu(menu)` method. Doing so allows Android to implicitly add additional items for you, such as the "back arrow" button.

Following that step, you can add your own particular featuers to the `Menu` object using its `add()` method. This is a highly overloaded method, meaning its many variants won't be apparent to you immediately, but here are some of the common parameters taken by the most commonly used forms of `add()` for a `Menu` object:

- A choice identifier, which is a unique `int` value for each menu item, and is passed to the `onOptionsItemSelected()` callback when the relevant menu item is selected.

- An order identifier, which is an `int` value specifying the placement of your item in the menu hierarchy, based on the lowest order identifier being at the top. This is especially useful when interspersing your own custom menu items with those Android provides for the call to the super class. You can also use the value `NONE` to allow Android to manage ordering implicitly.

- The menu text, which can be a resource ID reference or `String` value. You should get used to using resource ID references to allow for future language changes, internationalization and localization.

Your call to the add() method for a Menu object will return a MenuItem object, which itself has several interesting methods. Some of the most commonly used are the setAlphabeticShortcut() and setNumericShortcut() methods, which enable you to provide a one-character/digit shortcut for chosing your menu item when the UI has invoked keyboard (IME) menu input using the setQwertyMode() method for the menu.

The options you choose from to populate your menu are not limited to simple text. You also have the option of invoking the menu's setCheckable() method, passing in a choice identifier, to nominate that menu item as having a checkbox associated with it. This gives your user immediate information and feedback on the setting that a given menu item controls, such as whether WiFi is on or off. This concept can be extended further by the introduction of group identifiers and the setGroupCheckable() method. A group identifier is also an int property that can be assigned when using the menu's add() method, and you can provide the same group identifier to more than one menu item. You can then use setGroupCheckable() to create a radio button that covers all items with that group identifier, such that only one of those menu items can be turned "on" at a time. Using the WiFi example again, you could implement available networks as menu items with the same group identifier, and cover the selection of the user's preferred network with setGroupCheckable().

> **Tip**   You can create submenus within menus by using the addSubMenu() method. Your submenus require choice identifiers, but in other respects you are free to add other entries such as checkboxes, and to control a submenu's behavior much as any other menu. Android prevents you going crazy with nested submenus, limiting you to one extra level below the main menu.

Whatever form your menu takes, when a user actually chooses an item from your menu, you are notified through the onOptionsItemSelected() callback. The callback will pass the MenuItem object corresponding with the user's choice. You can then invoke your desired behavior, and can use common patterns such as a switch statement to handle all the options available to the user and your consequential reactions to their choice.

Working With Context Menus

Context menus are conceptually similar to ordinary menus. The main areas that differ are in flagging which of your UI elements will support a context menu, how menu items are constructed, and how your application gets notified of the user's choice. Let's deal with these in order.

To nominate that a particular UI element will support a context menu, make a call to registerForContextMenu() from your activity's onCreate() implementation passing as a parameter the View that will host a context menu. Obviously, if you have multiple on-screen elements that you want to have context menus, you will need to make multiple calls.

Regardless of how many widgets in your activity have context menus, they will all call onCreateContextMenu(), at the point the user invokes the context menu on a given widget. This is unlike regular activity/options menus that are instantiated once at activity creation time. You need to implement the onCreateContextMenu() and based on the View object passed (that is, the widget the user has selected), you will need to then build the necessary context menu. The typical pattern for doing this involves using a `switch` block in your Java code to handle which item needs its context menu, and then to proceed with the necessary creation.

When a user chooses a context menu item, the `onContextItemSelected()` callback is fired. It's incumbent on you to implement this method in your activity, and as with the regular menu case, you will be passed the `MenuItem` instance that the user chose. You can use the `switch` statement again to trigger the desired program logic at this point.

Caution   Because you are only given the `MenuItem` that the user chose, and not immediately given the relevant widget, it is best to ensure every menu item has a unique choice identifier across the entire scope of your activity. You can make calls to `getMenuInfo()` for the `MenuItem` passed in the `onContextItemSelected()` callback, which will return a `ContextMenu.ContextMenuInfo` structure from which you can determine which widget had its context menu invoked, but it is far easier to spare yourself the need for this logic by using activity-wide unique identifiers.

Menus In Action

With all of that theory now digested, let's examine what a working application with menus looks like. In the following example, I have used the `ListViewExample` application from Chapter 7, and I have adapted the Java implementation to illustrate a range of the menu capabilities introduced so far in this chapter.

```
package com.artifexdigital.android.menuexample;

import android.app.ListActivity;
import android.os.Bundle;
import android.view.ContextMenu;
import android.view.Menu;
import android.view.MenuItem;
import android.view.View;
import android.widget.AdapterView;
import android.widget.ArrayAdapter;
import java.util.ArrayList;

public class MenuExampleActivity extends ListActivity {
    private static final String[] items={"To", "be",
            "or", "not", "to", "be",
            "that", "is", "the", "question"};
    public static final int MENU_RESET = Menu.FIRST+1;
    public static final int MENU_UPPER = Menu.FIRST+2;
    public static final int MENU_REMOVE = Menu.FIRST+3 ;
```

```java
private ArrayList<String> words=null;

@Override
protected void onCreate(Bundle savedInstanceState) {
    super.onCreate(savedInstanceState);
    setContentView(R.layout.activity_menu_example);
    setupAdapter();
    registerForContextMenu(getListView());
}

@Override
public boolean onCreateOptionsMenu(Menu menu) {
    menu.add(Menu.NONE, MENU_RESET, Menu.NONE, "Reset");
    return(super.onCreateOptionsMenu(menu));
}

@Override
public void onCreateContextMenu(ContextMenu menu,
                                View v,
                                ContextMenu.ContextMenuInfo menuInfo) {
    menu.add(Menu.NONE, MENU_UPPER, Menu.NONE, "Upper Case");
    menu.add(Menu.NONE, MENU_REMOVE, Menu.NONE, "Remove Word");
}

@Override
public boolean onOptionsItemSelected(MenuItem item) {
    switch (item.getItemId()) {
        case MENU_RESET:
            setupAdapter();
            return(true);
    }

    return(super.onOptionsItemSelected(item));
}

public boolean onContextItemSelected(MenuItem item) {
    AdapterView.AdapterContextMenuInfo menuInfo=
            (AdapterView.AdapterContextMenuInfo)item.getMenuInfo();
    ArrayAdapter<String> adapter=(ArrayAdapter<String>)getListAdapter();

    switch (item.getItemId()) {
        case MENU_UPPER:
            String word=words.get(menuInfo.position);
            word=word.toUpperCase();
            adapter.remove(words.get(menuInfo.position));
            adapter.insert(word, menuInfo.position);
            return(true);

        case MENU_REMOVE:
            adapter.remove(words.get(menuInfo.position));
            return(true);
    }
```

```
            return(super.onContextItemSelected(item));
    }

    private void setupAdapter() {
        words=new ArrayList<>();

        for (String someItem : items) {
            words.add(someItem);
        }

        setListAdapter(new ArrayAdapter<>(this,
                android.R.layout.simple_list_item_1, words));
    }

}
```

This example is deceptively long, so let's get to the heart of the menu logic. First, we are using a simple ListView and an ArrayAdapter to present the familiar list of words from Shakespeare's Hamlet soliloquy. So you can refer back to Chapter 6 for the various details on the behavior of the ListView and adapter logic. That leaves the actual code setting up the options menu and the context menu, and then dealing with their invocation.

The methods onCreateContextMenu() and onCreateOptionsMenu() are very straight-forward, simply adding the items we wish to appear in each type of menu. The options menu receives the MENU_RESET entry, with the label "Reset Word List", while the context menu gets the "Upper Case" and "Remove Word" entries tied to the the MENU_UPPER and MENU_REMOVE references.

Just as the menu setup methods are paired for the options menu and context menu, so too are the selection handlers. The onContextItemSelected() method deals with the logic of capitalizing entries for the MENU_UPPER selection, and removing items from the ListView for the MENU_REMOVE selection. Similarly, onOptionsItemSelected() deals with the MENU_RESET logic to return the ListView to the originally populated version from the ArrayAdapter.

You can run the MenuExample application yourself and experiment with the menus. Figure 8-6 shows the running application with the context menu showing after a long-click on one of the items in the ListView.

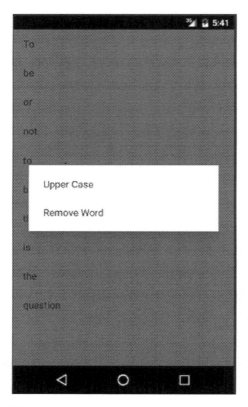

Figure 8-6. *Displaying the Context Menu*

As you click and choose multiple "Upper Case" and "Remove Word" items from the context menu, the ListView population will eventually change to appear more like that shown in Figure 8-7.

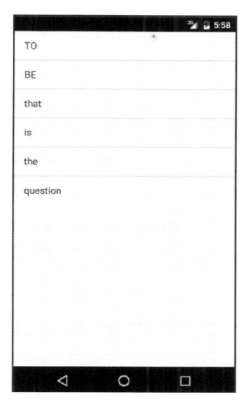

Figure 8-7. The MenuExample UI after multiple uses of the menus

Inflating Menus from XML

In earlier chapters I demonstrated how any UI widget can be defined purely using XML in your res folder. From there I showed how you can rely on Android to "inflate" your XML definition into a real UI widget. The same principle applies to menus: You can fully describe menus in XML, and then rely on Android to inflate them into existence.

Menu XML files are held in your project's res/menu folder. As with other XML resources such as layouts, you can create as many menu variants as you like, and have your chosen variant inflated whenever you need, such as in response to a user initiating a context menu. Listing 8-5 shows the ch08/MenuXMLExample application's menu definition.

Listing 8-5. Defining a Menu in XML

```
<menu xmlns:android="http://schemas.android.com/apk/res/android">
  <item android:id="@+id/respond"
    android:title="Respond"
    android:icon="@drawable/ic_menu_respond" />
  <item android:id="@+id/echo"
    android:title="Echo"
    android:icon="@drawable/ic_menu_echo" />
</menu>
```

A menu definition has as its root a <menu> element. Within the <menu> element, you can then specify any number of <item> elements to appear as menu items in your menu. You can also use the <group> element to manage a set of menu items as a group, just as you can in Java by providing a group identifier int for each item.

All of the behavior we explored with Java coded menus is available with XML definition for run-time inflation, including the submenu structures and options. To create a submenu, add a <menu> element as a child of the root <menu>. You can then add items, groups, and so forth to the submenu just as you would to its parent.

To be able to refer to your menu in code, and to find out when and what menus items are selected by your application's user, be sure to include an android:id attribute with a unique ID for each menu item.

Further Options for XML-Based Menus

The XML-based approach to menu definition provides all of the power of Java-coded menus, which means support for all the optional methods we introduced for menus earlier in the chapter. Table 8-1 shows the optional attributes you can apply to menu item elements in your XML definition, and the corresponding behavior.

Table 8-1. XML Menu Options

XML Menu Attribute	Behavior
android:title	The visible label for your menu item, when shown in the activity's UI. This can be a hard-coded String or a resource reference (e.g. @string/MenuText1)
android:icon	The icon to display adjacent to the android:title text. This is a reference to a drawable resource.
android:orderInCategory	Used to override the order of menu items in the XML definition. This is a zero-based reference to allow Android to re-order your menu at runtime. You might want to do this for instance so in your XML menu layout file you group items by function, but in you menu UI they are presented alphabetically.
android:enabled	True and False values for the the android:enabled attribute provide the same control that the Java methods setEnabled() and setGroupEnabled() offer. The XML definition will control the initial rendering of the menu item. To enable and disable a menu item subsequently, you will need to invoke the relevant logic and Java method in response to your user's actions.

(continued)

Table 8-1. *(continued)*

XML Menu Attribute	Behavior
android:visible	You can optional decided to hide menu items when first rendered (not just disable them through a android:enabled="false" attribute). This is often used in combination with a parent menu item that has a checkbox, which went activated invokes the Java logic via setVisible() or setGroupVisible() methods to make a previously invisible group or submenu item visible.
android:alphabeticShortcut	Nominate a letter shortcut from a soft or hard keyboard to activate this menu item.
android:numericShortcut	Nominate a digit shortcut from a soft or hard keyboard to select a desired menu item.

Inflating an XML-Defined Menu

With a XML definition for your menu, the next step is to wire up the necessary application behavior to inflate your menu into existence as and when required. The key Java class involved in inflating you definition into a useable menu is MenuInflater. Listing 8-6 shows the complementary code listing for the XML menu from the ch08/MenuXMLExample project we introduced in Listing 8-5.

Listing 8-6. Java logic to complement the XML-defined menu

```
@Override
public boolean onCreateOptionsMenu(Menu menu) {
  new MenuInflater(this).inflate(R.menu.option, menu);

  return(super.onCreateOptionsMenu(menu));
}

@Override
public void onCreateContextMenu(ContextMenu menu, View v,
                                ContextMenu.ContextMenuInfo menuInfo) {
  new MenuInflater(this).inflate(R.menu.context, menu);
}
```

Here, we see how MenuInflater "pours" the menu items specified in the menu resource (e.g., R.menu.option) into the supplied Menu or ContextMenu object.

We also need to change onOptionsItemSelected() and onContextItemSelected() to use the android:id values specified in the XML:

```
@Override
public boolean onOptionsItemSelected(MenuItem item) {
  switch (item.getItemId()) {
    case R.id.add:
      add();
      return(true);
```

```
      case R.id.reset:
        initAdapter();
        return(true);
    }

  return(super.onOptionsItemSelected(item));
}

@Override
public boolean onContextItemSelected(MenuItem item) {
  AdapterView.AdapterContextMenuInfo info=
    (AdapterView.AdapterContextMenuInfo)item.getMenuInfo();
  ArrayAdapter<String> adapter=(ArrayAdapter<String>)getListAdapter();

  switch (item.getItemId()) {
    case R.id.cap:
      String word=words.get(info.position);

      word=word.toUpperCase();

      adapter.remove(words.get(info.position));
      adapter.insert(word, info.position);

      return(true);

    case R.id.remove:
      adapter.remove(words.get(info.position));

      return(true);
  }

  return(super.onContextItemSelected(item));
}
```

You should notice the resulting menu UI in your application is broadly similar to the Java-based menu creation examples.

Interacting with Dialogs

There are times when you need to interrupt your user's normal use of your application, to notify them of an important event, change, or error. Anyone familiar with traditional desktop or web development will recognize dialog boxes and overlays in web pages that provide status or error information. Android provides two different kinds of pop-up dialog for use when notifying or interacting with the user: A Toast object for transient notification, and Alert objects for full dialog-style interaction.

In addition to these UI-centric approaches, Android also has a fully-fledged notifications system that facilitates communication for intents and services which we will cover later in the book. For now, let's examine what the user will see with toasts and alerts.

Creating Toast Notifications

Toast messages appear as an overlay to the current activity without interrupting its focus or the user's input. This means things like keyboard entry, touch actions and so forth won't be lost if a Toast notification is displayed.

Because of its non-interfering nature, as an application developer you need to keep in mind a few other characteristics of a Toast. First, you can't control for how long the Toast will be present. Android will manage the Toast's lifetime on your behalf, and typically presents a Toast message for several seconds before it fades from existence. As the user need not press a button or otherwise dismiss a Toast, you will also not receive any notification or callback that the user has seen the Toast, or responded to it. This means you typically want to use a Toast to present non-critical, advisory information.

To create and configure a Toast object, simply call the class' static makeText() method with the following three parameters:

* The text you wish to display, as either a String or resource ID reference
* The Activity or Context with which the Toast is to be associated
* A duration value, using either of the constants LENGTH_SHORT or LENGTH_LONG

You can also create more elaborate or sophisticated Toast notifications that go beyond simple text. For instance, you can create a Toast the presents an ImageView by creating a new Toast instance, invoking the constructor, and then calling the methods setView() and setDuration() to provide the View object for the Toast to use and its desired lifetime. With these values configured, calling show() will the present the final form of the Toast to your user.

Generating Traditional Dialog Alerts

The one drawback of Toast alerts is the lack of interactivity with the user. You may need to explicitly gather a response in your application. And sometimes you just want the traditional look, feel and behavior of a dialog box. Android covers these requirements with the AlertDialog class.

An AlertDialog has fundamentally well-known behavior when compared with dialog boxes on other platforms. It creates a pop-up overlaying the current UI, acts in "modal" form where the user is forced to interact with the AlertDialog before returning to the Activity or Context, and can be constructed with a range of buttons and other Views to prompt the user for meaningful interaction.

There are two general approaches to constructing your AlertDialog. The first approach is to use the Builder class to stitch together calls to the various options (and their methods) which suit the kind of dialog you would like to display. The second approach is to instantiate an AlertDialog instance, using its create() method, and then make subsequent calls to the methods needed.

Whichever approach you take, you ultimately call the show() method for your AlertDialog to finally present the dialog to the user of your application, and await their response of clicking one of the available buttons. You can configure listeners for any button on your AlertDialog if you want to catch the user's response and perform some subsequent action, or use the null listener where you don't have actions to perform.

> **Note**   Android will automatically dismiss the AlertDialog once a button is pressed, regardless
> of listener configuration. There is no way to have the dialog persist on-screen while your listener
> callback is processed.

Here are some of the useful methods that are commonly used when constructing
AlertDialogs:

- setTitle() Configure the caption that appears as the title of the
  AlertDialog

- setMessage() Configure the body text that appears in the AlertDialog

- setIcon() Configure an icon to appear in the leading corner of the
  AlertDialog, where leading corner is adapted by Android depending on
  left-to-right or right-to-left layout.

- setPositiveButton(), setNegativeButton() Choose the buttons that
  appear beneath the message text, along with the button text to display
  and the logic to invoke when selected.

- show() This method has a number of overloaded forms, but they all act
  to show a configured AlertDialog instance.

Pardon The Interruption

It is time to see both the Toast and AlertDialog options in action. Listing 8-7 introduces the basic
layout for a Button that I will then use to trigger an AlertDialog, followed by a Toast pop up.
You can find this code and the subsequent Java logic in the ch08/PopUpExamples project.

Listing 8-7. The Button definition that triggers AlertDialog and Toast popups

```
<RelativeLayout xmlns:android="http://schemas.android.com/apk/res/android"
    xmlns:tools="http://schemas.android.com/tools"
    android:layout_width="match_parent"
    android:layout_height="match_parent"
    tools:context="com.artifexdigital.android.popupexamples.PopUpExampleActivity" >

    <Button
        android:id="@+id/alertbutton"
        android:text="Press for AlertDialog"
        android:onClick="showAlertDialog" />

</RelativeLayout>
```

The logic of creating and displaying our AlertDialog and Toast notifications is in the actual
Java code shown in Listing 8-8.

Listing 8-8. Java code for AlertDialog and Toast popups

```java
package com.artifexdigital.android.popupexamples;

import android.app.Activity;
import android.app.AlertDialog;
import android.content.DialogInterface;
import android.os.Bundle;
import android.view.View;
import android.widget.Toast;

public class PopUpExampleActivity extends Activity {

    @Override
    protected void onCreate(Bundle savedInstanceState) {
        super.onCreate(savedInstanceState);
        setContentView(R.layout.activity_pop_up_example);
    }

    public void showAlertDialog(View view) {
        new AlertDialog.Builder(this)
        .setTitle("AlertDialog Exmaple")
        .setMessage("This is the example AlertDialog.
                            Press the button to see the Toast notification")
        .setPositiveButton("Show Toast", new DialogInterface.OnClickListener() {

            @Override
            public void onClick(DialogInterface dialog, int which) {
                Toast.makeText(PopUpExampleActivity.this,
                "The Toast Message", Toast.LENGTH_LONG)
                .show();

            }
        }).show();
    }
```

The logic here is straight-forward, and is driven by the simple button in our layout. When the button is pressed, we use the `Builder()` approach to construct the `AlertDialog`, giving the dialog a caption, text, and a Button of its own which in turn triggers the `Toast`. Our PopUpExample application showing the `AlertDialog` after the initial button press is shown in Figure 8-8.

Figure 8-8. *The AlertDialog presented to the user*

Once the "positive" button on the AlertDialog is pressed, the dialog is dismissed and the listener bound to the button press activates the creation of our Toast message. You can see the Toast displayed in Figure 8-9.

Figure 8-9. A Toast message popping up over the Activity

Summary

In this chapter you have seen all manner of UI elements that leap to the user's attention: IMEs, menus, and dialogs. You will continue to use these items in examples throughout the rest of the book.

Adopting the Action Bar

The previous chapter introduced the traditional notion of menus, giving you some common understanding across all Android versions of how a traditional menu would work. Starting with traditional menus has also set you up to take the next logical step into Android's (relatively) new and more advanced approach to menu-like interaction with users: The Action Bar.

The Action Bar works to incorporate the most intuitive menu options that users might wish to use at a given point in time, together with a standard set of navigation and option elements to bring consistency across Android devices of all sizes and types. Your users will not need to worry about screen size, layout, or where to find the most obvious actions to take. The Action Bar solves all! (Well, almost all).

We will take a look at the Action Bar appearance and behavior, and how to develop applications to use and take advantage of the Action Bar.

Recognizing the Action Bar

Depending on how you have tested the examples introduced earlier in the book, and on which AVD or real device, you might have already seen the Action Bar reveal itself. But to be absolutely sure, and for those who know they haven't seen it, Figure 9-1 shows a typical Android screen for contacts management that is running on an emulation of moderately-sized tablet in landscape mode. The Action Bar is at the top.

Figure 9-1. The Action Bar displayed at the top of a Contact detail screen

Some of the key features of Figure 9-1's Action Bar to note are the incorporation of the DONE button that would otherwise be a menu option, and the < symbol representing the back button (which may or may not display depending on context and other factors). Items like the back button are added by Android as part of the Action Bar framework, meaning no coding is required by you. Android will implicitly return to the previous activity. Or if there is no prior activity (e.g., when first starting the application and working with the launch activity) then the user is returned to the launcher.

Managing Android Versions for Action Bar

Support for the Action Bar was introduced in Android 3.0, otherwise known as Honeycomb. The support was implemented as a new feature in the Android SDK, meaning inevitable questions about version requirements arise.

Specifying SDK level for Native Action Bar Support

Honeycomb was released along with version 11 of the SDK for Android. To ensure your application can work with the Action Bar natively, you should do one of two things. The most common is to set the android:minSdkVersion to 11 in your android manifest file, in the <uses-sdk> element, like this:

```
<uses-sdk
    android:minSdkVersion="11" />
```

Alternatively, you can specify a lower `android:minSdkVersion` setting, and use an `android:targetSdkVersion` of 11 or higher to indicate you desire SDK level 11 functionality such as the Action Bar, but will settle for something lower if that's all the device has available. The two settings would look like this:

```
<uses-sdk
    android:minSdkVersion="8"
    android:targetSdkVersion="11" />
```

Utilizing the Support Library for Older Android Versions

One option for older versions of Android is to make use of the support library, which we discussed in Chapter 2. Through the support library and the classes it offers (notably, `android.support.v7.app.ActionBarActivity`) you can bring Action Bar behavior to devices with SDK support as far back as version 8. We will explore some examples that use this option later in this chapter.

Creating Action Bar Applications

You have seen examples of stock Android applicatoins using the Action Bar in Figure 9-1. Now it is time to create your own. We will start by defining menu items to "migrate" to the Action Bar, and then move on to more advanced topics of custom views and dealing with menu-based input.

Enabling the Action Bar for your Application

As introduced earlier in the chapter, you will need to ensure the your manifest specifies at least SDK level 11, if not higher, as the target SDK version in order to make the Action Bar available to your application. Listing 9-1 shows the manifest for our example menu application from chapter 8 converted to using the Action Bar.

Listing 9-1. Manifest with target SDK set correctly for Action Bar

```
<?xml version="1.0" encoding="utf-8"?>
<manifest xmlns:android="http://schemas.android.com/apk/res/android"
    package="com.artifexdigital.android.actionbarexample"
    android:versionCode="1"
    android:versionName="1.0" >
    <uses-sdk
        android:minSdkVersion="11"
        android:targetSdkVersion="21" />
    <application
        android:allowBackup="true"
        android:icon="@drawable/ic_launcher"
        android:label="@string/app_name"
        android:theme="@style/AppTheme" >
```

```
        <activity
            android:name=".ActionBarExampleActivity"
            android:label="@string/app_name" >
            <intent-filter>
                <action android:name="android.intent.action.MAIN" />
                <category android:name="android.intent.category.LAUNCHER" />
            </intent-filter>
        </activity>
    </application>
</manifest>
```

With the Action Bar enabled implicitly, things like options menus will appear under the control of a vertical ellipsis icon in the top-right of the Action Bar, revealing themselves when the icon is pressed. You can see this in action in Figure 9-2, and compare the behavior to earlier examples in the book that had no Action Bar at all

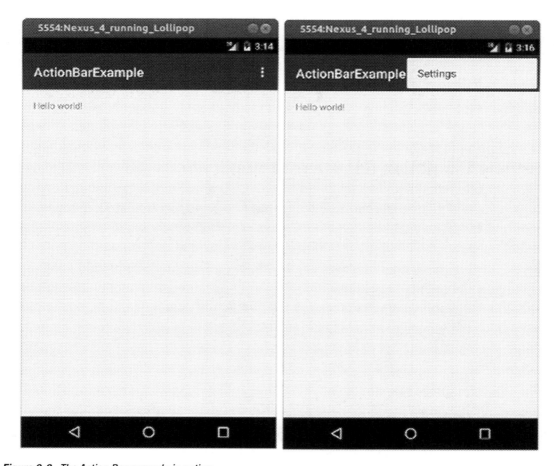

Figure 9-2. The Action Bar example in action

Having your options menu migrate automatically to the Action Bar is great, but that migration doesn't deal with any other custom menus you have created. Rather than leave the user with a "split" experience, the next step is to move all of your key menu-like options to the Action Bar.

Moving Menu Functionality to the Action Bar

The key to enabling a menu item to appear in the Action Bar is to include the attribute android:showAsAction in your menu item's <item> element. This is a simple stackable attribute that takes a mandatory value of always,never, ifRoom, and a few others to control whether the menu item is displayed. As the values suggest, an attribute of always indicates the menu item should always be displayed in the Action Bar, never means it is never promoted to the Action Bar, and lastly ifRoom indicates that you would like the menu item shown if there is room, and your application's functionality will not be compromised if the Android system decides there is no space to display it.

One stackable optional attribute you can include is the withText option, which instructs Android to include the menu text adjacent to the icon on the Action Bar. The withText option can be used with either always or ifRoom, but obviously increases your chances of not having room and therefore not being displayed with the ifRoom|showText combination.

Listing 9-2 shows our custom menu XML configuration to show variety of Action Bar behavior in action.

Listing 9-2. Manifest with target SDK set correctly for Action Bar

```
<menu xmlns:android="http://schemas.android.com/apk/res/android"
    xmlns:app="http://schemas.android.com/apk/res-auto"
    xmlns:tools="http://schemas.android.com/tools"
    tools:context="com.artifexdigital.android.actionbarexample.ActionBarExampleActivity" >
    <item android:id="@+id/newcolor"
        android:title="Set Color Red"
        android:icon="@drawable/ic_red"
        android:actionLayout="@layout/red"
        android:showAsAction="always|withText"/>
    <item android:id="@+id/reset"
        android:title="Set Color Blue"
        android:icon="@drawable/ic_blue"
        android:showAsAction="ifRoom"/>
    <item android:id="@+id/about"
        android:title="About"
        android:icon="@drawable/ic_menu_about_colors" />
    <item
        android:id="@+id/action_settings"
        android:orderInCategory="100"
        android:title="@string/action_settings"
        app:showAsAction="never"/>
</menu>
```

From here, there are no Java code changes necessary (assuming you are not also looking to alter your menu item functionality). Action Bar use and preferences are expressed entirely in the XML layout for your menu, which makes adoption even easier. You can see the new-look Action Bar for our ActionBarExample application in Figure 9-3.

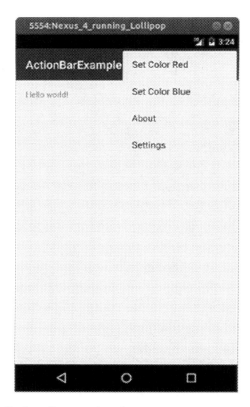

Figure 9-3. A customized Action Bar from the example code

Using Java to Manage Action Bars

As with almost all aspects of Android, programmatic creation and control of the Action Bar is provided in situations where you want to go beyond the augmented menu XML definition, or you want to allow for some kind of run-time dynamic changes to your Action Bar and its menus.

Android provides the ActionBar object to easily define and manipulate your activity's Action Bar at run-time. There is even a subclassed version of Activity, known as ActionBarActivity, for those circumstances where your activity is solely focused on the Action Bar and you are not interested in other widgets.

Working with a Standard Action Bar in Java

While you can manipulate Action Bar state anywhere in your code, you most often will want to do this as part of activity creation in onCreate() or shortly thereafter. Listing 9-3 introduces a little manipulation of the stock Action Bar through use of several of the methods for ActionBar objects. The code for this can be found in the ch09/ActionBarExample2 folder.

Listing 9-3. Manipulating behavior of an Action Bar in Java

```
package com.artifexdigital.android.actionbarexample;

import android.app.Activity;
import android.os.Bundle;
import android.view.Menu;
import android.view.MenuItem;

public class ActionBarExampleActivity extends Activity {

    @Override
    protected void onCreate(Bundle savedInstanceState) {
        super.onCreate(savedInstanceState);
        ActionBar bar = this.getActionBar();
        bar.setTitle("The Colorful ActionBar Title");
        bar.setNavigationMode(ActionBar.NAVIGATION_MODE_STANDARD);
        setContentView(R.layout.activity_action_bar_example);
    }

    @Override
    public boolean onCreateOptionsMenu(Menu menu) {
        // Inflate the menu as usual if Action Bar present
        getMenuInflater().inflate(R.menu.action_bar_example, menu);
        return true;
    }
}
```

Let's examine how each piece of the Java code affects the Action Bar for our example activity. First, after normal activity setup in onCreate(), we instantiate and ActionBar object named bar using the getActionBar() method to ask the activity to hand us the reference for its Action Bar. Thankfully, there are no tricky ID numbers or similar abstractions to track; an activity has only one Action Bar.

With our ActionBar object in place, we use several of its methods to set our preferences. The setTitle() method is quite self-explanatory, changing the ActionBar's title to the phrase we have chosen. Be careful how wordy you are when you do this, because you can run into problems due to screen width, especially on narrow devices.

Lastly, we use the setNavigationMode() method to set our prefered behavior for the Action Bar. In this instance we have chosen NAVIGATION_MENU_STANDARD, which is the vanilla version of an Action Bar that attempts nothing more than to elevate your otherwise-normal menus to be placed within the rendered Action Bar. We'll explore some other options shortly.

As already mentioned, Android provides a variety of child classes of `Activity` tailored to specific views. When it comes to the Action Bar, there is an `ActionBarActivity` child class that can be used in much the same way, and is useful if that's where most of you logic for your activity will reside. Listing 9-4 shows a reworked version of Listing 9-3 changed to use `ActionBarActivity`.

Listing 9-4. Adopting the ActionBarActivity for action bars

```
package com.artifexdigital.android.actionbarexample;

import android.support.v7.app.ActionBarActivity;
import android.os.Bundle;
import android.view.Menu;
import android.view.MenuItem;

public class ActionBarExampleActivity extends ActionBarActivity {

    @Override
    protected void onCreate(Bundle savedInstanceState) {
        super.onCreate(savedInstanceState);
        ActionBar bar = this.getActionBar();
        bar.setTitle("The Colorful ActionBar Title");
        bar.setNavigationMode(ActionBar.NAVIGATION_MODE_STANDARD);
        setContentView(R.layout.activity_action_bar_example);
    }

    @Override
    public boolean onCreateOptionsMenu(Menu menu) {
        // Inflate the menu; this adds items to the Action Bar if it is present.
        getMenuInflater().inflate(R.menu.action_bar_example, menu);
        return true;
    }
}
```

When we run the `ActionBarExample2` to generate menus programmatically, we see the results depicted in Figure 9-4.

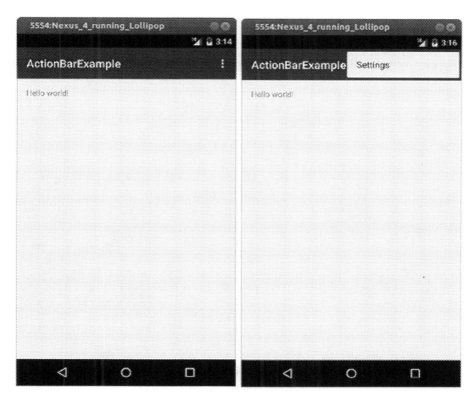

Figure 9-4. *The Action Bar controlled from Java code*

Choosing a Tab Layout for the Action Bar

If you have used any of the contemporary stock applications that come with an Android phone, you might have encountered a different layout for Action Bars that includes multiple tabs of menus or other custom views. For example, Figure 9-5 displays an application showing a tabbed Action Bar.

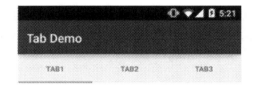

Figure 9-5. An example application with tabbed Action Bar

Using a tabbed Action Bar allows you to offer many more UI options in a small space, by allowing the tabs to house a subset of views and widgets, and display them only when that particular tab of the Action Bar is selected.

We can flag our desire to have a tabbed Action Bar by altering the parameter to the setNavigationMode() method to NAVIGATION_MODE_TABS. This forewarns Android that we'll be constructing tabs and adding the necessary logic to make them work.

To implement a tabbed Action Bar, we need three things:

■ First, the layouts you want each tab to inflate, such as menus, images, etc.

■ Then the code that defines each Tab object, and its key parameters.

■ Lastly, a custom listener that implements the TabListener interface, and provides our logic for what to do when one of our tabs is selected.

You already know how to define a menu layout or other set of Views, so we're left with the Tab definition logic and behavior logic as new things to learn about.

Defining Action Bar Tab Objects

In order to define the tabs that will consitute a tabbed Action Bar, we need to obtain the activity's Action Bar object, and then use the newTab() method to instantiate the Tab object which represents a tab. You will need to issue newTab() calls for as many tabs as you wish to have in your Action Bar. Listing 9-5 shows the changes to a regular activity's onCreate() method that enable such tab creation.

Listing 9-5. Configuring an Action Bar to use tabs

```
@Override
protected void onCreate(Bundle savedInstanceState) {
  super.onCreate(savedInstanceState);
  setContentView(R.layout.activity_tabbed_action_bar);

  ActionBar tabbed = getActionBar();
  tabbed.setTitle("Tabbed ActionBar");
  tabbed.setNavigationMode(ActionBar.NAVIGATION_MODE_TABS);

  CustomTabListener tabl = new CustomTabListener();
  // We can define as many tabs as we think necessary
  Tab tab1 = tabbed.newTab();
  tab1.setText("Tab One");
  tab1.setTabListener(tabl);
  tabbed.addTab(tab1);

  Tab tab2 = tabbed.newTab();
  tab2.setText("Tab Two");
  tab2.setTabListener(tabl);
  tabbed.addTab(tab2);

  Tab tab3 = tabbed.newTab();
  tab3.setText("Tab Three");
  tab3.setTabListener(tabl);
  tabbed.addTab(tab3);
}
```

We've created three tabs: tab1, tab2, and tab3. These will be added to our Action Bar when each Tab object is passed to an addTab() method call on the Action Bar's object, which we've called tabbed. You will note I also perform two other set up steps for the tabs. The setText() call provides a caption for each tab when presented on the Action Bar, and is fairly self-explanatory. The other method invoked is the setTabListener() method, which refers to the mysterious CustomTabListener object.

Coding the TabListener Behavior

When we configure the Action Bar to function in tabbed mode by using the setNavigationMode() method option NAVIGATION_MODE_TABS, we also implicitly flag that we'll implement the necessary listener to detect and respond to user interaction with the tabs and their content. The listener we need to implement is the ActionBar.TabListener interface. For those of you using Android Studio or Eclipse with ADT, you will get a useful code-time warning that you need to implement this interface. Text editor die-hards can refer to developer.android.com for the details, but the essentials are as shown in Listing 9-6.

Listing 9-6. Implementing the ActionBar.TabListener interface

```
package com.artifexdigital.android.tabbedactionbarexample;

import android.app.Activity;
import android.app.FragmentTransaction;
import android.app.ActionBar;
import android.app.ActionBar.Tab;

public class CustomTabListener implements ActionBar.TabListener{

  @Override
  public void onTabSelected(Tab tab, FragmentTransaction ft) {
    // implement your logic here to deal with tab selection
    // typically this will be a nested switch on which tab is passed
    // and then logic to display/respond to tab menu items
  }

  @Override
  public void onTabUnselected(Tab tab, FragmentTransaction ft) {
    // provide any cleanup logic needed when a tab is no longer selected
  }

  @Override
  public void onTabReselected(Tab tab, FragmentTransaction ft) {
    // provide logic to deal with state issues on tab reselection
  }

}
```

We can call our TabListener implementation anything we like. In my case, I've chosen the name CustomTabListener to make it obvious. We need to cover the implementation of the three methods defined in the interface, though for some of the methods you may not need specific logic. If you d o not need specific logic, then simply leave an empty method.

- onTabSelected() This method is the workhorse of the TabListener, typcially implementing the logic to determine which tab was selected. That's done via the Tab parameter. Then further code detects which menu item is selected and what subsequent action to take. The process is identical to normal menu management which I introduced in Chapter 8. In essence, onTabSelected follows a common coding pattern of a switch statement for Tab identification, and further switch logic for menu item detection and follow-up action

- onTabUnselected() There are times when you need to perform cleanup work or change UI behavior when a tab is no longer the focus. For example, one common design flourish is to bold the text caption of the Tab when it is selected, and unbold it when it is no longer selected (i.e. when another tab is selected and its caption is bolded).

※   onTabReselected() If you maintain any state for menu items, or even the Tab object itself, and you maintain that state through Java logic changes at run time that alter the initial menu layout for a given tab, then you might need to reinstate those changes when a tab is reselected. This callback is rarely used, but is presented here for completeness.

The FragmentTransaction parameter enables the use of fragments for the UI design and behavior for your tabs. The parameter is optional, and at this point in the book will make little sense. However, we will move on to cover fragments in-depth in Chapter11, at which point the capabilities will make perfect sense.

Future Changes For Action Bar Tabs

With the announcement of Android "M", the yet-to-be-released version 5.x of Android, Google has flagged that it will deprecate traditional tabbed Action Bar implementation in favour of a new set of APIs called TabLayout. You might think this deprecation makes all of the above discussion of tabbed Action Bars obsolete. Let me put your mind at ease. The traditional Action Bar and tab construction will still be present in future SDK levels (deprecated doesn't mean removed, after all), and the *vast* bulk of devices in circulation will be using pre-Android-M for *many* years. You can continue to build using the current approach to tabs for some time.

Using Other Layouts for the Action Bar

There are a range of other more advanced layout options available for Action Bars. Two that you will see from time are a list-based Action Bar, and an embedded custom view in the Action Bar.

Adopting a list-based Action Bar is done through setting the setNavigationMode() method option to NAVIGATION_MODE_LIST. With the Action Bar object configured to expect a list, the developer (that is, you) implement the ActionBar.OnNavigationListener interface and provide list adapter (such as those introduced in Chapter 7) to populate your Action Bar.

> **Note**   You are familiar now with lists, adapters, and the concept of a listener for an Action Bar. Rather than showing another example, I will point you to the excellent references online at developer.android.com/guide/topics/ui/actionbar.html for more details.

The Action Bar URL is also a good starting point for exploring adding custom views to your Action Bars (and tabs!)

Summary

With all of the options offered by the ActionBar now added to your Android know-how, you can start adding increasingly ambitious functionality to your application design and behavior. I incorporate the ActionBar in many more examples later in the book to show you some further possibilities.

The Life of an Activity

Up to this point in the book, I have a approached activities in a very practical and tactical way. The examples explored in the earlier chapters introduced activities as the basic UI building blocks, and you've seen how the Java code for an activity implements the Android framework and brings to life, through code, selected points in an activity's lifecycle and the logic to drive your application.

Now that you have a growing understanding of Android, activities, layout. and logic, let's delve in to the full background on activities, their lifecycle, and all of the common and not-so-common behaviors you should appreciate when building applications. This tour of the deeper fundamentals of activities will help expand your expertise. It also also lays the groundwork for later discussions on services, notifications, intents, and more.

Understanding the Activity Lifecycle

All of the example Android applications so far explored in the book have consisted of only one activity. But remember way back to the introductory chapter, where I stated that applications consist of one or more activities. So your application can have as many activities as you want, and each is governed by its own lifecycle. We'll cover an example later in this chapter where we have multiple activities in an application.

If all activities have lifecycle stages, what are these stages? I'm glad you asked. Figure 10-1 shows a graphic representation of the stages of an activity, and the callback methods related to the transitions between these stages, or states as they are sometimes called. Thinking of your activities in terms of both the stage they are in, as well as the callback methods called to get it there, is very common once you are familiar with Android.

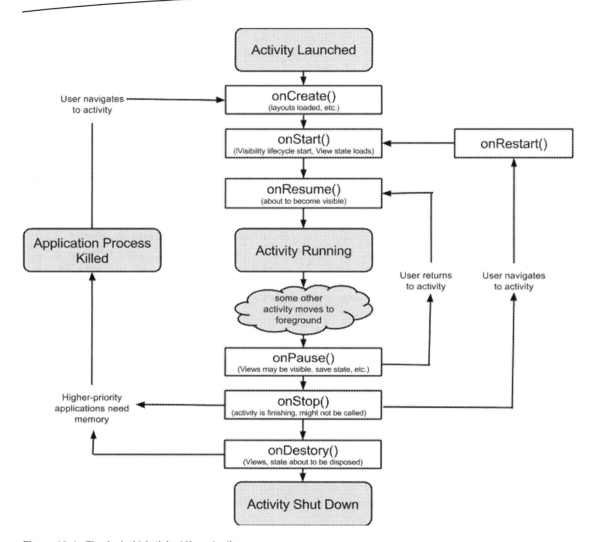

Figure 10-1. The Android Activity Lifecycle diagram

You can see that there are broadly four major states in which an activity can find itself:

- **Launched**: The point at which an activity comes in to existence, usually as the result of your user performing some action in your application (or starting your application)

- **Running**: The point at which your users actually sees your activity, after all of the various logistics and setup steps are performed (or re-performed)

- **Killed**: A state in which the Android OS has determined it needs to recoup the resources from your application, either from user-initiated load or some other trigger.

- **Shutdown**: The point at which all persistent state information, View hierarchy, etc. is gone.

The various activity stages are fairly simple to understand. The main complexity comes from the interplay of the various callback methods that govern transition between the stages and control intermediary points along the way.

Working with Activity Callback Methods

We will work through each of the callback methods from Figure 10-1, and explore their various behaviors and uses. There are some common characteristics of many of the callbacks that you should know. In almost all cases it is common practice to chain up to the parent class's equivalent method as the first action in implementing the callback. You have already sees examples of this in preceding chapters' examples that invoked `super.onCreate()` as the first action in the `onCreate()` implementation. I will call out those exceptions where that isn't done, but in general calling the super-method should be your first action within any callback.

onCreate()

This is where an activity's lifecycle starts. It may be that a user has invoked the activity for the very first time, or the activity may be restarting due to some environmental change such as a rotation event. The possibility of a restart is why the full method signature `void onCreate(Bundle savedInstanceState)` includes the Bundle object. There might be previous state information that you have saved in your code prior to a memory-related shutdown, for instance, that you need to recover for your activity. This Bundle object is typically known as the instance state for a given instance of an activity.

The key actions you should take within your method logic for `onCreate()` are:

- Load all of the layouts you plan to use in the activity into the content view so that the UI can be constructed in readiness for the `onStart()` call.

- Initialize any global activity-level variables listed in the activity's class definition

There are some other nuances to the use of `onCreate()` as part of recreating an activity. These have to do with managing existing global resources from the possible earlier incarnation of the activity, and dealing with remembering changes to views that happen in your logic *after* `onCreate()`. For instance, if you programmatically change your View layout dependent on user interaction, you might need to persist the user's choices so you can walk through such changes again in the case of an activity recreation scenario. We'll cover the global resource topic shortly under the `onRetainNonConfigurationInstance()`, and talk about the use of the instance state and preferences later in this chapter.

onStart()

Once onCreate() has built the necessary objects from your layout definitions, associated these with context views, and done other initialization work, it is then the job of onStart() to actually present the resulting UI to the user. I like to think of this method as the "OK, Show Me The UI" method, though that doesn't fit with the typical naming pattern for Android callback methods. If you examine Figure 10-1 closely, you'll see that onStart() can be called on the path from onRestart().

There is rarely a need to override this method and provide your own implementation. If you are tempted to fiddle with some of your logic and get things "done" before the UI shows up, be aware that if your activity is following the onRestart() path, then the instance state is still not fully restored and won't be until the subsequent call to onRestoreInstanceState() is made. If that leaves you struggling to think what you might actually add to an override at this point, good! Like I said, it is rare to need to override the onStart() method.

One of the few cases that does warrant implementing your own onStart() override is when you have some manner of custom resource that is long-lived, and that you have decided to pause or freeze when the activity is not in view so as to minimize memory or other resource consumption. If you decide to control such a resource through the onStop() or onPause() callbacks, then the onStart() method would be where you would wake or thaw such a custom resource. Be sure to call the super.onStart() method to invoke the parent's equivalent, even if you know there is no override code in the parent. Android itself still needs to do its own internal chores in this case.

onRestoreInstanceState()

When a user dismisses an activity, whether by hitting the back button or some other logic you have coded into your application, then they have indicated they are done with the activity itself, and any instance state associated with it. You as a developer have nothing to worry about, and certainly nothing to retain and restore. But when the Android system itself closes an activity, for instance because it is going to re-render it due to an orientation change, then the act of recreating that activity for the users needs to do just that! Re-create, including instance state.

It is important to note that the instance state is not long-term storage, nor is it designed to persist in any permanent fashion. Where you need to store user data or preferences, the Android Preference system is a perfect choice for small settings-like or option/choice values.

onResume()

Just as a magician has that moment of revealing the culmination of her or his trick, so too Android has onResume() as the magic-wand moment that occurs just before your UI becomes visible. Why have onResume() and onStart() both trigger in the lead up to UI visibility? Referring to Figure 10-1 again, you will notice onResume() in the boundary of the shaded region labeled Foreground. Along with onResume and onPause(), these transitions can be expected to happen many times in the life of your activity as others pre-empt it, are themselves pre-empted and dismissed, and so on.

The only actions typically coded into an override for onResume() are those that affect real-time visible activity, including:

- Animation
- Video
- Custom view transition effects

There is no state to manipulate or tinker with here, so resist the urge to meddle any further during onResume().

onPause()

A key building block of the multi-process architecture of Android is the ability to pause applications and their activities to help maintain responsiveness and preserve battery life. An activity's onPause() callback occurs just before it enters background state (see onStop() later in this chapter). There is also the possibility of immediately resuming through onResume(), which I have already covered.

Importantly, the onPause() call also marks the point beyond which Android can unilaterally terminate your activity and reclaim its resources. Key steps you should be taking during the onPause() call include saving state, deliberately deciding what to do with any running animation, video, audio, etc. Once the onPause() call exits, there is no guarantee your process and activity will ever receive an event again. So be prepared!

Careful observers will note that there is no parameter passed to onPause(). This is a deliberate attempt to guide you to be as light-weight as you can at the time the method is invoked.

onStop()

The onStop() method has the task of actually pushing your activity to the background. You can think of this method as the complement to the onStart() method introduced earlier. Once the onStop() call completes, your activity is no longer visible to the user, though its view hierarchy and properties still exist - and are fed in to onResume() and onStart() if called.

Remember that onStop() might never be called at all for your activity, for instance if the Android system is under severe memory pressure and Android decides to reclaim your paused activity for its memory resources. It is for this reason you should rarely attempt to override the onStop() method, and you should think carefully before relying on any custom logic in this method. One of the few types of logic added to onStop() includes service interaction with stock Android services or your own custom service, where lack of foreground activity is no impediment.

onSaveInstanceState()

From the picture painted in Figure 10-1, and the "paired" nature of many of the callback methods discussed so far, it should come as no surprise that onSaveInstanceState() exists. It is also reasonably self-explanatory as methods go. The primary purpose of of onSaveInstanceState() is to preserve state information when an activity is about to be destroyed through onDestroy() without the user realizing state information might be about to be lost.

You might think that would be a rare situation. However, there's a common behavior that users perform that unknowingly (to most) induces activity destruction and recreation. That behavior is an orientation change, most typically through the user rotating the device while your activity is running.

The good news is that the default implementation of onSaveInstanceState() already deals with handling view preservation. Any other custom state data you would want to save should be handled explicitly. Because of the potential I/O involved in saving state, be warned that calls to onSaveInstanceState() can take a variable, and sometimes long, duration.

onRestart()

The onRestart() callback method is triggered in the transition from stopped to started states. This gives you some options to deal with how you choose to start your activity. For instance, you can split your logic between a fresh start and a restart from stopped state. In the latter case, you will have access to preserved view and other state data, giving you some options to speed up or make things more efficient.

onRetainNonConfigurationInstance()

Not only does this method have a ridiculously long name, but if you refer to the state information in Figure 10-1, you'll see that onRetainNonConfigurationInstance() isn't mentioned. That is not an accident, as it falls somewhat outside the normal flow of activity state changes.

To understand why this method exists, you need to know a little more about what happens when an activity undergoes a configuration change. The most obvious form of configuration change is when we need to "redraw" an activity due to a rotation of the interface. Other triggers for configuration change include docking the device in some form of cradle, or adding or removing an SD card from the device. The term *redraw* is a misnomer, because Android actually casts aside your existing activity, recreates it, and then expects you to pick up from there as if (almost) nothing had happened. It doesn't stretch or tweak your layouts; it expects you to re-inflate them if you want to make use of additional or changed UI space. The need to pick up and carry on doesn't stop there.

There are potentially a range of resources you might have acquired for your activity that you still want to use should a configuration change occur. Think things like open files, database connections, objects supporting service interactions, and so forth. The onRetainNonConfigurationInstance() method is the traditional way to retain those types of resources. The method returns an object that includes references to all of the old activity's various resources, so you can carry them forward to use when the activity is recreated. If you look at many of the examples already introduced in the book, you'll see the onCreate() method almost always calls getLastNonConfiguationInstance(), which is the step required to gain access to the old activity's reference object, and all the resources it contains.

> **Note** The approach described with onRetainNonConfigurationInstance() is slowly being replaced by the use of headless fragments. However, the traditional approach will be supported for some time to come.

onDestroy()

Whether through an explicit user action, like clicking a "close" button you might have provided, or unexpectedly due to low resources or similar circumstances, there comes a time when your activity will be destroyed. Destruction is not a catastrophic as you might think. Remember, activities are cheap and easy to create, so just because your user is destroying the activity doesn't mean your whole application is being shut down. Your user could just as easily interact with and invoke this activity again in short order, and your application's resources will still persist.

The main logic you can consider adding to your override of onDestory() is any activity-centric cleanup. Don't try to interact with outside services or other resources that don't belong to your activity. Remember, there's no guarantee that onDestroy() will be called, so you should not rely on it.

Understanding the Goals of Android Activity Behavior

From a development perspective, having a grasp of the callback methods that control and guide state is useful. But if you only think in terms of which call takes you between various states, you might miss the bigger picture.

The number one goal of the activity state callback methods is to help you create and maintain the impression of one seamless application when a user is working with your code. It is great to have the power and flexibility to create and discard activities left, right, and center for your app. But remember your is almost certainly thinking in terms of an application and its "screens", rather than in terms of a loosely coupled group of activities that live and die multiple times.

Keep these guiding principles in mind as you create applications from more and more activities:

- Keep activities focused. That doesn't necessarily mean simple, but rather ensure an activity doesn't become the application version of the kitchen sink. This will help you manage other facets like resource use, state, and performance.

- Save state often. You will be surprised how often users do things like switch apps, jump back to the launcher, or take some other step outside your activity. Don't think of saving state as something onerous, nor like saving a long document that's being written. Save early; save often.

- Ensure all UI Views have android:id attributes. This helps Android automatically save instance state, including for mutable objects like an EditText field into which a user might already have entered some text.

- Remember paused activities can vanish! Even your best-designed application can run on a device in which the user has dozens of other poorly designed applications running. And the moment your application is paused, Android could decide it needs your application's memory to use somewhere else.

Working with Activity Configuration Changes

In the descriptions of activity lifecycle callback methods earlier in this chapter, I mentioned several times that one change that happens outside the normal activity lifecycle is activity configuration change. In a nutshell, a configuration change is something that affects the fundamental baseline of your application and the Android device itself. The most obvious example is a user rotating the device to give it a different orientation such as landscape instead of portrait.

But orientation is not the limit of possible configuration change. The Android developer documentation includes exhaustive notes on what constitutes a configuration change. Other key changes include the user changing the language setting, plugging in a power source such as a USB cable, docking the device, and more.

Understanding the Default Configuration Change Approach

One of the many things that Android does for your application is to track any configuration changes that happen to the device on which your code is running. Rotation, device pairing, charging, and more are all monitored. Should a configuration change occur, all running applications are notified by callback that a change is in progress.

Ordinarily, you might think that notification then forces you to do a great deal of work to deal with a configuration change. Nothing could be further from the truth. Along with monitoring and managing configuration changes, Android provides other useful default and/or automatic capabilities that make life easier for you, the developer.

Remember back to our discussion of the various resource folders within your project, including those that cover layouts. Android does all of the work required to get you the layout for a given configuration. You get portrait-orientated layouts when the device is rotated to a portrait orientation, and landscape-orientated layouts for landscape. You don't need to personally do the coding to detect the orientation and change the UI to cope. You simply ask for your resource by name, and Android sorts things out.

The one thing you as a developer do need to concern yourself with is the question of which other resources you have acquired for your existing activity. This is because any configuration change triggers Android to destroy the current activity and recreate it. You are given the chance to gracefully save state and resources so they can be reloaded.

Following is the callback sequence for configuration change:

1. onSaveInstanceState() This will be called when the configuration change is triggered, immediately before Android destroys the current activity. This is the appropriate time to save any resources or other transient user input or data you wish to keep. Use a Bundle object to collect all of the various items you wish to preserve. You have seen examples in this book where the Bundle is used, and older Android examples you might find on line often refer to this Bundle by the name icicle, which is meant to evoke the idea that you are

"freezing" state before thawing it again when the activity is recreated. The superclass ancestor for onSaveInstanceState() does many convenient things for you automatically, including saving View state for any object with an ID (as mentioned previously), so it can be recreated intact.

2. onCreate() This method invocation is passed the Bundle object created in onSaveInstanceState(). As you've seen in each example in the book so far, you needn't do any more with this call other than ensure it calls up to the parent class via super.oncreate(). If you have any custom state saved, you can elect to implement your restore logic here, or you can wait for the onRestoreInstanceState() callback which occurs immediately following the onCreate() call.

3. onRestoreInstanceState() This method is also passed the Bundle object created by onSaveInstanceState(), and you are free to retrieve your various resources in this call if you prefer. One advantage to waiting for the onRestoreInstanceState() call is that you can be sure the content view has been set, and any layout inflation has occurred prior to this call.

Saving Custom State

What data or objects can be saved as part of your instance state Bundle object? A quick inspection of the Bundle class shows a plethora of put- and get-style methods for storing integers, strings, complex objects and more. The pattern used is traditional key-value storage, where each resource you wish to place is the Bundle is keyed by a String name you provide. Example methods (not exhaustive) include:

* putInt() Store an integer value in the Bundle

* putFloat() Store a float value in the Bundle

* putString() Store a string value in the Bundle (beware a common pitfall here, of accidentally confusing which string is you value, and which is your key).

* putParcelable() Store a complex or custom object as a Parcelable in the Bundle.

There are many more options for putting values into your Bundle object, and the complementary get methods are self-explanatory.

Listing 10-1 shows a simple override of onSaveInstanceState() implementing the preservation of some custom data during configuration change (e.g. inserting an SD card).

Listing 10-1. Saving activity state during configuration change

```
@Override
    public void onSaveInstanceState(Bundle myBundle) {
    super.onSaveInstanceState(myBundle);
    myBundle.putInt("presses", 3);
}
```

Here we have simply saved an integer for later restoration once the configuration change has completed. Think back to the very first example you explored in Chapter 2, tracking button presses. We could use this approach to keep track of button presses in horizontal and vertical orientation, for instance by keeping the two integer values and passing them through successive configuration changes (though naturally we could use application-level variables to do the same job). Listing 10-2 shows a simple override for onRestoreInstanceState() that does the logic for this sort of button press tracking.

Listing 10-2. Restoring activity state during configuration change

```
@Override
    public void onRestoreInstanceState(Bundle myBundle) {
    super.onRestoreInstanceState(myBundle);
    int buttonPresses = myBundle.getInt("presses");
    // do some other logic here to display or use the retrieved value
}
```

This is a deliberately simple example. Remember to keep your custom logic to a minimum when handling configuration changes for your application's activities.

A World of Wonderful Devices and Screens

Android Fragments

Your journey through Android fundamentals so far has explored all of the main aspects of an Android application's user interface, from layout to choice of widgets, and including the creation and flow of activities through sample applications and your own testing. For quite a few of the early years of Android the UI development only became complex when more advanced widgets and screen elements were added to the tiny phone screens we were all using.

Then along came tablets. Big tablets, medium-sized tablets, things that would one day be called "phablets" and "jumbophones". 2011 saw the introduction of devices with screens up to – and in a few rare cases beyond – a foot in diagonal screen size. Google hurriedly pushed out a major change to Android that would solve some of the issues being seen. This was the dawn of the Fragments system.

The problems with tablets and large devices are easily visualized. Activities designed to show header information like a person's photo and name in a contacts activity, and then more detailed address information in another activity, looked like a huge waste of space on these giant screens. Even worse, initial adaptations to "fill" the big screens were done through scaling layouts, which meant poor image fidelity with lots of janky edges and pixelation, and users were left wondering why Android was making such poor use of all that space.

Why wasn't all that contact information on one well-designed screen? Fragments answers that question by helping Android make smart choices about how to render groups of objects on screen depending on the screen size, and whether to do that all in one activity, or through many. Read on to learn how.

Introducing the Fragment Class

A little more background is in order to help you appreciate how Fragments not only helps with the endless array of screen sizes Android now supports, but also how Fragments promotes tremendous reuse of existing layouts and designs to save you hour upon hour of additional design effort.

Up to this point in the book, if I asked you to deal with a new, much larger screen size, you might think that one way of tackling this would be to define another layout dimension, such as xxhdpi, and choose a layout container like RelativeLayout, meticulously laying out your widgets on this larger canvas for users of larger tablets of an appropriate size. Of course, tablets come in 7-inch, 10-inch, 13-inch and other sizes, so maybe you'd need a few of these extra layouts. Next you'll suddenly realise tablets can be rotated just like phones, and big-and-tall layouts should really have a short-and-wide equivalent. All of sudden, you are managing a dozen or more layouts for every activity within your application. Our example applications have had just one or two activities up to this point. Imagine an application with a dozen, or twenty, or one hundred activities. Do you want to maintain a thousand different layouts just to deal with tablets? I didn't think so.

Fragments solve the runaway layout issue by introducing an intermediary layer between activities and the layout containers, and widgets that are rendered within those containers. Fragments go a long way to reducing the complexity of dealing with multiple screen sizes and the desire to compose layout differently for those different sizes.

Backwards Compatibility with Fragments

Fragments were introduced with Android v3.0 "Honeycomb" and have steadily been improved since that rather hurried release. If you do find yourself targeting very old versions of Android on devices with tablet-sized screens, Google makes available the Android Compatibility library with SDKs for supporting older devices with newer features. While these kinds of devices are rare in the tablet realm, they can be found in some strange embedded-device use cases that make any kind of Android upgrade impossible. Examples I have seen include a home telephone address book device, and very basic resistive-touch tablets from manufacturers such as ZTE.

Designing with Fragments in Mind

The first thing to note about designing with Fragments is that they are entirely optional. If you really love designing lots of layouts, you can stick with that approach. However, if you want to save your creative energy for other parts of you application, then adopt Fragments wherever you have identifiable chunks of your interface that you would like to appear in multiple screen-size-dependent activities. Those activities can work with Fragment objects to work out what fragments to show and not show.

An illustration will make much of the preceding discussion clearer, and let you grasp how designing with fragments might be done. Figure 11-1 shows multiple possible renderings of widgets, within fragments, attached to activities for devices in different sizes and orientation.

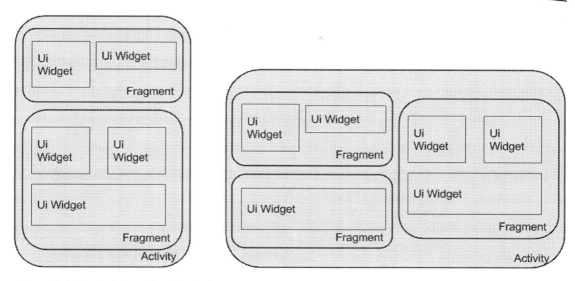

Figure 11-1. The logical nesting of Activities, Fragments, and UI Widgets

The larger displays capable of incorporating more on the screen can show fragments side-by-side, or one above the other, depending on the landscape or portrait orientation of the device. But only one of the fragments would be visible at a time on a traditional smaller phone screen, with the other triggered by some application logic. In the first instance, this is achieved by generating the XML for your layouts in <fragment> elements, as we will see in the examples later in the chapter, and then letting Android, in conjuction with your activity and its fragment manager, take on the work of what to show when. This means you still get to code your layouts much as before; they just sit in a different place. The views inside can have all the same simplicity or complexity, hierarchy, and so forth. The view hierarchy in the layout is still used to create the UI that the user sees.

Along with the layouts and view hierarchy, a Bundle object is used with a Fragment to provide initialization. This is in a very similar way to Activity in all of the examples we have seen so far. Fragments have a range of other qualities that will seem very similar to activities, with some subtle differences. For example:

- The need for a default constructor for any Fragment-derived class you choose to create

- The strong recommondation of an additional Bundle of arguments and properties that can be used to set up your Fragment, different to the Bundle that is used to recreate it successfully after events such as rotation

- Knowledge of the Fragment Manager that belongs to the Activity hosting the Fragment, enabling bidirectional interplay as required.

Now that we are talking about Fragment creation, instantiation and initialization, destruction and recreation, we should look at how Fragments have their own lifecycle and related callback methods. We'll also consider what to look out for in comparison to the Activity lifecycle discussed in Chapter 10.

Introducing the Fragment Lifecycle

There are areas of commonality between the Fragment lifecycle and that of an Activity, but it is useful to visualize where things are more complicated. This will help you appreciate the extra possibilities available when working with Fragments, and also the extra limitations you will run in to that dictate when and where you can do things you would assume are possible from your Activity experience. Figure 11-2 shows the full Fragment lifecycle.

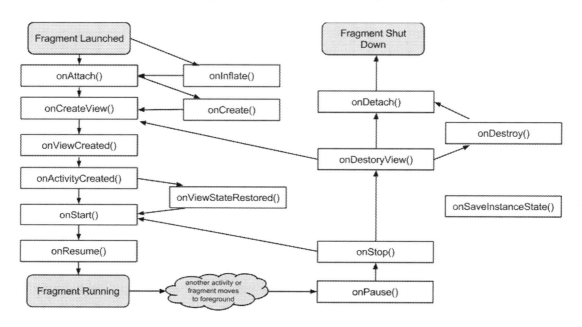

Figure 11-2. The Full Fragment Lifecycle

Most of the differences you see when compared to the Activity lifecycle in the previous chapter are to do with the interaction between a host Activity and its Fragments. There is not necessarily a 1-to-1 relationship between lifecycle events at both levels. An Activity experiencing one event might contain Fragments that have to transition multiple events and stages for the same trigger.

Understanding Fragment Lifecycle Callback Methods

Even though many of the lifecycle callbacks share identical names to the ones we saw for activities in Chapter 10, be careful not to be trapped into assuming those callbacks are exactly the same. The following subsections describe the key differences, as well as the Fragment-specific callbacks.

onInflate()

The onInflate() method is called in order to inflate the layout of fragments defined in your layout XML files using the <fragment> element. onInflate() is also called if you explicitly create new fragments programmatically in your code via the newInstance() call. Parameters passed include the reference activity in which the fragment will live, and an AttributeSet with any additional XML attributes from the <fragment> tag. You can think of onInflate()'s execution as a render-but-don't-display step in which Android works out what the fragment will look like, but actual UI creation and association with the activity does not happen until onAttach().

onCreate()

The fragment variant of onCreate() is similar to its activity cousin, but there are a few subtleties. The main difference is that you cannot rely on any activity view hierarchy being in place to reference in the onCreate() call. That's mostly because the activity with which the fragment is associated is transiting through its own lifecycle. And just when you think you can start relying on the activity, it may well cease to exist – or at least, it might transition or undergo configuration change, causing the activity view hierarchy to be destroyed or recreated.

onAttach()

The onAttach() callback happens immediately following Android's determination of which activity a fragment is attached to. At this point you can safely do things with the activity relationship, such as get and use context for other operations. Any fragment has an inherited method getActivity() that will return the activity to which it is attached. Your fragment can also use the getArguments() method to fetch and work with any initialization paramters.

onCreateView()

The onCreateView() callback allows you to return some sort of view hierarchy for your fragment. It takes a LayoutInfater object, and ViewGroup and the Bundle of instance state, and then relies on Android to choose a suitable layout based on all the usual screen size and density attributes. Android inflates that layout with the .inflate() method of the LayoutInflater, then modifies the layout in whatever way you think necessary, and then hands back the resultant View object for rendering.

onViewCreated()

Immediately after onCreateView() returns, onViewCreated() can perform further post-processing work before any saved state is used to modify the View.

onViewStateRestored()

This method is called in the cases when your fragment's view hierarchy has all of its state restored. This is handy for differentiating cases of new creation versus resumption, etc.

onStart()

The fragment's onStart() callback is linked to the activity's equivalent onStart(), and is called immediately after the fragment is displayed in the user's UI. Any logic you think of placing in an activity-level onStart() callback should in most cases be pushed down into the fragment onStart() methods.

onResume()

Another closely coupled callback between fragment and activity, onResume() is the last call made before the user takes full control of the activity and its fragments.

onPause()

The onPause() callback is also closely coupled with the overall Activity's equivalent. If you move logic to your fragments, then the rules from the Activity variant about pausing audio or video, halting or releasing other actions, and the like all apply here.

onSaveInstanceState()

Conceptually identical to the Activity equivalent, in the onSaveInstanceState() callback you should be persisting any resources or data you want to keep between Fragment incarnations to the Bundle object for the Fragment. Do not go crazy saving enormous amounts of information. Remember that you can use identifier references for long-lived objects outside the Fragment itself. You can just refer to, and save, those.

onStop()

Identical to the equivalent for an Activity.

onDestroyView()

This method is called in the pathway to end-of-life for the fragment. When Android has detached the view hierarchy associated with the fragment, onDestroyView() is then triggered.

onDestroy()

When a fragment is no longer being used, the onDestroy() method is called. Technically the fragment is still attached to and associated with its Activity at this point.

onDetach()

Breaking the bonds with the Activity is the last part of ending the life of a Fragment. This signals the point at which all other resources, references, and other lingering identifiers should be detroyed, removed, or released.

Keeping Sane with Fragment Lifecycles

While there are many more lifecycle stages to consider with fragments, you do not necessarily need to deal with every single state transition and lifecycle callback in your code. Just as with the Activity discussion in Chapter 10, you are free to override only the mandatory callbacks and select the others that you think are important to your application and its functionality. At a minimum, you can stick to just overriding onCreateView() and be done.

You can see for yourself with the FragmentsExample application that we can pare down the coding requirements to a much more manageable volume.

Implementing Your Own Fragment-Based Application

An example can help illustrate many of the concepts around fragments, and also give you a starting point from which to expand to explore the many options for working with fragments. I will use the simple set of colors from previous examples and rework their display into a familiar master-detail UI design pattern.

Creating Layouts for the Fragments Examples

Our example ColorFragmentExample application will aim to show a list of colors, and when clicked will present details on a given color. In order to make best use of screen space available, we will use fragments to do the "heavy lifting". This will ensure that users on smaller screens see the color list initially. Then when they select a color, another activity will host the fragment showing that color's detail. Tablet users will have one activity that hosts the fragment displaying the list of colors as well as the detail fragment, much like the depiction in Figure 11-1.

The Color List Layout

Listing 11-1 shows the fragment layout that will be used in different ways to show the list of colors.

Listing 11-1. The universal fragment for showing colors in a list

```
<fragment xmlns:android="http://schemas.android.com/apk/res/android"
    xmlns:tools="http://schemas.android.com/tools"
    android:id="@+id/color_list"
    android:name="com.artifexdigital.android.colorfragmentsexample.ColorListFragment"
    android:layout_width="match_parent"
    android:layout_height="match_parent"
    android:layout_marginLeft="16dp"
    android:layout_marginRight="16dp"
    tools:context=".ColorListActivity"
    tools:layout="@android:layout/list_content" />
```

This is a simple `<fragment>` definition that in turn calls on the stock Android layout `list_content`, which will show `TextView` entries in a list. This fragment layout will be used by both the "single-pane" view layout on small devices where an activity will have this fragment attached as the only UI, and by the "two-pane" view layout on large tablets for listing the colors side-by-side with details.

The Color Detail Layout

Showing details of a color will be handled by a `TextView`, wrapped in a fragment and placed in an Activity. The layout for the TextView is very straight-forward, and you can find this in the `fragment_color_detail.xml` file, the contents of which are shown in Listing 11-2.

Listing 11-2. The common TextView layout for color details

```
<TextView xmlns:android="http://schemas.android.com/apk/res/android"
    xmlns:tools="http://schemas.android.com/tools"
    android:id="@+id/color_detail"
    style="?android:attr/textAppearanceLarge"
    android:layout_width="match_parent"
    android:layout_height="match_parent"
    android:padding="16dp"
    android:textIsSelectable="true"
    tools:context=".ColorDetailFragment" />
```

A Host Activity For Color Details

In the circumstances where color details (laid out with the `TextView` from the previous section) need to be shown in an Activity in its own right on a small screen, we need to provide the layout for that Activity. The only job this Activity will have is to create the fragment that then displays the `TextView`. You can see the relevant code in `activity_color_detail.xml`, shown next in listing 11-3.

Listing 11-3. The activity_color_detail.xml layout

```
<FrameLayout xmlns:android="http://schemas.android.com/apk/res/android"
    xmlns:tools="http://schemas.android.com/tools"
    android:id="@+id/color_detail_container"
    android:layout_width="match_parent"
    android:layout_height="match_parent"
    tools:context=".ColorDetailActivity"
    tools:ignore="MergeRootFrame" />
```

As you can see, this is a simple `<FrameLayout>` with some simple styling. The `TextView` will be injected into this via a fragment.

The Large-screen Multi-fragment Layout

For those situations when our example application is running on a large screen, we need a layout capable of hosting all the fragments and UI widgets we want on one screen. The `activity_color_twopane.xml` layout file might look like yet another complication in the fragment story. But if you look closely at Listing 11-4, you will see that the layout file really is just a composition that includes the `<fragment>` and `<FrameLayout>` that we pulled into separate layouts for smaller screens.

Listing 11-4. The activity_color_twopane.xml layout

```
<LinearLayout xmlns:android="http://schemas.android.com/apk/res/android"
    xmlns:tools="http://schemas.android.com/tools"
    android:layout_width="match_parent"
    android:layout_height="match_parent"
    android:layout_marginLeft="16dp"
    android:layout_marginRight="16dp"
    android:baselineAligned="false"
    android:divider="?android:attr/dividerHorizontal"
    android:orientation="horizontal"
    android:showDividers="middle"
    tools:context=".ColorListActivity">

    <fragment android:id="@+id/color_list"
        android:name="com.artifexdigital.android.colorfragmentsexample.ColorListFragment"
        android:layout_width="0dp"
        android:layout_height="match_parent"
        android:layout_weight="1"
        tools:layout="@android:layout/list_content" />

    <FrameLayout android:id="@+id/color_detail_container"
        android:layout_width="0dp"
        android:layout_height="match_parent"
        android:layout_weight="3" />

</LinearLayout>
```

The only differences compared to the (combined) separate layouts from earlier in this chapter are the `android:layout_weight` values which will be used to control the comparative screen real estate used by the two fragments when presented together in a single Activity. A 1:3 ratio means the master list fragment will take a quarter of the space, and the detail fragment will take three-quarters (the remainder).

Controlling Which Layout Is Chosen

At this point you are probably wondering how our application will decide which layout to use, and therefore what arrangement of fragments, for different sized devices. The secret is in the `refs.xml` files (plural), under each of the `res/values-large` and `res/values-sw600dp` folders respectively. When our code runs on any device or emulator, Android will check at run-time for any size-specific XML resources across all of the different size-specific resource

directories, including all of those mentioned in Chapter 3. There is only one child element in
refs.xml for large and sw600dp sized-screens, and it reads:

```
<item type="layout" name="activity_color_list">@layout/activity_color_twopane</item>
```

Any screen that is categorized as large, or meeting sw600dp resolution standard, will implicitly
pick up the instruction in the attributes to use the activity_color_twopane layout from the
XML file of the same name.

Coding Differences for Fragments

The good news regarding the Java you write for a fragment-based design is that by and large
there are few differences compared to working with Activities alone. The main differences were
already discussed earlier: Any UI-centric logic, data manipulation, use of content providers,
services, and so forth, moves to the fragments in your application. The activities are then still
important for application lifecycle handling and functionality that spans fragments.

Regardless of whether our application ends up displaying one or two fragments
simultaneously, it will run the ColorListActivity shown in Listing 11-5.

Listing 11-5. The code for the ColorListActivity

```
package com.artifexdigital.android.colorfragmentsexample;

import android.content.Intent;
import android.os.Bundle;
import android.support.v4.app.FragmentActivity;

public class ColorListActivity extends FragmentActivity
        implements ColorListFragment.Callbacks {

    private boolean mTwoPane;

    @Override
    protected void onCreate(Bundle savedInstanceState) {
        super.onCreate(savedInstanceState);
        setContentView(R.layout.activity_color_list);

        if (findViewById(R.id.color_detail_container) != null) {
            mTwoPane = true;

            ((ColorListFragment) getSupportFragmentManager()
                    .findFragmentById(R.id.color_list))
                    .setActivateOnItemClick(true);
        }
    }
```

```
@Override
public void onItemSelected(String id) {
    if (mTwoPane) {
        Bundle arguments = new Bundle();
        arguments.putString(ColorDetailFragment.ARG_ITEM_ID, id);
        ColorDetailFragment fragment = new ColorDetailFragment();
        fragment.setArguments(arguments);
        getSupportFragmentManager().beginTransaction()
                .replace(R.id.color_detail_container, fragment)
                .commit();
    } else {
        Intent detailIntent = new Intent(this, ColorDetailActivity.class);
        detailIntent.putExtra(ColorDetailFragment.ARG_ITEM_ID, id);
        startActivity(detailIntent);
    }
}
}
```

Listing 11-5 is more straight-forward than it looks. Our onCreate() logic is very simple. First the activity_color_list layout is inflated into the UI. Then we run a quick test to see if the color_detail_container view object has been instantiated (even if it is not displayed), and use the result as a proxy to determine whether we are running within the activity_color_twopane layout triggered from our refs.xml rules. If we are, then we set the mTwoPane Boolean to true and the the getSupportFragmentManager() to set up click handling via the .setActivateOnItemClick() method.

The onItemSelected() override then does the subtle work of deciding what to do when a user clicks a color. Should we create an additional fragment using the color_detail_fragment layout and associated code in ColorDetailFragment.java, or should we fire off startActivity() with the intent explicitly calling for the color_detail_activity layout and associated ColorDetailActivity.java code?

You can look at those source files as well to see the basics for showing color details, and also of the supporting ColorContent class which is just a fancy packaging of an item set for colors and some management functions. I will spare you the endless pages of code for what is some fairly straight-forward Java. Take a look at the source files in ch11/ColorFragmentsExample, and do run them in different-sized emulators with some breakpoints set so you can see the size-determining logic and fragment creation steps being taken.

Seeing Differing Fragment Behavior in Action

There's nothing like seeing the results on different sized devices or emulators to get an appreciation of the fragment behavior in action. Figures 11-3 and 11-4 show the Color list and Color detail fragments within separate activities on a small device (in this case, a Nexus-5 AVD).

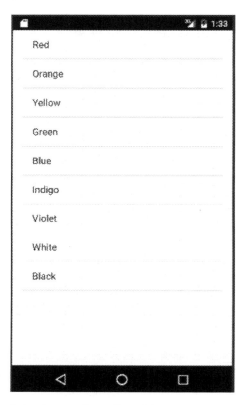

Figure 11-3. *The color list fragment showing on a Nexus 5 emulator*

Figure 11-4. *The new activity triggered to show the color detail fragment*

By comparison, when running the ColorFragmentsExample application on a large 10-inch screen emulator, we see the behavior in Figures 11-5 and 11-6, where the fragments are created and used within just the ColorListActivity activity.

Figure 11-5. The starting display for ColorListActivity with one fragment on a large screen

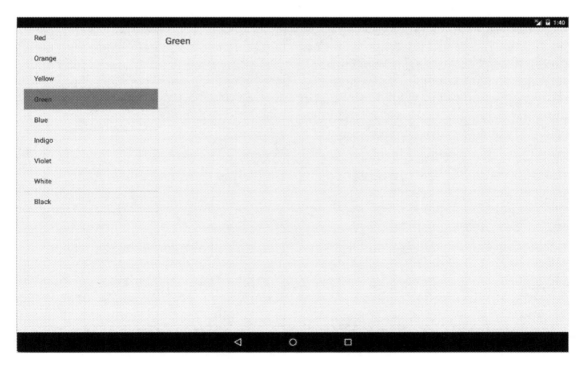

Figure 11-6. Having detected the large screen, the second fragment is added to the activity

Summary

Learning to use fragments is best done by working through more and more examples. You have the solid foundation of the fundamentals for fragments thanks to this chapter, as well as your first working example. Further examples throughout this book use Fragments in different ways, and I encourage you to explore those examples too to expand your Fragments skills. In particular, take a look at the maps example applications in Chapter 15, and the preferences example application in Chapter 19.

12

Intents and Receivers

You have learned many of the techniques for designing activities. Thanks to the preceding chapter, you now also know about the lifecycle of an activity: when and how it starts, pauses, and ends.

All of the examples presented so far have consisted of just one activity. But if you remember the early part of the book, you will recall that I said Android's architecture was built around the assumption that activities are cheap, easy to create and destroy, and should be plentiful to help build out the capabilities of any application you might wish to build. Activities, in the plural.

Each of our example applications, from button counters to phone dialers, has used a single activity to display its functionality (with the odd menu or action bar included). The single activity was displayed when you launched the application from the Android launcher. But if we create other activities for applications, how do we launch them? It is clearly too cumbersome to have dozens or hundreds of activities within an application each have their own launcher icon, so what's a mobile platform to do?

Introducing Intents

The answer is in Android's equivalent to a messaging and events system, known as *intents*. Android intents are built around concepts used in other event-based operating systems and environments such as Windows. Yet there are some key differences, which we will cover shortly.

At its heart, an intent is a message sent to the Android system indicating you want to do something. What the something is happens to be the first subtle difference between Android intents and other messaging and event systems. At times you might know exactly what action your application should take in response to a user request, and can pinpoint the precise activity to summon in response. But there are other times when your application won't have precise control over what a user might want, nor have all the necessary data to directly invoke another activity, but the user is expecting something. Android has both cases covered by using the complementary part of the messaging system, known as the receiver.

Receivers are coded into an application in order to listen for various intents and respond in various ways. Receivers will be covered later in this chapter once intents are fully introduced. Intents and receivers together form the core of how multiple activities are wired together to create seamless applications, and how activities from other applications can be harnessed within your application to do work on your user's behalf.

The Anatomy of an Intent

An Android intent is composed of two conceptual elements. First is the action desired, and second is the context associated with the desired action. There are a wide variety of actions, which we'll cover shortly, but they include such straight forward concepts as "view this thing", "make a new one of these", and so forth. Context is more variable, but can best be thought of as a range of data to help make sense of the intent, direct the intent, and fuel the resulting activity.

At its simplest, the data takes the form of a `Uri`, such as `content://contacts/people/1`, which is the Uri for the first person in Android's contact storage. If you bundle that `Uri` with an action like `ACTION_VIEW`, you have formed an intent. Android is able to interpret the intent, and will find an activity able to show the user a contact. Make the action something like `ACTION_PICK` on a `Uri` that points to a collection such as `content://contacts/people`, and Android looks for an activity that can present multiple contacts and provide the ability to pick from them.

A Uri with an action is not all that can be packaged in the context of an intent. There are four main additional elements you can include to expand the intent payload, and what Android and applications can do with it. These are part of an `Intent` object.

Specifying an Intent Category

Your intent's category helps govern what activity can satisfy it. For instance, the activity where you intend your users to begin interacting with your applications should be of category `LAUNCHER`. This category is what marks an activity as being suitable for placement on the Launcher menu (home screens) for Android. Other activity/intent categories include `DEFAULT` and `ALTERNATIVE`.

Specifying a MIME Type

There are times when you will not have, or will not know, a specific `Uri` for a collection of items such as contacts or wifi networks. To help Android find a suitable activity that can deal with sets of data in these situations, you can specify a MIME type. For instance, `image-jpeg` for an image file.

Nominating a Component

There are times when you know exactly which activity you want to invoke with your intent. One method is to specify the class of the activity in the component of the intent. Doing so makes life easier in that you no longer need to include other data elements in your intent. However, the approach is considered risky as it assumes knowledge about the implementation of the component class that violates the encapsulation programming principle.

Including Extras

Sometimes you have a mixed bag of additional data you wish to provide to the receiver for a variety of reasons. Where such data doesn't fit into a Uri scheme or other part of the Intent object, you can provide a Bundle object that includes arbitrary additional information. There is, however, no way to force your receiver to make use of such a Bundle. The receiver might or might not use the Bundle based on how the activity was written.

Intent Actions for all Kinds of Purposes

There is an exhaustive list of intent actions and categories provided with the Android documentation at developer.android.com. I do not propose to rewrite all of that material here, but I will highlight some notable and interesting actions so have more idea of what is possible as we continue with the rest of the book.

- ACTION_AIRPLANE_MODE_CHANGED: The user of the device has toggled the airplane mode setting from on to off, or vice versa.

- ACTION_CAMERA_BUTTON: The camera button (hard button or soft button) was pressed.

- ACTION_DATE_CHANGED: The date has changed, meaning any application logic you have written that users timers, elapsed time, and so forth might be affected.

- ACTION_HEADSET_PLUG: The user of the device has attached or removed headphones from the headphone socket.

As you can see, intent actions cover not just what happens in your application, but also its environment on the device and even further.

> **Caution** Google adds new actions to the set available for intents with each new release of Android. It also deprecates some older actions it deems no longer useful. As you maintain your application over time, it is prudent to check if any actions on which your application depends have been deprecated.

Understanding Intent Routing

The component approach is not a reliable nor safe approach with activities from other applications. My point about the encapsulation principle is at the heart of this advice. Just as you wouldn't want other people relying on your internal class names within your application, you shouldn't rely on them in others' applications. They can change in both signature and behavior, and indeed be removed entirely in subsequent versions.

The recommended pattern for targetting the application or service of your choice is to use Uris and MIME types appropriately. How then does one help Android determine which activites or receivers (such as a service) should receive a given intent? Android uses a scheme known as implicit routing to pass an intent on to all of the activities and so forth that should receive it. Implicit routing is based on a set of eligibility rules that must all be met. These rules are:

1. The activity must signal its ability to handle the intent through the appropriate manifest entry (which we will discuss shortly)

2. If a MIME type is part of the intent context, the activity must support the MIME type

3. Every category in the event context must also be supported by the activity.

You can see how these rules helps narrow down the possible set of matching activities that can receive your intent.

Adding Intents to Your Manifest

Android uses a specification of intent filters placed in your AndroidManifest.xml file to indicate which components in a given application are able to be notified and respond appropriately to which intents. If your component's manifest entry doesn't list the intent action, it won't be picked to receive such an intent. Think of it this way: the easiest way to filter-out all of the many intents that you don't wish to handle is to use a "filter-in" approach to list the intents you do wish to consume.

When you create a new Android project, you actually create (or your IDE creates for you) your first intent filter as part of the base manifest file. For instance, Listing 12-1 is the manifest from your very first application, BeginningAndroid, in chapter 2. In bold you can see the activity MainActivity and its specified intent file.

Listing 12-1. Example intent filters from an AndroidManifest.xml file

```
<?xml version="1.0" encoding="utf-8"?>
<manifest xmlns:android="http://schemas.android.com/apk/res/android"
    package="com.artifexdigital.android.beginningandroid"
    android:versionCode="1"
    android:versionName="1.0" >
```

```
<uses-sdk
    android:minSdkVersion="9"
    android:targetSdkVersion="21" />

<supports-screens android:smallScreens="true" android:normalScreens="true"
    android:largeScreens="true" android:xlargeScreens="true" />

<application
    android:allowBackup="true"
    android:icon="@drawable/ic_launcher"
    android:label="@string/app_name"
    android:theme="@style/AppTheme" >
    <activity
        android:name=".MainActivity"
        android:label="@string/app_name" >
        <intent-filter>
            <action android:name="android.intent.action.MAIN" />
            <category android:name="android.intent.category.LAUNCHER" />
        </intent-filter>
    </activity>
</application>

</manifest>
```

There are two key things to note here in the intent filter. We specify the `MainActivity` activity is of the LAUNCHER category, meaning any intent must also be of that category. We also specify the action `android.intent.action.MAIN`, which is used to signify that any intent looking for a MAIN-capable activity may be accepted. Your `MainActivity` could have more possible actions, and more categories, signifying it has more capabilities (assuming you've coded for them in the component class logic).

Your other activities for your application would not use the MAIN/LAUNCHER combination for action and category. While there are many actions and categories from which to chose, as mentioned earlier, a very common category is the DEFAULT category. The DEFAULT category is often used with view- and edit-style actions in combination with a `<data>` element describing the `mimeType` that an activity can deal with for viewing or editing. For example, Listing 12-2 shows an intent filter for a Notepad-like application.

Listing 12-2. An intent filter for an example secondary activity in your application

```
<activity
    android:name=".NotesViewActivity"
    <intent-filter>
        <action android:name="android.intent.action.VIEW" />
        <category android:name="android.intent.category.DEFAULT" />
        <data android:mimeType="vnd.android.cursor.dir/vnd.google.note" />
    </intent-filter>
</activity>
```

Here in Listing 12-2 we have defined an activity, and through its intent filter nominated that the activity can be launched to deal with an intent asking to view content using the Uri for content with a vnd.android.cursor.dir/vnd.google.note mimeType. This intent could obviously come from your own application, such as following a user action from your launcher activity. Other applications that can create a well-formed Uri for this activity can also trigger it through an intent using that Uri.

ANDROID VERSION 6.0 MARSHMALLOW AND VERIFIED LINKS

With the launch of Android 6.0, known as Marshmallow, Google have enhanced some of the behavior regarding intents triggered from URLs. Historically, if you included a URL in your application as a link that your user could click, and they had an application installed that identified itself as synonymous with the URL's website, then they would then see a system dialog asking if they wanted to complete the action with the application or the website. They would also be asked if they wanted this to happen just once, or always for the give application and website. Users became very frustrated at the unpredictable nature of whether they would see this dialog or not, and whether their preference would "stick".

With Android 6.0, Google has introduced auto-verified links, which is a feature you can add to your code explicitly to make the link between URLs from a specific website and the companion application. This feature includes "smarts" to enable seamless authentication and save the user any extraneous dialogs when Android, the application, and the website team up to deal with the intent. The Android developer documentation is still being updated to cover this feature of auto-verified links.

Seeing Intent-launched Activities in Action

You have now seen enough of the theory and structure of intents to work on an example that should illustrate their power and convenience to you. You know that Android's design philosophy is to have many activities to support the varied functionality of your application, such as a photo album application having one activity to view a single picture, another activity to view groups or albums (perhaps using the GridView), and maybe more activities for tagging, sharing with friends, and so on.

Before we get to implementation, there's one last design choice to consider. If you launch an activity via an intent from another activity, how much knowledge about the state of the launched activity should the invoking activity be concerned with? Does your launching activity need to know when the second (or subsequent) activities are completed, and be passed some result?

Deciding on Activity Dependency.

Android answers the dependency-vs-no-dependency issue by providing two main ways to invoke an activity with an intent. The StartActivity() method is used to trigger Android to find the activity that best meets the criteria of the intent (remember the discussion earlier in the chapter, on action, category and mime types). That activity will be started, the intent will be passed to it for possible data processing, and the new and old activity will then continue on their separate lives. The activity from which you call StartActivity() will not be notified about the called activity's eventual end. No data will be available to inspect, and so forth.

If that just-described approach sounds unappealing, perhaps because you want to mimic a parent-and-child relationship between your activities, there is an alternative. Let's assume you decide to include a social media sharing option in your photo album application. To achieve this, you might need the user to complete a login process, and then return them to the sharing activity and provide it the details of the successful login (such as a login cookie, token, etc.). To support this closer dependency, Android provides the startActivityForResult() method.

The startActivityForResult() method passes not only the intent to the activity selected as the most appropriate, but also a calling number unique to the activity invocation. Your parent activity is then notified when the called activity ends through the onActivityResult() callback. The callback includes:

- The unique calling number associated with the specific child activity and the original startActivityForResult() method. You would typically use a switch pattern to determine which of your child activities had completed, and continue with your application logic appropriately

- A numeric result code from the stock Android-provide results of RESULT_ OK and RESULT_CANCELED, plus any custom results you care to nominate of the form RESULT_FIRST_USER, RESULT_FIRST_USER + 1, etc.

- An optional String object with any data your called activity should return, such as the item chosen from a ListAdapter.

- An optional Bundle containing any additional information not found in the above options.

You should decide at design/coding time when to use either startActivity() or startActivityForResult(). While you can code to dynamically choose either at runtime, it can become quite elaborate to handle all the possible outcomes.

Creating an Intent

Now that you know how to choose the appropriate activity invocation method, you must first create the Intent object to use as the vessel from which to trigger the launch. If your aim is to launch another activity from within your own application, the most straight-forward technique is to create your intent directly and explicitly state the component you wish to reach. You would create a new Intent object as follows:

```
new Intent(this, myOtherActivity.class);
```

Here, you are explicitly referencing that you want to invoke your myOtherActivity activity. You do not need an intent filter in your manifest for this explicit invocation to work. Your myOtherActivity will be started whether it likes it or not! Obviously the onus is on you as the developer to ensure your myOtherActivity can respond accordingly.

Earlier in the chapter I explained how it was far more elegant to use a Uri and criteria-matching approach to have Android find an appropriate activity. You can create a Uri for any of the support schemes in Android. For example, here is a snippet creating a Uri for a contact in the contacts system:

```
Int myContactNumber = 1;
Uri myUri = Uri.parse("content://contacts/people/"+myContactNumber.toString());
Intent myIntent = new Intent(Intent.ACTION_VIEW, myUri);
```

We are using the number for the first contact, and then constructing the Uri string for referencing a contact. Finally, we pass the string to the new Intent object.

Starting the Intent-Invoked Activity

With the Intent created, you decide which of startActivity() or startActivityForResult() to call. There are additional, more advanced options here Listing 12-3 shows the example layout from the ch11/IntentExample project. It is a very simple layout with one label, one field, and one button.

Listing 12-3. An example layout involving intents

```
<RelativeLayout xmlns:android="http://schemas.android.com/apk/res/android"
    xmlns:tools="http://schemas.android.com/tools"
    android:layout_width="match_parent"
    android:layout_height="match_parent"
    android:paddingBottom="@dimen/activity_vertical_margin"
    android:paddingLeft="@dimen/activity_horizontal_margin"
    android:paddingRight="@dimen/activity_horizontal_margin"
    android:paddingTop="@dimen/activity_vertical_margin"
    tools:context="com.artifexdigital.android.intentexample.IntentExampleActivity" >

    <TextView
        android:id="@+id/textView1"
        android:layout_width="wrap_content"
        android:layout_height="wrap_content"
        android:layout_alignBaseline="@+id/myContact"
        android:layout_alignBottom="@+id/myContact"
        android:layout_alignLeft="@+id/button1"
        android:text="Contact Number:" />

    <EditText
        android:id="@+id/myContact"
        android:layout_width="wrap_content"
        android:layout_height="wrap_content"
        android:layout_alignParentTop="true"
        android:layout_marginLeft="28dp"
        android:layout_toRightOf="@+id/textView1"
        android:ems="10"
        android:inputType="number" >
```

```
        <requestFocus />
    </EditText>

    <Button
        android:id="@+id/button1"
        android:layout_width="match_parent"
        android:layout_height="wrap_content"
        android:layout_below="@+id/myContact"
        android:layout_marginTop="30dp"
        android:text="View Contact"
        android:onClick="viewContact" />

</RelativeLayout>
```

The viewContact() method for the button creates a contact Uri as explained above, then creates the Intent object that will use the Uri, and finally starts an activity expecting no follow-up results. You can see the code in listing 12-4.

Listing 12-4. An activity expecting no follow-up results

```
package com.artifexdigital.android.intentexample;

import android.app.Activity;
import android.content.Intent;
import android.net.Uri;
import android.os.Bundle;
import android.view.View;
import android.widget.EditText;

public class IntentExampleActivity extends Activity {
    private EditText myContact;

    @Override
    protected void onCreate(Bundle savedInstanceState) {
        super.onCreate(savedInstanceState);
        setContentView(R.layout.activity_intent_example);
        myContact=(EditText)findViewById(R.id.myContact);
    }

    public void viewContact(View view) {
        String myContactNumber=myContact.getText().toString();
        Uri myUri = Uri.parse("content://contacts/people/"+myContactNumber);
        startActivity(new Intent(Intent.ACTION_VIEW, myUri));
    }
}
```

I have intentionally kept the logic that's not related to the actual business of intents very simple. That's so you can focus on what we have discussed in this chapter.

> **Note** Before running Listing 12-4's activity, be sure to have used an existing virtual device where you have added at least one contact using the built-in contacts application, and do not wipe the AVD state when (re)starting the virtual device. This way, you will have contacts in the contact database for the example to display

When you run the IntentExample project, you should see the IntentExample activity as shown in Figure 12-1.

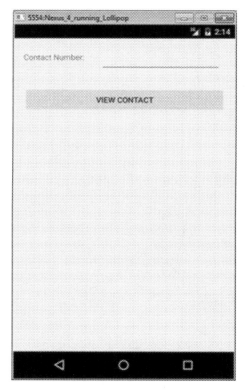

Figure 12-1. Our main activity triggered from launching the application

Remember, you are seeing this activity first, because Android Studio, Eclipse, or your Android project creation tool of choice added it as the LAUNCHER category in your manifest file.

When you attempt to enter a number for a contact, you'll see the appropriate digit-restricted IME thanks to our layout specification for the EditText widget. This appears as shown in Figure 12-2.

Figure 12-2. Submitting the data for Uri creation and intent triggering

Enter the number for a contact (for example, type in the digit 1 for the first contact in the system) and hit the "View Contact" button. Your contact Uri is parceled up in your Intent, and startActivity() sends Android off on the hunt to find the most appropriate activity to handle the ACTION_VIEW action for your intent. You can see the result in Figure 12-3.

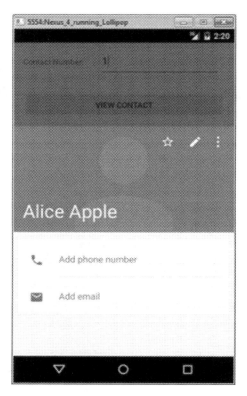

Figure 12-3. The contact activity selected to satisfy our intent

Figure 12-3 shows the built-in contact view activity, and not something included in the IntentExample project. Ours was a "safe" invocation because of our use of the Uri and our trust in Android to find the right activity. We didn't try to force things by using the explicit, component-naming method.

Introducing Receivers

The bulk of this chapter has covered how to use intents to create and launch multiple activities within your application in order to trigger a wide variety of actions in response to your user's demands and interaction with your program. But not every response to an intent needs to be within the scope of an activity.

Indeed, there are a number of concrete examples of times when you do not really need the bells and whistles of an activity to complete the desired outcome for an intent. Some examples include performing calculations, data manipulation, and other tasks having no need for any UI. You may also want to drect an intent at an Android service rather than atany end-user-facing application. For instance, you may want to build a photo-sharing service that sends all photos to a cloud storage provider for backup without any UI interaction. There are even times when you will not know until run-time whether or not an activity is required, and need to design for both an activity-related response and one with no activity involved.

Using Receivers When No UI is Needed

To deal with these "activity-less" scenarios, Android provides the `BroadcastReceiver` interface, and the concept of receivers. Just as activities are described as being light-weight UI screens for quickly dealing with a user's interactions, receivers are similarly meant to be light-weight objects that are created to receive and process a broadcast intent, and then be thrown away.

If you examine the definition for the `BroadcastReceiver` in the Android documentation, you will see that it consists of only one method named `onReceive()`. You can think of the `onReceive()` method as the "OK, do stuff" method for your receiver. You implement the method using whatever logic you decide needs to happen to deal with the associated intent.

Just as activities are declared in you manifest file, so too are declarations for any implementations of `BroadcastReceiver` you plan to have in your application. The element name is `<receiver>`, with an `android:name` attribute of the class that implements `BroadcastReceiver`. For example:

```
<receiver android:name=".MyReceiverClass" />
```

Your receiver will persist only for the time it takes to actually execute the logic in your implementation of `onReceive()`, and then will be discarded for garbage collection. There are also limitations in the base form of a receiver that mean you cannot issue callbacks, nor invoke UI elements such as dialog boxes.

The exception to this what I've just described comes when you implement a receiver on a service (or even an activity). In that case, the receiver will live for the lifetime of the related object. The receiver will live either until the service stops, which is rare, or until the activity is destroyed.

Receivers cannot be created via the manifest for services or activities. Instead, you'll need to invoke the `registerReceiver()` within `onResume()` to indicate your activity would like to receive intents (again, based on definted actions, categories and mime types), and similarly clean up with a call to `unregisterReceiver()` during the `onPause()` callback.

Navigating Receiver Limitations

As well as the limitations noted above for receivers, there is one other important aspect to note about their use in combination with intents. You might be imagining a world where you can use intent definitions and broadcast receivers as a general-purpose messaging system for an application. The one gotcha with that approach is that when activities are paused, as described in the lifecycle in Chapter 10, they will not receive intents.

That paused activities won't receive intents means that if you care about missed messages via intents, then you will specifically need to avoid activity-bound receivers and declare your receivers in the manifest as outlined at the start of this discussion. You will also need to think about how you can otherwise be re-notified of, or recover, any "messages" that occurred and were lost while activities were paused.

There are alternative approaches to a message bus for Android that rely on the Google Play Services APIs. These are better suited to message bus metaphor, namely Google Cloud Messaging. That product has its own quirks and limitations that are beyond the scope of this book, but interested readers can find out more on the Android developer website.

Making Phone Calls

Of all the capabilities, applications and features available to users of Android, and to you as a developer, the one "original" feature that is still pervasive is the ability to make telephone calls. Even now when Android is appearing in cars, planes, home appliances, and more, the very large majority of devices running Android are phones, and will be for some time.

Checking for Phones and "Phonies"

I claimed in the opening to the chapter that the vast majority of devices for Android are phones. That is true, but the growth of tablets and other non-cellular devices means you should think in advance about what telephony support your application must have, what is nice to have, and what it can live without. In short, checking if the device is really a phone will help you as a developer, and your users.

Mandating Telephony Support

Requiring phone support for your application is done by specifying the relevant uses-feature option in your application's manifest. For phone support, the hardware feature is named *telephony*, and is specified as shown in Listing 13-1

Listing 13-1. Including telephony as a requirement in your AndroidManifest.xml file

```
<uses-feature
  android:name="android.hardware.telephony"
  android:required="true"
/>
```

Specifying the telephony requirement ensures your application will run only on devices that have cellular support, and that the Google Play store and other application stores can filter results shown to people looking for applications such that your application isn't shown as available for install to devices that don't have telephony support.

Optional Telephony Support

Obviously an all-or-nothing approach to requiring telephony is fine in some circumstances, but you might have in mind an application where telephony is nice to have, but not strictly required. In those circumstances, instead of specifying the hardware requirement in your manifest, you can check for detected telephony support on a given device at run time, and code Java logic to handle both its presence and absence. The key to detecting various device capabilities at run-time is the PackageManager class, and its most-frequently-used method is hasSystemFeature().

Listing 13-2 is an example fragment of code showing PackageManager in action, using a common if block pattern. The example detects the presence or absence of telephony support at run-time.

Listing 13-2. Detecting telephony support at run-time

```
PackageManager myDevice = getPackageManager();
if (myDevice.hasSystemFeature(PackageManager.FEATURE_TELEPHONY) {
    // the user's device has telephony support
    // add your call-related logic here
} else {
    // the user's device lacks telephony support
    // do something that doesn't require making calls
};
```

There are several other useful variants of telephony for which you can check. These include whether a device is running on a GSM, CDMA, or other style of cellular network providing telephony for the device.

Making Outbound Calls

With the device capabilities determined, you can now start doing interesting things like making an outbound phone call. This is actually far simpler than you might imagine, as Android is built around telephony as a core feature. You do not have to personally build low-level components like radio firmware, network handshakes, etc. In fact, there is almost no code required at all!

The secret to almost all of the telephony and phone call handling you might want to undertake is the TelephonyManager class. Its methods include the ability to determine a wide variety of details and state information about the phone and calls. Some of the most useful methods are:

- getPhoneType() Returns the phone's radio type (GSM, etc.)

- getNetworkType() Provides information on the data capabilities of the network, including its categorization as 4G, LTE, 3G, GPRS, EDGE, etc.

- getCallState() Can determine whether the phone is idle (not in a call), in the process of making a call by ringing a number, or connected in a call (known as offhook).

> **Tip**   It is very good practice to use `getCallState()` and examine the result before your application tries to initiate a call, to avoid the embarrassing situation of interrupting an existing call or forgetting that your user might be doing other call-related activities outside of your application. There are ways to deal with multiple incoming or active calls, but they stretch beyond the scope of this book. You can always check out the advanced call handling options at `developer.android.com`

The actual task of dialing a number and initiating the call is performed by invoking an `ACTION_DIAL` or `ACTION_CALL` intent. We will cover the differences in the two approaches shortly. Either intent takes a Uri representing the number your user wishes to call, taking the string format `tel:nnnnnnnn`, where nnnnnnnn are the digits of the desired phone number. Explaining the setup and behavior is easier with an example.

The folder `ch13/PhoneCallExample` contains working code, and a simple custom layout that shows the various calling and dialing options in action. From that example code, Listing 13-3 presents a simple layout that allows a user to enter a number and make a call.

Listing 13-3. Layout for a simple phone call example

```xml
<LinearLayout xmlns:android="http://schemas.android.com/apk/res/android"
    xmlns:tools="http://schemas.android.com/tools"
    android:layout_width="match_parent"
    android:layout_height="match_parent"
    android:orientation="vertical"
    android:paddingBottom="@dimen/activity_vertical_margin"
    android:paddingLeft="@dimen/activity_horizontal_margin"
    android:paddingRight="@dimen/activity_horizontal_margin"
    android:paddingTop="@dimen/activity_vertical_margin"
    tools:context="com.artifexdigital.com.phonecallexample.PhoneCallExample" >

    <TextView
        android:layout_width="wrap_content"
        android:layout_height="wrap_content"
        android:text="Phone Number:" />

    <EditText
        android:id="@+id/phonenumber"
        android:layout_width="match_parent"
        android:layout_height="wrap_content"
        android:inputType="number" />

    <Button
        android:id="@+id/usedialintent"
        android:layout_width="match_parent"
        android:layout_height="wrap_content"
        android:text="Call with ACTION_DIAL"
        android:onClick="callWithActionDialIntent" />
```

```
<Button
    android:id="@+id/usecallintent"
    android:layout_width="match_parent"
    android:layout_height="wrap_content"
    android:text="Call with ACTION_CALL"
    android:onClick="callWithActionCallIntent" />
</LinearLayout>
```

The layout has a label and an `EditText` field, into which the user can enter their desired phone number. It also has two buttons, with each used to call a method invoking the relevant intent. Figure 13-1 shows the layout as rendered in a virtual device.

Figure 13-1. A simple layout for entering and dialing or calling a number

There are a few things to note about this example so as not to confuse you. First, the EditText field has the inputType="number" attribute, which means it will restrict its input to digits and some limited punctuation. This inputType is also why the IME shown for input into the EditText field is limited in the same way. It looks like a phone dialer pad, but is just a normal number EditText IME soft keyboard.

The two buttons are labeled to explicitly inform you what each one does when pressed. The first button, labeled CALL WITH ACTION_DIAL, will use the ACTION_DIAL intent, and the other button, labeled CALL WITH ACTION_CALL uses the alternative intent. So what's the difference? The ACTION_DIAL intent will trigger Android to display the phone dialer interface to the user (see Figure 13-2 later in the chapter). Whereas the ACTION_CALL intent moves immediately to dialing the number and placing the call, with no additional UI step.

Figure 13-2. *The Android dialer invoked through ACTION_DIAL intent*

Why have these alternatives? You can probably think of many reasons, but the ACTION_DIAL intent means the user will actually see the number, and have to hit the call button to go ahead and place the call. This means it is the user who actually completes the steps to make the call. The ACTION_DIAL intent needs no special permissions, as it's the user who has the final say.

In contrast, ACTION_CALL will proceed immediately to calling with no further user interaction. You can probably imagine various ways this can be abused, or accidentally cause issues. As such, Android protects the ACTION_CALL intent with the CALL_PHONE permission. You must have this in your manifest in order for a startActivity() call with ACTION_CALL intent to work.

Listing 13-4 shows the Java code that wires up the logic for the PhoneCallExample app.

Listing 13-4. Java logic to implement phone dialing/calling example

```java
package com.artifexdigital.com.phonecallexample;

import android.app.Activity;
import android.os.Bundle;
import android.content.Intent;
import android.net.Uri;
import android.view.View;
import android.widget.EditText;

public class PhoneCallExample extends Activity {

    @Override
    protected void onCreate(Bundle savedInstanceState) {
        super.onCreate(savedInstanceState);
        setContentView(R.layout.activity_phone_call_example);
    }

    public void callWithActionDialIntent(View view) {
        EditText targetNumber=(EditText)findViewById(R.id.phonenumber);
        String dialThisNumber="tel:"+targetNumber.getText().toString();
        startActivity(new Intent(Intent.ACTION_DIAL, Uri.parse(dialThisNumber)));
    }

    public void callWithActionCallIntent(View view) {
        EditText targetNumber=(EditText)findViewById(R.id.phonenumber);
        String callThisNumber="tel:"+targetNumber.getText().toString();
        //the following intent only works with CALL_PHONE permission in place
        startActivity(new Intent(Intent.ACTION_CALL, Uri.parse(callThisNumber)));
    }

}
```

Both methods triggered by the two buttons, usedialintent and usecallintent, follow the same pattern of logic: Find the phonenumber view into which the user has typed their number and extract the digits to format in the pattern expected by the Uri format introduced earlier in the chapter. With the Uri properly constructed, then fire the relevant intent through startActivity().

Using ACTION_DIAL

Figure 13-2 shows the result of the user pressing the usedialintent button, and therefore triggering the ACTION_DIAL intent and the presentation of the dialer UI to the user.

At first glance, the dialer in Figure 13-2 is very similar to the numeric IME shown as part of Figure 13-1. However, there are some key differences over and above the color and alignment of the digits. This is the *real* Android system dialer. It has extra flourishes such as the ability to add the number entered as a contact. The number is also formatted automatically depending on the device's regional and language settings, the number of digits entered, use of IDD codes, etc. In this example, Android has detected that the number 5551234567 looks like a North American number. Android has added the idiomatic brackets, spacing, and hyphen expected in the USA and Canada.

The other UI element to note is the big green phone symbol centered at the bottom. This is the call button that actually places the call using the number entered.

Using ACTION_CALL

There is no figure to show for pressing the usecallintent button, because we skip the dialer and go straight to the call. I am going to assume you as a developer have probably made at least one phone call from an Android device. You can imagine what the screen then looks like.

Working with Incoming Calls

Intercepting and handling an incoming call is a somewhat advanced endeavor, and beyond the scope of this book. However, there are other actions your application can take when a call is being received.

The main way in which your application can respond to incoming calls is by registering a broadcast receiver for the broadcast intent ACTION_PHONE_STATE_CHANGED in your application manifest file. This intent is fired by the Telephony Manager framework when a call is received. Listing 13-5 demonstrates the receiver declaration in your AndroidManifest.xml file.

Listing 13-5. Specifying a receiver for incoming calls in AndroidManifest.xml

```
<receiver android:name="MyPhoneStateChangedReceiver">
    <intent-filter>
        <action
            android:name="android.intent.action.PHONE_STATE"  />
    </intent-filter>
</receiver>
```

When the call is made to the device, the intent is fired, and your receiver is notified by way of callback to the specified method. Along with the intent, two possible extras are included. First is a state value for the call, such as CALL_STATE_OFFHOOK to indicate the call has been answered, or CALL_STATE_RINGING to indicate the phone is still ringing. In the latter case, the second extra will be EXTRA_INCOMING_NUMBER which provides the caller ID if such is passed by the network.

Listing 13-6 shows a simple fragment of Java code for the `MyPhoneStateChangedReceiver` class to give you an idea of what you can do with the callbacks.

Listing 13-6. Working with an incoming call

```
public class MyPhoneStateChangedReceiver extends BroadcastReceiver {
    @override
    public void onReceive(Context context, Intent intent) {
        String deviceCallState = intent.getStringExtra(TelephonyManager.EXTRA_STATE);
        if (deviceCallState.equals(TelephonyManager.EXTRA_STATE_RINGING) {
            // phone is still ringing, we have access to caller ID if provided
            String callerID =
              intent.getStringExtra(TelephonyManager.EXTRA_INCOMING_NUMBER);
            // go display the number, etc.
        } else {
            // do some other stuff
        }
    }
}
```

Because working with incoming calls is considered potentially sensitive from a security perspective, your application must also include the permission `READ_PHONE_STATE` in the manifest file in order to receive the `ACTION_PHONE_STATE_CHANGED` intent.

14

Making Noise with Audio for Android

In the previous chapter, you began to explore Android beyond the simple programming environment, branching out and using device features such as the ability to make phone calls. We are going to continue expanding you Android reach, and your knowledge of how to leverage the devices on which Android runs, by turning to the topic of audio and sound.

Introducing the Media package

Android provides a rich set of classes supporting the playback and recording of media of all sorts, both audio and video. At the core of Android support is the Media package, which provides everything from basic MP3 audio playback, MPEG video playback, and similar support for a variety of other audio and video formats, through to recording audio and video, and even specialized support for audio routing (choosing headphones over speakers) and image recognition in image formats.

At the heart of the Media package are the MediaPlayer and MediaRecorder objects. These two objects manage all the heavy lifting of playing back and recording. Let's take a look at managing audio with the Media package, before we move on to video in the next chapter.

Building Your First Audio Application

To start your musical journey, let's consider one of the very basic uses your users might have for audio playback and your application. If you think of devices like iPods, and even older MP3 players, they effectively provided a mechanism to play back an audio file from the device to the listener – the user of the application or device. We will build our own application to do exactly that. Later in the chapter we will extend the functionality to mimic contemporary streaming services like Spotify, and play back audio directly from a web location.

Using Resources or Assets

We are about to use an audio file to demonstrate playback in an Android application, and you as the developer have the option of using an "assets" folder in which to store your audio files , or the "raw" folder as discussed in Chapter 3. If you are using Eclipse and the ADT, you will find your projects are already created with a raw folder, and this is the most straight-forward option to use. If you are using Android Studio, particularly after the v1.0 release, your projects will be lacking both the raw and assets folders. While this simplifies your project folder structure, it is probably taking things too far into the realm of absurdly simplified.

To create a raw folder for holding audio files in Android Studio, navigate to the res folder in the hierarchy, and choose the menu option File ➤ New ➤ Directory. Name the directory "raw", and your raw folder will now be in place.

If you prefer to use an asset folder and are using Android Studio, you should navigate to the File ➤ New ➤ Folder ➤ Assets Folder option in Android Studio, which will then prompt for the creation of an assests folder for your project, as shown in Figure 14-1.

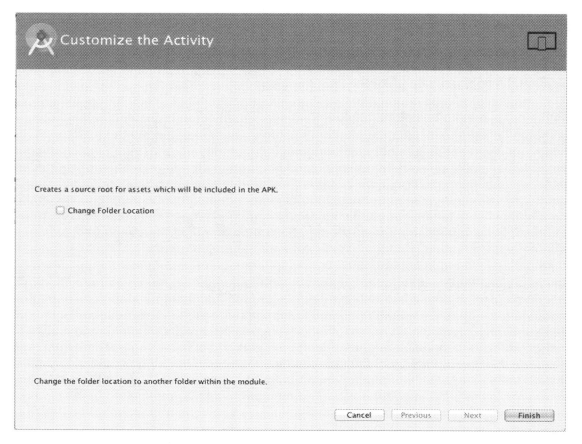

Figure 14-1. Creating a new asset folder for you audio file in Android Studio 1.0 or later

Allow Android Studio to keep the default location. You should see a new folder pop into existing in your project tree named assets, as shown in Figure 14-2.

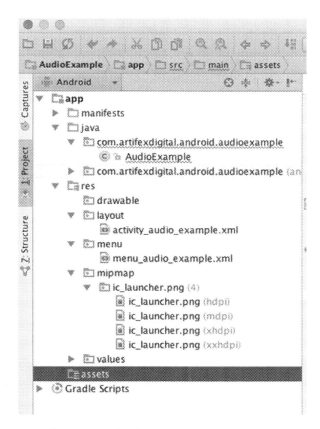

Figure 14-2. Assets folder created in an Android Studio 1.0 or later project

The corresponding filesystem location for you Android Studio assets folder within your project is ./app/src/main/assets (or .\app\source\main\assets under Windows).

If you want to continue using the traditional raw folder, you can find (or create) it under the ./app/src/main/res folder of your project.

Coding for Audio Playback Using the Media Framework

Delve into the special-case UI widgets and parts of the Media framework and you will find a very slick, all-in-one audio player widget that is complete with stubs for implementing the common playback functions people use when listening to music. Using that widget would get you an application very quickly, but using it would completely rob you of understanding how the parts of the media framework do their thing. You would miss learning the fundamentals that you need to master as a budding Android developer.

So instead of presenting the fully polished application with no scope for learning these things, we will build our own widget. We'll explore the Media framework properly as we go.

Starting With A Simple Audio Player Layout

In order to start exploring the use of the Media player framework for audio playback, we will need a simple interface of our own construction. Figure 14-3 presents what is probably the world's most straight-forward audio player application.

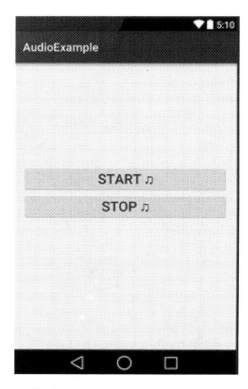

Figure 14-3. *A simple audio player application*

The layout provides just enough to begin the exploration of the Media framework: a "Start" button, and a "Stop" button. The layout for the interface from Figure 14-3 is shown in Listing 14-1.

Listing 14-1. The layout for the AudioExample application

```
<RelativeLayout xmlns:android="http://schemas.android.com/apk/res/android"
    xmlns:tools="http://schemas.android.com/tools"
    android:layout_width="match_parent"
    android:layout_height="match_parent"
    android:paddingLeft="@dimen/activity_horizontal_margin"
    android:paddingRight="@dimen/activity_horizontal_margin"
    android:paddingTop="@dimen/activity_vertical_margin"
    android:paddingBottom="@dimen/activity_vertical_margin"
    tools:context=".AudioExample">
```

```
<Button android:id="@+id/startButton"
    android:layout_width="match_parent"
    android:layout_height="wrap_content"
    android:text="Start &#9835;"
    android:textSize="24sp"
    android:onClick="onClick"
    android:layout_above="@+id/stopButton" />

<Button android:id="@+id/stopButton"
    android:layout_width="match_parent"
    android:layout_height="wrap_content"
    android:text="Stop &#9835;"
    android:textSize="24sp"
    android:onClick="onClick"
    android:layout_centerVertical="true"
    android:layout_alignParentLeft="true"
    android:layout_alignParentStart="true" />
```

```
</RelativeLayout>
```

The layout is a straight forward RelativeLayout with two Button views placed within it. These buttons have android:id values of startButton for Start, and stopButton for Stop. You can also see a range of additional attributes used to style the look and feel, such as the android:layout_above attribute to place the Start button above the Stop button, and font sizing to make the text large and obvious.

> **Note**   You will also see in the android:text attribute values of each button the text ♫ This isn't some mysterious Android code, but rather is simple Unicode for the little musical symbol you see on the buttons in Figure 14-3. Remember, layouts are XML, and XML is Unicode based, so you have the freedom to include "text" like this. (See http://unicode-table.com for a list of such codes).

Each of the buttons also has the same value for the method to invoke when clicked. This method is named in the android:onClick="onClick" attribute.

Coding the AudioExample Behavior

Let's look at the application now. You can see the code in Listing 14-2, and in the ch14/AudioExample folder.

Listing 14-2. Java code for the AudioExample application

```java
package com.artifexdigital.android.audioexample;

import android.app.Activity;
import android.media.AudioManager;
import android.media.MediaPlayer;
import android.media.MediaPlayer.OnPreparedListener;
import android.os.Bundle;
import android.view.View;
```

```java
public class AudioExample extends Activity implements OnPreparedListener {
    private MediaPlayer mp;

    @Override
    protected void onCreate(Bundle savedInstanceState) {
        super.onCreate(savedInstanceState);
        setContentView(R.layout.activity_audio_example);
    }

    public void onClick(View view) {
        switch(view.getId()) {
            case R.id.startButton:
                doPlayAudio();
                break;
            case R.id.stopButton:
                doStopAudio();
                break;
        }
    }

    private void doPlayAudio() {
        mp = MediaPlayer.create(this, R.raw.audio_file);
        mp.setAudioStreamType(AudioManager.STREAM_MUSIC);
        mp.start();
    }

    private void doStopAudio() {
        if (mp != null) {
            mp.stop();
        }
    }

    // The onPrepared callback is for you to implement
    // as part of the OnPreparedListener interface
    public void onPrepared(MediaPlayer mp) {
        mp.start();
    }

    @Override
    protected void onDestroy() {
        super.onDestroy();
        if(mp != null) {
            mp.release();
        }
    }

}
```

Let's walk through what each method does to build the features of our simple audio file player application. First, our package imports some familiar dependencies such as view.View and os.Bundle. You will also see three key Media framework packages installed, which were alluded to in the chapter introduction. These are:

- Android.media.AudioManager: The AudioManager provides a range of support functions to make audio handling of all sorts of audio easier. You use AudioManager to flag that an audio source is a stream, voice, machine-generated tone, and so on.

- Android.media.MediaPlayer: The work-horse of the Media package, MediaPlayer gives you total control over preparing and playing back audio from local and remote sources.

- Android.media.MediaPlayer.OnPreparedListener: The key to asynchronous playback, OnPreparedListener is the interface that enables callbacks to playback music after off-thread preparation has been done.

Our class implements the OnPreparedListener interface, which obliges us to to eventually provide the logic for the the onPrepared callback. We will come to that shortly.

The onCreate() callback implementation does the by-now familiar inflation of our layout into a fully-fledged UI for the application. All of the interesting logic is in the other methods.

The onClick() method uses a very common design pattern to channel to the appropriate application logic on the basis of the View passed to it. When the user of the application actually clicks either of the startButton or stopButton buttons, Android passes the respective View representing the clicked button to the onClick() method. We simply perform switch logic to detect which View was passed to the method, and by implication which button was pressed. For the startButton we then call the doPlayAudio() method. Similarly, for the stopButton, we call the doStopAudio() method.

When a user of the application clicks the startButton, and doPlayAudio() is called, some obvious things happen. For example, we get the file to play. But some not-so-obvious things also happen. First we create a new MediaPlayer object, and bind our audio file resource to it. The R.raw.audio_file notation is conceptually similar to the layout inflation notation you've already seen, such as R.layout.activity_audio_example. Android will examine the raw folder packaged with the application in the .apk file and try to find an asset named audio_file.<some extension>.

Having found and bound our audio_file.m4a example file, we then introduce the use of the AudioManager class through the mp.setAudioStreamType() method. AudioManager has a range of tasks it performs for you, one of the most common being to set the stream type for the given audio resource. Android supports a range of audio stream types, with the goal of ensuring a given stream gets the fidelity and other audio characteristics needed for a given purpose. For instance, the STREAM_DTMF audio stream is used for DTMF tones, and Android filters any streams marked this way to conform to the DTMF standard. Similarly, the STREAM_VOICE_CALL stream type triggers Android to invoke or suppress various echo-cancelling techniques on voice audio.

The AudioExample application sets the stream type to STREAM_MUSIC, meaning our source file is some kind of music recording. Because we are playing our audio file from an asset packaged with the .apk, we can then move straight ahead and start actually playing back the audio. The final call in doPlayAudio() is the mp.start() call. That call has the MediaPlayer object start actually playing the file, sending audio to the speaker or headphones.

The doStopAudio() method is pretty self explanatory. It calls the stop() method on the MediaPlayer object if it is instantiated. The reason for the if{} block testing for instantiation is to ensure we don't try to stop anything if the user has never pressed Start (i.e. they open the application and press Stop, just for kicks).

Next in the code is the onPrepared() callback method. This is linked to the package definition where AudioExample implements the OnPreparedListener interface. Strictly we aren't using the onPrepared() callback in this first pass of the AudioExample application, but I wanted to include this deliberately to highlight that there are times where you cannot immediately begin playback after the MediaPlayer object is instantiated and the AudioManager has been invoked to set the stream type. Fear not, we will expand this example in the next section to illustrate how and why to use the onPrepared() callback.

Lastly, we include logic in the onDestroy() callback to release the MediaPlayer object if it has been previously created.

Obviously there's no way to "show" what the running application is doing with audio playback in a printed book, so you should go ahead and run the example to satisfy yourself that the final working product actually makes some noise!

Building Your Own Android Music Streaming Application

It would be a little strange if Android audio playback was limited to just what was on a device. As you would expect from a smartphone platform born in the internet age, off-device assets and resources are fair game for audio (and video), and the Media framework has you covered.

Altering the existing AudioExample application is easy, and if you peruse the ch14/AudioExample2 project you can see some straight forward changes to the UI, and some not-so-straight-forward adaptations of the Java logic. Figure 14-4 shows the new layout as it appears to the user running the application.

Figure 14-4. A simple layout that accepts a URL for playback

I will omit the layout XML in full for the sake of saving space, but the key changes you should note in AudioExample2 are the TextView for the field label, and the EditText view with an android:id of "@+id/sourceFile".

The changes to the Java logic are somewhat more extensive, and the code can be seen in Listing 14-3.

Listing 14-3. AudioExample2 logic

```
package com.artifexdigital.android.audioexample2;

import android.app.Activity;
import android.media.AudioManager;
import android.media.MediaPlayer;
import android.media.MediaPlayer.OnPreparedListener;
import android.os.Bundle;
import android.view.View;
import android.widget.EditText;

public class AudioExample2 extends Activity implements OnPreparedListener {
    // useful for debugging
    // String mySourceFile=
    // "https://ia801400.us.archive.org/2/items/rhapblue11924/rhapblue11924_64kb.mp3";
    private MediaPlayer mp;
```

```java
@Override
protected void onCreate(Bundle savedInstanceState) {
    super.onCreate(savedInstanceState);
    setContentView(R.layout.activity_audio_example2);
}

public void onClick(View view) {
    switch(view.getId()) {
        case R.id.startButton:
            try {
                EditText mySourceFile=(EditText)findViewById(R.id.sourceFile);
                doPlayAudio(mySourceFile.toString());
            } catch (Exception e) {
                // error handling logic here
            }
            break;
        case R.id.stopButton:
            doStopAudio();
            break;
    }
}

private void doPlayAudio(String audioUrl) throws Exception {
    mp = new MediaPlayer();
    mp.setAudioStreamType(AudioManager.STREAM_MUSIC);
    mp.setDataSource(audioUrl);
    mp.setOnPreparedListener(this);
    mp.prepareAsync();
}

private void doStopAudio() {
    if (mp != null) {
        mp.stop();
    }
}

// The onPrepared callback is for you to implement
// as part of the OnPreparedListener interface
public void onPrepared(MediaPlayer mp) {
    mp.start();
}

@Override
protected void onDestroy() {
    super.onDestroy();
    if(mp != null) {
        mp.release();
    }
}
}
```

The main changes you should notice between AudioExample and AudioExample2 are the differences in the doClick() and doStartAudio() methods. There are a few other minor changes that support the major changes in those two methods. We include the android.widget.EditText import so that we can access and manipulate the text the user enters into the UI, and we finally make use of the onPrepared() callback introduced in the AudioExample application.

The doClick() method has two main changes. First, we create an EditText object, named mySourceFile to work with the UI EditText field into which the application user types the URL of their chosen audio file. We use the String value of the EditText to pass to the modified doPlayAudio() method in the subsequent call. The try-catch block is in place to cover the exceptions that doPlayAudio() can now throw.

As for doPlayAudio(), its ability to throw exceptions is just one of the many changes. Instead of creating a MediaPlayer object pointing directly to a file in the .apk, we simply create the new mp MediaPlayer object. We invoke the AudioManager package as before to declare that the eventual data source will be STREAM_MUSIC.

The code then calls setDataSource() on the URL passed to doPlayAudio() from onClick(). The setDataSource() method is a very powerful tool, having quite a few overloaded forms to handle source data presented as strings. Also present are FileDescriptor objects, AssetFileDescriptor objects, and many other resource forms.

Using setDataSource() by implication gives us more power and flexibility with the MediaPlayer object. We can interrogate the object with getDataSource() to see what is currently allocated. We can also change the source data, which cannot be done if the MediaPlayer object is passed a raw resource or asset directly at instantiation-time as in the original AudioExample case.

There are more playback options that stem from using a data source, such as the ability to define playback windows for only part of the source file. No matter how the MediaPlayer object was created, the .seekTo() method can find an exact point in the data, and .getCurrentPosition() can be used to determine the current playback point. Both .getCurrentPosition() and .seekTo() work with millisecond precision.

In order for the setDataSource() call to successfully resolve and fetch the resource (music file) at the URL given, we need to grant our application the android.permission.INTERNET permission in the manifest file. I will cover permissions in much more detail in Chapter 19, but for now all you need to do is add the following to your project's AndroidManifest.xml file.

```
<uses-permission android:name="android.permission.INTERNET" />
```

Note that this line should be the first child element after the <manifest> root element. Put it before the <application> child element that Eclipse or Android Studio created for you.

The next two changes to doStartAudio() work in tandem to ensure that we can play back our audio file from the internet while accommodating all the vagaries of problematic networks, slow connections, and an Android device busy with many parallel tasks. The first of the calls is to .setOnPreparedListener(), indicating that it is our activity itself that will deal with the registered callback. We're finally working in anger with the implementation of OnPreparedListener that the package definition has carried around since the first example.

Lastly, a call is made to `.prepareAsync()` on the `MediaPlayer` object. This brings us to the concept of immediate versus asynchronous playback, so we should deal with that now.

Synchronous versus Asynchronous Playback

As a developer, you have one important choice to make when working with a data source of a `MediaPlayer` object. The choice is all about what behaviour the user will experience from the point in time the intent to playback is triggered, up to when the actual source data has successfully been accessed and any related playback UI has been prepared. Fundamentally, the choice is this: Should the application (and UI) block and wait until the data source has been reached and playback is ready, or should this happen asynchronously allowing your application to do other things in the time the preparation takes?

Android provides for both approaches through the `.prepare()` and `.prepareAsync()` methods. The `.prepare()` method does all of its work synchronously, forcing the user to wait until such time as it is ready to invoke the `onPrepared()` callback. This is usually fine for resources or assets you know to be on the device, either packaged with `.apk` or available on the filesystem. The `.prepareAsync()` method, as the name suggests, is an asynchronous, non-blocking version for data source preparation. Control is returned immediately, and at some later point the `onPrepared()` callback will eventually be invoked.

Using `.prepareAsync()` is principally designed to cope with off-device resources (though you can use it for local items as well). As a developer, you never know when the end-point for a URL is going to be available, how responsive it will be, and how all of that changes from any one day to another. Adopting the asynchronous approach is desirable in the circumstances, and it is a design pattern you will see recur throughout your Android development.

Playing at Last

With all of the changes so far described for AudioExample2, your application will eventually receive the callback to `onPrepared()`, and the logic here is unchanged from the previous unused example. For AudioExample2, `onPrepared()` is actually called once `.prepareAsync()` from `onStartAudio()` completes, and a simple call to the `MediaPlayer`'s `.start()` method gets the music rolling.

There are more details and nuances to the various states in which your `MediaPlayer` objects and related data source can exist. Rather than repeat the fine documentation here in the Beginning Android book, feel free to take a look a the state diagram and flow of callbacks and transitions on the Android Developer website at:

`http://developer.android.com/reference/android/media/MediaPlayer.html`

As before, there is nothing to show in the interface here on the printed page that lets you experience the audio, so you should go ahead and run the example to hear for yourself. I have included a link to a public domain mp3 file in the comment at the top of the AudioExample2 package. It is to Gershwin's Rhapsody in Blue, which is such a great track that everyone should hear it... possibly through their own Android app!

Alternative Audio Playback Approaches

The Media package and MediaPlayer object are great for playing back audio, and even video as we will discover in the next chapter. As good as they are, there are some limitation to MediaPlayer in particular. As a developer you should be aware of the alternatives at your disposal.

The principal limitation of MediaPlayer is that it can only deal with one audio/video track at a time. This is fine in many circumstances, but I'm sure you can think of a range of applications where this will be a moderate to severe limitation.

For example, creating a game application that uses many sounds and music tracks, and a desire to have these play simultaneously isn't possible with MediaPlayer. The good news is that Android provides other options for a variety of special-case playback needs.

Using SoundPool for Simultaneous Playback

While the MediaPlayer class has enormous power and capabilities, sometimes you are after just the basics. In particular, you might want to only worry about playing back audio tracks local to the device – whether packaged as a resource or asset, or from the file system accessed directly or via FileDescriptor.

Enter the SoundPool class, which is a cut-down wrapper class that encapsulates a subset of the MediaPlayer functionality. SoundPool has the following very useful features:

- Simple playback from on-device: Because SoundPool doesn't need to handle off-device complications, the more complex methods and capabilities of MediaPlayer are removed.

- Straight-forward File/Resource Access: Resources or assets packaged with the .apk are accessed through SoundPool's simple .load() method for resources, or the activity context's .getAssets().openFd() method for gaining a FileDescriptor for the local asset. For the filesystem-inclined developer, .load() has an overloaded version to take a full filesystem filepath to access audio files directly.

- Simultaneous Playback: As a developer, you can load as many sounds as you like, with one limitation we will come to shortly. If you want drums and guitar, you can have both!

There are other benefits of SoundPool you can read about from the documentation, but there is also one major limitation to be aware of. This limitation is the overall limit on the memory footprint of all the audio souces loaded into a SoundPool instance. The total internal buffer for all audio is capped at 1MB. This sounds like a reasonable amount, but there's more to the SoundPool storage limits than meets the eye.

SoundPool tries to do everything it can to make playback fast and efficient. One of the approaches it takes is to expand audio from whatever compression format it was compressed with into an uncompressed in-memory representation. This means the amount of buffer used by your audio tracks depends on things like number of channels, bit rates, and duration. You might be surprised how quickly you can fill the 1MB buffer.

If you can work within the buffer size limitation, then SoundPool is an excellent alternative for simple local-to-device playback.

Going Fully-Asynchronous with AsyncPlayer

While MediaPlayer has support for asynchronous preparation of an audio source, much of the other setup and management is synchronous or uses the main application thread to manage click handling and related stop, start, and pause behaviour. Sometimes, audio is really not the focus of your application. Maybe you just want some "background music" as a flourish or minor addition.

When you want audio handled entirely in the background, with little need for direct control, then the AsyncPlayer class is the perfect option. The AsyncPlayer is capable of dealing with the same data sources as MediaPlayer, meaning it can use on-device or remotely-accessed items.

In practice, AsyncPlayer makes your work simple by limiting your options and your control. All you do is to first create the AsyncPlayer, and then ask it to play a selection. That's it. For example:

```
ap = new AsyncPlayer("AsyncPlayerExample");
ap.play(this, Uri.parse( <some filepath or URL location > ), false,
    AudioManager.STREAM_MUSIC);
```

This snippet declares a new AsyncPlayer. Then it invokes the .play() method to set an audio resource to be played. The resource wil be accessed asynchronously, and played when it can be played, which is typically shortly after the call completes, but you have no control over the precise timing of playback. You basically have no other control than to specify what is to be played. AsyncPlayer doesn't give you callbacks, lacks seekTo() and other useful methods, and frees itself of other baggage. It just plays the audio track, eventually.

AsyncPlayer does provide a .stop() method. You can guess what it does. It stops the playback, and kills the background thread. It is the only management method provided.

Recording Audio with Android

The flipside of playing back audio is making your own, and recording it to share with others, or to replay at a later time. Android supports a range of approaches to recording audio, to suit various levels of complexity and fidelity.

Making Recordings with MediaRecorder

The MediaRecorder class is the complement to MediaPlayer introduced earlier in this chapter. MediaRecorder gives you a set of useful features to capture sound and record it. To show its capabilities, you will find one more variant of our on-going example application in ch14/AudioExample3. Figure 14-5 shows the user interface, which incorporates buttons for recording and playback.

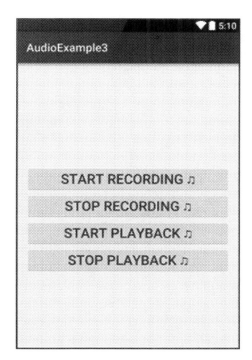

Figure 14-5. The AudioExample3 UI for recording and playback

Listing 14-4 gives the `layout.xml` for the UI. You should note that I have extended the pattern from the earlier examples, with all of the buttons triggering the `onClick()` method.

Listing 14-4. The AudioExample3 layout definition

```
<RelativeLayout xmlns:android="http://schemas.android.com/apk/res/android"
    xmlns:tools="http://schemas.android.com/tools"
    android:layout_width="match_parent"
    android:layout_height="match_parent"
    android:paddingLeft="@dimen/activity_horizontal_margin"
    android:paddingRight="@dimen/activity_horizontal_margin"
    android:paddingTop="@dimen/activity_vertical_margin"
    android:paddingBottom="@dimen/activity_vertical_margin"
    tools:context=".AudioExample">

    <Button android:id="@+id/startRecordingButton"
        android:layout_width="match_parent"
        android:layout_height="wrap_content"
        android:text="Start Recording &#9835;"
        android:textSize="24sp"
        android:onClick="onClick"
        android:layout_above="@+id/stopRecordingButton" />
```

```
<Button android:id="@+id/stopRecordingButton"
    android:layout_width="match_parent"
    android:layout_height="wrap_content"
    android:text="Stop Recording &#9835;"
    android:textSize="24sp"
    android:onClick="onClick"
    android:layout_centerVertical="true"
    android:layout_alignParentLeft="true"
    android:layout_alignParentStart="true" />

<Button android:id="@+id/startButton"
    android:layout_width="match_parent"
    android:layout_height="wrap_content"
    android:text="Start Playback &#9835;"
    android:textSize="24sp"
    android:onClick="onClick"
    android:layout_below="@+id/stopRecordingButton" />

<Button android:id="@+id/stopButton"
    android:layout_width="match_parent"
    android:layout_height="wrap_content"
    android:text="Stop Playback &#9835;"
    android:textSize="24sp"
    android:layout_below="@+id/startButton"
    android:onClick="onClick" />
```

```
</RelativeLayout>
```

The layout is more closely related to the original AudioExample project, as we don't need an EditText widget to take a URL. We have two new permissions that will be required in order for our application to be able to first record the audio from a microphone, and then store the recording on the device. Your AndroidManifest.xml will need the two following privileges:

```
<uses-permission android:name="android.permission.RECORD_AUDIO" />
<uses-permission android:name="android.permission.WRITE_EXTERNAL_STORAGE" />
```

With these permissions in place, our Java logic can do the work required. Listing 14-5 shows the Java code for AudioExample3.

Listing 14-5. Java logic for recording and playing back audio

```
package com.artifexdigital.android.audioexample3;

import android.app.Activity;
import android.media.AudioManager;
import android.media.MediaPlayer;
import android.media.MediaRecorder;
import android.os.Bundle;
import android.view.View;
import java.io.File;
```

```java
public class AudioExample3 extends Activity {
    private MediaRecorder mr;
    private MediaPlayer mp;
    private String myRecording="myAudioRecording";

    @Override
    protected void onCreate(Bundle savedInstanceState) {
        super.onCreate(savedInstanceState);
        setContentView(R.layout.activity_audio_example3);
    }

    public void onClick(View view) {
        switch(view.getId()) {
            case R.id.startRecordingButton:
                doStartRecording();
                break;
            case R.id.stopRecordingButton:
                doStopRecording();
                break;
            case R.id.startButton:
                doPlayAudio();
                break;
            case R.id.stopButton:
                doStopAudio();
                break;
        }
    }

    private void doStartRecording() {
        File recFile = new File(myRecording);
        if(recFile.exists()) {
            try {
                recFile.delete();
            } catch (Exception e) {
                // do exception handling here
            }
        }

        mr = new MediaRecorder();
        mr.setAudioSource(MediaRecorder.AudioSource.MIC);
        mr.setOutputFormat(MediaRecorder.OutputFormat.DEFAULT);
        mr.setAudioEncoder(MediaRecorder.AudioEncoder.DEFAULT);
        mr.setOutputFile(myRecording);
        try {
            mr.prepare();
        } catch (Exception e) {
            // do exception handling here
        }
        mr.start();
    }
```

```
    private void doStopRecording() {
        if (mr != null) {
            mr.stop();
        }
    }

    private void doPlayAudio() {
        mp = new MediaPlayer();
        try {
            mp.setDataSource(myRecording);
        } catch (Exception e) {
            // do exception handling here
        }
        mp.setAudioStreamType(AudioManager.STREAM_MUSIC);
        try {
            mp.prepare();
        } catch (Exception e) {
            // do exception handling here
        }
        mp.start();
    }

    private void doStopAudio() {
        if (mp != null) {
            mp.stop();
        }
    }

    @Override
    protected void onDestroy() {
        super.onDestroy();
        if(mr != null) {
            mr.release();
        }
        if(mp != null) {
            mp.release();
        }
    }

}
```

By now you are familiar with many of the logic constructs shown here. The onClick()
method switches on the button clicked by the user, our playback and stop methods
are almost identical to before. Interestingly, if you examine the doStopRecording() and
doStopAudio() methods, you see exactly the same logic applied to the MediaRecorder
and MediaPlayer objects respectively. One of the neat parallels of the two classes is that
common goals are served by logically matching methods.

The main expansion of the Java code is through the doStartRecording() method. This
method starts by ensuring the File object, myRecording, is created afresh, deleting any
previously existing object in the process. Notably, we are relying on the java.io.File
package to provide basic file handling capabilities. This is one example of stepping outside

the bounds of Android to include other useful libraries. We will cover more of the capabilities of using standard Java libraries in Chapter 20.

The code goes to create the MediaRecorder object named mr. Then the code invokes the .setAudioSource() method to indicate that the application wants to access the MIC in order to record sound. It is this call that necessitates the RECORD_AUDIO permission.

With the microphone accessed, a pair of calls are then made to select the desired output container format for the audio, and the desired codec to use to encode the audio that will be placed in the container. These are the .setOutputFormat() and .setAudioEncoder() calls. The example shown takes the DEFAULT option in each case, which typically varies depending in particular on the audio codecs supported by the hardware device and version of Android in use.

Some commonly-used output formats include:

- **AAC_ADTS:** The container popularlized by Apple and AAC audio format.

- **AMR_NB:** The AMR Narrow Band container type is recommended when you would like maximum portability across Android devices.

- **MPEG_4:** MPEG4 container format is one of the most venerable, but also the most likely to be misinterpreted on older platforms and devices. Use with caution.

- **THREE_GPP:** Another recommended container format for broad Android support.

- **WEBM:** The container synonymous for both Google's much-advertised but little-used WEBM format, and also the default used with Ogg encoded files

The topic of container formats and audio and video codecs could, and does, literally fill entire books by themselves. I will wrap up this area by highlighting the popular codecs used for audio (and video) encoding in Android. They are:

- **AAC:** (And also AAC_ELD and HE_AAC) audio codecs for the Advanced Audio Codec standard. Widely supported by Apple and other devices and platforms.

- **AMR_NB:** The actual audio encoder for AMR narrow band. While not widely used outside Android, this codec provides broad support across Android versions and devices.

- **VORBIS:** The Ogg Vorbis audio codec format

Returning to our examination of the .doStartRecording() method, the .setOutputFile() call configures the Java File object previously created as the repository for the audio stream the user will record.

Lastly we come to the familiar pattern of calling `.prepare()` and `.start()` for our `MediaRecorder` object. Just as the `MediaPlayer` object has to deal with a variety of obstacles and delays, so too does the `MediaRecorder`. Whether it's a slow local filesystem, or remote end point that is not responding, the `.prepare()` method takes care of the work to allow your recording to be stored, and returns control once all is in place. The call to `.start()` actually begins capturing the audio input.

As with our earlier playback examples, a printed book cannot demonstrate audio capture. So try the example for yourself to see how each of the pieces described works in action.

15

Locations and Mapping with Android

If I asked you what the most common task anyone performs on a mobile device is, I'm guessing that using maps would be high on your list of responses. Of course there are other popular tasks—like watching videos, messaging friends, searching in general, and making calls—but searching for locations and seeking directions to them are some of the most common activities people perform.

From their inception in 2008, Android devices have supported and promoted a range of options for working with locations and maps. The most obvious and most used service is Google Maps, which not only exists as a standalone application on most (but not all) Android devices, but which you can also use to power a range of Android components for your own location-powered application. The main components available to you as a developer are `MapView` and `MapActivity`, but you can also use other approaches to include alternative mapping and location services and functionality into your applications.

Choosing Map Providers for Your Application

Over the course of the history of Android, mapping and location has grown from defaulting to and being synonymous with Google Maps, to offering a rich category of technology with several strong contenders from which you, as the developer, can choose. Each option has benefits and drawbacks, so it is worth spending a moment to consider in which technology you want to invest your time and effort.

Google Maps

Although it is easy to think of Google Maps on Android as part of Android itself, this is not the case. From early on in Android's history, Google Maps was split from the platform and now it exists as part of the separately-packaged Google APIs. The principal reason for this split was the competing desire to "strongly encourage" handset manufacturers to license Google's bundle of higher-order applications and APIs with any Android device, and the desire to promote and ship as many Android devices as possible, regardless of whether they included separately-licensed Google applications.

Google Maps bundled within the Google APIs is very simple to install, since Google provides it in the same repository as the normal Android SDK components and the other additional APIs it offers. Fire up your SDK Manager from Android Studio, Eclipse, or straight from the command line, and you will see the Google APIs as an install candidate, as shown in Figure 15-1.

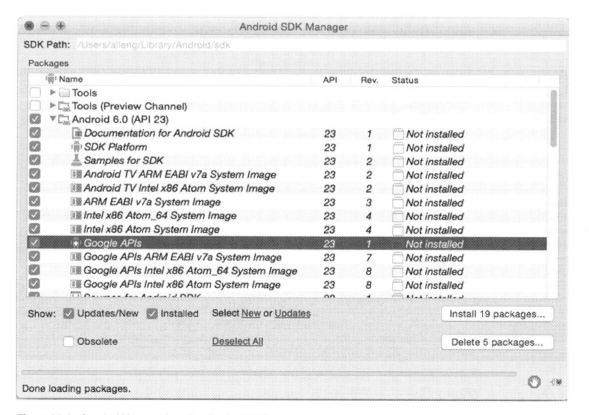

Figure 15-1. Google APIs as an install option in SDK Manager

The main drawback to using the Google Maps APIs then immediately becomes apparent. Because Google Maps is not part of the Android open source package, it is not licensed in an open source fashion. Instead, the Google APIs (including Google Maps) carry a range of much more commercial-style licensing, and I would strongly encourage you to actually read the fine print and ensure that you are happy with its meaning and implications.

If Google Maps will form part of the applications you plan to sell in the Google Play store or elsewhere, be aware that there are cost implications that you need to factor in to your calculations.

The OpenStreetMap Project

Steve Coast started the OpenStreetMap project as a small volunteer effort in 2004 as an way to crowd-source map and location data. OpenStreetMap began in response to the comparatively high cost of licensing map and location data at the time, but it has since exploded to become one of the biggest examples of high-quality crowd-sourced data on the Internet today. Thousands upon thousands of volunteers collect data as they travel to work, home, school, and beyond, using every conceivable GPS-capable device you can imagine, including Android phones.

Using OpenStreetMap in your projects is a little more convoluted, because the OpenStreetMap project has not made any neatly-packaged library or Android API available itself. However, because the data for OpenStreetMap is licensed using the Open Data Commons Open Database License, anyone is free to take it and use it as long as they provide the necessary attribution to the source. A number of people have packaged the OpenStreetMap data into useful Android libraries that they maintain and share themselves.

The most popular third-party libraries that provide OpenStreetMap data and APIs for Android are OpenTouchMap and TouchMapLight. You can find out more about these packages on the OpenStreetMap developer wiki at `http://wiki.openstreetmap.org/wiki/Android#Developer_tools`.

HERE/Ovi Maps

Now owned by a consortium of German car manufacturers, HERE Maps (formerly Ovi Maps) was, for a long time, the mapping and location technology owned by Nokia. HERE Maps provides rich map data and APIs for multiple platforms, including Android. You can source the APIs and documentation from the HERE developer website at `https://developer.here.com/native-apis`.

Like Google Maps, HERE comes with a commercial license with a range of legal implications and obligations. If you plan to include HERE Maps in your applications, read and understand the license. If you are in any doubt, seek professional legal advice.

Which Technology to Choose?

Although the ultimate choice of mapping and location technology is up to you, I only have finite space in this book to cover the mapping and location topic. For now, I will delve into the Google Maps APIs since they are the most commonly used by beginner Android developers. But you now know you have options, and you can even include multiple mapping APIs in your application. I know of at least one fitness tracking application that does exactly that.

Preparing for Google Maps Development

In order to use Google Maps from any form of application (not just Android ones), you as the developer need to source and use a Google API key and configure your Google account for the Maps API. You also need to extract the necessary cryptographic signature for you map widgets to use so they can reference your account and map data can flow. Let's cover these steps briefly now; much more information on this setup is available from the general Google developer site at `https://developer.google.com`.

Creating Your API Project

Head to `https://console.developers.google.com` and create a new project under your Google account. You can call the project anything you like, although you might want to think about how this will relate to your maps application and any other applications you plan to write that make use of Google's web-based APIs.

Enabling a Maps API on Your Google API Project

From your new API Project's dashboard, follow the link named "Enable APIs and get credentials like keys." Doing so displays a very large list of the ever-changing set of APIs Google builds for all of its services. In fact, this list and its layout changes so frequently that I'm going to save some paper and not include a screen shot that will be out of date within days. Look for the "Google Maps Android API" entry, and enable that API for your project. You will see a confirmation that looks like the response shown in Figure 15-2.

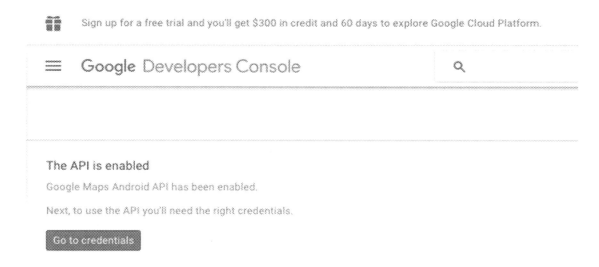

Figure 15-2. Confirmation of Google Maps Android API enabled

Once you have the Maps API enabled, you need some further cryptographic keys to ensure that only your approved applications can use your API Project (and incur any costs that might be triggered).

Getting the API Key

Press the Go To Credentials button to see the details for your proposed API key. Make sure to enter a meaningful key name and nominate the Android package that you will be using for this key. You can have many, many keys for different applications, so do not feel like this is a once-in-a-lifetime naming event. For the example that follows later in the chapter, I have used com.artifexdigital.android.mapsexample, as you can see if Figure 15-3.

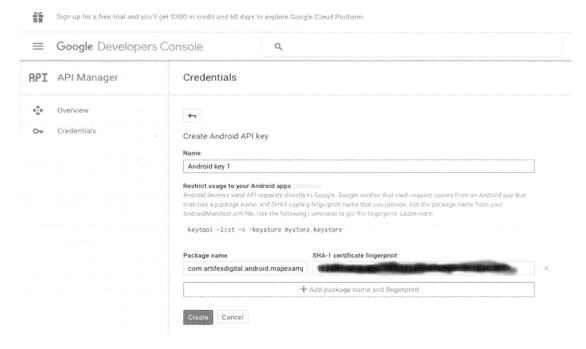

Figure 15-3. Confirming API key details

Once you are happy with the details, click the Create button.

Retrieving Your API Key

The developer console then presents the API key it is has generated for you as I have partially shown in Figure 15-4.

Figure 15-4. API key presented by the Google Developer Console

> **Caution**   *Never* share your API key with anyone. Even though it is nominally tied to your Android
> package, and you notionally have a unique package namespace that prevents others from abusing
> your API Project (and your credit card), sophisticated attacks can use this information to your detriment.
> Keep your API key secret, and use it only where needed in manifest files, layouts, or resource files.

All current Google Maps API keys begin with the substring 'Alza', though I have obscured
my API key for the reasons I mentioned in the caution statement.

Building Your First Maps Application

After you've completed the tasks of setting up your Google developer account and API key,
you might be wondering how much different a maps-based application is from the regular
Android development you have learned so far. The good news is that conceptually you are
now on very familiar ground, with all the earlier topics in this book are perfectly applicable to
building maps-based applications.

However, there are a few nuances to be aware of when it comes to composing layouts and
choosing permissions and device sensor options. Let's delve into all of these choices as we
build our first maps-based application.

Using MapActivity or FragmentActivity with MapView

Historically, in order for a MapView widget to display a map in your application, it needed to
be placed within the purpose-built MapActivity subclass that you'd have needed to define
from the base class provided with the Android framework. A MapActivity subclass acts to
do a bunch of the stitching behind the scenes, and thus it handles much of the logistics
surrounding the "tiles" that make up a Google map and their display within your layout.

With the advent of fragments, which I covered in Chapter 11, much more flexible ways of
working with maps were introduced that allowed a MapView to inhabit a fragment and retain
much of the behind-the-scenes magic that makes using maps so easy. Let's explore this
approach so that you are armed with the latest and greatest way of building and working
with map-based applications.

We'll now explore the contemporary approach in some example applications so you become
familiar with the current preferred development style and adapt it to your needs.

Permissions and Manifest Settings for Maps

Regardless of whether you use an old-style or new-style approach to creating location-aware applications with Google Maps, you need to include several permissions in your manifest file. We cover permissions in more detail in Chapter 20, but for now, you need to adhere to these recommendations.

At a minimum, your application needs `android.permission.INTERNET` and `android.permission.ACCESS_COURSE_LOCATION`. The latter allows you to use the APIs that let Android talk to on-device sensors and radios that can approximate location at a course level. This includes cellular (tower) data and wi-fi signals, but not GPS. IF you wish to have GPS location data included "under the hood" when Android satisfies various location-style API calls, you need to include `android.permission.ACCESS_FINE_LOCATION`.

Strictly speaking, some maps-based functionality will work without these permissions, but I'd strongly advise you to include them so that features that maps expose (directions, journey time calculations) can work seamlessly for your users.

Using the external Google APIs library also requires a custom permission that it enforces (more on this in Chapter 20 as well). You need to include the `com.google.android.providers.gsf.permission.READ_GSERVICES` permission in order to be able to include and use the Google APIs.

Your `<application>` element also needs to include a `<meta-data>` custom child element that specifies version information for the Google API library that you will set as a minimum for using your application. For example, when building applications to target the Google APIs released as part of Google Play services for Android version 6.0 Marshmallow, the `<meta-data>` element would look as follows:

```
<meta-data
    android:name="com.google.android.gms.version"
    android:value="8298000"
 />
```

The `android:name` value has not changed since Android KitKat 4.2, but the `android:value` changes with Google API (and implicitly Google Play services) versions. The current value for Android version 6.0 Marshmallow is 8298000,but you should check for updates periodically and decide if you wish to increase your target API level, just as you do for the Android API level, or whether you want to set a more flexible API level tolerance as I describe a little later in the chapter.

The final entry that you should add to your manifest is the API key you generated for your application from the Google Developers Console. This is another `<meta-data>` element, and it takes the following form:

```
<meta-data
    android:name="com.google.android.maps.v2.API_KEY"
    android:value="PUT_YOUR_API_KEY_VALUE_HERE"
/>
```

You can also reference a key value stored as a string in the `strings.xml` resource file (e.g., `android:value="@string/my_secret_maps_api_key"`).

Building the Layout for Your Map Application

Creating a map-based application with `FragmentActivity` is very similar to some of the other activity helper subclasses you have used throughout the book, such as `ActionBarActivity` for building an `ActionBar`-centric application, and `ListActivity` for building activities that are dominated by a `ListView` widget and the data populating it.

Listing 15-1 shows the layout for a straightforward map application named `MapsExample`, which you can find in the `ch15/MapsExample` folder. Note in particular the way in which the `SupportMapFragment` (that implicitly houses a `MapView` for you) is referenced. Because our desired map classes are provided by a separate library (the Google APIs) outside of the Android API and its widget namespace, we need to use the fully-qualified package name reference in the layout XML.

Listing 15-1. The Layout for a Maps-based Activity

```
<fragment xmlns:android="http://schemas.android.com/apk/res/android"
    xmlns:tools="http://schemas.android.com/tools"
    android:layout_width="match_parent"
    android:layout_height="match_parent"
    android:id="@+id/map"
    tools:context=".MapsExampleActivity"
    android:name="com.google.android.gms.maps.SupportMapFragment" />
```

The `com.google.android.gms.maps.SupportMapFragment` takes care rendering the map canvas for us and placing a `MapView`. You can add other normal attributes to this `<fragment>`, although some of them may be overridden implicitly when the fragment enters various parts of its lifecycle.

Adding Code for a Basic Map

The code for rendering a map is unbelievably simple, although there are a few traps that you as a developer should watch out for; we will cover those shortly. Listing 15-2 shows the bare-minimum code to draw a map and puts one embellishment upon it.

Listing 15-2. Code to Render a Map and Add a Push-Pin for London

```
package com.artifexdigital.android.mapsexample;

import android.support.v4.app.FragmentActivity;
import android.os.Bundle;
import com.google.android.gms.maps.GoogleMap;
import com.google.android.gms.maps.SupportMapFragment;
import com.google.android.gms.maps.model.LatLng;
import com.google.android.gms.maps.model.MarkerOptions;
```

```
public class MapsExampleActivity extends FragmentActivity {

    private GoogleMap myMap;

    @Override
    protected void onCreate(Bundle savedInstanceState) {
        super.onCreate(savedInstanceState);
        setContentView(R.layout.activity_maps_example);
        createMap();
    }

    @Override
    protected void onResume() {
        super.onResume();
        createMap();
    }

    private void createMap() {
        myMap = ((SupportMapFragment) getSupportFragmentManager().findFragmentById
        (R.id.map))
                .getMap();
        myMap.addMarker(new MarkerOptions().position(new LatLng(51.5, 0)).title("London"));
    }
}
```

That is all it takes to render a basic map. You can run this code (from the ch15/MapsExample folder) on an emulator that includes the Google APIs. If you haven't already done so, you should create at least one AVD based on the Google-API-enhanced device images.

In our onCreate() override, we perform the normal steps to restore any state and inflate our layout. We then call the createMap() method to do the work of putting together the map itself. We do this from onResume() as well to ensure our map is re-created if any configurations change, especially those triggered from rotation.

The createMap() method uses the SupportMapFragment library and the regular findFragmentById() method to find the ID of the com.google.android.gms.maps. SupportMapFragment from our layout. The .getMap() call does the work of actually getting the map tiles, rendering them, and so forth.

I have added one extra to this map, by using the .addMarker() method for a map to create a Marker object and position it over London, in the UK. I did this by passing a latitude and longitude pair as either integers or floats.

GOOGLE APIS, GOOGLE PLAY, ANDROID APIS, AND VERSIONING CHAOS

If you attempt to use an AVD based on the Level 22 APIs and Google APIs, you will encounter an issue that the combination of those APIs throws at developers; in these cases, the maps library expects a later version of the Google APIs than the device images provide. This is a convoluted problem but you can fix it. If you have this problem while you are attempting to run the example application (or any application that includes the Google APIs), you can spot it by looking for the following LogCat entry when the application fails to show a map:

```
Google Play services out of date. Requires 7095000 but found 6774470
```

Instead of showing a map, your activity will probably show a warning about Play Services needing to be updated and offer an update button. So save yourself some pain and use a Level 21- or Level 23-based AVD instead. Even then, you will have instances when this problem can strike, mainly due to the frequent updates Google pushes for Google Play services and the hoops a developer needs to go through to update those services on an AVD. In those circumstances, the easiest solution is to change the Google Play services dependency to be far more forgiving of different versions. If you encounter this problem with your AVD, open your `build.gradle` file for the app module, and change the dependency for "play services" to the following:

```
compile 'com.google.android.gms:play-services:6+'
```

You'll likely see a far more specific version to start with, such as 8.3.0. By using the value 6+, you are telling gradle to tolerate any build of Google Play services from the last few years.

When run, the MapsExample application shows a simple map, as you can see in Figure 15-5.

Figure 15-5. *The Basic MapsExample application running*

After all the effort of setting up your API keys, and adding a little code, you have maps at your disposal.

This looks deceptive. Problems can and do crop up due to the lack of the Google APIs on a device, and that means it is prudent to add some checks to your code to handle cases in which the map object is null because the original instantiation failed as a result of missing APIs. Listing 15-3 shows a slightly modified version of the stock Google example that is created for you if you use the Google Maps template when you create a new project in Android Studio or Eclipse.

Listing 15-3. Simple Map Code with Missing-API Handling

```
package com.artifexdigital.android.mapsexample;

import android.support.v4.app.FragmentActivity;
import android.os.Bundle;

import com.google.android.gms.maps.GoogleMap;
import com.google.android.gms.maps.SupportMapFragment;
import com.google.android.gms.maps.model.LatLng;
import com.google.android.gms.maps.model.MarkerOptions;

public class MapsExampleActivity extends FragmentActivity {

    private GoogleMap myMap; // Might be null if Google Play services APK is not available.

    @Override
    protected void onCreate(Bundle savedInstanceState) {
        super.onCreate(savedInstanceState);
        setContentView(R.layout.activity_maps_example);
        setUpMapIfNeeded();
    }

    @Override
    protected void onResume() {
        super.onResume();
        setUpMapIfNeeded();
    }

    private void setUpMapIfNeeded() {
        // Do a null check to confirm that we have not already instantiated the map.
        if (myMap == null) {
            // Try to obtain the map from the SupportMapFragment.
            myMap = ((SupportMapFragment) getSupportFragmentManager().findFragmentById
            (R.id.map))
                    .getMap();
            // Check if we were successful in obtaining the map.
            if (myMap != null) {
                setUpMap();
            }
        }
    }

    private void setUpMap() {
        myMap.addMarker(new MarkerOptions().position(new LatLng(51.5, 0)).title("London"));
    }
}
```

Here I split the initial `myMap` object setup from the other code that adds the marker. In `setUpMapIfNeeded()`, Google's example code shows the typical way to test if the `GoogleMap` object is still null after attempting the `.getMap()` call; it then shows how to skip any additional map method calls if the object is null (because they would fail). In general, you should add this kind of protection to your code so the rest of your application logic can continue to function on devices that lack the Google APIs.

Obviously you can add a lot more to the map to suit your every need, so let's cover a range of the most popular options.

Adding Flair and Features to Your Maps

The market pin added to the map in the `MapsExample` application is one of the familiar flourishes that you have no doubt experienced in your own use of maps. There are many more tricks and treats that you can include when devising functionality for your maps. You can configure many of these options in the layout file and/or in your Java code. I will mix and match to get you comfortable with both approaches for some of the most common additions to maps.

Zoomin'

The initial map depicted in Figure 15-5 shows London from the aerial perspective of half of planet Earth. This is probably not so useful if, for instance, you are looking for the nearest supermarket. You can add zoom controls to your map through the `getUiSettings().setZoomControlsEnabled()` method. This takes a simple `Boolean`, which you set to `true` to enable zoom controls.

True North

Before the advent of spoken turn-by-turn directions in your favorite mapping applications, a good percentage of users used the compass on a map to help orient themselves. You can add the compass to your map using another of the `getUiSettings()` submethods—the `.setCompassEnabled()` option, which also takes a `Boolean`.

Toolbars and theMy Location Button

You can enable other normal features, like the maps toolbar and the My Location button, by using additional `getUiSettings()` calls. The `setMapToolbarEnabled()` and `setMyLocationButtonEnabled()` methods do exactly what their names describe.

Shakin' It!

There is more than one way to interact with a map on an Android device. One of the more interesting ways is to use gestures and device movement to control maps and related information. Additional getUiSettings() calls can handle shakes, rattles, and rolls to let your user play with your maps. Some of the major options are as follows:

- setRotateGesturesEnabled(): This method allows users to use a two-finger spin gesture to have the compass orientation rotate for your map.

- setScrollGesturesEnabled(): With this method, swiping up and down on the map allows scrolling through (virtual) space.

- setTiltGesturesEnabled(): This is particularly useful with building map types and satellite/street-view maps. This alters the viewer's perspective from the default bird's eye view to one of their own choosing based on the titling gesture they use.

- setZoomGesturesEnabled(): The infamous "pinch to zoom" feature. This is very handy for the user, and was once a minefield of patent litigation between Google and one other notable mobile technology company.

Changing Map Type

The default map type for MapView objects in fragments or standalone is very useful for many situations. But there are times when seeing building outlines, real satellite imagery, or some hybrid combination of map type is more suited for the use you have in mind.

Your map object includes the .setMapType() method to indicate which of the supported map types you wish to display. This takes an integer value, with these constants provided as part of the GoogleMap package:

- MAP_TYPE_NORMAL: The default cartoon-style map with roads, parks, street names, and so on.

- MAP_TYPE_SATELLITE: Uses the satellite imagery from Google Earth to show real images of the map area. This includes the place names, street names, and so on from a normal map.

- MAP_TYPE_TERRAIN: The terrain view shows all of the geographic features of your map area, but it omits label overlays like street names by default.

- MAP_TYPE_HYBRID: The mix of everything—satellite imagery, street outlines and names, terrain features, the works!

Your maps are of type MAP_TYPE_NORMAL by default. You can change types at any time.

Listeners for Every Conceivable Type of Map Interaction

There are no fewer than 10 different listeners you can configure to interact with maps and user actions. These range from the straightforward—such as the map equivalent of an onClickListener, named, as you might suspect, the onMapClickListener—to esoteric options like the onIndoorStateChangeListener for dealing with transitions to and from indoor maps.

As with other listeners, you can configure a range of responses to deal with the events the listener captures. In a straightforward example, we can register an onMapClickListener with the .setOnMapClickListener() method like this:

```
myMap.setOnMapClickListener(this);
```

This sets the fragment to be its own handler and requires us to extend the class definition to implement OnMapClickListener and to implement an onMapClick() method to deal with the associated callback. We could structure a very simple example as follows:

```
public void onMapClick(LatLng point) {
    myMap.animateCamera(CameraUpdateFactory.newLatLng(point));
    Toast.makeText(getApplicationContext(), point.toString(),
        Toast.LENGTH_LONG).show();
}
```

The calls of note here include using the animateCamera() method to move the map to the point the user clicked, and using the LatLng object passed to the call back to populate a Toast message that tells the user what latitude and longitude they clicked.

Even More Map Options

There are so many more options for maps that they could fill a book. In fact, several books have been written just on Google Maps APIs and using them with Android. I would suggest *Beginning Google Maps API 3*, by Gabriel Svennerberg (Apress, 2010). Rather than turn this book into a clone of Gabriel's book, let us finish by looking at an updated MapsExample2 application that includes all of the preceding options and a few more (see Listing 15-4).

Listing 15-4. Implementing a Range of Map Features in MapsExample2

```
package com.artifexdigital.android.mapsexample;

import android.support.v4.app.FragmentActivity;
import android.os.Bundle;
import android.widget.Toast;
import com.google.android.gms.maps.CameraUpdateFactory;
import com.google.android.gms.maps.GoogleMap;
import com.google.android.gms.maps.SupportMapFragment;
import com.google.android.gms.maps.model.LatLng;
import com.google.android.gms.maps.model.MarkerOptions;
```

```java
public class MapsExampleActivity extends FragmentActivity implements GoogleMap.
OnMapClickListener {

    private GoogleMap myMap;

    @Override
    protected void onCreate(Bundle savedInstanceState) {
        super.onCreate(savedInstanceState);
        setContentView(R.layout.activity_maps_example);
        setUpMapIfNeeded();
    }

    @Override
    protected void onResume() {
        super.onResume();
        setUpMapIfNeeded();
    }

    private void setUpMapIfNeeded() {
        if (myMap == null) {
            // Try to obtain the map from the SupportMapFragment.
            myMap = ((SupportMapFragment) getSupportFragmentManager().findFragmentById(R.
            id.map))
                    .getMap();
            // Check if map is found
            if (myMap != null) {
                createMap();
            }
        }
    }

    private void createMap() {
        myMap.addMarker(new MarkerOptions().position(new LatLng(51.5, 0)).title("London"));
        myMap.getUiSettings().setZoomControlsEnabled(true);
        myMap.getUiSettings().setCompassEnabled(true);
        myMap.setMapType(GoogleMap.MAP_TYPE_SATELLITE);
        myMap.setOnMapClickListener(this);
    }

    @Override
    public void onMapClick(LatLng point) {
        myMap.animateCamera(CameraUpdateFactory.newLatLng(point));
        Toast.makeText(getApplicationContext(), point.toString(),
                Toast.LENGTH_LONG).show();
    }
}
```

You can run this example yourself from the ch15/MapsExample2 folder (do not forget to substitute your own API key); you should see the results that appear in Figure 15-6.

Figure 15-6. *The MapsExample2 application showing our maps enhancements*

Summary

This chapter provided you with a very fast crash course on mapping and location for Android, as well as much of the background and history on how today's state-of-affairs came to be. If you want to learn more, the developer.google.com and developer.android.com sites have copious information on incorporating maps, and the OpenStreetMap and HERE Maps sites include even more. Happy mapping!

Working with Resources and Services

Weaving the Web with Android

Your journey through Android's capabilities has already taken you through many of the widgets and UI elements that form your basic toolkit for building applications. It has also introduced you to device capabilities that will bring features and functionality to your applications. There is, however, an 800-pound gorilla in the Android application development room, and that is the Internet.

Whether you want to bring HTML-based interfaces to your application, use services and capabilities on the Internet, or just work to download files and data to your application from a web server, Android has you covered. In this chapter, I explore three key building blocks for incorporating Internet-based data and features into your Android applications: the WebView widget for displaying web pages, the AndroidHttpClient and HttpURLConnection for richer manipulation of web services, and the DownloadManager for working with data in bulk.

Working with the WebView Widget

You can think of the WebView widget as being like most other UI components in Android—it provides a particular kind of UI experience for relevant data and functionality. With the appropriate layout in place, you can then drive a web-browser-like display to show the content of a page you specify. I say "web-browser-like" because under the hood, Android is using the WebKit plumbing that forms the core of the Chrome browser to provide the parsing and rendering capabilities needed to show web content. Interestingly, Chrome for Android itself uses a separate parsing and rendering engine, just to keep things a little complicated.

There are some limitations and additional points for you to consider when using a WebView widget, so let's explore an example I can use as the basis for covering these.

Creating a Simple Application with a WebView

You can place a WebView in a layout much as you would any other component, either by itself or as one of a number of widgets in your activity. Listing 16-1 shows a straightforward layout where the WebView is the only widget, and it takes pretty much all of the available screen space.

Listing 16-1. A Layout Incorporating a WebView

```
<RelativeLayout xmlns:android="http://schemas.android.com/apk/res/android"
    xmlns:tools="http://schemas.android.com/tools" android:layout_width="match_parent"
    android:layout_height="match_parent"
    android:paddingLeft="@dimen/activity_horizontal_margin"
    android:paddingRight="@dimen/activity_horizontal_margin"
    android:paddingTop="@dimen/activity_vertical_margin"
    android:paddingBottom="@dimen/activity_vertical_margin"
    tools:context=".WebViewExample">

    <WebView
        android:layout_width="wrap_content"
        android:layout_height="match_parent"
        android:id="@+id/webView" />

</RelativeLayout>
```

No surprises here, although at this point it is worth flagging the first limitation of a WebView. If you look at the android:layout_height attribute, you can see I have chosen match_parent. This is the normal recommendation for WebView widgets. You can choose wrap_content, but there are known issues with both the WebView and its parent being set to wrap_content that result in incorrect sizing and scaling—and that basically result in a poor UI.

With a working layout defined, some Java logic is required to inflate the layout and do something useful with the WebView. The WebViewExample sample application in the ch16/WebViewExample folder uses the Java shown in Listing 16-2.

Listing 16-2. The WebViewExample Implementation

```
package com.artifexdigital.android.webviewexample;

import android.app.Activity;
import android.os.Bundle;
import android.webkit.WebView;

public class WebViewExample extends Activity {
    WebView myWV;

    @Override
    protected void onCreate(Bundle savedInstanceState) {
        super.onCreate(savedInstanceState);
        setContentView(R.layout.activity_web_view_example);
```

```
    myWV = (WebView)findViewById(R.id.webView);
    myWV.loadUrl("http://www.artifexdigital.com");
  }

}
```

Such a small amount of code is capable of a great deal, depending on what the target URL provided in the .loadUrl() call returns. The myWV object is an instance of the android.webkit.WebView class, and that is worthy of comment. The Internet and Android's WebKit plumbing are considered first class citizens (apologies for the "class" joke), such that WebKit has its own highest-level package in Android.

In other respects, the onCreate() method is quite simple, defining the myWV object for later use, inflating the layout—including the WebView defined—and retrieving the ID of the WebView for the instantiation call. That puts the code at the point where .loadUrl() can be called.

Normally .loadUrl() is called using the incarnation that takes a simple string parameter. There is a variant of .loadUrl() that takes both the desired URL and a second parameter as a String collection of additional HTTP headers to use.

Simple and Not-So-Simple WebView Security

At this point the WebViewExample application is almost ready to run. What remains is for us to add the necessary permissions to the manifest to allow access to the Internet. Providing the permission is as simple as adding the <uses-permission> option for the android.permission.INTERNET option in our AndroidManifest.xml file, as shown in Listing 16-3.

Listing 16-3. Adding the Permissions Needed to Access URLs through WebView

```
<?xml version="1.0" encoding="utf-8"?>
<manifest xmlns:android="http://schemas.android.com/apk/res/android"
    package="com.artifexdigital.android.webviewexample" >

    <uses-permission android:name="android.permission.INTERNET" />

    <application
        android:allowBackup="true"
        android:icon="@mipmap/ic_launcher"
        android:label="@string/app_name"
        android:theme="@style/AppTheme" >
        <activity
            android:name=".WebViewExample"
            android:label="@string/app_name" >
            <intent-filter>
                <action android:name="android.intent.action.MAIN" />

                <category android:name="android.intent.category.LAUNCHER" />
            </intent-filter>
        </activity>
    </application>

</manifest>
```

Without the android.permission.INTERNET permission in place, your application throws a range of unpredictable errors depending on the version of Android on which you run it and the API levels specified in the manifest file. Modern versions of Android, including Marshmallow 6.0 and Lollipop 5.0, show the error depicted in Figure 16-1.

Figure 16-1. Errors showing in later versions of Android when the INTERNET permission is missing

You will probably confuse most lay users with a message like net:ERR_CACHE_MISS. Even somewhat web-savvy users might be mistaken and think the problem is with caching or something unrelated to permissions. You are also unlikely to actually ship an application with this problem, since hopefully you test your applications before you ship them and when you do, you notice the web page you are requesting is definitely not shown.

With the correct permissions in place in your manifest file, the WebViewExample application should behave as expected and actually load the page. Figure 16-2 shows the successful loading and rendering of the target URL.

Figure 16-2. Successfully loading a URL with WebView

Android's security regime with WebView does not end with the android.permission.INTERNET setting. If you look at both Figures 16-1 and 16-2, you should notice that the WebView might have used the WebKit browser underpinnings to render output, but some other notable parts of typical web browsers are missing.

For instance, there is no address bar shown in the WebViewExample application. This is the default with WebView widgets; it prevents the WebView from being rerouted to other URLs unless you explicitly override this behavior. You will also notice there are no scroll bars. This is not a security measure, but rather a pragmatic interface choice on devices with no pointer. Instead, users of your application can scroll by touch-and-drag with their finger.

By default, Android also prohibits JavaScript execution in a WebView. You can change this restriction by invoking the method getSettings().setJavaScriptEnabled(true) on the WebView object.

| GOOGLE, ANDROID, AND WEBVIEW SECURITY FLAWS |

The history of security issues with WebView goes back some time, with a number of instances mentioned widely online. Google's current practice is to patch WebView bugs promptly, which is in line with its overall security practice. Unfortunately, the combination of working through many handset manufacturers who do not use Google's patching priorities and historic issues with poor upgrade paths means that older versions of Android have unpatched WebView bugs. You can help yourself protect your code and your users in a variety of ways, but it is worth keeping in mind Google's official stance on WebView for older pre-Android 4.4 devices:

> *"If the affected version [of WebView] is before 4.4, we generally do not develop the patches ourselves, but welcome patches with the report for consideration. Other than notifying OEMs, we will not be able to take action on any report that is affecting versions before 4.4 that are not accompanied with a patch."*

How's that for commitment to the long tail of Android versions? Android Lollipop 5.0 and Marshmallow 6.0 benefit from a rearchitecting of WebView by Google; in fact, Google is now releasing WebView as a stand-alone application so that, in the future, it can be updated separately from the Android version of the device.

Building HTML Layouts with WebView

An alternative to simply pointing your WebView to a URL is to provide the HTML that can be rendered within the WebView widget yourself and load it so it can be used with the loadData() method. Although you may see this as duplicating capabilities, it opens up a range of possibilities. You can, for instance, use HTML fragments to draw UI elements that stock Android widgets do not cover. You can also use it to display data fetched from a file, a database, or somewhere else online that is too big or otherwise cumbersome to bundle at application install time. And, of course, you can go so far as to design the entire layout of your application in HTML. There are pros and cons to this approach, which are argued about extensively in many fine books and websites. I'll spare you a long diatribe on this point and assume you can judge for yourself if HTML is a useful interface design approach.

The loadData() method has several overloaded forms. The simplest version takes three parameters, all of which are string values.

- The HTML content, which is parsed and rendered to display in the WebView.

- A MIME type for the content, which is almost always text/HTML.

- The encoding used for the HTML content. UTF-8 is a safe option in almost all cases.

It is easy to experiment with HTML-based layouts assuming you have some knowledge of HTML. I have adapted the original WebViewExample application to replace the loadUrl() call with a loadData() call, which you can find in the ch16/WebViewExample2 folder. The layout for WebViewExample2 is exactly the same as it was for WebViewExample. The Java code differs, as shown in bold in Listing 16-4.

Listing 16-4. The Modified WebViewExample2 Using loadData()

```java
package com.artifexdigital.android.webviewexample2;

import android.app.Activity;
import android.os.Bundle;
import android.webkit.WebView;

public class WebViewExample2 extends Activity {
    WebView myWV;

    @Override
    protected void onCreate(Bundle savedInstanceState) {
        super.onCreate(savedInstanceState);
        setContentView(R.layout.activity_web_view_example2);

        myWV = (WebView)findViewById(R.id.webView);
        myWV.loadData("<html><p><b>A WebView HTML Page</b></p></html>",
                "text/html",
                "UTF-8");
    }

}
```

Here you can see the HTML payload provided to the loadData() method. Although the example HTML is simple, you can use almost all of the HTML5 elements with only a few minor exceptions. These include some quirks and limitations for <canvas> and the HTML5 video viewport extensions. (The Android developer website has more details on the particular supported behavior.) For easier reading, I have also written the HTML payload directly into the Java method call. In reality, it is far better to create string resources for your HTML in your strings.xml file and refer to them by ID.

When you run the WebViewExample2 application, you should see output similar to that shown in Figure 16-3.

Figure 16-3. HTML rendered in a WebView using loadData()

As with the earlier WebViewExample application, there is no address bar and no scroll bars. As mentioned earlier in the chapter, a user can scroll using swipe gestures on the screen. As a developer, you also have a range of programmatic controls over scrolling and web page behavior, via methods on the WebView object such as these:

- goBack(), which is analogous to hitting the back button in a browser, sends the user back to the previous page visited in the WebView.

- goForward() moves forward one page in the history of pages visited in the WebView, assuming at least one page forward has been visited.

- canGoBack() returns a boolean indicating if the WebView has any history, and therefore whether goBack() would do anything.

- canGoForward(), like canGoBack(), returns a boolean indicating if there's a "future history" to which the WebView can progress.

- reload() reloads the content of the WebView from the source (HTML or URL).

- clearCache() removes all cached items from the WebView's inventory of form entries, images, and so on.

- clearHistory() clears the history of URLs visited within the WebView object.

Many more methods are available for WebView; an exhaustive list is at `http://developer.`
`android.com/reference/android/webkit/WebView.html`.

UI-less Internet Interaction with Android

Displaying web content in a `WebView` widget is a common way of integrating various Internet-
based sources into Android applications. However, there are many cases in which an
application's interaction with a website or other Internet resource is all about consuming
data, or accessing web-exposed APIs, such as SOAP web services or RESTful JSON API
end points. In these cases, functionality and interaction are all possible without any UI to
speak of, although the results of these actions probably get communicated to the user in
some way. For instance, a music playlist might be updated, new features of a game might be
exposed, or the results of an online purchase might be displayed.

Whatever the need, Android provides a multitude of techniques so you can interact with
the Internet without a UI. The three principle approaches are via the Apache `HttpClient`
interface, the `AndroidHttpClient` object, and the `HttpURLConnection` object.

Why Multiple Approaches to Web Interaction?

As is the case when they discuss any technology that is entering its fourth or fifth decade
(depending on how you count), many people have differing opinions on the "best" way to
incorporate Internet capabilities into software and libraries developers use. Each package,
library, or class Android supports has its benefits and drawbacks, and you will not find a
consensus on which is "best" to use. The following sections discuss the three most popular
approaches at a high level.

The Apache HttpClient Approach

The venerable approach to Internet connectivity in Android is the Apache `HttpClient`. As
the name suggests, this was sourced from an Apache-sponsored project and featured in the
earliest Android devices. As far back as Android 2.2 Froyo, Google began signaling that this
interface's days were numbered when it introduced the parallel `AndroidHttpClient` object.
Most of the capabilities you would expect are present with `HttpClient`-derived objects and
the related `HttpRequest` and `HttpResponse` implementations, which allows you to conduct
common Internet-enabled tasks.

These are the main issues with using Apache `HttpClient`:

- No default handing of SSL; the interface instead relies on you as the
developer to do the hard work of certificate management.

- Single-threaded by default, with significant overhead to work in a
multithreaded Android application.

- Marked as deprecated from Android API level 22 on (and will be
removed from the Android SDK at some imminent point).

You can still use Apache `HttpClient` as your Internet connectivity approach today, and it is a good option if you are targeting the many older Android 2.2 Froyo and 2.3 Gingerbread devices on the market. But be aware that its days are numbered, and other approaches target Android devices of all vintages.

The AndroidHttpClient Approach

With the release of Android 2.2, Google introduced the `AndroidHttpClient` as its preferred approach to HTTP-and-friends interaction. Bundled as part of the `android.net.http` package, it is an optimized implementation of `DefaultHttpClient` that tries to help you, the developer, make good design choices. The following are among the many things it does for you:

- Integrated SSL handling with Android certificate management capabilities, which means you do not need to handcraft the certificate handling seen in Apache `HttpClient`.

- Better threading capabilities and the "benefit" of enforced performance controls; it provides these by insisting that all activity happens off the main UI thread. We will explore this more later in the chapter.

- Control over various HTTP connection and header attributes, such as the user agent string.

- Various utility methods to handle more elaborate HTTP payloads (`GZIP`, for example), date manipulation, and more.

One of the drawbacks for `AndroidHttpClient` is the loss of default cookie handling. Instead of seamlessly caching cookies for the life of the object, as a developer, you need to use a `HttpContext` object to persist cookies. The other principal thing to consider is whether only targeting devices running Android 2.2 or later suits you. As of this writing, this decision would encompass around 70 percent of the Android devices in circulation; but if you are aiming for all 100 percent, there are other options.

The HttpURLConnection Approach

If I told you there was a "venerable" approach to Internet integration in your application that was also as future-proof as Android itself, would you be interested? I hope the answer is "yes," because that is what we explore next. The Internet predates Android by decades, and Java has provided a variety of approaches to working with Internet-based resources for many years longer than Android has existed. The `HttpURLConnection` package has been a mainstay of Java for a while, and because of Android's Java underpinnings, it is also available as a viable option to help you develop Internet-powered applications.

`HttpURLConnection` has advantages and disadvantages, just as `HttpClient` and `AndroidHttpClient` have. For instance, Android enforces all network activity on non-main-UI thread code. But its universality in being available for all versions of Android, and, of course, wherever else Java is used, make it powerful and attractive. A huge number of examples of using `HttpClient` and `AndroidHttpClient` are online and in other books, including the Android Developer website. To help you expand to cover the fullest possible range of approaches to Internet interaction, I'll now explore an example with `HttpURLConnection` so you can judge for yourself when you are comparing using this to those other examples.

Building a JSON-based Application with HttpURLConnection

The advent of JavaScript Object Notation, or JSON, has somewhat revolutionized many forms of application development. Many databases now support it natively, many developers use it to describe objects, and many APIs—particularly REST-based APIs on the Internet—use it as the data format for sending information to and fro. You could use JSON from APIs like this in any number of ways, but how would you fetch and send JSON to these distant REST APIs? A tour through the `HttpUrlConnectionExample` application should shine a light on the mechanics.

Layout or No Layout?

As mentioned earlier in the chapter, although you will want some form of UI for the user, such as a `WebView`, you don't necessarily want to show UI components exposing the plumbing of how a web connection goes about its work (regardless of library or package in use). The layout for our `HttpUrlConnectionExample` application is very straightforward, and you can see it in Figure 16-4.

Figure 16-4. The UI provided as a courtesy for the HttpUrlConnectionExample application

I will spare you the layout XML file—as you can imagine, it is quite sparse. Check the ch16/HttpUrlConnectionExample folder if you are curious. The real activity in the application happens soon after launch, when all the promise of the HttpURLConnection approach is harnessed.

More Than Just a Series of Tubes

The plumbing for our application demonstrates the essential pieces of the HttpURLConnection technique. Listing 16-5 covers the Java logic for the example.

Listing 16-5. The Java Code Powering the HttpUrlConnectionExample Application

```java
package com.artifexdigital.android.httpurlconnectionexample;

import android.app.Activity;
import android.os.AsyncTask;
import android.os.Bundle;
import android.widget.Toast;

import java.io.BufferedReader;
import java.io.IOException;
import java.io.InputStream;
import java.io.InputStreamReader;
import java.net.HttpURLConnection;
import java.net.URL;

public class HttpUrlConnectionExample extends Activity {

    @Override
    protected void onCreate(Bundle savedInstanceState) {
        super.onCreate(savedInstanceState);
        setContentView(R.layout.activity_http_url_connection_example);

        //invoke an asyncTask-based object to do work off main UI thread
        //note the blank string placeholder, for easy conversation to take user input
        new InternetOperation().execute("");
    }

    private String fetchUrl(String url) {
        String urlContent = "";
        StringBuilder myStrBuff = new StringBuilder();

        try{
            URL myUrl = new URL(url);
            HttpURLConnection myConn = (HttpURLConnection)myUrl.openConnection();
            myConn.setRequestProperty("User-Agent", "");
            myConn.setRequestMethod("GET");
            myConn.setDoInput(true);
            myConn.connect();
```

```
            InputStream myInStrm = myConn.getInputStream();
            BufferedReader myBuffRdr = new BufferedReader
                    (new InputStreamReader(myInStrm));

            while ((urlContent = myBuffRdr.readLine()) != null) {
                myStrBuff.append(urlContent);
            }

        } catch (IOException e) {
            // do error handling here
            e.printStackTrace();
        }

        return myStrBuff.toString();
    }

    private class InternetOperation extends AsyncTask<String, Void, String> {

        @Override
        protected void onPreExecute() {}

        @Override
        protected String doInBackground(String... params) {
            String myJson = "";
            myJson = fetchUrl("http://api.openweathermap.org/data/2.5/weather?q=London,uk");
            return myJson;
        }

        @Override
        protected void onPostExecute(String result) {
            int duration = Toast.LENGTH_LONG;

            Toast toast = Toast.makeText(getApplicationContext(), result, duration);
            toast.show();
        }
        @Override
        protected void onProgressUpdate(Void... values) {}
    }
}
```

That might seem like a lot of code for what I promised was a simple example, but in reality, it is easy to digest. The action happens across three distinct parts of the code.

The onCreate() method has very little content. It inflates a layout that is not strictly needed but that is helpful in this example as a container for showing some of the trace information about what happens in other parts of the code. The last line of code in onCreate() is the secret sauce that drives the rest of the fetching and display of a URL and its content. Here, I create a new InternetOperation object, which is a subclass of the AsyncTask<> base class Android provides for invoking additional threads.

Jumping to the InternetOperation implementation itself, I have chosen the overloaded form of AsyncTask<> that takes a String collection for the doInBackground() phase and also uses a string for onPostExecute(). We pass the URL provided in the first String to the fetchUrl() method—which I cover shortly—and pass back the returned payload in the results member of InternetOperation (inherited from the parent class). The onPostExecute() method takes the result and creates a toast to display that onscreen. Obviously this is a little contrived, since in real life, you would likely want to parse the resulting payload from the URL, interrogate the HTTP return code (200 for OK, 404 for not found, and so on), and decide whether to render the response as a web page, a transaction result, or as some other action.

The fetchUrl() method does the bulk of the work preparing for the URL retrieval; it performs the actual work of contacting the URL and streaming and processing its content into a String object to return to the caller. The conceptual order of the code is as follows:

1. Define a new URL object and assign the user-provided URL String to it.

2. Define a new HttpURLConnection object, named myConn, for the URL object.

3. Set the desired paramaters and attributes that the connection should have and use. This is done with various calls to myConn's methods.

4. myConn.setRequestProperty() can set a wide range of HTTP-related values, and in the case shown, it adds a blank User-Agent string for identifying the client application. Obviously you can use any User-Agent string you like to mimic well-known browsers, crawlers, and so on.

5. myConn.setReqeustMethod() sets the HTTP verb to GET. This implies that various other settings are included in the header of the HTTP call when it is made, rather than the payload being used as it is in the POST method. This is a much larger topic in its own right; you'll find plenty of additional information online.

6. myConn.setDoInput() is set to true, which flags to the server that the response body will be consumed and used. There are times when you wish to set this to false to indicate that only the header of the response is important and that performance can be improved by discarding the response body.

7. With the HttpURLConnection properties set as desired, invoke .connect() to actually connect to the URL and see what its server does in response.

8. The response is gathered via a BufferedReader and InputStream for ultimately returning as a string of the web page content or as a server response.

Many, many more options and methods are available to `HttpURLConnection` objects, and Oracle, as the current "owner" of Java, provides an extensive set of documentation on them at `http://docs.oracle.com/javase/<insert your java version here>/docs/api/java/net/URLConnection.html`.

Running HttpUrlConnectionExample and Its Results

With the logic explained, and the world's sparsest UI in place, running the code is as easy as launching it in your chosen AVD. For this example, I have included a URL for publicly available weather data from the Open Weathermap project.

`http://api.openweathermap.org/data/2.5/weather?q=London,uk`

If you check this URL in any browser, you should see a resulting JSON object returned as the "web page." The content should look something like Listing 16-6 (depending on the day you look for the weather). Note that I have compressed the normally white-space-heavy JSON layout to save space.

Listing 16-6. The JSON Payload Returned from Open Weathermap

```
{"coord":{"lon":-0.13,"lat":51.51},"weather":[{"id":801,"main":"Clouds",
  "description":"few clouds","icon":"02d"}],"base":"stations","main":
  {"temp":288.59,"pressure":1037,"humidity":82,"temp_min":285.37,
  "temp_max":291.48},"visibility":10000,"wind":{"speed":4.1,"deg":80},
  "clouds":{"all":20},"dt":1443432329,"sys":{"type":1,"id":5089,
  "message":0.0192,"country":"GB","sunrise":1443419776,"sunset":1443462305},
  "id":2643743,"name":"London","cod":200}


        return "{\"coord\":{\"lon\":-0.13,\"lat\":51.51},\"weather\":
        [{\"id\":801,\"main\":\"Clouds\",\"description\":\"few clouds\",
        \"icon\":\"02d\"}],
        \"base\":\"stations\",\"main\":{\"temp\":288.59,\"pressure\":1037,
        \"humidity\":82,\"temp_min\":285.37,\"temp_max\":291.48},
        \"visibility\":10000,\"wind\":{\"speed\":4.1,\"deg\":80},
        \"clouds\":{\"all\":20},\"dt\":1443432329,\"sys\":{\"type\":1,
        \"id\":5089,\"message\":0.0192,\"country\":\"GB\",
        \"sunrise\":1443419776,\"sunset\":1443462305},\"id\":2643743,
        \"name\":\"London\",\"cod\":200}";
```

Let us see if the `HttpUrlConnectionExample` returns the same information via the logic I described. Figure 16-5 shows the toast generated with the returned results from a successful run of the application.

Figure 16-5. The JSON response showing in HttpUrlConnectionExample

Success! Obviously showing a user raw JSON is not the best application experience, so you would probably parse the JSON to extract temperatures, wind, sunrise and sunset, and so forth, to create a more pleasant experience.

Troubleshooting Issues with Internet Connections

If you have done any other form of development with Internet-based resources, web services, or pretty much anything online, you realize that there are a myriad of different ways in which things can go wrong. As a general strategy, definitely employ a liberal dose of exception handling across any use of `HttpURLRequest` and the data or payload you gather as you use it.

Rather than have the `HttpUrlRequestExample` application blow out to dozens of pages of mainly try-catch blocks, I have deliberately kept it simple so you can understand the mechanics, but in any real-world application, I would look to address these common types of exceptions and code for appropriate behavior and mitigation.

Correct and Fully-Formed URLs

For many years, browsers have been trying to make users lives easier and easier. Whether it is friendly interpretation of 400-series and 500-series HTTP error codes, or the not-so-friendly hijacking of NXDOMAIN responses to show advertisements when a URL is not found, the general thrust has been to get the users to their destination (or any destination) rather than just leave them hanging.

One of the most pervasive forms of assistance is the browser assuming which protocol the user meant to use when they omitted that from the URL they entered. For instance, if the user types www.apress.com into the browser, it assumes the user meant to use HTTP, it adds the missing http:// preamble to the string, and it implicitly directs the request to the correctly formed http://www.apress.com URL instead. Great for the user, and for Apress!

That habit and its assumed behavior can cause you grief as a developer, however, because packages like java.net.URL and java.net.HttpURLConnection mean HTTP when they say HTTP. In practice, this means that although helper methods and the like exist to "fill in the gaps," if a URL isn't entered correctly, by default if you just attempt to use the String api.openweathermap.org you will get errors thrown akin to those in Listing 16-7.

Listing 16-7. Partial LogCat Output Showing Malformed URL Errors

```
<date and time> com.artifexdigital.android.httpurlrequestexample W/System.err:
    java.net.MalformedURLException: Protocol not found:
        api.openweathermap.org/data/2.5/weather?q=London,uk
<date and time> com.artifexdigital.android.httpurlrequestexample W/System.err:
    at java.net.URL.<init>(URL.java:176)
<date and time> com.artifexdigital.android.httpurlrequestexample W/System.err:
    at java.net.URL.<init>(URL.java:125)
<date and time> com.artifexdigital.android.httpurlrequestexample W/System.err:
    at com.artifexdigital.android.httpurlrequestexample.HttpUrlRequestExample
        .fetchUrl(HttpUrlRequestExample.java:38)
...
```

The key error is shown in bold on the second line of the LogCat snippet. By not specifying the protocol (http://) in the URL string, we technically attempted to use a malformed URL. The upshot is that you either need to add the protocols explicitly or dynamically via helper methods (your own, or the java.net.* ones), or help your users specify which protocol they want, so you avoid the issue up front. Catching MalformedURLException errors should also be part of your normal code patterns when you're working with Internet connections.

Misbehaving on the Main Thread

Earlier in the chapter, when discussing the various libraries and packages that are available to you for working with the Internet, I mentioned that any use of AndroidHttpClient must use a background thread for any network connection. This same stricture is true for HttpURLConnection—any network activity must happen off the main UI thread.

In the HttpUrlConnectionExample application, you can easily see how we use an AsyncTask<> implementation to make our fetchUrl() call on a dedicated thread. As your code gets more and more complicated and your applications add many activities, private classes, and more, it can become tricky to know for sure that you have spawned a separate thread for all attempts to invoke .connect() and its parallels in other classes.

I mentioned that network connections on the main UI thread are a performance no-no. They are bad for the users and bad for their impression of Android. In fact, Google was so concerned that they didn't just forcefully recommend that network activity happen elsewhere—they changed Android to detect any attempt to do this and throw errors at the unlucky developers. Listing 16-8 shows the partial error stack you will see if you accidentally (or purposefully) try to invoke any form of network connection on the main thread. The formatting is wrapped to fit the page.

Listing 16-8. Proactive Catching and Error Reporting of Network Activity on the Main UI Thread

```
com.artifexdigital.android.httpurlrequestexample E/AndroidRuntime:
    FATAL EXCEPTION: main
    Process: com.artifexdigital.android.httpurlrequestexample, PID: 26207
    java.lang.RuntimeException: Unable to start activity
        ComponentInfo{com.artifexdigital.android.httpurlrequestexample/
            com.artifexdigital.android.httpurlrequestexample.HttpUrlRequestExample}:
            android.os.NetworkOnMainThreadException
        at android.app.ActivityThread.performLaunchActivity
...
```

The second to last line, shown in bold, holds the key. We run straight into the NetworkOnMainThreadException with any attempt to use any kind of network connection (from any package or library) on the main thread. This means no sneaky Internet calls in onCreate() or any other callback without them being wrapped in AsyncTask<> or similar thread-management libraries.

Mastering Downloads with DownloadManager

As well as providing the many different foundational packages and libraries for network and Internet connectivity, Android also gives you access to a number of Internet-aware components to deal with common, higher-order concepts like maps, downloads, and more. To complete the current chapter, let's explore the built-in DownloadManager facility for dealing with large and complex downloads.

Introducing the DownloadManager System Service

In old versions of Android, up to version 2.3, if you wanted to download any significant file or volume of data from an online source, you had to code your own tools and classes and do all the work yourself; it was a little like building a glorified example of the preceding HttpURLConnectionExample application. That got really painful for developers who werestruggling to cope with ever-expanding file types, network issues, and more, however. There had to be a better way; Android delivered this with the introduction of DownloadManager in version 2.3, and improvements have been made to it ever since.

The DownloadManager system service give you access to a lot of features that take the complexity out of managing large downloads, including the following:

* Network connectivity differentiation gives you options to allow, throttle, postpone, or end downloads depending on your network connection type (LTE, 4G, 3G, etc.), wifi signal strength, and so on.

* Cost-sensitivity controls allow you to avoid downloads if data roaming is in use and if there is a risk of excessive cost to the application's user.

* Device keep-alive ensures that the device doesn't disable radios or enter sleep mode.

* Download resumption for interrupted downloads.

* Connectivity-mode handoff, when the device transitions from cellular, to wifi, and so on.

The service taking on these tasks for you frees you to simply deal with the request in general and the resulting file.

Selecting Permissions for DownloadManager Use

The entire point of downloading something from the Internet is to take it from a server somewhere and place it locally on some storage for later use. At a minimum, this implies the following two permissions are needed to successfully work with DownloadManager.

1. android.permission.INTERNET for accessing the Internet, just as with the other examples in this chapter

2. android.permission.WRITE_EXTERNAL_STORAGE, which is the typical permission you need to write to your device's user-accessible storage or SD card

I cover the WRITE_EXTERNAL_STORAGE permission in detail in Chapter 17 and the topic of managing and using files. For now, make sure you have the necessary entries in your AndroidManifest.XML file, as shown in Listing 16-9.

Listing 16-9. Manifest Permissions for Using DownloadManager

```
<?xml version="1.0" encoding="utf-8"?>
<manifest xmlns:android="http://schemas.android.com/apk/res/android"
    package="com.artifexdigital.android.downloadmanagerexample" >

    <uses-permission android:name="android.permission.INTERNET" />
    <uses-permission android:name="android.permission.WRITE_EXTERNAL_STORAGE" />
...
</manifest>
```

The DownloadManager also supports several other permissions, notably android.permission. DOWNLOAD_WITHOUT_NOTIFICATION. This permission allows an application to avoid posting notifications about downloads, which otherwise are always shown. This clearly has security implications for silent downloads, thus the protection offered by this additional permission.

A Simple Downloader Example

The manifest shown earlier in Listing 16-9 is for the example application, `DownloadManagerExample`, which you can find in the `ch16/DownloadManagerExample` folder of the sample code. Any good downloader needs a UI, and Listing 16-10 shows the layout for a simple two-button display to start and view downloads.

Listing 16-9. The DownloadManagerExample Layout

```xml
<?xml version="1.0" encoding="utf-8"?>
<manifest xmlns:android="http://schemas.android.com/apk/res/android"
    package="com.artifexdigital.android.downloadmanagerexample" >

    <uses-permission android:name="android.permission.INTERNET" />
    <uses-permission android:name="android.permission.WRITE_EXTERNAL_STORAGE" />

    android.permission.DOWNLOAD_WITHOUT_NOTIFICATION

    <RelativeLayout xmlns:android="http://schemas.android.com/apk/res/android"
    xmlns:tools="http://schemas.android.com/tools"
    android:layout_width="match_parent"
    android:layout_height="match_parent"
    android:paddingLeft="@dimen/activity_horizontal_margin"
    android:paddingRight="@dimen/activity_horizontal_margin"
    android:paddingTop="@dimen/activity_vertical_margin"
    android:paddingBottom="@dimen/activity_vertical_margin"
    tools:context=".DownloadManagerExample">

        <Button
            android:id="@+id/startDownload"
            android:layout_width="match_parent"
            android:layout_height="wrap_content"
            android:text="Start Download"
            android:onClick="onClick" />

        <Button
            android:id="@+id/viewDownloads"
            android:layout_width="fill_parent"
            android:layout_height="wrap_content"
            android:text="View Downloads"
            android:layout_below="@id/startDownload"
            android:onClick="onClick" />

</RelativeLayout>
```

My two-button example layouts should start to become familiar after a while. Here we have a Start Download button and a View Downloads button, which are pretty self explanatory. The secret sauce is in the Java implementation. The layout renders the UI shown in Figure 16-6.

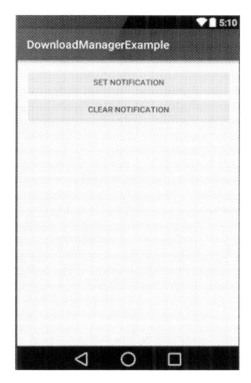

Figure 16-6. *The DownloadManagerExample application UI*

Coding DownloadManager Behavior

To give a user the ability to download is great, but you can also provide additional features that let them know when the download is in progress, when it is done, and even ways to work with downloads when they are complete. Our code covers some of these extended features and sets you up to expand even further.

Listing 16-10 is the complete code for the DownloadManagerExample application, with some areas already ripe for you to expand. I am also including techniques from earlier chapters to show, in particular, the use of broadcast intents and receivers to handle communication flow and some aspects of behavior.

Listing 16-10. *Code Implementing the DownloadManagerExample Project*

```
package com.artifexdigital.android.downloadmanagerexample;

import android.app.DownloadManager;
import android.content.BroadcastReceiver;
import android.content.Context;
import android.content.Intent;
import android.content.IntentFilter;
import android.net.Uri;
```

```java
import android.os.Environment;
import android.support.v7.app.ActionBarActivity;
import android.os.Bundle;
import android.view.View;
import android.widget.Button;

public class DownloadManagerExample extends ActionBarActivity {
    Uri myUri = Uri.parse("https://ia801400.us.archive.org/2/items/" +
                          "rhapblue11924/rhapblue11924_64kb.mp3");
    private DownloadManager myDLManager = null;
    private long downloadTarget = -1L;

    @Override
    protected void onCreate(Bundle savedInstanceState) {
        super.onCreate(savedInstanceState);
        setContentView(R.layout.activity_download_manager_example);

        myDLManager = (DownloadManager) getSystemService(DOWNLOAD_SERVICE);
        registerReceiver(onDownloaded,
                new IntentFilter(DownloadManager.ACTION_DOWNLOAD_COMPLETE));
    }

    public void onClick(View view) {
        switch(view.getId()) {
            case R.id.startDownload:
                if (downloadStatus != -1L) {
                    // Consider logic here for simultaneous downloads
                    // But for now we will keep it simple
                }
                else {
                    startDownload(view);
                }
                break;
            case R.id.viewDownloads:
                viewDownloads(view);
                break;
        }
    }

    @Override
    public void onDestroy() {
        super.onDestroy();
        unregisterReceiver(onDownloaded);
    }

    public void startDownload(View view) {

        downloadTarget = myDLManager.enqueue(new DownloadManager.Request(myUri)
                        .setAllowedNetworkTypes
                            (DownloadManager.Request.NETWORK_MOBILE |
                            DownloadManager.Request.NETWORK_WIFI )
```

```
                        .setTitle("Amazing Tunes")
                        .setDescription("Rhapsody in Blue")
                        .setDestinationInExternalPublicDir(
                                Environment.DIRECTORY_DOWNLOADS,
                                "rhapsody.mp4"));

            //Disable the Start Download button until current download ends
            Button myStartButton=(Button)findViewById(R.id.startDownload);
            myStartButton.setText("Downloading...");
            myStartButton.setEnabled(false);
    }

    public void viewDownloads(View view) {
        startActivity(new Intent(DownloadManager.ACTION_VIEW_DOWNLOADS));
    }

    BroadcastReceiver onDownloaded =new BroadcastReceiver() {
        public void onReceive(Context context, Intent intent) {
            //return Start Button to enabled state
            Button myStartButton=(Button)findViewById(R.id.startDownload);
            myStartButton.setText("Start Download");
            myStartButton.setEnabled(true);
        }
    };

}
```

Let's break this down into sections to ensure you understand what each area covers. The activity setup and onCreate() method put in place some useful constants and inflate our basic layout. The myUri value is set to the same mp3 track we played with in Chapter 14 on Audio, and a DownloadManager object is created and then used to bind to the system service using the getSystemService(DOWNLOAD_SERVICE) call.

The activity is also flagged as a receiver with a filter for ACTION_DOWNLOAD_COMPLETE broadcast intents, which happens to be the intent fired when a download completes (you could have guessed that from the name). We could have configured this in the manifest instead, but it helps to see alternatives in practice. The onDownloaded method implements the logic for the BroadcastReceiver, which I cover shortly.

With the activity live, we have an onClick() method to implement a little logic around which button has been clicked. The Start Download button triggers the startDownload() method, and I've placed a little stub of if/then logic here if you wish to experiment with multiple simultaneous downloads and what happens when the user clicks Start Download more than once. For now, the logic in startDownload() prevents this, but you are free to change it.

The startDownload() method is where the action happens. Any download performed through DownloadManager relies on the notion of queuing items to be downloaded and having the system service work through its queue asynchronously. Your enqueed download might start instantaneously, but it might not, depending on what other activity is happening, what

other downloads are in progress, and so on. If you revisit the enqueue() method, you will
note that it takes a DownloadManager.Request object that looks and acts like a builder-style
object—because that is exactly what it is.

```
downloadTarget = myDLManager.enqueue(new DownloadManager.Request(myUri)
                .setAllowedNetworkTypes
                    (DownloadManager.Request.NETWORK_MOBILE |
                     DownloadManager.Request.NETWORK_WIFI )
                .setTitle("Amazing Tunes")
                .setDescription("Rhapsody in Blue")
                .setDestinationInExternalPublicDir(
                        Environment.DIRECTORY_DOWNLOADS,
                        "rhapsody.mp4"));
```

Here we are using a combination of .setAllowedNetworkTypes() to specify that mobile and
wifi are acceptable connectivity levels from which to initiate the download. For very large
downloads, consider what network charges a user might need to pay, and allow them some
control over whether NETWORK_MOBILE is included. There is also a .setAllowOverRoaming()
Boolean to control dreaded roaming charges. The .setTitle() and .setDescription() calls
add some useful text to the download when you are viewing its progress and the completed
file, which you can see on the following pages in the screenshots of the example in action.
These can be any strings you like. Lastly, we use .setDestinationInExternalPublicDir()
to choose one of the system-provided locations for the file. We cover this in significantly
more detail in Chapter 17 when we cover files and file systems for Android. For now, you can
proceed knowing that your download will be called rhapsody.mp4 and will be placed in the
common downloads folder used by all applications.

The startDownload() method is rounded out with some UI tricks to prevent multiple
simultaneous downloads. I have done this only to keep the example simple to understand
at first use—there is no Android limitation at play here. Using findViewById(), we find the
reference for the Start Download button, change its text to "Downloading…," and disable
the button itself. Starting a download, therefore, changes the look of the UI, as shown
in Figure 16-7.

Figure 16-7. A download in progress. Note also the system-generated arrow in notification bar

These UI steps are reversed in the onDownloaded() broadcast receiver implementation. Assuming a download completes normally, our UI returns to the original form shown in Figure 16-6. Of course, that assumption is a little risky, and we will talk more about that in a moment. Android itself adds the animated downloading arrow to the notification bar at the top of the screen. At any point during a download, your user can swipe down to see the notification drawer (which we cover in-depth in Chapter 23) to see the progress of their downloads. This is depicted in Figure 16-8, where you can see the title and description text we used in the enqueue() method and Request object.

Figure 16-8. Download in progress shown in the notification drawer

We have implemented an onDestroy() override, which ensures our broadcast receiver is unregistered. This prevents stray receivers from consuming resources and causing problems, and it also means that your activity will not be triggered if it is not already running when some other application decides to perform a download with DownloadManager. Note that we do nothing with the DownloadManager object itself. We don't dispose or destroy or unassign the myDLManager object, because we don't have to. Android is designed to garbage collect objects referencing any system service, so we can simply leave the housekeeping to the system.

Last up is the viewDownloads() method. It is deceptively simple, attempting to start an activity that responds to the broadcast intent filter of DownloadManager.ACTION_VIEW_DOWNLOADS.

```
startActivity(new Intent(DownloadManager.ACTION_VIEW_DOWNLOADS));
```

Absent any other application that has already registered a receiver that can handle this intent, you are likely to trigger the system-provided Downloads management activity, as show in Figure 16-9.

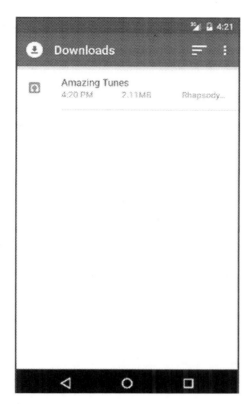

Figure 16-9. Our successful download in the general Downloads activity

In the spirit of liberally using plenty of activities, this Downloads activity can also fire off an intent for a playback activity just by touching the download. Figure 16-10 shows and example of this using one of the built-in playback activities. You can, of course, tweak your audio examples from Chapter 14, register a receiver, and see if you can trigger your own playback code.

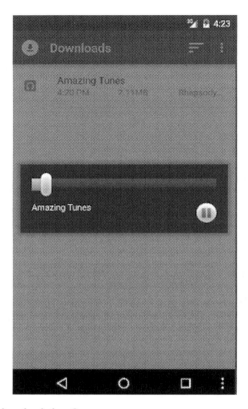

Figure 16-10. Playing back the downloaded mp3

When everything works normally, the user of your application gets all the benefit of smooth downloads, and you get the benefit of writing comparatively little code and letting the DownloadManager service do all the hard work. Of course, things do not always work smoothly, and I cover dealing with those circumstances next.

Dealing with Download Problems

The download manager offers a range of methods and data to help you keep tabs on the progress and status of your downloads, as well as see resulting information about what went right, and what might have gone wrong. Your DownloadManager object includes a .query() method that takes a Query object. By providing the reference to the relevant download, you will be returned a Cursor object that can be "walked through" to gather all kinds of information.

```
Cursor myDLCursor = myDLManager.query(new DownloadManager
                                .Query()
                                .setFilterById(downloadTarget));
```

Data available from the cursor includes the following:

- COLUMN_BYTES_DOWNLOADED_SO_FAR: The number of bytes already downloaded for the file
- COLUMN_LAST_MODIFIED_TIMESTAMP: The last modified time of the file
- COLUMN_LOCAL_URI: The local Uri reference for the local file
- COLUMN_STATUS: The status value for the download (more on this shortly)
- COLUMN_REASON: Any additional reason information for the COLUMN_STATUS

Even though a successfully completed download fires the DownloadManager.ACTION_DOWNLOAD_COMPLETE intent, it is still prudent to check the COLUMN_STATUS of your download to ensure its value is STATUS_SUCCESSFUL.

Here are other possible values for COLUMN_STATUS:

- STATUS_FAILED: Where the download failed for some reason, and will not be retried automatically.
- STATUS_PAUSED: A download is waiting to retry, or for the user to resume it.
- STATUS_PENDING: When your download is successfully queued via enqueue() but has not yet started.
- STATUS_RUNNING: The download is in progress.

Some of the Query object columns are only populated in some COLUMN_STATUS states. For example, COLUMN_BYTES_DOWNLOADED_SO_FAR does not have any data while the download is in STATUS_PENDING state, and COLUMN_REASON is only populated in STATUS_FAILED states, hopefully with useful diagnostic information.

Remember to keep the user's perspective in mind when things go wrong; be careful not to let coding for the perfect situation cause further issues. The DownloadManagerExample application leaves the Start Download button disabled in some failure modes, so you can practice your skills expanding the code to cover STATUS_FAILED states and return the button to enabled. Figure 16-11 shows a failed download in the Downloads activity. Note the differing text inserted from STATUS_REASON automatically by Android (our code did not do this).

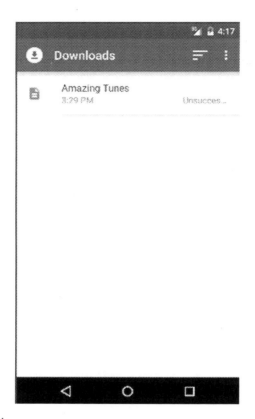

Figure 16-11. A failed download

Chapter

17

Chapter

Working with Files

Android offers quite a wide range of approaches to the topic of dealing with storing, and retrieving, data for you applications. In the next three chapters, I cover the major features that allow you to store data away, to process it, to use it for logic and other functions in your application. Android offers a built-in preference system for maintaining state about a user's settings, options, and preferences. Bundled with all Android installations is a fully working SQLite library, which provides embedded relational database capability. The last main data storage technology Android supports is the traditional file, stored on a file system.

In this chapter I cover the basics of working with files in Android; to do this, I work with the two broad approaches to thinking about file-based data when you build Android applications. The first of these two approaches is what I call the "application embedded" model, which uses raw resources and assets packaged with your application; and the second is what I term the "Java I/O" approach, which enlists the venerable java.io package to manipulate files, data streams, and so on using all the traditional methods you might be used to from Java and working with Linux file systems.

There is no "better" or "best" approach. Each technique has its pros and cons, which I cover as we discuss the relative file handling capabilities and build a few example applications along the way. Let's get started.

Using Raw and Asset-based Files

In Chapters 14 and 15, you saw examples of how to use raw resources in the res/raw project directory and asset resources from the assets project directory when you are working with audio and video. However, your use of the raw and asset locations is not limited to just media files like audio, images, and video.

You can place any file you like in these locations, but the burden is then on you as a developer to ensure you know how to access their content. For instance, you can store a text file or an XML representation of some data. Android makes accessing such a file easy through the Resources class and its getResources() method. Once you have your raw resource file, you can present its content through an InputStream by calling the openRawResources() method. Interpreting that InputStream is then your job as a developer. We'll look at an example that drawings on the ListView and Adapter example from Chapter 7 shortly. First, let me cover some important advantages and disadvantages to working with data sources from raw or asset files.

The advantages to the raw-based approach include the following:

  ▓ Easy packaging with your application and its .apk file, thanks to the Android Asset Packaging Tool (AAPT).

  ▓ Ability to place resources in a library project so they are accessible from a range of applications.

  ▓ Simple static data is easily represented in human-readable and machine-manageable formats like XML.

There are also some important disadvantages to be aware of if you take this approach:

  ▓ By default, read-only. Editing existing resources packaged with the application is not trivial, and creating dynamic assets at runtime is complex.

  ▓ Not designed for wide sharing with other on-device applications

  ▓ Static nature raises questions about keeping information up to date.

You might decide that for your application and functionality, the benefits of a raw-based approach outweigh the disadvantages. As I highlighted in this chapter'sintroduction, the choice of a file-like data management technique is subjective, and you are free to adopt this approach when you think it suits your application.

Populating Lists from Resource Files

Let's look at a practical example of using an XML file packaged as a resource to populate a list dynamically at runtime. Recall the ListViewExample application from Chapter 7. In its first incarnation, it used a string array defined in the Java code, which is populated with the opening words of a soliloquy from Shakespeare's *Hamlet*. The output appears in Figure 7-1. Later versions showed lists of colors. That was all fine for demonstrating ListViews and Adapter logic, but in reality, you will almost certainly want to manage your data separate from your code, so let's place those words into an XML resource instead.

Listing 17-1 shows a simple layout that provides a ListView to ultimately display the content of our XML resource file.

Listing 17-1. The Layout for the RawFileExample

```
<RelativeLayout xmlns:android="http://schemas.android.com/apk/res/android"
    xmlns:tools="http://schemas.android.com/tools"
    android:layout_width="match_parent"
    android:layout_height="match_parent"
    tools:context=".RawFileExample" >
```

```
<TextView
    android:id="@+id/mySelection"
    android:layout_width="match_parent"
    android:layout_height="wrap_content" />
<ListView
    android:id="@android:id/list"
    android:layout_width="match_parent"
    android:layout_height="match_parent"
    android:drawSelectorOnTop="false" />

</RelativeLayout>
```

Let's focus on the color list example, for which the application uses the data in the colors.xml file in the ch17/RawFileExample project. The content of colors.xml is in Listing 17-2.

Listing 17-2. The colors.xml File Content

```
<colors>
    <color value="red" />
    <color value="orange" />
    <color value="yellow" />
    <color value="green" />
    <color value="blue" />
    <color value="indigo" />
    <color value="violet" />
    <color value="black" />
    <color value="white" />
</colors>
```

The colors.xml file is deliberately simple because I want us to focus on the logic we need to actually open this file, read and parse its content, and place it in an appropriate data structure so we can use it in the application. Listing 17-3 shows the logic for a very simple ListActivity-based application that shows the colors from the file in a list and allows the user to click to choose a particular color.

Listing 17-3. RawFileExample Java Logic for Processing the XML Resource File

```
package com.artifexdigital.android.rawfileexample;

import android.app.ListActivity;
import android.os.Bundle;
import android.view.View;
import android.widget.ArrayAdapter;
import android.widget.ListView;
import android.widget.TextView;
import org.w3c.dom.Document;
import org.w3c.dom.Element;
import org.w3c.dom.NodeList;
import java.io.InputStream;
import java.util.ArrayList;
import javax.xml.parsers.DocumentBuilder;
import javax.xml.parsers.DocumentBuilderFactory;
```

```
public class RawFileExample extends ListActivity {
    private TextView mySelection;
    ArrayList<String> colorItems=new ArrayList<String>();

    @Override
    protected void onCreate(Bundle savedInstanceState) {
        super.onCreate(savedInstanceState);
        setContentView(R.layout.activity_raw_file_example);
        mySelection=(TextView)findViewById(R.id.mySelection);

        try {
            InputStream inStream=getResources().openRawResource(R.raw.colors);
            DocumentBuilder docBuild=DocumentBuilderFactory
                    .newInstance().newDocumentBuilder();
            Document myDoc=docBuild.parse(inStream, null);
            NodeList colors=myDoc.getElementsByTagName("color");
            for (int i=0;i<colors.getLength();i++) {
                colorItems.add(((Element)colors.item(i)).getAttribute("value"));
            }
            inStream.close();
        }
        catch (Exception e) {
            e.printStackTrace();
        }

        setListAdapter(new ArrayAdapter<String>(this,
            android.R.layout.simple_list_item_1, colorItems));
    }

    public void onListItemClick(ListView parent, View v, int position,
                                long id) {
        mySelection.setText(colorItems.get(position).toString());
    }

}
```

The first thing you should notice about this code is the number of external libraries I am importing to handle file I/O and XML parsing. I return to the topic of employing the power of external libraries in Chapter 20, but you should make the most of opportunities like this to pull in existing well-built libraries rather than reinvent XML parsing.

The onCreate() method has changed significantly from the examples back in Chapter 7, so let's examine what is going on. The first line of the method is the actual file-handling in action. I created an InputStream object, and the getResources().openRawResource() call carries out the heavy lifting of finding the file within the .apk, allocating file descriptors, associating them with the InputStream, and readying the system for subsequent use of the data stream from the file. Everything that follows is the logic you need to interpret what is in the file.

Next I use a `DocumentBuilder` object to parse the content of the file and store the resulting DOM representation in a `Document` object, `myDoc`. I invoke the `getElementsByTagName()` method to collect all of the `<color>` elements into the `NodeList` object. This might seem excessively pedantic, but imagine a more complicated XML schema with other elements, child elements, and so on, and you can see how this does the sifting work quite efficiently.

Lastly, I use a `for` loop to iterate through the `NodeList` `<color>` entries, extracting the `value` attribute's text—which happens to be the color names I want to present in the `ListView`. With this in place, I can now inflate the `ListView` with the `ArrayAdapter` configured to use my list of color names, asking it to render things using the default `simple_list_item_1` built-in XML layout.

The logic for handling the user clicking a color is unchanged from Chapter 7, apart from the variable names. I could make XML handling even easier by using specialist XML resource calls, but I'll save that topic for later.

If we run our application, it shows the content of the `colors.xml` file rendered in our `ListView`, as shown in Figure 17-1.

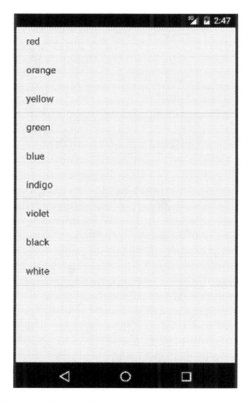

Figure 17-1. The RawFileExample application showing the contents of an XML file

Working with Files from the File System

If you are used to reading and writing files on file systems from traditional Java applications, then performing the same work in Android will be very familiar to you. For those of you not familiar with Java-based file I/O, here is a quick crash course, in one paragraph.

From the Java perspective, files are treated as streams of data, and the key pair of objects you will use are InputStream and OutputStream, for reading and writing data to/from files, respectively. These streams are provided by calling the openFileInput() or openFileOutput() methods from your context or activity. When a stream is available, your program logic is then responsible for actions such as reading in from the InputStream or writing out to the OutputStream and tidying up all of the resources when you are done.

Android's File System Model

In the very early days of Android, a representation of the built-in file system was presented to developers, together with some rudimentary controls for reserving part of the file system for Android's internal use; this left developers using the remainder of the file system for storing other files.

This roughly mapped to the notion of on-board storage being "internal," and plugged-in storage, such as an SD card, being "external." Then a funny thing happened as the 2.x and 3.x releases of Android came to market. Google decided to discourage the use of add-on SD cards, though manufacturers could push to include them and many still do. This meant that Android had to deal with both possible scenarios—devices with dedicated external storage, and devices without. Google's solution was to abstract the presence or absence of physical removable storage and present the system with internal and external partitions. Now, "external" actually maps to part of the on-board storage, and any removable SD card or similar hardware is silently mounted to a subdirectory under the "external" partition.

In addition to the "internal" area being used for system-related purposes, other differences also represent advantages and disadvantages to both internal and external storage.

Here is a description of the pros and cons of internal storage:

- Internal storage is found on every Android device and is always in place.

- The default security boundary for internally-saved files is private to your application. You need to take explicit steps to share files.

- Files that form the part of your application designated to be placed on internal storage are considered a hermetic part of your application. The files are installed when the application is installed and are removed when the application is removed.

- Internal storage might be significantly smaller than the available external storage, and often it is the area that fills first, causing users issues with space management, even when they have ample external storage available.

External storage differs in these ways:

- Android provides a USB abstraction layer and interface for external storage. When an Android device is in use as a USB device, applications on the device cannot access external storage.

- The default security boundary is to make all files on external storage world-readable. Other applications can read your externally-stored files without developer or user knowledge or permission.

- Depending on the save method invoked, externally-stored files might not be removed when your application is uninstalled.

With these benefits and costs in mind, whether you choose to use internal or external files for your project, read on.

Permissions for Reading and Writing Files

If you choose to use internal storage, your application always has permissions to write to, and read from, the portion of internal storage reserved for it. You can request details of your application's internal storage by calling getFilesDir(). More usefully, you can use getDir() to create a named (sub)directory for you to use.

When you call openFileOutput(), a file itself is opened for output streaming, otherwise known as writing (and one is created if it doesn't already exist). The openFileInput() method performs file opening—but not creating—for an InputStream to satisfy your reading requirements.

Both openFileOutput() and openFileInput() accept a number of MODE_* options to fine tune the file and stream behavior. The mostly commonly used include these:

- MODE_APPEND: With this option, none of the existing data in the file is changed; the data from the string is appended to the existing content in the file.

- MODE_PRIVATE: Permissions on the file are set so only the application that creates it (and any other that runs as the same user) is allowed to access the file. This is the default.

- MODE_WORLD_READABLE: This option opens permissions for reading to all applications and users on the device. This is considered poor security practice but often crops up when a user considers using content providers or services overkill.

- MODE_WORLD_WRITABLE: Even more dangerous than world-readable is world-writable. Any application or user can write to the file. Just because other developers use this, doesn't mean you should!

It is important to remember that, you as a developer, and you application user, do not need any specific permissions to create, open, or write to an internal file within the application's allocated internal file system space. The simplest example of creating a file stored within the internal device storage looks like this:

```
FILE myFile = new FILE(context.getFilesDir(), "myFileName");
```

When working with external storage, a different set of methods are at your disposal, and the permission model is somewhat more strict; it is even undergoing a steady shift as this book is written.

In order to write to external storage, your Android manifest needs to include the privilege `android.permission.WRITE_EXTERNAL_STORAGE`. You should already be familiar with this permission from the audio and video examples in Chapters 14 and 15.

All Android versions up to and including Android M allow your application to read freely from external storage without specifying or requiring any particular permission. But do not be complacent about this. Google has flagged that it intends to introduce and enforce read permissions in a future Android release. To that end, it already supports the inclusion of the permission name it plans to use to allow reading from external storage— `android.permission.READ_EXTERNAL_STORAGE`. You should definitely start including this privilege now in your manifest, even though it is effectively a no-op. Doing so future-proofs your applications so that when Google finally flicks the switch to start enforcing permission-based reading from external storage, you are ready.

The methods used to access external storage closely mirror the methods I previously introduced for internal storage, but the words "external" or "public" are added as part of the method name.

The `getExternalStoragePublicDirectory()` method is designed to allocate well-structured directories and files into which you can store documents, audio, pictures, video, and more. The method takes an `enum` signifying one of the predefined application directories and a filename of your choosing. Android provides nearly a dozen application directories, including the following:

- `DIRECTORY_DOCUMENTS`: For storing traditional text or other editable documents created by the user
- `DIRECTORY_MUSIC`: A place to keep all kinds of music and audio files
- `DIRECTORY_PICTURES`: For storing still-image files such as photos, drawings, and so on

Although these predefined locations are helpful and provide some predictability, at times, you will have distinctly different types of files you want to store on the device. You'll use the general-purpose `getExternalStorageDirectory()` method in these circumstances; it provides similar functionality to the `getFilesDir()` I noted earlier in the chapter for internal storage.

Examining External Files in Action

You now have enough exposure to the theory of external files to examine a working example. The ExternalFilesExample app, which you'll find in ch17/ExternalFilesExample, is a very simple walk through of the mechanics of saving a file and reading back its content.

Figure 17-2 shows the layout for providing a text entry field, buttons for file writing and reading, and a text reading field. The corresponding layout XML flle is in the ch17/ExternalFilesExample project, but I omit it here for brevity.

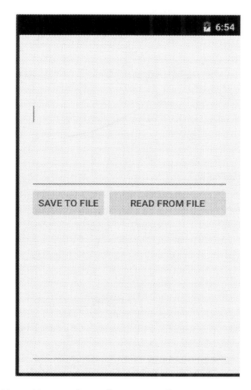

Figure 17-2. An activity with fields and buttons for testing external file management

The Java logic that supports our little application follows the pattern I have used several times. A common onClick() method handles the button clicks and switches to the appropriate method based on which button the user chooses at runtime. The code is shown in Listing 17-4.

Listing 17-4. The ExternalFilesExample Java Code

```
package com.artifexdigital.android.externalfilesexample;

import android.app.Activity;
import android.content.Context;
import android.os.Bundle;
import android.view.View;
```

```java
import android.view.inputmethod.InputMethodManager;
import android.widget.EditText;

import java.io.BufferedReader;
import java.io.IOException;
import java.io.InputStream;
import java.io.InputStreamReader;
import java.io.OutputStreamWriter;

public class MainActivity extends Activity {
    public final static String FILENAME="ExternalFilesExample.txt";

    @Override
    protected void onCreate(Bundle savedInstanceState) {
        super.onCreate(savedInstanceState);
        setContentView(R.layout.activity_main);
    }

    public void onClick(View view) {
        switch(view.getId()) {
            case R.id.btnRead:
                try {
                    doReadFromFile();
                }
                catch (Exception e) {
                    e.printStackTrace();
                }
                break;
            case R.id.btnSave:
                doSaveToFile();
                break;
        }
    }

    public void doReadFromFile() throws Exception {
        doHideKeyboard();
        EditText readField;
        readField=(EditText)findViewById(R.id.editTextRead);
        try {
            InputStream inStrm=openFileInput(FILENAME);
            if (inStrm!=null) {
                // We will use the traditional Java I/O streams and builders.
                // This is cumbersome, and we'll return with a better version
                // in Chapter 20 using the IOUtils external library

                InputStreamReader inStrmRdr=new InputStreamReader(inStrm);
                BufferedReader buffRdr=new BufferedReader(inStrmRdr);
                String fileContent;
                StringBuilder strBldr=new StringBuilder();
```

```java
            while ((fileContent=buffRdr.readLine())!=null) {
                strBldr.append(fileContent);
            }
            inStrm.close();
            readField.setText(strBldr.toString());
        }


    }
    catch (Throwable t) {
        // perform exception handling here
    }
}

public void doSaveToFile() {
    doHideKeyboard();
    EditText saveField;
    saveField=(EditText)findViewById(R.id.editText);
    try {
        OutputStreamWriter outStrm=
            new OutputStreamWriter(openFileOutput
                (FILENAME, Context.MODE_PRIVATE));
        try {
            outStrm.write(saveField.getText().toString());
        }
        catch (IOException i) {
            i.printStackTrace();
        }
        outStrm.close();
    }
    catch (Exception e) {
        e.printStackTrace();
    }
}

public void doHideKeyboard() {
    View view = this.getCurrentFocus();
    if (view != null) {
        InputMethodManager myIMM=(InputMethodManager)
            this.getSystemService(Context.INPUT_METHOD_SERVICE);
        myIMM.hideSoftInputFromWindow
            (view.getWindowToken(), InputMethodManager.HIDE_NOT_ALWAYS);
    }
}


}
```

What Goes in to Saving and Reading Files

Let's focus on the key methods in the ExternalFilesExample project, starting with the doSaveToFile() method. We need to perform some preparation and housekeeping prior to defining the method; we do this by first calling doHideKeyboard() (which I explain shortly), followed by creating our local saveField variable and binding it to the EditTextView in our layout. We do this so we can eventually reference the text we want to save in the UI.

The try/catch block that follows defines the output stream we will use to stream the text to the file nominated by the variable FILENAME, which is set globally to whatever meaning we need. We then invoke the .write() method to attempt to actually write out the text through the stream to the file.

You should also notice the multiple layers of exception handling. There are many, many reasons writing to files can run into issues, whether they involve full partitions or users spontaneously removing the volume to which you were writing—sometimes halfway through the writing process! In short, you can never have too much exception handling around file access.

Reading from the file is handled by the doReadFromFile() method. As with the doSaveToFile() method, the initial work you perform is some necessary setup and housekeeping. First you need to call the doHideKeyboard() method. When you do, the local variable readField is created and bound to the editTextRead widget in the UI. We use this to display the contents of the file once they have been read.

What follows in the try/catch block is almost entirely classic Java file handling, in all its cumbersome glory. A stream reader is used to access the file, which is then passed to a buffer. We use the buffer to access the stream one line at a time in the while block, and slowly we build up the file content in the string builder. Once we have read all of the lines from the stream (and therefore, the file), we close the stream and transfer everything that has been buffered in the strBldr object to the readField EditText widget in our Android UI.

I have deliberately taken the old-fashioned Java approach to be sure you appreciate everything that is happening when you access a file. I will return to this example in Chapter 20 to demonstrate a third-party Java library that does all of the messy work in one simple method call. If Java was being designed today, I hope file handling would be one of the things that was radically simplified.

Helping Hands with IMEs

When your user is busy typing text in the EditText field, the IME is triggered to present the soft keyboard for text entry. We could go to some effort to code for an accessory button (as covered in Chapter 8) to provide a "done" option that then hides the IME, but that's an additional key-press to ask of your users.

Instead, I have been a little subtle in ensuring the layout still includes the Save (and Read) button even when the IME is presented. This means the user can type to her heart's content and then immediately hit the Save button. The call to doSaveToFile() invokes doHideKeyboard, which determines first, what view the user interacted with, and second, whether or not the Input Method Framework is active and presenting an IME (keyboard) to the user. Any keyboard currently being shown will be closed automatically, representing a convenience to the user.

Seeing File Save and Read Behavior in Action

Now that I've described the logic and layout, it is time for you to see the finished product in action. Figure 17-3 shows the initial display of the ExternalFilesExample application when the user first starts to enter text into the top field.

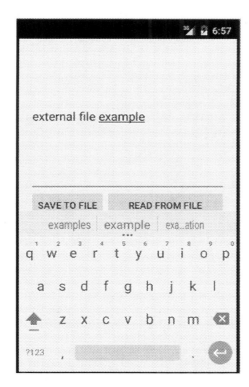

Figure 17-3. Entering text to be saved to an external file

The IME displays over the lower half of the screen, but our buttons are still visible. This really only works in this example as a hack—it is not the polished UI a fully-fledged application would use, but it is sufficient to show the file I/O in which we are interested.

At any point, the user can hit the "Save to File" button, and the doSaveToFile() method kicks in. As I discussed earlier in the chapter, this invokes the doHideKeyboard() method, and our UI then appears as shown in Figure 17-4.

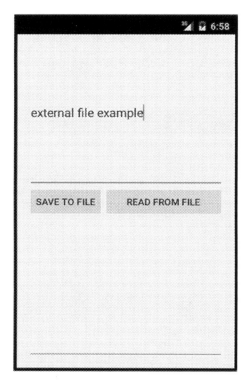

Figure 17-4. The IME is hidden when the user saves the file

The text the user typed into the EditText field is saved in the external file
ExternalFilesExample.txt. The user can recall its content at any time by hitting the
Read from File button. If they do, the contents of the file are read and displayed by the
doReadFromFile() method, and they show in the lower EditText field, as in Figure 17-5.

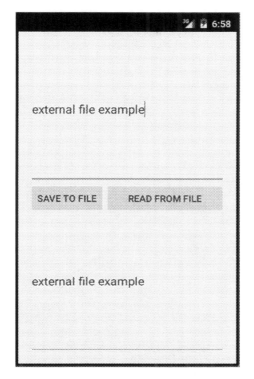

Figure 17-5. Recalling the contents of the external file

That covers all of the behavior within the ExternalFilesExample application.

Ensuring External Storage Is Available When Needed

Earlier in the chapter I mentioned that one of the potential drawbacks of using external storage is the uncertain nature of whether you can rely on it being there when you need it. Remember that your users can physically remove SD cards from their devices, and even for those devices that mimic external storage as a separate partition on internal memory, Android still allows that external storage to be mounted as a USB device elsewhere, which makes that part of the storage unavailable to applications while it is so mounted.

To develop well-behaved applications, you should perform some sanity checks on the presences and availability of your external storage before your application attempts to use it.

Android provides some useful environment methods to help with this. The principal method you want to use is Environment.getExternalStorageState(), which returns a string from a predefined enum that describes the current state of the external storage. This external storage state can have many states, including one of the following commonly seen values:

- MEDIA_BAD_REMOVAL: This state indicates the physical SD card was removed before it was unmounted, possibly leaving files in an inconsistent state due to cached pages not being flushed (see the file system discussion later in this chapter).

- MEDIA_CHECKING: When an SD card is inserted, checks are performed to determine if the card has been formatted, and if so with which file system. This is the value returned while these processed take place.

- MEDIA_MOUNTED: The normal state for external storage that can be used.

- MEDIA_MOUNTED_READ_ONLY: Typically seen when the SD card's physical switch is set to the read only position, which means that no writing to that part of external storage can be performed.

- MEDIA_REMOVED: This value is returned when no external storage is mapped from the on-board device and no SD card is present.

- MEDIA_SHARED: When the device has its external storage mounted as a USB device to some other external platform, this is the value returned to indicate that external storage is not available to be used at this time, even though it is present in the device.

You can check the Android documentation for a full list of all the possible external storage state values.

Other Considerations with Android File Systems

Now that you are familiar with a variety of approaches to working with files in Android, I need to make you aware of a few subtle and not-so-subtle management considerations that you should think about to ensure the long-term viability of using files on the file system.

Android Filesystems Throughout History

When the original Android systems were launched, their NAND-based on-board storage was presented to the devices through a file system designed to better support flash-based storage. At the time, the file system chosen was YAFFS, or Yet Another Flash File System. This file system offered a number of useful benefits, including wear-leveling support so that the decay over time of flash storage from multiple writes was managed, and to some extent, hidden from the operating system and applications, as well as file system–level garbage collection tools to help move bad regions of storage to a "dead pool" so they would not be used for meaningful storage.

YAFFS has evolved over time to become YAFFS2, with some tweaks and enhancements along the way. There is one significant drawback to the YAFFS file system, which is tied up in its locking behavior and impact on application responsiveness. YAFFS has no file-locking semantics; instead it relies on locking the entire files system to ensure consistent access to a file being modified. That means, in practice, that only one file can be written to by any application at a time, and any other application, or threads of applications, is blocked and has to wait its turn to write. This has negative consequences for any device capable of issuing parallel I/O calls, such as multiprocessor devices capable of running processes or threads simultaneously. As most Android devices in the last few years have sported dual-core or quad-core processors, this is becoming a more prevalent issue.

Newer Android devices have had a choice of underlying solid-state storage technology, and device manufacturers have added ext4 as a file system in a range of cases. This file system comes with traditional file-level locking semantics, which means concurrency issues are greatly reduced. Unfortunately, there is no easy way for you to determine from your application which file system is being used by a user's device. If you run into concurrency or I/O delay issues with the underlying storage when you are performing read or write operations from your application's main UI thread, all your user will notice is a slow or unresponsive application. As a developer, you are likely to get the blame, even when it might be Android itself that is causing the issue.

Controlling UI Delays with File I/O

As a developer, you can take several approaches to mitigate locking and contention issues with the YAFFS file system. These techniques can also assist in general with other types of I/O to network end points.

Using StrictMode to Profile an Application

We will explore a range of developer-focused tools and utilities in the coming chapters, but the most relevant for any I/O delay issues is the StrictMode policy system that profiles the operation of all of your code looking for issues defined in its policies.

StrictMode currently has only two sets of policies on which you can call. The first are the virtual machine policies that cover generally poor behavior or practices across an entire application, such as leaking database connection objects. The second set of policies are the thread policies, and these look specifically for poorly behaved code happening on the main UI thread. The policies I've just mentioned can help spot code—both yours, and Android's—that is going to slow or interrupt a user's smooth experience with the UI.

Activating a StrictMode policy can be as simple as calling the static `StrictMode.enableDefaults()` method from your `onCreate()` callback. Doing so reports all kinds of useful information in your LogCat output regarding UI thread issues including file I/O concerns. You can also define your own policies if you desire; the Android documentation has many more details on this.

> **Caution**   Never leave StrictMode policies defined in your final, publicly-available, application. Either use application logic such as if/then/else to skip setting policies in released applications, or simply comment the code out of any final version. Leaving StrictMode in place creates significant amounts of log data on user devices that can cause issues with full devices.

Moving Logic to Asynchronous Threads

StrictMode is an excellent tool for finding candidate logic that you can move away from the main UI thread and interface. You might also know of other logic in your application that doesn't need to happen on the critical path, such as the background lookup of data from a web service, or messaging and polling-style work for maintaining lists, cached items, and so forth.

Android provides a method for spawning asynchronous threads called AsyncTask(). This is well worth mastering as part of your Android learning, since most developers use it as the workhorse for managing threading across their applications.

The AsyncTask() class is provided in a form that means you, as the developer, must subclass it to create specific implementations for the work you want to do. In its most basic form, it provides a doInBackground() method to encapsulate the actual logic your want performed on another thread. You can implement optional additional methods to provide pre- and post-execution logic, interact with the UI in a controlled way, and so on.

Listing 17-5 outlines a subclassing of AsyncTast() to illustrate how you can use it to perform file-saving operations. This is only one of countless ways you can implement this, and I'll return to the subject of threading and task management in more depth later in the book.

Listing 17-5. An Example AsyncTask Subclassing

```
private class SmartFileSaver extends AsyncTask<Void, Void, Void> {

    protected void onPreExecute() {
        // This method will fire on the UI thread
        // Show a Toast message
        Toast.makeText(this, "Saving File", Toast.LENGTH_LONG).show();
    }

    protected void doInBackground() {
        // This method will spawn a background thread
        // All work happens off the UI thread
        // create output stream
        // call .write()
        // catch exceptions
        // etc.
    }

    protected void onPostExecute() {
        // This method will fire on the UI thread
        // Show a Toast message
        Toast.makeText(this, "File Saved", Toast.LENGTH_LONG).show();
    }
}
```

Using the SmartFileSaver.execute() method invokes your various onPreExecute(), doInBackground(), and onPostExecute() methods with Android managing the related thread lifetime and UI interaction.

Managing Databases with Android

Files are not the only way to store information from your application onto an Android device. Every Android device ships with an embedded and embeddable database known as SQLite. Those of you familiar with SQLite know that it represents a rock-solid database engine that ships as a single library, and that it can be included in all manner of applications. SQLite has been around for almost 20 years and has proven itself one of the winners in the "small but mighty" database category.

For those of you not familiar with SQLite, or its Android capabilities, let me quickly walk you through the database fundamentals of using SQLite, and how to use it with Android to build up a simple database-driven application.

> **Note** If you would like to delve deeper into the world of SQLite, beyond what I cover in this chapter, I recommend *The Definitive Guide to SQLite,* Second Edition. In the interests of full disclosure, I should admit that the authors of that book are Michael Owens and Grant Allen. That second name should look familiar to you, as that is none other than the author of the book you are now reading.

SQLite: A Seriously Popular Database

If you are questioning whether you should invest your time learning about SQLite as part of your Android education, let me provide some reassurance. SQLite is, without a doubt, the most popular database platform shipped with, or used by, software today. Some of its adherents include the following:

- **Google** (well, obviously, we're talking Android here). Not only does SQLite ship built in to Android, but it is also the database the Chrome Web browser uses for storing all kinds of profile information, from bookmarks to cookies. It is also used for supporting the "local storage" option of HTML5.

▓ **Apple**. Android's great competitor, the iPhone, ships with SQLite as a standard library as well. As do iPads, all recent Macintosh machines, and even devices like Apple TV.

▓ **Mozilla**. The Firefox browser uses SQLite for many tasks similar to what Chrome uses it for, including options for HTML5 local storage support.

▓ **Symbian**. If you remember Nokia phones before the Microsoft era, then you will certainly know of and have used Symbian. It, too, shipped with SQLite.

▓ **Oracle**. Yes, the database behemoth best known for being one of the giants (in both reputation and resource consumption) of the database world. Many of Oracle's products ship with SQLite embedded, particularly the range of products it acquired from the Sun acquisition.

And this is just a sample of the incredibly broad use and support for SQLite across the technology industry. Even if all of these names don't sway you to learn about SQLite for Android use, the millions of Android applications that already use it and that are available from the Google Play store should convince you it's a solid technology foundation for data storage needs in your Android applications.

A Crash Course in SQLite

SQLite is designed to be a very familiar database library that provides the relational database query and transaction capabilities to whatever application loads the library. It uses a fairly standards-compliant implementation of SQL as the query language, as you probably guessed from the name.

As a language, SQL has steadily evolved in various date-stamped versions, such as SQL-92 and SQL-99, and SQLite supports all the usual SELECT, INSERT, UPDATE, and DELETE commands, but there are some key features of later SQL standards it doesn't support. Here are some of the support restrictions:

▓ Only a subset of ANSI outer join syntax is supported.

▓ There is minimal alter table support—basically just what you need to rename and add columns—so you won't be able to drop columns or perform data type morphing (more on this later).

▓ Row-centric triggers are OK, but you won't be able to use statement-centric triggers.

▓ Views are strictly read-only.

▓ There isn't any support for any windowing or OLAP capabilities (LAG, LEAD, etc.).

To be honest, these few missing features are all at the higher end of typical database usage, and for a very small embeddable database library, you still get the huge range of the power that SQL offers.

In this list, note that in the second item on altering tables flags, you cannot play with existing data types for a table. This isn't because of any ideological reason; rather, it has to do with the one fundamentally different—and some would say strange—area of the design of SQLite.

When you are specifying data types for a column, such as `integer` or `char`, SQLite happily accepts such syntax, but under the hood, it implements a data typing system it calls *manifest typing*. In layperson's terms, what this really means is that the notion of prescribed data types really isn't present;instead, SQLite simply uses them as guides and allows you to create data of any "type" in a given column.

This is very close in concept to the data type flexibility you might have experienced in contemporary NoSQL-style databases. The data type isn't enforced across the whole column; instead, it is simply another attribute of each individual value in that column for the rows in a table.

Creating SQLite Databases for Your Application

There are two main approaches to bootstrapping a SQLite database for your application: you can either create a SQLite database file from somewhere else, such as your development machine, and copy it as a resource in your Android project, or you can have your application create and populate a database for you.

The drawback of the packaging approach is that as a developer, you find it becomes more difficult to keep the database schema and code development in sync—this is a problem not unique to Android. Ordinarily, you might think that having to manage the creation and initial population in you Android code would be a similar burden, but Android comes to the rescue with some excellent setup assistance.

As part of Android's SQLite support, the `SQLiteOpenHelper` class is provided for you to subclass in your application. This class takes care of all the initial setup of a SQLite database, and it deals with future changes and upgrades. You need to implement at least three of the methods from the parent class, and a fourth method for downgrades is also available as an option.

First, you need to add any logic to the `SQLiteOpenHelper` constructor (calling that parent constructor as a basis). The parent takes care of checking to see if the nominated database file itself actually exists and creates the file if it needs to. It also performs a version check against the provided version and calls the `onUpgrade` and `onDowngrade` methods as determined. It can also do some other fancy tricks, but those are the essentials.

Second, you need to implement the `onCreate()` method. Here you actually perform the SQL commands to create the tables, indexes, views, and so forth that you want in your database. You should also perform any inserts, updates, and the like that you need to seed your database.

Lastly, you have to provide an implementation for `onUpgrade()`, and you can optionally also provide one for `onDowngrade()`. The point of these methods is to handle the schema changes and any related data changes you wish to have occur as you upgrade your application over time (and presumably, change the SQLite database to support the new application logic). You will often see a quick hack that uses the "drop and re-create" approach. This is not something I recommend performing unless the data is really unimportant to your user and you know you can create it again if you need to—for example, if you have backed up the user's data to a web service or end point.

It is one thing to read a few paragraphs that dryly describe what should be in the code; it's another to...... So let's improve the situation by taking a look at the example application I use throughout this chapter to explore Android and SQLite.

Introducing the SQLiteExample Application

The ch18/SQLiteExample application highlights all of the key SQLite capabilities you might want to use when you're building database-driven Android applications, and it builds on some of the list-based UIs we explored in earlier chapters. Figure 18-1 shows the UI comprised of a ListView for showing known Android device models from a SQLite database, along with buttons for adding new device models and showing information about known devices.

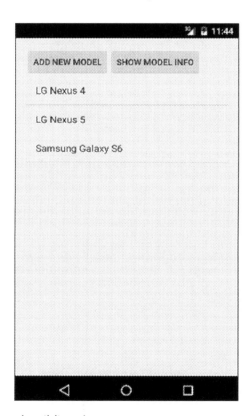

Figure 18-1. The SQLiteExample main activity and appearance

Since you are already familiar with this kind of UI design, I won't dwell on it in huge detail. Listing 18-1 shows the layout.

Listing 18-1. The SQLite Example Main Activity Layout

```xml
<LinearLayout xmlns:android="http://schemas.android.com/apk/res/android"
    xmlns:tools="http://schemas.android.com/tools"
    android:layout_width="match_parent"
    android:layout_height="match_parent"
    android:paddingLeft="@dimen/activity_horizontal_margin"
    android:paddingRight="@dimen/activity_horizontal_margin"
    android:paddingTop="@dimen/activity_vertical_margin"
    android:paddingBottom="@dimen/activity_vertical_margin"
    android:orientation="vertical"
    tools:context=".SQLiteExample">

    <LinearLayout
        android:id="@+id/buttonGroup"
        android:layout_width="wrap_content"
        android:layout_height="wrap_content"
        android:orientation="horizontal">

        <Button
            android:id="@+id/addNewModel"
            android:layout_width="wrap_content"
            android:layout_height="wrap_content"
            android:text="Add New Model"
            android:onClick="onClick"/>

        <Button
            android:id="@+id/getModelInfo"
            android:layout_width="wrap_content"
            android:layout_height="wrap_content"
            android:text="Show Model Info"
            android:onClick="onClick"/>

    </LinearLayout>

    <ListView
        android:id="@android:id/list"
        android:layout_width="wrap_content"
        android:layout_height="match_parent" />

</LinearLayout>
```

When you look at this code you should notice two quick points. First, note that I define two nested LinearLayouts. The outer-most LinearLayout uses orientation=vertical, and contains the inner LinearLayout and the ListView with the stock Android id. The inner LinearLayout houses the two buttons, addNewModel and getModelInfo, with orientation=horizontal. This is a quick layout hack to have the UI widgets flow as I want them, but you can devise a more elegant solution with suitable weightings, gravity, and layout references.

The second point to note is the presence of the by-now normal pattern of both buttons registering the same method to handle clicks. As usual, when we delve into the supporting Java code, our onClick() method determines which button was pressed and directs the logic from there.

Look again at Figure 18-1; you can see several devices already listed, which suggests that there is data in a database somewhere that I am already using to demonstrate the application. This data was placed there when I implemented the SQLiteOpenHelper I used in the SQLiteExample application. The Java for my implementation appears in Listing 18-2.

Listing 18-2. The MySQLiteHelper SQLiteOpenHelper Implementation

```
package com.artifexdigital.android.sqliteexample;

import android.content.Context;
import android.database.sqlite.SQLiteDatabase;
import android.database.sqlite.SQLiteOpenHelper;

public class MySQLiteHelper extends SQLiteOpenHelper {
    public static final String TABLE_NAME="devices";
    public static final int COLNO__ID = 0;
    public static final int COLNO_MODEL_NAME = 1;
    public static final int COLNO_RELEASE_YEAR = 2;
    public static final String[] TABLE_COLUMNS =
            new String[]{"_id","model_name","release_year"};

    private static final String DBFILENAME="devices.db";
    private static final int DBVERSION = 1;
    private static final String INITIAL_SCHEMA=
            "create table devices (" +
                    "_id integer primary key autoincrement," +
                    "model_name varchar(100) not null," +
                    "release_year integer not null" +
                    ")";
    private static final String INITIAL_DATA_INSERT=
            "insert into devices (model_name, release_year) values " +
                    "('LG Nexus 4', 2012)," +
                    "('LG Nexus 5', 2013)," +
                    "('Samsung Galaxy S6', 2015)";

    public MySQLiteHelper(Context context) {
        super(context, DBFILENAME, null, DBVERSION);
    }

    @Override
    public void onCreate(SQLiteDatabase db) {
        db.execSQL(INITIAL_SCHEMA);
        db.execSQL(INITIAL_DATA_INSERT);
    }
```

```
@Override
public void onUpgrade(SQLiteDatabase db, int oldVersion, int newVersion) {
    // perform upgrade logic here
    // This can get quite complex
    if (oldVersion==1) {
        // do upgrade logic to new version
    }
    // and so on
}

}
```

From the Java listing, you can see the various mandatory helper requirements that I introduced earlier in the chapter. The constructor takes the file name and version information so that it can check to see if the SQLite database file exists and can create it if it needs to. In our case, I have called the database file "devices.db".

The onCreate() implementation looks deceptively simple. Two calls are made to the execSQL() method; this is your introduction to the first of many of the methods that are used to actually issue SQL commands and work with results. In its most basic and common form, the execSQL() method takes a string SQL statement as a parameter, which is the SQL command executed by the SQLite library. Normally there is nothing returned, assuming the execution is successful.

The SQL statements passed to the execSQL() calls are built up in the constant declarations at the beginning of the class. The constant-based approach is not a new one, but you should take note of the few additional constants the application uses:

- The three COLNO_* constants represent the ordinal position of the columns in the table as defined. These positions are important for some of the access methods that implicitly use the default column order for returning data.

- TABLE_COLUMNS is a String array of the column names in the table. A number of the methods we are about to explore make use of this collection of names.

You should also note the _id column of the table. This uses the autoincrement feature of SQLite to have it generate a unique integer value as the primary key for your table. A number of the built-in Android tools, helper classes, and so on use and expect the name _id convention to be available, so it's a design choice you should adopt for all of your SQLite tables.

The other SQL statement issued through execSQL() is the INITIAL_DATA_INSERT statement that performs a multirow insert to bootstrap some data into the one table in our schema. This statement is entirely optional and specific to this example. Your own application might have no initial data, or enormous amounts. The syntax used for the insert statement itself is only supported in later versions of SQLite, and, therefore, later versions of Android. I return to the SQLite versions and features versus Android versions toward the end of the chapter.

The last method in the helper class implementation is a skeleton for onUpgrade(). In the example application, we are dealing with the first version of the application (DBVERSION equals 1 and is used in the constructor call). However, you can see the outline of the logic you can use to work with the provided oldVersion and newVersion values in order to decide what schema changes, data updates, or other actions you might need as part of an upgrade to your application. As I mentioned previously, you will see many examples online of people simply dropping and re-creating a database as the onUpgrade() implementation. It's lazy, but it works to a degree, so long as you don't care about your user's data. Beware this approach if you are storing any data of value!

Building a Database-Driven Activity

Now that you understand the structure and purpose of the SQLiteOpenHelper class, you can actually use it to build a database-driven application. The logic that sits behind the SQLiteExample application is shown in Listing 18-3. This is a fairly long listing, even though I have broken out the DialogWrapper class into a separate file and have not copied it here to save space—you can always view this yourself in the ch18/SQLiteExample source code.

Listing 18-3. The Main SQLiteExample Activity

```
package com.artifexdigital.android.sqliteexample;

import android.app.AlertDialog;
import android.app.ListActivity;
import android.content.ContentValues;
import android.content.DialogInterface;
import android.os.Bundle;
import android.database.Cursor;
import android.database.sqlite.SQLiteDatabase;
import android.view.LayoutInflater;
import android.view.View;
import android.widget.ArrayAdapter;
import android.widget.Toast;

import java.util.ArrayList;
import java.util.Calendar;
import java.util.List;

public class SQLiteExample extends ListActivity {
    private SQLiteDatabase myDB;
    private MySQLiteHelper myDBHelper;

    @Override
    protected void onCreate(Bundle savedInstanceState) {
        super.onCreate(savedInstanceState);
        setContentView(R.layout.activity_sqlite_example);

        myDBHelper = new MySQLiteHelper(this);
        myDB = myDBHelper.getWritableDatabase();

        displayModels();
    }
```

```java
public void onClick(View view) {
    switch(view.getId()) {
        case R.id.addNewModel:
            addModel();
            break;
        case R.id.getModelInfo:
            getModelInfo(view);
            break;
    }
}

public List<String> getModels() {
    List<String> models = new ArrayList<>();

    Cursor cursor = myDB.query(MySQLiteHelper.TABLE_NAME,
            MySQLiteHelper.TABLE_COLUMNS, null, null, null, null, null);

    cursor.moveToFirst();
    while (!cursor.isAfterLast()) {
        String model = cursor.getString(MySQLiteHelper.COLNO_MODEL_NAME);
        models.add(model);
        cursor.moveToNext();
    }

    cursor.close();
    return models;

}

public void displayModels() {
    List<String> modelEntries = getModels();

    ArrayAdapter<String> adapter = new ArrayAdapter<>(this,
            android.R.layout.simple_list_item_1, modelEntries);
    setListAdapter(adapter);
}

public void getModelInfo(View view) {

    Cursor cursor = myDB.rawQuery(
            "select _id, model_name, release_year " +
                    "from devices", null);

    cursor.moveToFirst();
    while (!cursor.isAfterLast()) {
        String model = cursor.getString(MySQLiteHelper.COLNO_MODEL_NAME);
        Integer year = cursor.getInt(MySQLiteHelper.COLNO_RELEASE_YEAR);
        Toast.makeText(this, "The " + model +
                " was released in " + year.toString(),
                Toast.LENGTH_LONG).show();
        cursor.moveToNext();
    }
```

```
        cursor.close();

    }

    private void addModel() {
        LayoutInflater myInflater=LayoutInflater.from(this);
        View addView=myInflater.inflate(R.layout.add_model_edittext, null);
        final DialogWrapper myWrapper=new DialogWrapper(addView);

        new AlertDialog.Builder(this)
                .setTitle(R.string.add_model_title)
                .setView(addView)
                .setPositiveButton(R.string.ok,
                    new DialogInterface.OnClickListener() {
                        public void onClick(DialogInterface dialog,
                                            int whichButton) {
                            insertModelRow(myWrapper);
                        }
                    })
                .setNegativeButton(R.string.cancel,
                    new DialogInterface.OnClickListener() {
                        public void onClick(DialogInterface dialog,
                                            int whichButton) {
                            // Nothing to do here
                        }
                    })
                .show();
    }

    private void insertModelRow(DialogWrapper wrapper) {
        ContentValues myValues=new ContentValues(2);

        myValues.put(MySQLiteHelper.COLNAME_MODEL, wrapper.getModel());
        myValues.put(MySQLiteHelper.COLNAME_YEAR,
            Calendar.getInstance().get(Calendar.YEAR));

        myDB.insert(MySQLiteHelper.TABLE_NAME,
            MySQLiteHelper.COLNAME_MODEL, myValues);
        //uncomment if you want inserts to be displayed immediately
        //displayModels();
    }

    @Override
    public void onDestroy() {
        super.onDestroy();

        myDB.close();
    }

}
```

The first and most important part of any SQLite-based Android application is creating an object from your helper class, and keeping it for the life of the activities that need it. Typically that's easily done, as is demonstrated here in our example application from within the launcher activity.

With your helper object available, any time you need to work with the database, all you need do is invoke its getReadableDatabase() or getWritableDatabase() method to return a database object for your underlying SQLite database. As the names suggest, a database object that is readable is used for only SELECT-style queries, whereas the writable version allows DML statements (INSERT, UPDATE, DELETE) and DDL statements like the ones used in our onCreate() helper class method.

When you are done with the immediate needs of using the database object, simply call its .close() method and the helper class tidies up. You typically do this as part of the process of your activity being finalized in onDestroy() or similar.

Our example application creates the helper object and uses getWriteableDatabase(), and then it proceeds to populate the modelEntries list using the getModels() method. With the results in hand, we feed our ArrayAdapter what it needs to inflate the ListView with the data returned from the database. The getModels() method is a deceptively short method, because is introduces and uses two major capabilities having to do with SQLite databases and Android. The first concept is the query helper approach to gathering data from your SQLite database, and the second concept involves the cursor object for managing the results that are returned. Let's look at the bigger picture of both these concepts in detail.

Choosing Query Approaches for SQLite and Android

When you are using SQLite in your application, you have to choose between two principal ways of actually retrieving the information stored in the database. Although the basis of both is the humble SELECT statement, your choice basically boils down to how much structure and hand-holding you want.

Walking Through the Query Building Process

The first approach, as seen in the getModels() method of the SQLiteExample application, is the query() method. The query() approach provides a very structured path to build up the necessary and desired column choices, tables, predicates, and so on for the query that will actually be issued against your SQLite database.

When using query(), you don't actually write the SQL SELECT statement itself. Instead, you step through the following constituent phases, and the query() method builds the equivalent SQL under the hood.

1. Provide the name of the table to be used in the query.

2. Provide the column names to select (or "project" if you are into official relational database nomenclature).

3. Provide predicates for the where clause, including any optional positional parameters.

4. If positional parameters are used, provide the values for the parameters.

5. Provide any GROUP BY, HAVING, or ORDER BY clauses.

Where one of the parts is not needed, you simply provide null. Thus, from SQLiteExample, you saw our call take this form:

```
myDB.query(MySQLiteHelper.TABLE_NAME, MySQLiteHelper.TABLE_COLUMNS,
    null, null, null, null, null)
```

This means we didn't use any predicates in a where clause, had no parameters, and didn't use any GROUP BY, HAVING, or ORDER BY options.

If this all seems very straightforward, I want you to go back and carefully read the first item in the preceding list of the steps for using query(). Note that you provide the name of the table—singular! That's right. The number one drawback of the query() approach is that it can only work with one table in a given call. This means you cannot use joins to other tables. More subtly, the predicates to the where clause must not implicitly invoke the use of other tables, meaning you cannot sneak in a subselect, an EXISTS predicate, or other approach that references another table or tables.

Using the Raw Power of SQL

If the query() method seems limiting, and you ache to use the full power of SQL, then rawQuery() is the alternative. As suggested by its name, rawQuery() takes a "raw" string representing a SQL statement. The second parameter is an optional array of positional parameters, if you choose to use them in your SQL statement. Where you don't need parameterization, simply pass null as the second parameter.

You can see the working example of rawQuery() in the getModelInfo() method of SQLiteExample:

```
myDB.rawQuery("select _id, model_name, release_year " + "from devices", null)
```

You are free to go wild with all the SQL complexity your heart desires. Everything SQLite supports can be included in rawQuery(), including nested subselects, joins, and more. Be aware, however, that the power of rawQuery() comes at a price. If you have a well-known set of static queries, then managing them with rawQuery() is fine. But as your query strings become more complex, and especially if you find yourself dynamically building SQL SELECT statements through string concatenation, then life becomes both more complex and more risky. The main danger to watch out for with string concatenation and dynamic SQL you run via rawQuery() is the risk of SQL injection.

SQL injection refers to the practice of malicious users inserting SQL database commands into text fields and application URLs in order to trigger (to deceive!) the application into executing those commands. Such exploits are among the most common, and SQL injection is at the root of many embarrassing breaches of security. This isn't an Android issue, nor really a SQLite issue—it affects every database where unsanitized dynamic SQL is used. Practice safe SQL!

Managing Data Results with Cursors

Regardless of which approach you use to query the database, your return object is a cursor, which I now cover. This concept is pretty much identical to the concept of cursors in other database programming libraries, so if you have used cursors in other databases, you already have a pretty good idea of how the SQLite cursor behaves with Android. For those of you who have not yet worked with cursors, the best way of thinking of them is as complete sets of data that result from a query, and a pointer (or cursor position) to the current row of interest within the result set.

The data-plus-positional-pointer metaphor is key to understanding the many capabilities a Cursor object gives you. Among the common tasks you can perform are the following:

- Move the cursor position and iterate over the result set with methods like moveToFirst() and moveToNext(); test the position with isAfterLast().

- Interrogate the result set to learn the names of columns, ordinal column positions, and so on with getColumnNames() and getColumnIndex().

- Extract individual column values from the current row with getString(), getInt(), and other similar methods for other data types.

- Get statistics about the result set with getCount(), but be aware that this forces the entire result set for the cursor to be read, which can consume considerable memory and take quite a bit of time for large results.

- Free all of the cursor resources using the close() method.

You typically process your cursor results in a loop, performing whatever application logic you need on each row. The SQLiteExample app does this in a few places, including in this snippet from getModels():

```
Cursor cursor = myDB.query(MySQLiteHelper.TABLE_NAME,
    MySQLiteHelper.TABLE_COLUMNS, null, null, null, null, null);

cursor.moveToFirst();
while (!cursor.isAfterLast()) {
    String model = cursor.getString(MySQLiteHelper.COLNO_MODEL_NAME);
    models.add(model);
    cursor.moveToNext();
}

cursor.close();
```

Here I use the query() method for a SQLite database object and pass it the name of the table and the String array with the column names that interest us. This means I get back a cursor with a result set that looks like Listing 18-4.

Listing 18-4. Sample Cursor Result Set for the SQLiteExample Activity

```
_id  model_name         release_year
---  -----------------  ------------
1    LG Nexus 4         2012
2    LG Nexus 5         2013
3    Samsung Galaxy S6  2015
```

I invoke the .moveToFirst() method before entering the loop, which means the current row for the cursor is the _id=1 row. Stepping through the loop, I test that we have not moved to the end of the result set for the cursor with isAfterLast(), and I call getString(), passing it the column position for the model_name column, which is represented by the COLNO_MODEL_NAME constant declared in the helper class. I add this string to our ArrayList, and use moveToNext() to continue processing the next row.

> **Tip**   This kind of iterative row processing is a very common programming practice, but it contains the most common performance peril in all database-related programming. Do not be seduced by the iterative logic of while loops or for loops if you can express the same logic declaratively in SQL. SQL is pretty much always the best choice for computation and crunching the data. Use the iterative approach in your Java code for non–data-processing logic, such as where data is bound to UI widgets or non–SQL-like processing is performed. Your performance will be preserved and your users will thank you for it.

You can also feed a Cursor object to a SimpleCursorAdapter so you can use it in binding with a ListView or other selection UI widget. In order to use any of the CursorAdapter options, or their subclasses, you must use the table structure pattern I introduced earlier in the chapter. You must create your table with a column named _id as the primary key, and you must set this key with the autoincrement property. This is the value that all of the adapter's methods expect, such as onListItemClick().

Inventing Cursors of Your Own

When the built-in Cursor class is not enough for your needs, you can branch out with the SQLiteDatabase.CursorFactory object and the queryWithFactory() and rawQueryWithFactory() methods that work with it. The factory object is responsible for generating new cursor objects with the newCursor() method. In all my years of working with Android, I have not yet found a real need to implement CursorFactory, so if you wish to know more, head over to the Android documentation.

Modifying Data with Your Android Application

A world in which you can only read existing data is usually not what you are after when you are building database-driven applications. At some stage, you will want your users to add, modify, and remove information from your SQLite database. This means you want to be able to run INSERT, UPDATE, and DELETE SQL DML statements against your database.

Android's SQLite support offers you two ways in which to carry out your DML desires. The first is to use the execSQL() method and pass a fully-formed SQL statement. This is what the SQLiteExample application does using the helper class when the database is first created. As discussed earlier, execSQL() is suitable for any kind of statement that doesn't expect to return a result. This means INSERT, UPDATE, and DELETE are just fine. If SQLite ever supports MERGE, and Android updates the SQLite library accordingly, that would also be a good candidate statement. I cover more about the nuances of Android versions and SQLite versions shortly.

The second option to using DML on your database is to use your SQLiteDatabase object's .insert(), .update(), and .delete() methods, taking the "guided-path" approach to DML in much the same way that .query() guides you to easier SELECT statements. All of these methods use a ContentValues object, which provides a SQLite-tailored map of values and columns.

Inserting Data

If you look at the insertModelRow() method from SQLiteExample, you can see the .insert() method in operation:

```
private void insertModelRow(DialogWrapper wrapper) {
    ContentValues myValues=new ContentValues(2);

    myValues.put(MySQLiteHelper.COLNAME_MODEL, wrapper.getModel());
    myValues.put(MySQLiteHelper.COLNAME_YEAR,
        Calendar.getInstance().get(Calendar.YEAR));

    myDB.insert(MySQLiteHelper.TABLE_NAME,
        MySQLiteHelper.COLNAME_MODEL, myValues);
    //uncomment if you want inserts to be displayed immediately
    //displayModels();
}
```

The .insert() method here is pretty readable thanks to the use of the helper class constants, but why those constants are there bears scrutiny. The first parameter is the name of the table into which you want your data inserted. The second parameter is an Android-required column from the table that can accept nulls, and it is known as the *null column hack*. This requirement is a workaround for some slightly strange insert behavior in SQLite itself. This hack is only used if the third parameter, the ContentValues object, is empty.

Ordinarily, the ContentValues object has some data added to it before it gets used. In our SQLiteExample application, you can see it is pulling string data from the DialogWrapper object using its .getModel() method. You can open up the class definition for yourself, but .getModel() is returning the text a user enters in the dialog box, which displays if they press the Add New Model button, as shown in Figure 18-2.

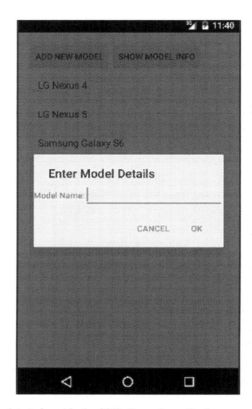

Figure 18-2. Prompting for new data to insert in the SQLiteExample application

The text the user enters becomes the value for the .put() call on the ContentValues object, and the COLNAME_MODEL column name String is used as the key. For the year of release value, we use a common Java technique to simply calculate the current year, though you can expand the complexity of the dialog to have the user input that as well.

Updating Data

Updating data with the .update() method is very similar in approach to how you do it with .insert(), with one additional consideration. Just as with .insert(), you call .update() with the String that represents the name of the table you wish to update, and you call a ContentValues object that represents the new values the column or columns you want to update should have. You can also provide an optional where clause to provide the criteria with which you can refine which rows to update. This where clause can include the question mark, ?, as a value placeholder, and you can pass a final parameter that is a list of values you can use to replace the ? parameter placeholders. This is a very common technique for parameter substitution in other database libraries, so it is likely to be familiar to many of you.

The main drawback of the .update() approach is the simplicity of the ContentValues object. It must contain actual values, and cannot use formulas or dynamically calculate the updated value as part of the executed update statement. If you need that level of sophistication, you should use a SQL update statement as part of the execSQL() method instead.

Deleting Data

Deleting data with .delete() is very similar to the process of updating with .update(); the only exception is that you do not need to provide any "new" values. Simply provide the name of the table you want to target for the delete, and optionally, provide the where clause and any parameter values it might need. This can be as simple as the following example:

```
myDB.delete(MySQLiteHelper.TABLE_NAME, "_id=?", args);
```

Assuming you provide something for args—for example, a list with one value in it, such as "2"—the delete() call will substitute that value for the ? marker, note the table name (in our case, "devices" is the MySQLiteHelper.TABLE_NAME value), and execute the resulting SQL. In our case, the SQL statement would be as follows:

```
delete from devices where _id=2
```

Again, for complex cases that requiring calculations, joins, subselects, and so on, to determine what rows to delete, you should use the execSQL() option instead.

Tracking SQLite Versions and Android Versions

Just as Android has released many versions over the years, so too has SQLite. Although SQLite is considered to be very mature and not in need of constant overhauling, at least three different library versions have shipped with various releases of Android.

All releases of Android since the initial release, up to and including versions 2.1.x, shipped with SQLite support that used the version 3.5.9 library. When Android 2.2 (Froyo) was released, the SQLite library changed to version 3.6.22. This version had very little impact; it mostly dealt with minor bug fixes and subtle improvements.

Things were static for some time again until the advent of Android 3.0 (Honeycomb). But from Honeycomb on, upgrades to the SQLite library have come thick and fast with new Android releases. Table 18-1 breaks down of all the Android versions at which SQLite versions changed.

Table 18-1. *Android Versions That Introduced New SQLite Versions*

Android Version	SQLite Version
1.0	3.5.9
2.2	3.6.22
3.0	3.7.4
4.1	3.7.11
5.0	3.8.4.3
5.1	3.8.6
6.0	3.8.11

From SQLite 3.7 on, significant enhancements and improvements have been made to features like locking, concurrency, and logging. You can decide not to worry about all the more powerful new features and just treat things as if you are using a common ancestor version of SQLite. However, there are two key things to note, even if you do want to ignore such library updates.

The database files SQLite creates include an internal version number. Historically, prior to version 3.7, this was always 1, but with the release of SQLite 3.7, it began to be incremented because at this point a newer format was required to support some of the new features. Ordinarily you can totally ignore this within an Android application. However, if you decide to package and ship a prebuilt SQLite database file with your application, you need to think about what older versions of Android you plan to support. If versions earlier than Android 3.0 Honeycomb interest you, ensure that you use the older SQLite database file format. Although all versions of the SQLite library happily work with the old format without requiring any kind of update or rebuild, shipping a newer format database to an old device with a pre-3.7 SQLite library version will cause unpredictable results, likely including program crashes and data corruption issues.

The second point you need to think about is any situations in which you want to use rawQuery() or execSQL() and newer SQL syntax that is supported by later versions of SQLite. A concrete example of this is the insert statement I constructed in the MySQLiteHelper class. This example uses the newer multirow insert syntax that was only introduced in SQLite 3.8:

```
insert into devices (model_name, release_year) values
  ('LG Nexus 4', 2012),
  ('LG Nexus 5', 2013),
  ('Samsung Galaxy S6', 2015)
```

Usually, you will find ways of working around this if you want to provide the broadest possible support. For example, I can perform our multirow insert using a hack with unions and subselects, as follows:

```
insert into devices (model_name, release_year)
  select 'LG Nexus 4', 2012
  union
  select 'LG Nexus 5', 2013
  union
  select 'Samsung Galaxy S6', 2015
```

This is far less elegant, but it is supported in all versions of SQLite. The main point here is that you need to check whether you plan to use any recently added SQL features in your statements, and you need to decide whether to set an appropriate `minSdkVersion` value in your application manifest to ensure you target versions of Android with the SQLite library capabilities you need, or code your SQL to the lowest common denominator.

Packaging and Managing SQLite Databases for Android

You are now well on your way to mastering the use of SQLite for your Android applications. But in addition to learning simple coding, make sure to acquaint yourself with design considerations and the topic of the "care and feeding" of databases, so that your users enjoy using your database-driven applications over time. Whether it's ensuring that I/O performance doesn't hinder your UI thread, or preparing the perfect database to include in your application, a little attention to detail here goes a long way.

Managing Performance and Android Storage

In Chapter 17, I covered various aspects of using and managing files and file systems on Android in detail, including SQLite database files. I won't repeat everything from that chapter here, but I do want to point out one thing that you will hear again. Most Android devices ship with onboard storage based on flash (using NAND hardware).

As you build Android applications using SQLite databases, and as you merrily have your users inserting, updating, and deleting data, remember that they will be reliant on the flash storage to manage the writes to "disk." Unfortunately, flash storage is notoriously fickle and consistent fast writes. Often you might get great write performance, and then suddenly see a speed decrease because the flash storage is managing some internal properties such as wear leveling and the like. This means a write could suddenly take hundreds of milliseconds or even whole seconds.

Don't be fooled by the behavior of your application when you are running it in the emulator. It might look fast, but it is almost certainly using an AVD completely cached in your computer's very fast memory, including the simulated storage and file system. Writes in the emulator are not really writes to disk, and they will seem much faster than any write your application performs when it is actually deployed to a device.

To mitigate the performance risk, use the `AsnycTask()` approach described in Chapter 17 so that database changes happen on an asynchronous thread, away from the main UI thread.

You should also think about what happens to flash, and to your application's data, in low-power situations. If a device loses power, SQLite's abilities to recover from crashes and preserve the "durability" property of ACID should protect your actual data. But you may need to know this is happening, and you may also want to check to see if any transactions were rolled back because they failed to commit during a power-down or power-up situation.

You can add some smarts to your application to track and take action in low-power situations. You can register a receiver in your application to watch for broadcasts like ACTION_BATTERY_ CHANGED. You can also examine the intent payload, determine what is going on with the power and battery, and take action such as warning the user or deferring write-heavy tasks.

Packaging Your Own SQLite Database with Your Application

In the SQLiteExample application, the helper class adds three rows of data to the devices table to seed the database. But what if I want to add a few hundred devices? Indeed, currently thousands of known Android devices have been released. Trying to insert all of these at database creation time when the application first runs will be cumbersome, will possibly provide a terrible performance experience, and could run into a variety of runtime errors.

In situations in which you want a nontrival database to be used from the beginning with your application, you can ship a SQLite database in place, packaging it with your other assets within the .apk file.

You are already familiar with the assets/ folder in your project. You can place an already-created-and-populated SQLite database file into the assets/ folder and then pass the path and filename to the overloaded openDatabase() method that accepts a full file location as its first parameter.

To create the full path and filename for your SQLite database file, you need to know that database assets get placed into the file system folder /data/data/your.package.name/ databases/. Append the string representing your file name (e.g., devices.db from our example application) and you have the value to pass as a parameter to openDatabase(). In our example application, this would be the following:

```
/data/data/com.artifexdigital.android.sqliteexample/devices.db
```

Preparing SQLite Databases for Packaging

Handcrafting databases of any type is a tedious affair, so you will almost certainly want some tools to help design your database and populate it if you want to package a database file with your Android application.

SQLite has a wealth of options to choose from, including the sqlite3 shell program that ships with almost all operating systems (Windows is the exception here). Even the Android emulator provides access to the sqlite3 utility. You can invoke it from the adb shell utility once you are connected to your emulated device. For example,

```
sqlite3 /data/data/com.artifexdigital.android.sqliteexample/devices.db
```

A lot of options are available within the `sqlite3` utility. Check out the documentation at `sqlite.org` for more details. The adb tool also provides some other useful general file management commands that you can harness for your SQLite database files, such as adb push to move a file to a device, and adb pull to copy a file from a device.

Of course, you may want to use a fancier GUI tool, and there are many to choose from. One of the most popular is a plug-in for Firefox known as the SQLite Manager. Figure 18-3 shows the SQLite Manager in action.

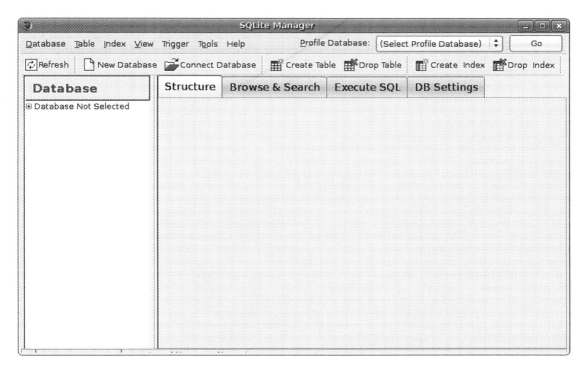

Figure 18-3. *The GUI for SQLite Manager in Firefox*

One nice aspect of using browser extensions like this is that they work on all the platforms the browser itself supports.

For a wider list of GUI tools for SQLite database management, check out sqlite.org.

Using Preferences

In the previous chapters you learned how to store, modify, and retrieve information from the Android file system and using SQLite databases. Android has multiple ways of storing information that suit many different purposes and goals. One of the simplest pieces of information you may want to store on behalf of your users is a simple preference or option setting. For instance, you may want to store a preference for date format, or a nickname in a chat program.

Using a dedicated file or database for storing very small preference data is overkill, so Android provides the preferences system as a way of storing and using simple key/value items that persist across repeated activity lifecycles. Although the system and technique are called preferences, you can, in fact, store anything you like, so long as it can be mapped to simple key/value pairs. The main limitation, as you will explore in the examples that follow, is that the key values must be strings, and the values must be in one of the primitive Java data types such as int, Boolean, and so on.

Everything Old Is New Again

Before we delve into the details of coding and controlling preferences, here's a little history lesson to help you understand how preferences have changed over Android's lifetime.

With the original release of Android, preferences were controlled by the PreferenceActivity subclass, which had the job of loading preferences from resource XML files. This process was very straightforward, and simple. As a developer, you'd use PreferenceActivity to directly determine, based on individual preferences, what behavior your application should perform.

Things changed to a degree when Google released Android 3.0 (Honeycomb). Although the PreferenceActivity subclass (and its fragment parallels, PreferenceFragment and others) still has the job of controlling preferences, it does so by loading preference headers from your resource files.

As we explore both new and old approaches, you'll see how things differ. The reason you as a developer still need to be familiar with both approaches is two-fold. First and foremost, the new `PreferenceActivity` approach is not included in the Android support library for older versions, meaning there is no system-provided way to mimic the new behavior in an older Android version. The second reason is related to the first—old versions of Android, particularly Android 2.2 and 2.3, still abound, and you need to make some design choices about whether you want to target those old versions. Let's explore both new and old preference approaches, and you can then decide what you should use for your application.

Starting with Preferences

Preferences can be conceptually grouped into three "tiers" or "scopes" that target different levels of sharing and availability.

The lowest level of preferences work at the level of an activity and are accessed via the `getPreferences()` method. `getPreferences()` uses the activity class name to associate the preference with the activity (this process is transparent to you—more on this in a moment). A security visibility parameter is also passed to `getPreferences()`, and normally you would choose the `MODE_PRIVATE` constant to mark the preference as private so that no other application can access it.

The next highest level of preferences targets your entire application or application-level context. Preferences at this level are controlled with the `getSharedPreferences()` method, which takes a similar privacy marker to `getPreferences()` and an explicit preference set name. This means you can create and use multiple preference sets at the application level. If you return to `getPreferences()` at the activity level for the moment, you should know that it actually calls `getSharedPreferences()` and uses the activity class name as the preference set value.

The last scope or tier of preferences falls under the `PreferenceManager` object and its governance of shared preferences across the entire Android device and its preference framework. Interaction here is normally via the `getDefaultSharedPreferences()` method and its variants. Calls to `getDefaultSharedPreferences()` take a context, such as your activity.

Whichever level you work at, the associated method call returns a `SharedPreferences` object representing the complete map of relevant key/value pairs. A `SharedPreferences` object comes equipped with getter helper methods such as `getInt`, `getString`, and `getBoolean`, each of which takes a `String` as the key to look for among the preferences. A second "defValue" parameter is also provided, and it represents the default to return if the key is not found (by implication, that preference has not yet been set).

In practice it is almost always worth working with your preferences at the highest level using `getDefaultSharedPreferences()`. This has two benefits. First, you get a fully-formed `SharedPreferences` object that works seamlessly with a `PreferenceActivity`. Second, as a developer, you save yourself from the ongoing mental gymnastics of having to remember the various tiers of preferences and where you might have stashed away a given preference key/value pair.

Recording Preferences

Once you have your SharedPreferences object in hand, you can modify the value or values you desire by calling the edit() method to invoke the editor for your preferences. This provides you with a SharedPreferences.Editor object, which has setter methods that match the getters mentioned earlier, such as setString(), setBoolean(), and so forth.

A number of additional methods are crucial to editing your preferences:

- ▓ commit() actually saves the changes you have made via setter calls. This returns a Boolean indicating success or failure.

- ▓ apply() is a faster version of commit(), effectively doing a "fire and forget" attempt to persist your changes. There is no return value.

- ▓ remove() is used to purge a single preference key and its value.

- ▓ clear() deletes all of your preference keys and values. Use with caution!

The main behavior to note is that you must code your application to use commit() or apply() after you use any combination of setter calls in order to actually save your changes to preferences. Without such a call, your efforts are lost when the SharedPreferences.Editor object loses scope.

On the flip side of needing to commit, once you do call commit() or apply(), preference changes are instantly visible. This means, for instance, that a preference set in one fragment of a visible activity is instantly available in another fragment within the same activity.

Working with Preference-Specific Activities and Fragments

The preferred way to incorporate preferences into your application is through the use of PreferenceActivity and PreferenceFragment contexts. There are lots of good reasons to use this approach that become apparent in the example we explore shortly. However, there is a non-code reason to use the activity and fragment approach provided by Android: consistency.

It is possible to design and build your own system of managing preferences. You might think you have a good approach that uses some kind of local storage, a database, or even a remote web service. But if you think about this from the user's perspective, when they work with a device, they work with lots of applications, not just yours, and if each does preferences in a distinct and different way, the user experience becomes confusing, disjointed, and quite likely, a mess.

If you use the PreferenceActivity approach, along with PreferenceFragment and the related preference header and preferences XML resource files, you provide your users with a consistent and very slick preference experience. As a reminder, the preference system was revamped with Android 3.0, so you will find many old references online and in books to the previous technique. I will talk about the old approach briefly toward the end of the chapter so that those of you developing for older devices are covered. For now, let's explore the contemporary approach in the sample application, FragmentPreferencesExample, which you can find in ch19/FragmentPreferencesExample.

Seeing the Big Picture with Preferences

I have designed the sample application, FragmentPreferencesExample, to show the many options you have with preferences in action, as well as to let you visualize the behind-the-scenes preference values as you interact with the a PreferenceActivity and its PreferenceFragments.

Figure 19-1 shows the initial view of the launcher activity.

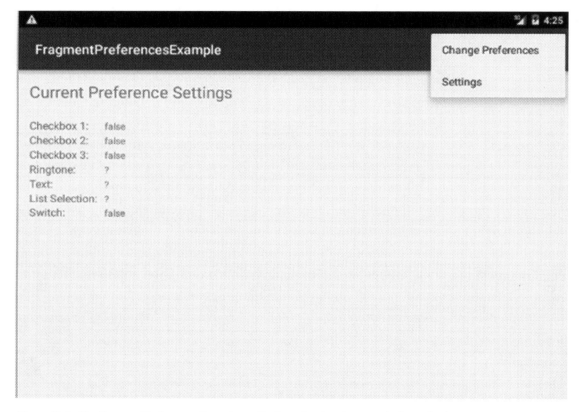

Figure 19-1. *The FragmentPreferencesExample application, showing the menu in the action bar*

We will discuss the use of getDefaultSharedPreferences, the SharedPreferences object, and using the getters to populate what you see in Figure 19-1 shortly. Of immediate interest is the simple menu that has been promoted to the action bar, offering you the option to change preferences.

Invoking the Change Preferences menu item results in the activity shown in Figure 19-2, which reveals preferences in all their glory.

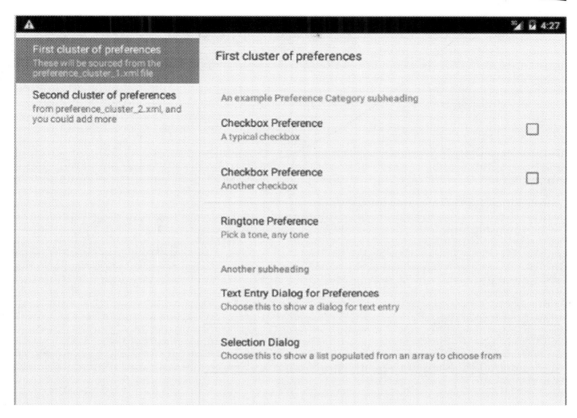

Figure 19-2. Preference headers and the preference screen in fragments

The layout and detail shown in Figure 19-2 demonstrate `PreferenceFragments` in all their glory and the controlling preference headers that define and manage them. Let's start our exploration of the code from the vantage of the preference headers.

Using Preference and Preference Header Resources

In Listing 19-1, I took the layout and entries for the left-side preference headings from configuration data in the `preference_headers.xml` file.

Listing 19-1. Contents of the preference_headers.xml File

```
<preference-headers xmlns:android="http://schemas.android.com/apk/res/android">
    <header
        android:fragment="com.artifexdigital.android.fragmentpreferencesexample.
        DefaultPreferenceFragment"
        android:title="First cluster of preferences"
        android:summary="These will be sourced from the preference_cluster_1.xml file">
        <extra android:name="fragprefresource" android:value="preference_cluster_1" />
    </header>
    <header
```

```
        android:fragment="com.artifexdigital.android.fragmentpreferencesexample.
        DefaultPreferenceFragment"
        android:title="Second cluster of preferences"
        android:summary="from preference_cluster_2.xml, and you could add more">
        <extra android:name="fragprefresource" android:value="preference_cluster_2" />
    </header>
</preference-headers>
```

Dissecting this preference header resource file is straightforward and should illuminate how control over all of the ultimate low-level preferences is performed. Within the <preference-headers> element, you can define one or more <header> elements that act to visually group individual collections of preferences. You can see that in this case, I have two <header> elements, but I could have one, five, or dozens.

This preference header resource file is loaded from a PreferenceActivity context and controls all of the preference headings, options, display, and so forth you see in Figure 19-2. Each header has a handful of attributes, including the title used for display text and a summary to further explain that header's purpose. A child <extra> element is the secret that links a given header to the subordinate preferences it controls through a trick I introduce later in the chapter.

In the example application, the two <header> elements each include an <extra> element, named preference_cluster_1 and preference_cluster_2, respectively. These map to resource XML files preference_cluster_1.xml and preference_cluster_2.xml. You can name these files anything you like, so long as you ensure matching android:value attributes within the <extra> child element. These are used to create the PreferenceFragment subclass that will contain the respective clusters of preferences.

> **Note**　For Android Studio users, to use the naming and referencing approach from the FragmentPreferencesExample application, you need to create a folder named xml within the res folder of your project to hold your preference-related XML files. Eclipse users with the traditional ADT should already see this folder in their project hierarchy.

You might have noticed that I have strenuously avoided using the term *category* when describing preference headers and preference resource files. I have used the terms *cluster* or *group*, because there is no logical restriction on what preferences can be placed together in a preference resource file, nor are there any coding or logic implications from grouping things together. The word *category* can be misleading when used with preferences, as developers start to think that perhaps all checkbox preferences need to be placed together, or anything that affects program logic, such as font characteristics, must be placed together. No such requirement exists—you are free to group preferences in any way you like, just as in the example application.

Returning to the two clusters of preferences defined in preference_headers.xml, Listing 19-2 shows the preference_cluster_1.xml file.

Listing 19-2. The Preferences Described in preference_cluster_1.xml

```
<PreferenceScreen
    xmlns:android="http://schemas.android.com/apk/res/android">
    <PreferenceCategory android:title="An example Preference Category subheading">
        <CheckBoxPreference
            android:key="checkbox1"
            android:title="Checkbox Preference"
            android:summary="A typical checkbox"
            />
        <CheckBoxPreference
            android:key="checkbox2"
            android:title="Checkbox Preference"
            android:summary="Another checkbox"
            />
        <RingtonePreference
            android:key="ringtone"
            android:title="Ringtone Preference"
            android:showDefault="true"
            android:showSilent="true"
            android:summary="Pick a tone, any tone"
            />
    </PreferenceCategory>
    <PreferenceCategory android:title="Another subheading">
        <EditTextPreference
            android:key="text"
            android:title="Text Entry Dialog for Preferences"
            android:summary="Choose this to show a dialog for text entry"
            android:dialogTitle="Enter your text value"
            />
        <ListPreference
            android:key="list"
            android:title="Selection Dialog"
            android:summary="Choose this to show a list populated from an array to
            choose from"
            android:entries="@array/colors"
            android:entryValues="@array/color_codes"
            android:dialogTitle="What is your favorite color?" />
    </PreferenceCategory>
</PreferenceScreen>
```

Its partner file, preference_cluster_2.xml, is shown in Listing 19-3.

Listing 19-3. The Preferences Described in preference_cluster_2.xml

```
<PreferenceScreen
    xmlns:android="http:// schemas.android.com/apk/res/android">
    <CheckBoxPreference
        android:key="checkbox3"
        android:title="More Checkbox"
        android:summary="Another typical checkbox"
        />
```

```
<SwitchPreference
    android:key="switch"
    android:title="A Switch"
    android:summary="A switch instead."
    />
</PreferenceScreen>
```

Each file includes the root <PreferenceScreen> element, portraying what one onscreen display of preferences will include. Each child element is a preference variant of some sort, based on the standard widgets with which you are already familiar, such as Checkbox, EditText, and so on. When the PreferenceFragment subclass is instantiated, it takes care of inflating the preference UI items into widgets on the screen. You do not need to define your own layouts in general—the only exception is where you wish to use a custom layout for list elements in a ListView rendering for ListPreference. If you are happy with the defaults, you will see a ListPreference preference rendered with the contents of the array resource named in the android:entries attribute. These act as the key to the equivalent positional entry in the android:entryValues array. That sounds a little clunky, but it works.

For instance, if you look in the arrays.xml resource from the example project, you will see an array named colors like this:

```
<string-array name="colors">
    <item>Red</item>
    <item>Orange</item>
    <item>Yellow</item>
    <item>Green</item>
    <item>Blue</item>
    <item>Indigo</item>
    <item>Violet</item>
</string-array>
```

Following the colors array is the color-code array, which provides the possible parameter values associated with each display key:

```
<string-array name="color_codes">
    <item>#FF0000</item>
    <item>#FFA500</item>
    <item>#FFFF00</item>
    <item>#00FF00</item>
    <item>#0000FF</item>
    <item>#4B0082</item>
    <item>#EE82EE</item>
</string-array>
```

With the default ListView row layout, if you choose the Selection Dialog preference item in the first cluster of preferences, you will see the ListView dialog rendered in Figure 19-3.

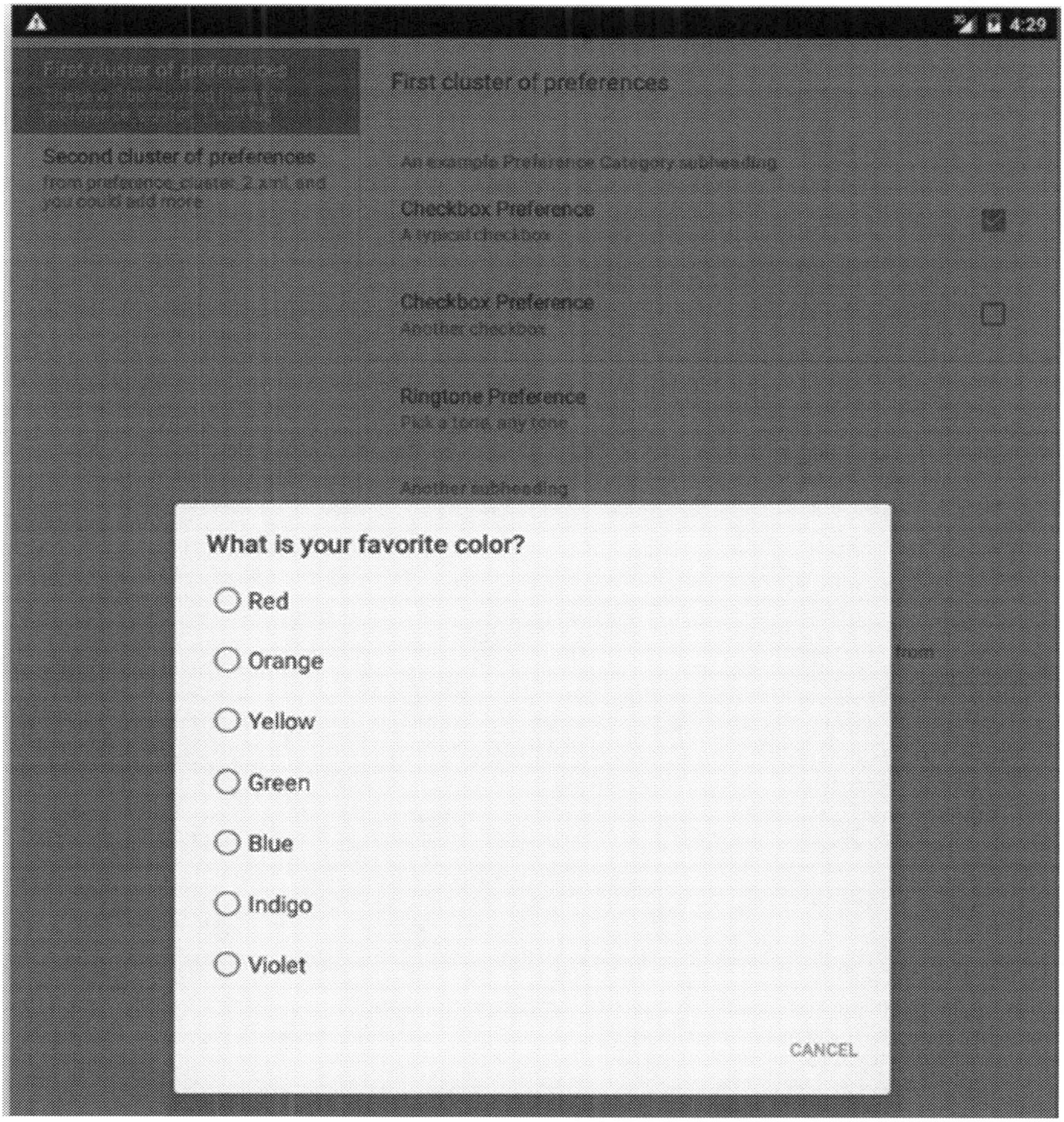

First cluster of preferences

Second cluster of preferences
from preference_cluster_2.xml, and
you could add more

First cluster of preferences

An example Preference Category subheading

Checkbox Preference
A typical checkbox

Checkbox Preference
Another checkbox

Ringtone Preference
Pick a tone, any tone

Another subheading

What is your favorite color?

○ Red

○ Orange

○ Yellow

○ Green

○ Blue

○ Indigo

○ Violet

CANCEL

Figure 19-3. A preference that selects from an array presented in ListView fashion

The main attribute to note about all the preference types is android:key, which is the reference half of the key/value pair that constitutes a preference. Note that you do not strictly need to use reference files to break up the preference headers and resource XML files in the fashion shown. You can include bare key/value preference items in multiple <extra> elements within the <header> if you prefer. But I think you'll agree the separation makes sense, and it is much more readable when your collection of preferences grows to moderate or large in size.

Because the Android preference framework and the preference header and individual preference screen files do much (but not all!) of the background work to bring everything together, the ChangePreferences PreferenceActivity just needs to call the loadHeadersFromResource() method in your implementation of the override for onBuildHeaders, as you can see in Listing 19-4.

Listing 19-4. The PreferenceActivity Implementation in ChangePreferences

```
package com.artifexdigital.android.fragmentpreferencesexample;

import android.preference.PreferenceActivity;
import java.util.List;

public class ChangePreferences extends PreferenceActivity {
    @Override
    public void onBuildHeaders(List<Header> myPrefHeaders) {
        loadHeadersFromResource(R.xml.preference_headers, myPrefHeaders);
    }

    @Override
    protected boolean isValidFragment(String fragmentName) {
        return DefaultPreferenceFragment.class.getName().equals(fragmentName);
    }
}
```

The second override within ChangePreferences is the isValidFragment method. This method was introduced in Android 4.1 in response to a security vulnerability that allowed arbitrary fragments to be injected at runtime when a PreferenceActivity loaded a PreferenceFragment. You need to implement logic to ensure the fully qualified name of the fragment being loaded is the one you intended when the fragment is invoked. Do not fall into the trap of simply returning true in the isValidFragment method. Although this is syntactically correct, it leaves the original vulnerability available for exploit.

Filling in the Blanks with PreferenceFragment

You will see shortly that when we examine the launcher activity for the FragmentPreferencesExample application, we simply start the ChangePreferences activity when the user selects the Change Preferences menu item, by dint of directly starting the ChangePreferences activity with a call to startActivity(). Because it is a PreferenceActivity, it will invoke the onBuildHeaders() callback and elegantly map out all of the preference headers you decided to declare in the related XML resource. No fuss, no extra coding required. For each header, the related preference screen elements will be parsed—whether from a nominated resource file or from direct key/value entries—and then something a little jarring occurs. The Android preference framework then expects to find the custom subclass you have coded to process the items from the resource file and call addPreferenceFromResource(). You read that correctly. Android does a great job helping with the preference headers, and then it leaves you in the lurch with the individual preference screens.

You have a few choices in this situation, depending on the volume of preferences you plan for your application and your appetite for needless repetitive coding. You can

- Customize a `PreferenceFragment` subclass for each preference screen, calling `addPreferenceFromResource()` and any optional logic you might imagine.

- Design a single `PreferenceFragment` subclass that can navigate all of your preferences, for instance, via their headers using an agreed format for `<extra>` elements to enable them to be identified, and the associated `<preference-screen>` elements to be handled by the same subclass for fragment handling.

I know it seems crazy that you need to go to this additional level of effort when you would expect the Android preference framework to take care of this. Sadly, even after four major releases of Android since the advent of the new approach to preferences, this is still a work in progress.

Listing 19-5 shows an implementation of the `PreferenceFragment` subclass for the example application.

Listing 19-5.

```
package com.artifexdigital.android.fragmentpreferencesexample;

import android.os.Bundle;
import android.preference.PreferenceFragment;

public class DefaultPreferenceFragment extends PreferenceFragment {

    @Override
    public void onCreate(Bundle savedInstanceState) {
        super.onCreate (savedInstanceState);

        int myResource=getActivity().getResources().getIdentifier(
                    getArguments().getString("fragprefresource"),"xml",
                    getActivity().getPackageName());

        addPreferencesFromResource(myResource);
    }

}
```

You can find many alternative examples and approaches to the same write-once-use-everywhere approach to the `PreferenceFragment` subclassing issue. As `addPreferencesFromResource()` takes a resource identifier for the preferences to inflate in the fragment. This implementation tries to find the related `<header>` by expecting the `<extras>` element to include an `android:name` attribute with the value "fragprefresource" and uses the `getIdentifier()` trick to go from knowing a textual name of the related `android:value`, which is the preference file that Android will have automatically loaded, to finding its related resource ID at runtime. This is a reflection-based technique, which also relies on two other parameters: first, a resource type, which for our preference files is xml, and second, the package to hold the resulting resource, which is almost always your own package.

> **Tip**   Using reflection is a slow process in any language and system, and particularly in the case of Android with limited processing power and system resources. Use it sparingly, and never in frequently called code, loops, and so on.

Bringing the Preference Puzzle Pieces Together

Now that you understand how the internals of preferences are managed, and the pieces to fill in the blanks that Android has left, you can review the interesting parts of the example FragmentPreferencesExample application. Most of the code in Listing 19-6 is simple onscreen widget entry setup, so you can see the preference values, even when they are not interacting with the PreferenceActivity and fragments.

Listing 19-6. The Launcher Activity in FragmentPreferencesExample

```
package com.artifexdigital.android.fragmentpreferencesexample;

import android.support.v7.app.ActionBarActivity;
import android.content.Intent;
import android.content.SharedPreferences;
import android.os.Bundle;
import android.preference.PreferenceManager;
import android.view.Menu;
import android.view.MenuItem;
import android.widget.TextView;

public class FragmentPreferencesExample extends ActionBarActivity {
    private TextView checkbox1=null;
    private TextView checkbox2=null;
    private TextView checkbox3=null;
    private TextView ringtone=null;
    private TextView text=null;
    private TextView list=null;
    private TextView mySwitch=null;

    @Override
    protected void onCreate(Bundle savedInstanceState) {
        super.onCreate(savedInstanceState);
        setContentView(R.layout.activity_fragment_preferences_example);

        checkbox1=(TextView)findViewById(R.id.checkbox1);
        checkbox2=(TextView)findViewById(R.id.checkbox2);
        checkbox3=(TextView)findViewById(R.id.checkbox3);
        ringtone=(TextView)findViewById(R.id.ringtone);
        text=(TextView)findViewById(R.id.text);
```

```
        list=(TextView)findViewById(R.id.list);
        mySwitch=(TextView) findViewById(R.id.myswitch);
    }

    @Override
    public void onResume() {
        super.onResume();

        SharedPreferences myPrefs =
            PreferenceManager.getDefaultSharedPreferences(this);

        checkbox1.setText(new Boolean(myPrefs.getBoolean("checkbox1", false))
                .toString());
        checkbox2.setText(new Boolean(myPrefs.getBoolean("checkbox2", false))
                .toString());
        checkbox3.setText(new Boolean(myPrefs.getBoolean("checkbox3", false))
                .toString());
        ringtone.setText(myPrefs.getString("ringtone", "?"));
        text.setText(myPrefs.getString("text", "?"));
        list.setText(myPrefs.getString("list", "?"));
        mySwitch.setText(new Boolean(myPrefs.getBoolean("switch", false))
                .toString());
    }

    @Override
    public boolean onCreateOptionsMenu(Menu menu) {
        getMenuInflater().inflate(R.menu.menu_fragment_preferences_example, menu);
        return true;
    }

    @Override
    public boolean onOptionsItemSelected(MenuItem item) {
        int id = item.getItemId();

        if (id == R.id.change_preferences) {
            startActivity(new Intent(this, ChangePreferences.class));
            return true;
        }

        if (id == R.id.action_settings) {
            // We could invoke other preference changes here if desired
            return true;
        }
        return super.onOptionsItemSelected(item);
    }

}
```

The two areas of code worth noting are the onResume() override and the onOptionsItemSelected() override. In the case of onResume(), whether the application is starting for the first time, as shown in Figure 19-1, or resuming from running in the background or being paused, I used a SharedPreferences object and the getter methods described at the beginning of the chapter to update the onscreen widget values. If you do this as well, you can always see the details of your preference settings. You may never need to do this in a real application, but it is useful for learning and debugging. Figure 19-4 shows the activity once I have toyed with the preferences to some degree.

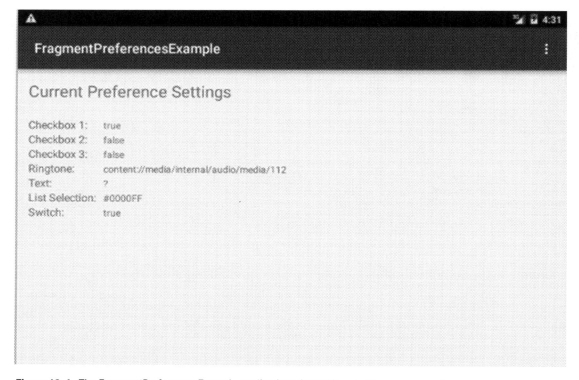

Figure 19-4. The FragmentPreferencesExample application after various preferences are set

In onOptionsItemSelected(), I test which menu item was chosen, and if it is the change_preferences resource identified in my menu layout, I explicitly launch my ChangePreferences() PreferenceActivity and the fun begins.

Other Preference Considerations

The Android preference framework continues to evolve; it received minor tweaks and changes in all of the releases up to Android 6.0 (Marshmallow). There are still areas where it pays to know the boundaries of what Android does and does not offer.

Customizing Preferences

There are two fundamental approaches to extending the preference framework if you find you are limited by the many options already offered in PreferenceActivity, PreferenceFragment, and the headers and screens of the preferences that populate them.

▒ Extend the `DialogPreference` class to create a custom preference dialog. For instance, you can create a dialog with multiple fields, performing calculations, and so forth, which then ultimately sets a preference value.

▒ Extend a `<header>` to include an `<intent>` child element, and include the attribute `android:action="your-fully-package-qualified-intent-here"`. When it is chosen, the intent is fired, and then whichever suitable activity has the relevant intent-filter set is selected to run.

Both of these approaches are a left as an exercise for you to experiment with.

Nesting Preferences and Display Quirks

If you develop applications with many preferences, it can be tempting to think about nesting one set of preferences inside another, and so on. Be aware that the modern themes, such as Holo and the various material-design inspired options shipped with Android versions 4.0, 5.0, and 6.0, do not provide nested preference screen thematics, so your nested `PreferenceScreen` items will appear unskinned and look very different from any other theme or design language you might have chosen.

Using the Old-School Approach to Preferences

Now that you have mastered the contemporary Android preference framework, let's take a quick look at the old approach to preferences so that you are familiar with it should you ever need to target pre-Android 3.0 with your applications, but also so you can spot outdated advice when you inevitably go searching the Internet for tweaks and tricks for preferences.

Losing Headers and Fragments

The main conceptual differences in the original Android preferences framework were the single "level" of preference resources, and the lack of fragments in general and the `PreferenceFragment` in particular. Remember that fragments themselves were only introduced in Android 3.0 as part of the scramble to address the then-booming tablet market.

The main help you receive is via the `PreferenceActivity` class, which still bootstraps most of the things you need to manage preferences; this includes offering shared access to the system's `SharedPreferences` object in a very smooth way.

In other respects, the main launcher activity can remain the same, and indeed, whatever activities you would otherwise code for a given application are not affected when you change to using the old approach to preferences.

Adapting PreferenceActivty for Older Behavior

You can change the ChangePreferences class to deal with multiple preference resource files by "stacking" calls to addPreferencesFromResource() in the standard onCreate() override, as shown in Listing 19-7.

Listing 19-7. Modifying ChangePreferences for the Old Approach to Preferences

```
package com.artifexdigital.android.oldpreferencesexample;

import android.preference.PreferenceActivity;

public class ChangePreferences extends PreferenceActivity {
    @Override
    public void onCreate(Bundle savedInstanceState) {
        super.onCreate(savedInstanceState);

        addPreferencesFromResouce(R.xml.preference_cluster_1);
        addPreferencesFromResouce(R.xml.preference_cluster_2);
        // and potentially many more calls to addPreferencesFromResouce()
    }

}
```

As you can see in Listing 19-7, you can call addPreferencesFromResource() to stack more and more preference UI widgets into the PreferenceActivity. This might become a bit silly if you get carried away, so you can either confine your preferences to a small collection, or use some switch logic in a menu callback to selectively load a few of the preference resources.

Android Security and Permissions

The fact that you are reading this book, and are thinking of developing applications for Android, means you have certainly been exposed to ongoing security issues that are an inescapable fact of modern operating systems and programs. Catchy names like Heartbleed and Shellshock have brought security to the forefront of even nontechnical consumers' thinking, so people looking to buy and use your applications will be more aware than ever that there are risks and problems that can lurk in an unexpected corner of the Internet, or the latest Android game they just downloaded.

The good news is that security is a fundamental part of all phases of development, deployment, and use of applications in Android, and there are lots of things Android does for you and many tools at your disposal to help you build robust, secure applications. In this chapter we explore the permissions system that allows you to safely share resources and interact with other parts of Android; we discuss the packaging and deployment of applications to a device; and we cover the protection offered by Android's package management, package signing, and related Google Play Store mechanisms. Let's get started!

Requesting Permissions for Your Application

You are already familiar with a few instances of requesting permissions for the example applications used earlier in the book. In Chapter 13, the PhoneCallExample application needed the CALL_PHONE permission in order to directly dial a number; and in Chapter 17, the example applications working to write data to storage needed the WRITE_EXTERNAL_STORAGE permission in order to change files.

These are just two examples of the dozens of permissions baked into Android with the goal of protecting sensitive data or powerful (and potentially costly) features. In addition to using the Android-provided set of permissions, you as a developer are also able to create custom permissions for your application, and you have control over whether and how other applications use your resources. I cover custom permissions more later in the chapter.

You need to request each permission you wish to be granted through a `<uses-permission>` element in your `AndroidManifest.xml` file. You may remember seeing these entries in the earlier examples, but now, so you get the complete picture, let me explain that you can have as few or as many permission requests as you deem fit in your manifest; each is a child element under the `<manifest>` root that takes this form:

```
<uses-permission android:name="<the permission name>"
   android:maxSdkVersion="<version number>"
```

When you are specifying the value for the `android:name` attribute, you have well over 100 separate permissions from which to choose. I won't waste pages repeating them all here, so to get an idea of your choices, you can check the full list in the Android developer documentation at `http://developer.android.com/guide/topics/manifest/uses-permission-element.html`. A few of the notable and interesting permissions that I haven't already covered in earlier chapters are as follows:

- ACCESS_FINE_LOCATION: Enables your application to get the maximum precision for device location from a range of sensors including GPS, wifi, cell tower triangulation, and more.

- BODY_SENSORS: Gain access to data about the device user's physical body, taken from sensors, such as skin temperature monitors, pulse monitors, pedometers, and so on.

- FLASHLIGHT: Allows access to camera flashes and dedicated flashlights that can be used as light sources and works (separate from any other function, like taking pictures).

- INTERNET: Talks to remote network IPs and services running remotely onthe device.

Any Android-provided permission lives in the `android.permission` namespace, so when you are specifying any permission value in the `android:name` attribute of `<uses-permission>`, you need to include the fully-qualified name, such as `android.permission.INTERNET`.

The `android:maxSdkVersion` attribute tells Android the threshold for version-checking when you are installing and running your application. A device that is running an Android release higher than the `maxSdkVersion` you specify ignores the permission request. The main use for this attribute is not to inadvertently fail permission checks and break your application; instead, it primarily works with known permission relaxation changes that happen in Android from release to release. For instance, from API version 19 on, an application no longer needs to request `WRITE_EXTERNAL_STORAGE` to write to its own application-scoped directories. In fact, we could add this to our example application from Chapter 17 and save the file system permission checks on newer API releases.

Listing 20-1 shows an excerpt of the `AndroidManifest.xml` file for the `PermissionsExample` application from the `ch19/PermissionsExample` folder. You can see it is as simple as directly editing the XML to add the desired permission entries.

Listing 20-1. Permissions Added to the Manifest of the PermissionsExample Project

```xml
<?xml version="1.0" encoding="utf-8"?>
<manifest xmlns:android="http://schemas.android.com/apk/res/android"
    package="com.artifexdigital.android.permissionsexample" >

    <uses-permission android:name="android.permission.INTERNET" />
    <uses-permission android:name="android.permission.CAMERA" />
    ...
```

For those nostalgic users who are fans of Eclipse and the ADT, there is a graphical XML editor that helps ensure that layouts, manifests, and other XML files are always valid and well-formed. For the `AndroidManifest.xml` and permissions in particular, this editor also provides a list of known platform-provided permissions from which you can just click to insert the selected permissions into the underlying manifest file. Figure 20-1 shows the editor in action.

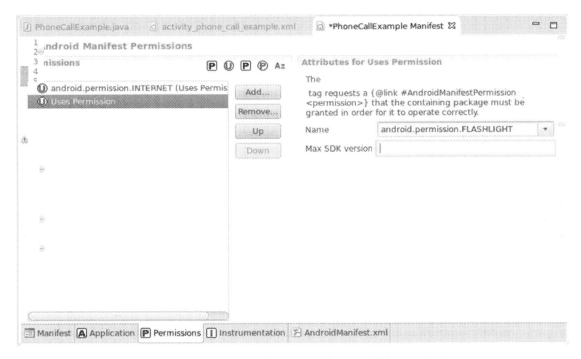

Figure 20-1. The graphical XML editor in Eclipse provides plenty of help specifying permissions

This might seem like needless UI gloss, but for Eclipse users, it ensures that permission typographical naming errors are avoided; you will find this functionality very useful once you understand the design-time limitations in debugging permissions (more on that later in the chapter). For Android Studio users, Google dispensed with a graphical editor for manifest files and instead relies on the content assistance feature to provide valid permission entries as you type. That strictly is just as good at getting permission names right, but it is an overall loss in ensuring that your XML file as a whole is valid and well-formed from the beginning.

Dealing with Debugging Permissions

When you are working with permissions for secured services and resources, one of the frustrations of Android development is the lack of design-time checks for required permissions as you write your Java code. This means that in the absence of any other tools or tricks, you typically first learn of any mistakes or omissions to required permissions when you are debugging on an emulated device.

In general, you see errors emitted in LogCat that describe the symptoms of what has gone wrong, and usually some suggestive steps indicate what permission your application is trying to use but currently lacks. This differs depending on the specifics of what you are trying to do, but as an example, if you attempt to use an Internet-based resource without the `android.permission.INTERNET` permission in your manifest, typically an error like this appears:

```
java.net.SocketException: Permission denied (maybe missing INTERNET permission)
```

Many of the permissions return a more generic `SecurityException`, but you get the idea.

Installing Applications and Accepting Permissions

Android's approach to bundling permissions and presenting them to the user for acceptance has historically been a fairly basic, even crude, approach. There have even been a few comical slip-ups as Google has moved to meet user demand that it provide much more control over runtime permission use, which has been a mainstay for other mobile platforms such as iOS.

Pre-Marshmallow Behavior

The vast majority of devices running in the wild are using Android versions 2.x, 3.x, or 4.x; all of these versions, with one minor exception, require the potential user of your application to accept all of your permission requests when they go to install, or else they abort any attempt to install. There is no halfway point, no optional permissions, and nothing as nuanced as the approach seen in other systems.

There are some subtle and not-so-subtle impacts of this approach. First and foremost, users are forced to make potentially important decisions about sharing data, such as contacts or location, all at once, and for an application that might request dozens of permissions, this can present a bewildering choice to the user.

A related issue is the users' perception, in general, of what the application may do with the permission they grant, and what it can do with multiple permissions they grant in combination. Great examples are what happens when the same application requests `android.permission.CAMERA` and `android.permission.INTERNET`. This makes sense for a Snapchat-style picture messaging system, but imagine this combination of requests from something like a streaming music app. Similarly, `android.permission.CONTACTS` and `android.permission.CALL_PHONE` makes sense for a phone book app, but what if an alarm clock application asked for that? Users are sensitive to combinations that they perceive as exposing their personal data and risking their privacy, and they are even more sensitive when the request combinations seem to bear no relation to the way expect to use the application.

As a developer, your best approach for all Android versions, but pre-Marshmallow Android 6.0 in particular, is to request as few permissions as possible. When you do request a permission, provide a clear rationale for why your application needs a given permission, and expect to lose a small set of potential users who might not be prepared to accept what you ask for.

APP OPS, OR APP OOPS?

Enduring criticism of the all-or-nothing approach to application permissions seemed to precipitate a change at Google with the Android 4.3 release, which included an intriguing new feature called App Ops. This was a permission management approach that allowed users to selectively revoke permissions after they installed applications, which gave the user the control many believed they rightful needed and deserved.

This was in keeping with Google's general "Put the User First" principle, but sadly, it seemed to clash with competing commercial and other objectives. Shortly after the release of Android 4.3, the 4.4.2 "update" was released; it reached out and hid all App Ops functionality from the end user. All the framework support was left in place, but as a functional user-controlled fine-grained permission system, App Ops disappeared as quickly as it appeared.

As a developer, even if you decide to detect release levels all the way down to minor point releases, I don't recommend coding specific behavior for the presence of App Ops on an Android 4.3 or 4.4 platform. Google eventually released App Ops in the guise of runtime permissions in Marshmallow.

Marshmallow and Beyond

With the release of Android 6.0 Marshmallow, Google has changed tack and has finally given users what they have long asked for in the form of selective permission granting when they install an application. This changed behavior is still very new, since Marshmallow is coming to market as this book goes to print.

What this means for you as a developer is that in addition to adhering to the principle of least privilege, meaning that you only ask for the permissions you strictly need, you should also prepare for how your application will behave if it is denied the expected permission to perform some action—write to a file, read contacts, take a picture, and so on. In such a situation, it's likely that your application's default behavior is that Android simply silently fails, and the next piece of code in your application then also fails with some form of unhandled exception, such as a null reference, because your expected resource isn't there when you ask for it.

Applications using the new permission model for Android Marshmallow trigger a system prompt to the user when they attempt to use a given permission, and Android triggers the new onRequestPermissionsResult() callback in your application so that you can perform your permission allowed/denied logic.

Google is gradually preparing for the full release of Android Marshmallow, but at this time, the final (third) preview is still ironing out issues in the new runtime security model. The behavior only changes if your application requests permissions using the special <uses-permission-sdk-m> value for the preview releases of Marshmallow in addition to checking the device's build of Android via Build.VERSION.CODENAME.

In the full release, users will also be able to revoke permissions they granted at installation time. This means that just because your application works initially, you can't take it for granted that it will always have the permissions it had when it was first installed. Android now supports the checkSelfPermission() method from any context, which allows you to test for granted permissions before you attempt to use them. This method takes the permission name as the parameter—for example:

```
Context.checkSelfPermission(Manifest.permission.CALL_PHONE);
```

Make sure you watch out for updates to forward and backward compatibility as Google irons out the bugs on the https://developer.android.com/preview/features/runtime-permissions.html page of the Android developer website.

Trading In Permissions

Android adds and even removes permissions from the platform over time. As you saw in Chapter 17, when we discussed file access, Google has flagged that it will introduce the READ_EXTERNAL_FILE permission at some future point. WRITE_EXTERNAL_STORAGE was introduced in Android 1.5, but its implementation was altered in Android 4.3, when the security model of Android changed to always allow an application to write to its own private-named file locations.

Implicit permissions are also bundled with your application automatically, depending on your setting for the android:minSdkVersion attribute in <uses-sdk> in your manifest. An SDK setting of 3 implicitly adds android.permission.READ_PHONE_STATE and android.permission.WRITE_EXTERNAL_STORAGE, even if your application doesn't care for, and doesn't use, those permissions. Your application users see these implicit permission requests, along with your explicit ones, at install time. When you change to a higher SDK version, these permissions are no longer implicitly requested, but others might be. You shouldn't rely on the implicit permissions for your application if you actually do need them. Instead, always explicitly add them to your manifest so that if Google does swap out the implicitly requested permission in some future SDK version, your application still requests what it needs and keeps working.

The release of Android Marshmallow introduces 11 new permissions, which you can read about in depth in the Android developer documentation. A few of the more notable new appearances are as follows:

- GET_ACCOUNTS_PRIVILEGED: Provides access to the set of all registered accounts on the device.

- PACKAGE_USAGE_STATS: Allows access to the metrics on how often components of a package, such as one of your activities or services, are called.

- USE_FINGERPRINT: Accesses the fingerprint scanner hardware on devices when it is present.

Creating Custom Permissions

You are not limited to the set of permissions Android provides with each release of the API. If you find yourself creating data, activities, services, content providers, or other assets over which you'd like to exert some control, then you can secure them with custom permissions you define.

Most often, you will want to consider custom security permissions if your application is storing and using sensitive or private user data. At the context level, you can also secure the content provider and other code you provide that supplies the logic to manipulate and use such data.

Using custom permissions is a two-part process. First, you declare the existence of the permission, and then you enforce its use.

Declaring Custom Permissions

To declare the permission you would like to create, add a `<permission>` element to your manifest. The `<permission>` element has eight attributes, of which you need to provide at least the following:

- `android:name`: This string will be the programmatic name of the permission, referred to in code and XML elements. By convention, use your package name and a meaningful permission name to create the fully-qualified name. This prevents name collisions across namespaces.

- `android:label`: This will be the permission name displayed to users at install time and at runtime in Android 6.0 and later. Being short and meaningful are key characteristics of a good label.

- `android:description`: This string provides some meaningful narrative to what your permission does. "Protects FoozApp" isn't a great description. "The FoozKey permission protects your personal player profile in the FoozApp game" is better.

> **Note**   You must define the `android:description` attribute as a resource reference to a string, such as `android:description="@string/my_desc"`. There is no literal text in the attribute within your manifest for this one.

We can expand the manifest I showed earlier in Listing 20-1 by adding a custom permission declaration, as shown in Listing 20-2.

Listing 20-2. Defining a Custom Permission in the PermissionsExample Application

```xml
<?xml version="1.0" encoding="utf-8"?>
<manifest xmlns:android="http://schemas.android.com/apk/res/android"
    package="com.artifexdigital.android.permissionsexample" >

    <uses-permission android:name="android.permission.INTERNET" />
    <uses-permission android:name="android.permission.CAMERA" />

    <permission
        android:name="com.artifexdigital.android.PE_SEE_HIDDEN"
        android:label="PE See Hidden Data"
        android:description="@string/pe_see_hidden_desc" />
...
```

You can also define a banner and an icon to use when prompting users and include your permission in Android's permission groups and levels as with the stock Android permission grouping approach.

Enforcing Custom Permissions

With your permission defined, you can then opt to enforce it to restrict access through either declarations in your manifest, or through code in the related Java classes.

You can protect an activity, receiver, or content provider by adding the `android:permission` attribute to the relevant context element in your manifest. For instance, to protect our `PermissionsExampleActivity` from the example application, we would further extend the manifest, as shown in Listing 20-3.

Listing 20-3. Enforcing a Custom Permission in the PermissionsExample Application

```xml
<?xml version="1.0" encoding="utf-8"?>
<manifest xmlns:android="http://schemas.android.com/apk/res/android"
    package="com.artifexdigital.android.permissionsexample" >

    <uses-permission android:name="android.permission.INTERNET" />
    <uses-permission android:name="android.permission.CAMERA" />

    <permission
        android:name="com.artifexdigital.android.PE_SEE_HIDDEN"
        android:label="PE See Hidden Data"
        android:description="@string/pe_see_hidden_desc" />

    <application
        android:allowBackup="true"
        android:icon="@mipmap/ic_launcher"
        android:label="@string/app_name"
        android:theme="@style/AppTheme"
        android:permission="com.artifexdigital.android.PE_SEE_HIDDEN" >
        <activity
```

```
            android:name=".PermissionsExampleActivity"
            android:label="@string/app_name" >
            <intent-filter>
                <action android:name="android.intent.action.MAIN" />
                <category android:name="android.intent.category.LAUNCHER" />
            </intent-filter>
        </activity>
    </application
</manifest>
```

With this permission in place, no other application can invoke our `PermissionsExampleActivity` through a `startActivity()` call without first requesting the `PE_SEE_HIDDEN` permission. If this is a service (which I cover in the next chapter), it can't be implicitly started, stopped, or bound in another context without the permission. If we modify the code and manifest to be a broadcast receiver, we ignore any intent designed to trigger invocation unless the intent initiator holds the `PE_SEE_HIDDEN` permission.

To achieve the same effect in code is a little harder, because the methods available are fairly primitive. You can check the permissions of the caller by using the `checkCallingPermissions()` method with a permission name to see if the caller holds that permission. You can also telegraph your permission requirements when sending broadcasts in your code via the `sendBroadcast()` method by using the optional permission name `parameter` to signal to receivers that you only want responses from those that hold the named permission.

Securing Applications for Publication and Execution

There is a great deal more to the security and protection mechanisms provided by Android than just the permission system. Two areas in particular where the security framework shows its mettle are in the signing requirements that guarantee and protect the provenance of a given application through the use of PKI and certificates, and in Android's Linux underpinnings, which means application process and user contexts enjoy strict boundaries and protection. We'll explore both of the aspects of Android security next.

Securing Your Application with Certificate Signing

Before you can publish your application to Google Play and make it available for download and installation to Android devices, you are required to sign you application with a suitable X.509-style PKI certificate. For those of you not familiar with PKI and digital certificates, PKI is a cryptographic system you can use to do things like assert identity, establish trust, and pass secrets. You can find many great descriptions online.

With you digital certificate in hand (or more accurately, on your machine), you can sign the `.apk` file that, in effect, is the zip-formatted container that holds you application code, manifest, resources, and assets, all ready for deployment.

Sourcing or Creating a Signing Certificate

Obviously to sign an `.apk` file with a digital certificate you actually need the certificate. You have two broad options: making a commercial purchase of a certificate issued from a publicly trusted root or intermediate Registry, or generating a self-signed certificate using a tool such as `keytool`.

With self-signed certificates, your main concern is that, by definition, no other party asserts the validity and trustworthiness of your signing certificate. For this reason, self-signed certificates are considered the poor cousins of the PKI world.

The Keystore

Whichever style of certificate you choose, you will likely want to use the keystore facility that `keytool` offers to manage your certificates and public/private key material.

You can tell `keytool` to store a (self-signed) certificate it is generating by passing the `-keystore` parameter and the path you would like to use as your keystore. A bunch of other parameters are offered by keystore; you can examine these at your leisure by reviewing the output of `keytool --help`.

Whether you realized it or not, you have already been using a certificate and a keystore when you have been working with the example applications from the book. Both Eclipse with the ADT and Android Studio automatically create a developer keystore known as the Debug Keystore, and both also create a self-signed certificate you use when deploying the `.apk` files from the example applications to a device emulator. You can examine this debug setup, and even change it so it uses a different keystore location and/or certificate by opening the Build options from the Android > Build menu. There are some "gotchas" to doing this, however, so keep reading to be sure you understand the implications.

Signing Your APK

With a certificate in place, and your build system (Eclipse, Android, Ant, or something else) capable of building your `.apk` file, you have multiple options in how you approach signing.

You can use the `jarsigner` tool that ships with the JDK to manually sign your `.apk` file, which needs a few relevant parameters to do its job.

```
jarsigner -keystore <path to your keystore> <necessary passwords> <path to your .apk>
<application name>
```

The pseudo-parameters shown here give you the basics, and obviously, more options are available for the `jarsigner` tool. The drawback is the finicky nature of using a command-line tool and the risk of exposing passwords when you are running command-line tools in general.

Android Studio users can generate the signed `.apk` directly from the project view by choosing the Build ➤ Generate Signed APK menu option. You are prompted for exactly the same information the `jarsigner` tool requires, just through a friendlier UI that helps avoid some of the mistakes. It should not surprise you to know that the information is used to actually run `jarsigner` itself under the hood.

With a signed .apk file, you can manually deploy your application through the "side loading" technique using the adb tool, or you can publish it to your developer account on Google Play for public download and use. Deploying with adb can be as simple as this:

```
adb install <path to signed .apk file>
```

You can entertain other options and considerations for deployment, such as optimizing the final .apk file using the zipalign tool. You can read more about this in the Android developer documentation.

Signing Is (Almost) Forever, So Take Care

You know already that you must sign your application with your chosen certificate before you can installed it on a device, and that Google helps this process with your emulator environments by automatically creating debug certificates and keystores. If you have an Android Developer account and plan to publish applications to Google Play, the certificate takes on additional importance.

The signing certificate along with the fully qualified package name for your application form the principal identifiers for your application. When you create updates in the future, either because you are adding features or fixing bugs, you need to sign the new-and-improved application with the same certificate in order for Google Play to consider it an upgrade for the same application, rather than a separate application in its own right.

This might seem onerous, but it's one of the most important guarantees user have that an update to their favorite application comes from you, and not someone impersonating you. For this reason, as well as for the general security imperatives of protecting yourself and your users, you should take a great deal of care with the key material for your certificate. Protect your private key and the keystore repository you are using, keep an offline backup, and do not upload this to any form of cloud service or repository. Should you ever lose your key material and be unable to use your existing certificate, there is no feasible way to re-create it. If you are forced to use a different certificate for signing updates to your applications, those applications will be considered completely separate applications by Android and Google Play.

The certificates you use for signing your application also need to be unusually long-lived. By default, the certificates you create with keytool are valid for around 20 years (14,000 days). You can opt to use a shorter or longer validity period, but Google Play checks to ensure a lifetime is valid to at least the 22nd of October, 2033. This is very different from certificates used for SSL, S/MIME, or other protocols, where generally shorter-lived certificates are preferred, and rotation to new certificates is performed regularly. You have probably guessed that because of the identification implications, certificate rotation is not practiced with Android applications and their signing certificates.

Protecting Android and Applications at Runtime

In addition to the certificate signing that attests to the authenticity and origin of your application and the permissions model that protects data and services, Android also uses its Linux underpinnings to enforce a runtime process and user model to provide even more security for your application and all the other applications that run on a given device. You can think of this as protecting applications from each other and Android itself from applications.

Every application loaded on to a device or emulator is automatically allocated its own user context and underlying user account. You as a developer do not control this, and the user of the device typically does not know this is happening. Your application runs under the ownership of this account for its entire lifetime on the device, so once its account is allocated at install time, that is a permanent attribute of the application.

Because each application uses its own user account, as with any Linux-based system where many applications are running, the processes are owned by many different users. Figure 20-2 depicts the user and process boundaries for Android applications on a device.

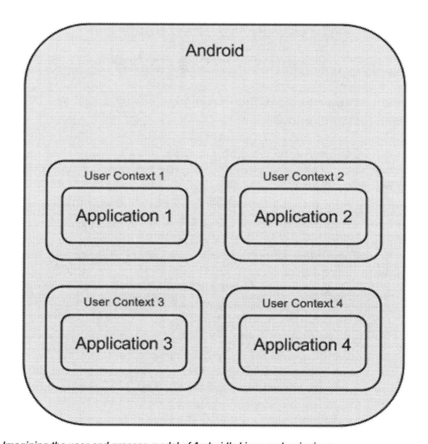

Figure 20-2. Imagining the user and process model of Android's Linux underpinnings

If this is transparent to you as a developer, and to the user running the applications, you might ask why this is important. The main benefit here is that you application's implicit user account has permissions over files and process artifacts for your application, but not for any other applications. If there is any kind of security vulnerability and one application starts misbehaving, this ownership separation provides another line of defense by ensuring the compromised application cannot automatically run rampant with the files and other resources of other applications at the Linux level.

Incorporating External Libraries with Android

Way back in time, long before Google bought Android, the founders of Android made the choice to use Java as the development language. This was for a host of reasons, including Java's widespread use, which meant many talented developers could write applications for the platform, but those developers could also write libraries and other tools that could be used by Java programs in general. Whether it's on a server, a desktop, or a mobile device, Java supports a wealth of libraries that rival any other development language.

Before you race off thinking that absolutely all of Java is at your disposal, there are a few limits and omissions of which you should be aware.

The ART of Android

When Android was originally released, one of the choices its designers made was to embed an Android-specific runtime to execute the Java-coded applications written to run on Android. Instead of a stock JVM, Android introduced Dalvik. Conceptually, the Android runtime does much the same job as the JVM, handling things like memory allocation, stack management, compilation functions, and garbage collection.

Dalvik was good for the job at hand, but as Android evolved, so too did the need to improve and update the runtime. With the release of Android 4.4, Google started testing the brand-new Android runtime, or ART, as the next incarnation of VM for code execution in Android.

There are some great improvements in ART and some key differences between ART and Dalvik, which makes for better application behavior and more efficient system resource use. Before I detail these key changes, the one thing about which you can relax is that as a developer, you basically do not need to worry about which runtime is present on a device. Dalvik is used by default on almost all contemporary devices, and newer devices running late KitKat 4.4 Android versions, 5.0 Lollipop, or 6.0 Marshmallow still all use 100-percent Dalvik-compatible byte code as the input for the VM—whether it's Dalvik or ART.

Here are the key improvements and new features you should know about in ART:

▓ Ahead-of-time (AOT) compilation. Dalvik used a snippet-based just-in-time compilation approach to small sections of code that resulted in compiled "traces." This sped up parts of applications that were frequently used, but it also left large tracts of applications unoptimized. ART performs AOT compilation at install time, which means the user is by and large oblivious to the one-time overhead.

▓ Strict Java Native Interface (JNI) health and hygiene, in which ART provides stricter enforcement of JNI precautions and also leverages compacting features in garbage collection. JNI is beyond the scope of this book, but some excellent articles online discuss the precautions you should take if you are writing C or C++ for use through JNI with Android applications in an ART-based environment.

▓ Unified stack model with thread-configurable stack sizes. Dalvik used separate stacks for Java and native code and also had some inflexible stack size defaults. ART provides a cleaner model that also has more configuration options.

▓ Better diagnostic and debugging options through better runtime exception logging, and better instrumentation of issues such as locks, live objects, and method testing using method-exit modeling.

By the time you need to know more about ART's inner workings, you will well and truly be in the realm of professional Android developer. More information is available at `developer.android.com`.

Choosing Library Sources or JARs

Broadly speaking, you can choose to use the raw source code of an external library or other piece of code, or you can use the packaged JAR (Java archive) file. You can mix and match when working with multiple libraries or external sources as you see fit.

Direct Source Inclusion

To incorporate Java source code in your application, you need to place the code in the source tree along with the rest of your Android Java code. Depending on your build tools and environment, the location might differ.

Android Studio

The Java source files for the library should be placed in the main source tree along with your Android Studio Java source files. Within you project's root folder, you should be able to follow the path `./app/src/main/java`. Within that Java folder, you will see further subfolders that represent your package namespace. In the example application `ExternalLibraryExample`, I used the fully-qualified package name `com.artifexdigital.android.externallibraryexample`. So the full path from the project root is `./app/src/main/java/com/artifexdigital/android/externallibraryexample`. This is where you'll see existing Java source for your project, and where you should place source files for external library source that you want included in the package context of your application (i.e., you want to just copy over portions of code rather than use the library as a separate package). You can opt to follow a fully-qualified package name from the `java` directory if you prefer to keep the packages separate.

Of course, you can also drag and drop the files through your GUI file manager and Android Studio, but knowing the plumbing that makes this work is crucial if you need to debug missing or misplaced source files.

Eclipse

Eclipse follows a similar conceptual approach to Android Studio, but the path structure is a little simpler. From the project root folder, the `src` folder contains all of the fully-qualified packages in folder hierarchy form. So for the example `ExternalLibraryExample` project, the full path to the source Java files is `./src/com/artifexdigital/android/externallibraryexample`.

Just as with Android Studio, you can take the easy approach and use a GUI file manager (Explorer for Windows, Finder for Mac OS X, Nautilus for Linux, and so on) and drag and drop your source files into the source folder in Eclipse. But where is the fun in that?

Other Development Environments

Ant or other build tools are usually structured as per the original Eclipse-style project layout, so use your application's equivalent to a `src` directory.

Incorporating JARs

The alternative to copying source directly into your code is to use prepackaged JAR files. The approach for JAR files is deceptively simple:

1. Acquire the JAR file for the external library you wish to use.

2. Copy it to the library location for your project (dependent on IDE or environment).

3. Configure your build tools to find and use the JAR.

4. Import the library into your code and start coding!

This is a deceptively simple approach, since the configuration step has not always been the most intuitive of tasks. Both Eclipse and Android Studio offer much better automated support for this in recent releases, but historically it has been a manual task with the pitfalls and chances for mistakes that entails.

In the interests of making the process well-understood, I will step you through explicit examples later in the chapter, adding a well-known external library to the `ExternalLibraryExample` project.

When Is Java not Java?

After the discussion on the ART environment earlier in the chapter, you should, by now, realize that ART is not a 100-percent like-for-like implementation of the official Oracle/Sun JVM, nor was Dalvik. There are some important differences and omissions of which you need to be aware, particularly when you start relying on external libraries and packages.

In essence, if those external sources expect an aspect of Java that ART does not provide or does not implement, you will end up with your application exhibiting uncertain behavior at best, and code that just does not work at worst. Consider these broad areas when you are thinking of the difference between ART and JVM.

Absent JVM Features

Each release of Android was built broadly targeting features from a JVM of a similar vintage. Obviously this has changed over time as both Android with ART/Dalvik and the JVM incorporate new features, and as Google decides whether or not to take up features of the JVM it wants to include.

The main features you will notice that are missing from ART (and Dalvik) are the Swing UI toolkit and a range of location and mobile-optimization packages. Notionally all of these have equivalents in Android.

Considering Java Performance for Android

There are three key performance considerations that you need to think through with an Android mindset so you avoid building a hog of an application that nobody likes.

Package Size

If you are incorporating code from non-Android origins, you might find that packages written for a traditional desktop or server environment are larger than anything you are writing yourself. The sheer size of the libraries can cause your application size to blow out—where anything larger than 50MB to 100MB when finally packaged on Google Play looks bloated. This also impacts memory footprint, discussed momentarily.

CPU Use

Lots of Java libraries have been written on ever-more-powerful x86 processors over the years, and often they liberally use threading in the expectation that multicore processors are commonplace. Although it is true that Android devices have moved to multicore in recent years, almost all Android devices are using ARM-based processor designs, and in general, they have much less power than a traditional desktop or server.

Memory Use

When you are dealing with Java on a desktop or server, memory is typically measured in gigabytes or tens of gigabytes, and it's not unusual for a Java application and its libraries to drive JVM memory to the limit. A typical Android handset has much less memory, and you also will not have tools at hand like `jstat` or `gcutil` to closely monitor memory use and garbage collection. Although there are some other tools that do help, watch out for especially memory-hungry libraries when you are thinking of external imports for your code.

Operating System or Native Dependencies

It is rare to find Java libraries that leverage the various forks seen on some operating systems (Windows, for example), but it is worth double-checking on any library just in case. Likewise, libraries that use the Native Development Kit (NDK) to leverage some native resource need careful scrutiny. NDK is available for use in Android, but the native resources being referenced might not be, so you need to do some digging through NDK layers to the underlying native code.

Unusual I/O or Interfaces

Some libraries expect to have control over logging locations and paths, which can have implications on Android and cause subtle quirks or failures. For instance, a library that assumes a /tmp-like shared scratch space is available could be in for a surprise. Some libraries also expect the existence of the console, which you certainly will not have under Android.

Versioning and Cascading Dependencies

Like your very own application, a Java library is created at a point in time and is likely itself relying on other libraries, all the way down to the oldest base classes and foundations. Whether it's a JAR compiled with an older JVM or a daisy-chain of library dependencies that lead to mysterious destinations, some investigation of the heritage of a library can save you pain in the future.

Overcoming Java Library Issues

In addition to the checks and vigilance described in the previous section, there are more things you can do to make life easier for yourself when you are using external libraries.

- Look at open source alternatives; they offer source transparency that makes spotting dependencies and issues easier.
- Extract only the source you need, if you have access to it.
- Repackage or strip down the JAR to remove unneeded dependencies.
- Use continuous integration and build tools to constantly test your application against changing library dependencies.
- Use a device library testing service to see what quirks might exist with libraries you think are packaged normally, but in fact might differ from one device manufacturer to another.

Adapting an Application to Use an External Library

In Chapter 17, I introduced some simple example applications that dealt with files and file systems. The examples from that chapter demonstrated a lot about the things you need to know when working with files. The `ExternalFilesExample` application also demonstrated one of the "high-fidelity" parts of Android's Java implantation: Android wholly adopted Java's original, traditionally cumbersome file I/O language.

Fortunately, many fine external Java libraries exist that provide a far more elegant and approachable way of dealing with file I/O, and these libraries work well in the Android context. One in particular, the Apache Commons IOUtils library, is a perfect example to use to demonstrate the power of using external libraries and the straightforward way in which you can incorporate them into your applications.

We will use IOUtils to retrofit the `ExternalFilesExample` application with nicer source code for the file I/O aspects, turning it into the `ExternalLibraryExample` application you will find in `ch21/ExternalLibraryExample`. Let's get stuck in to the retrofit!

Sourcing Apache Commons IOUtils

Apache publishes all of the Commons project source code and JAR files at `http://commons.apache.org`. The IOUtils main page is at `http://commons.apache.org/proper/commons-io/`. You will notice references to the current version of the package, Commons IO 2.4, and older versions. For our example, download the current version in binary form (either the `.zip` or `.tar.gz` file).

Unpack your chosen download when it completes; you should see contents including the following:

- `commons-io.2.4.jar`, which is the actual JAR file compiled from the source; it is ready for use in a Java project such as your Android application.

- `commons-io-sources.jar`, which is a JAR that provides the source code.

- `commons-io-2.4-tests.jar` and `commons-io-2.4-test-sources.jar`, which provide the `junit` and other tests used by the developers.

- `commons-io-2.4-javadoc.jar`, which provides the JavaDoc-style documentation for use in IDEs such as Eclipse and Android Studio.

- `docs` folder with API documentation, samples, and so on.

- `LICENCE.txt` and other text files, which contain the Apache license information, readme, and other notices.

We are really only interested in the `commons-io-2.4.jar` file to add to our project, although you can use the test-focused JARs if you are creating unit tests in your project and the JavaDoc JAR for contextual assistance and package documentation.

Adding the JAR to Your Project's Libraries

From your unpacked binary download, it is the commons-io-2.4.jar file you need to add to your project. The approach for doing this varies depending on the IDE or tools you are using, and obviously covering every esoteric development environment would exhaust the pages in the book quickly. However, I can demonstrate how it's done in Android Studio and Eclipse, and from this information, you can infer how to do it if you are using a different environment.

Adding JARs in Android Studio

To incorporate the commons-io-2.4.jar into your Android Studio project, or indeed to add JARs in general to any Android Studio project, follow these four steps.

1. Create a libs folder in the project hierarchy directly under the root, and copy the commons-io-2.4.jar file to the matching location on disk. Android Studio should update the project hierarchy automatically, but to see the library in your project, you need to switch to Project view.

2. From within the Project view of your project in Android Studio, right-click on the JAR and choose the Add As Library option, which is buried toward the bottom of the menu, as shown in Figure 21-1.

Figure 21-1. *The crucial Add Library step to incorporate an external JAR into your project*

3. At this point, you should see a confirmation to add the library to the app portion of your project. When you click OK, you see a Project Sync In Progress overlay message as Android Studio invokes the gradle build process to add the necessary build rules for the library to the future compilation of your project.

4. Strictly speaking, normally you should be able to trust your IDE to perform this build dependency configuration without a hitch. The reality, however, is that Android Studio has had a rapid rise, and its fair share of bugs and problems, and this is one of those areas

where older versions of Android Studio have had problems. When the gradle build success message appears, it is worth opening your `build.gradle` file to ensure the `commons-io-2.4.jar` library has been added as a dependency. You should see the entry in bold shown in Listing 21-1.

Listing 21-1. Ensuring the JAR Dependency Is Correctly Added to Your build.gradle File

```
apply plugin: 'com.android.application'

android {
    compileSdkVersion 22
    buildToolsVersion "22.0.1"

    defaultConfig {
        applicationId "com.artifexdigital.android.externallibraryexample"
        minSdkVersion 11
        targetSdkVersion 22
        versionCode 1
        versionName "1.0"
    }
    buildTypes {
        release {
            minifyEnabled false
            proguardFiles getDefaultProguardFile('proguard-android.txt'), 'proguard-rules.pro'
        }
    }
}

dependencies {
    compile fileTree(dir: 'libs', include: ['*.jar'])
    compile 'com.android.support:appcompat-v7:22.2.1'
    compile files('libs/commons-io-2.4.jar')
}
```

5. Lastly, it's prudent to ensure your project can build regardless of any prevail state. Invoke the Build ➤ Clean Project option to perform a clean build of your application.

At this point, you are ready to reference your included library, so in our example, we can now go ahead and import and use IOUtils for file I/O operations.

Adding JARs in Eclipse

The process for adding JARs to an Android project in Eclipse is similar to the way you would do it in an ordinary Java project.

1. To begin, download the `commons-io-2.4.zip` or `.tar.gz` file as in the Android Studio description in the previous section.

2. With the archive downloaded, extract the contents and copy the
   commons-io-2.4.jar file to the /libs folder of your project. In recent
   versions of ADT working with Eclipse, this should automatically
   trigger a build rule change to incorporate the JAR in the build path.
   In reality, this doesn't always work, or you may find yourself with an
   older environment and may want to set the build path explicitly.

3. To explicitly set the build path to include the commons-io-2.4.jar
   file in your /libs folder, choose the Project ➤ Properties menu
   option. In the Properties dialog, choose the Libraries tab. If you are
   using a newer version of Eclipse and the ADT, you should already
   see the library shown under Android Private Libraries, as shown in
   Figure 21-2. If your library isn't shown, click the Add JARs button
   and browse to find your .jar file, which in our example is
   commons-io-2.4.jar.

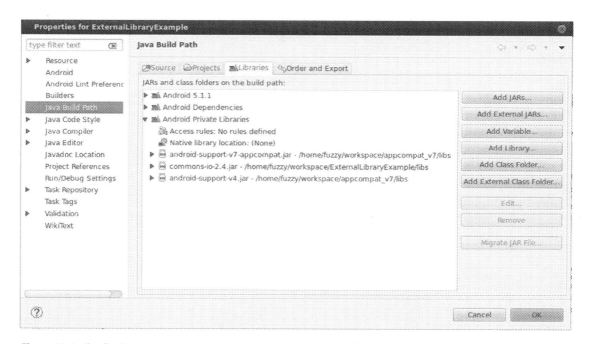

Figure 21-2. Confirming that the build path is set correctly for external libraries in Eclipse with the ADT

4. Whether you have added the commons-io-2.4.jar file manually,
   or it was automatically picked up and included, it is a good safety
   measure to perform a clean build of the project. Choose the
   Project ➤ Clean menu option. You are now ready to import and use
   the library in your code.

Referencing (or Refactoring for) Your External Libraries

The process of importing and using the packages and classes provided by an external library is basically the same in Android as with normal Java programming. A quick walk through the refactoring for our ExternalLibraryExample project should provide a refresher for anyone rusty on the details.

The layout for the application is the same for the ExternalFilesExample project from Chapter 17. When rendered, the layout in Figure 21-3 should look familiar to you.

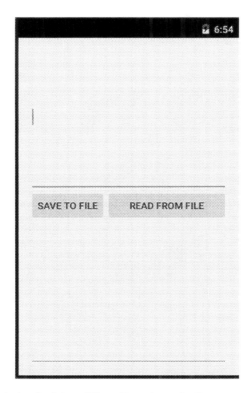

Figure 21-3. The unchanged UI design for ExternalLibraryExample application

The code required to use the IOUtils library features is fairly straightforward—remember, that was the entire reason for opting for this library, since it cleans up the mess that is vanilla Java I/O. Listing 21-2 shows the changes in the externallibraryexample.java code; the import of IOUtils and its use is in bold.

Listing 21-2. Modified Code to Use the IOUtils External Library

```
package com.artifexdigital.android.externallibraryexample;

import android.app.Activity;
import android.content.Context;
import android.os.Bundle;
```

```
import android.view.View;
import android.view.inputmethod.InputMethodManager;
import android.widget.EditText;

import java.io.IOException;
import java.io.InputStream;
import java.io.OutputStreamWriter;
import java.io.StringWriter;

//importing the IOUtils external library for use
import org.apache.commons.io.*;

public class ExternalLibraryExample extends Activity {
    public final static String FILENAME="ExternalLibraryExample.txt";

    @Override
    protected void onCreate(Bundle savedInstanceState) {
        super.onCreate(savedInstanceState);
        setContentView(R.layout.activity_external_library_example);
    }
    public void onClick(View view) {
        switch(view.getId()) {
            case R.id.btnRead:
                try {
                    doReadFromFile();
                }
                catch (Exception e) {
                    e.printStackTrace();
                }
                break;
            case R.id.btnSave:
                doSaveToFile();
                break;
        }
    }

    public void doReadFromFile() throws Exception {
        doHideKeyboard();
        EditText readField;
        readField=(EditText)findViewById(R.id.editTextRead);
        try {
            InputStream inStrm=openFileInput(FILENAME);
            if (inStrm!=null) {
                // File I/O using the much more elegant Apache IOUtils approach

                StringWriter myWriter = new StringWriter();
                IOUtils.copy(inStrm, myWriter);
                String fileContent = myWriter.toString();

                inStrm.close();
                readField.setText(fileContent);
            }
```

```
        }
        catch (Throwable t) {
            // perform exception handling here
        }
    }
}

// code continues unchanged from here
...
```

The proof of the external library use is, as you would expect, in building and running the application. You should definitely go ahead and run things; watch the LogCat output in particular to see if there are any issues packaging the JAR with your .apk and deploying it to the emulator. Assuming all of the configuration steps went smoothly, and you haven't made any errors in your code, you should end up with a running application that incorporates your desired JARs. Figure 21-4 shows the ExternalLibraryExample running, showing off our use of IOUtils.

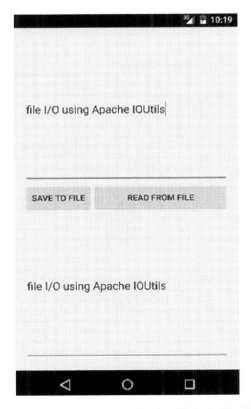

Figure 21-4. ExternalLibraryExample running successfully and using IOUtils for file I/O

It is true that the actual application here is not the most demanding in the world. But that is precisely so that you can appreciate the steps you must take to set up and use the external JAR without getting swamped with fancy application logic or UI.

Using Languages Beyond Java

One interesting and powerful result of building your own runtime environment and VM is your ability to take full control over what source languages can be supported. With Android's use or ART (and Dalvik before it), Google provided a great deal of openness in allowing you to use many different source languages, providing you with plumbing to help convert to Dalvik-compliant Java byte code and even providing you with interpreted language support through a few interesting approaches.

The most well-known Android technique for interpreted languages is the Scripting Language For Android module, or SL4A.

Scripting Layer for Android Overview

The SL4A was written and maintained by Damon Kohler and is now available from a repository on GitHub at `https://github.com/damonkohler/sl4a`. Active development has "paused" on SL4A, so what follows may begin to atrophy over time, though several forks of the work are still seeing activity.

SL4A provides support for quite a few interpreted scripting languages, including these:

- BeanShell
- JRuby
- Lua
- Perl
- Python
- Rhino (the Java-based JavaScript layer from Mozilla)
- Tcl

Historically SL4A also supported PHP, but for a variety of reasons later versions have deprecated support for it.

Choosing Your Approach to SL4A

If you are interested in using one of the languages supported by SL4A, you have two approaches from which to choose. You can embed support for SL4A in your own application by including the source or JAR forms as described earlier in this chapter. This allows you to then perform all kinds of tricks in the interpreted language of your choice, and you can even provide your own layout and UI for an IDE. Yes, you can write an application development environment in your chosen Android application development environment—nested IDEs.

The alternative approach is to install the full SL4A application onto your emulator or device, and then write your scripts within the application. Obviously, this approach doesn't result in separate fully-functional applications, but it does open up a range of control and management capabilities that are lacking in stock Android.

Testing SL4A on Your Emulator

To install the full SL4A environment and a supported language on an emulator, first download the source from GitHub and build the projects included. This will create a range of .apk files.

Assume for a moment you wanted to try Python in SL4A; you would need the following packaged .apk files from your SL4A project: sl4a_r4.apk and python_for_android_r4.apk.

Next, ensure your emulator AVD is running, and from the command shell in your host operating system, use the adb tool to install the .apk files as follows:

```
adb install <path_to_files>/sl4a_r4.apk
adb install <path_to_files>/python_for_android_r4.apk
```

> **Note**   The "r4" values refer to release number, and this may differ depending on which repository you take the source code from to build your .apk files.

Installing SL4A and any of its language modules will present a typical permissions overview acceptance dialog, which you should accept. Interestingly, the applications or script fragments you might write with SL4A inherit the permissions of the container application. This means if you build SL4A support into your own application and have permissions such as WRITE_EXTERNAL_FILE granted to the application, then the scripts you run inside the application using the SL4A library will enjoy that same write permission.

When SL4A is installed, you should see it available in the list of applications from the launcher in your emulator. When you start SL4A, you should see a home activity similar to the one shown in Figure 21-5.

Figure 21-5. The SL4A interpreter system started on an emulator

The interpreters for the languages installed are shown, so in our case, Python is listed along with the default basic shell. Start the Python interpreter, and you should see Python's familiar triple-greater-than prompt, >>>.

From here, you can play around with Python to your heart's content. To get you started, you should be aware that the Python SL4A library includes a dedicated "android" module that you can import and use to control Android features and classes from within your Python script.

Almost every attempt at coding in a new environment starts with the Hello World-style program, so here's the absolute based SL4A Python code to get you running.

```
>>> import android
>>> mySL4APyObj = android.Android()
>>> result = mySL4APyObj.makeToast('Hello World')
```

For more information, and to explore the possibilities of SL4A, I recommend the excellent book *Pro Android Python with SL4A*, by Paul Ferrill (Apress, 2011).

Leveraging Android Services

Android's underpinnings of the Linux operating system extend to multiple areas of the platform, many of which you have explored already. As with almost every operating system in existence, Android provides for a specific class of program that runs independently of any user interface, running in the background to provide crucial functionality regardless of other activity. In Android these programs are called *services*, similar to the services concept in Windows, or the daemon concept in Unix and Linux.

In this chapter, I explore the rationale and fundamentals of Android services, and the steps you need to take to create, start, work with, and control them. We also explore some simple service examples to help you complete your understanding not only of how to use services, but how to create your own.

Services Background

The need for services has numerous sources, most of which stem from any situation in which one or more applications require functionality without any specific need to see or access an activity or other user interface. Dozens of services run on a stock Android device, and undoubtedly you can think of many more possibilities you can code yourself, such as these:

- Provide a local interface to control a remote API such as a mapping service or social network.

- Maintain long-lived connections for chat-like applications that have "conversations" running over days, weeks, months, or more.

- Continue with processing a task or piece of work once invoked by a user, without further interaction. A great example is downloading an Android application update once the user has requested it.

There are, of course, many more examples, and you will often find that a more complex service pairs itself with some other application that can trigger its work, check its status, and so on. For instance, a home-screen audio player widget actually triggers a background service to do the main task of playing back an audio track.

There is no strict requirement mandating that you use services with your applications. Instead, you should think of them as a very useful kind of resource upon which you can call if you need to, but that you can forget about at other times. Many of the applications you write will have no need for services at all. But some of your applications will call out for the use of services, both of the stock Android variety and the ones you write yourself.

Defining Your Own Service

The process of defining and creating your own service application is very similar to the work you have already learned about when you created normal activity-based Android applications. The broad steps should look very familiar to you:

- Using an Android-provided base class, you extend and inherit to create your own specific service.

- Decide on the callback methods you need to override, and code the logic to implement your desired behavior.

- Update the `AndroidManifest.xml` file to provide the permissions, definitions, and links into the wider Android platform you need for your service to run and serve applications.

Let's take a look at these three areas in a little more detail.

Implementing Your Own Service Class

Android provides the basic `Service` class as a foundation from which you can build your own service, and it also offers several useful subclasses out of the box that deal with common service patterns. The most commonly used, and most useful, of these is the `IntentService` subclass. You are free to use the basic `Service` class or aim for one of the more-specific subclasses.

The basic code skeleton should not surprise you and is shown in Listing 22-1.

Listing 22-1. Skeleton of a Service Application in Android

```
package com.artifexdigital.android.serviceskeleton

import android.app.service
//more imports here

public class SkeletonService extends Service {
    //overrides and implementation logic here
}
```

Controlling Service Lifecycle via Callbacks

Android's Service class and its subclasses provide a range of callbacks designed to be overridden so that you can implement your own logic and service control behavior. This framework is conceptually similar to the Activity and Fragment lifecycle approach, but there are distinctly fewer states in which a service will find itself, and consequently, you need to concern yourself with only five main methods at coding time.

- onCreate(): Almost identical to the onCreate() method for Activities, the Service's onCreate() method is invoked when any trigger for service activity happens.

- onStartCommand(): When the related startService() method is called by a client application, the onStartCommand() method is invoked and its logic is processed.

- onBind(): When a client application attempts to bind to the service with a bindService() call, the onBind() method is invoked.

- onTrimMemory(): For devices running Android version 3.0 or later, services selected for resource reclamation while the device is under memory shortage have their onTrimMemory() method called. This is the somewhat-more-graceful approach to letting services try to return memory in a controlled fashion before more drastic measures are taken.

- onDestroy(): When performing a normal graceful shutdown, onDestroy() is invoked. Just as with normal Activities, graceful shutdown is not guaranteed, and therefore neither is a call to onDestroy().

The general approach to lifecycle management stays the same. Your service should create what it needs during its onCreate() call and clean up and dispose of any lingering resources during onDestroy().

You will notice that there are no equivalents to onPause() or onResume() for a service. Your service is either running or it's not, and there's no need to provide background-transition methods when a service is considered always in the background. You should ensure that you minimize any state held by the service or use preferences or other storage where appropriate. Not only can Android terminate a service at any time for resources—bypassing any call to onDestroy()—but users can also kill your services via the application management system's setting activity. This becomes more complicated if your clients decided to bind to your service in a long-lived fashion; I explore this in the examples in a moment.

Adding Manifest Entries for Your Service

To flag that you want your application recognized as a service by Android, you need to make a few modifications to your manifest file. The main change is that you need to define a <service> element as a child of the <application> element. Listing 22-2 shows the minimal entry for a service, providing the required android:name attribute, which in this case is "Skeleton".

Listing 22-2. A Minimal Service Definition in the AndroidManifest.xml File

```xml
<?xml version="1.0" encoding="utf-8"?>
<manifest xmlns:android="http://schemas.android.com/apk/res/android"
    package="com.artifexdigital.android.skeletonservice" >

    <uses-permission android:name="android.permission.INTERNET" />

    <application
        android:allowBackup="true"
        android:icon="@mipmap/ic_launcher"
        android:label="@string/app_name"
        android:theme="@style/AppTheme" >

        <!-- any other application child elements would go here -->

        <service android:name="Skeleton">

    </application>

</manifest>
```

You can freely define a service and activities in the same project (and therefore have them both in the manifest). This is very common for applications that are developed in conjunction with their own services. If you want to protect your service from being accessed indiscriminately, you can add permissions from the set described in Chapter 20, specifying an android:permission attribute in your <service> element.

Service Communication

Defining services is really as straightforward as it seems from the introduction in this chapter. Once you have created a service, however, controlling how client applications such as activities (and even other services) communicate with them is a little more involved. How clients communicate with a service takes one of two possible paths—they either use starting commands or binding—but the converse of services communicating with clients has a world of options and choices for you to make as a developer.

Client-to-Service Communication

When any kind of client wants to work with a service, whether that client is an activity, a fragment, or some other service, one fundamental question guides which of the two communication approaches is best suited to the task. Is this a one-time, fire-and-forget request for a service to do something for the client? In these cases, the command approach to service communication is best. If the client needs to work with the service over a series of actions and wants to maintain an ongoing interaction with the service, then the bind approach is preferable.

Invoking Commands with startService()

To have a service perform some action for your application, whether that's from an activity or some other context, a simple call to startService() is the easiest way to go. Just as the startActivity() method introduced earlier in the book can trigger an arbitrary activity by taking an intent and some parameters, startService() also accepts an intent as the first parameter, and a set of intent extras as the second parameter so that you can pass call-specific payload data to the service. The pseudo-code form looks like this:

```
startService(someSignatureIntent);
```

In the basic pattern for calling, startService() can use the simplest form of the Intent parameter—the class of the intent itself. startService() is an asynchronous call, meaning the main UI thread of your application continues immediately and does not block on the return from the method call.

If the service itself is not started, the Android service framework takes care of starting it for you and your application user. The intent passed as a parameter is provided to the onStartCommand() method so that you can inspect and use it as you see fit within the rest of the logic you code for the onStartCommand() method. Unlike the calling application, which is not blocked by the service invocation, the onStartCommand() method is processed on the service's main thread, so be careful not to burden your code with too much heavy processing, external calls with indeterminate timing, or anything else that might prevent a speedy response. If you need to perform such long-running work within your service, incorporate additional threads through the java.util.concurrent package and its Executor and related abilities.

Using the startService() approach does not provide return payloads in the normal sense to the calling client application. (I cover service-to-client communication later in the chapter.) The startService() call does return a value to the service instance from a range of predefined values that are mainly designed to signal whether the call completed successfully or was killed for resource-starvation or other reasons. Among the return values your service might see are these common responses:

- START_STICKY: Restart the service once Android has enough free memory to do so, but don't worry about the triggering intent; pass a null intent instead.

- START_NON_STICKY: Don't automatically restart the service at all, even if Android resource pressure drops to a low enough level to allow it. Implicitly this means the service is not started until your application or some other application explicitly calls startService() or otherwise invokes the need for the service again.

- START_REDELIVER_INTENT: Restart the service once Android has enough free memory, and also attempt to redeliver the original Intent object passed to the service when the original (failing) call was made.

A service that starts from a startService() invocation keeps running indefinitely, assuming no low-resource conditions cause Android to kill it and the user doesn't deactivate the device. This is in keeping with the fire-and-forget notions of startService() in that once your client has what it wants, it doesn't really care what happens to the service afterward.

As a developer, you might, from time to time, want to explicitly and gracefully shut down a service. For such a shut down, you have two options:

▓ Call the `stopService()` method, which is analogous to `startService()`, and provide either the same intent used to start the service as a parameter or an intent of a derived class. When you do, the service stops and all resources are released, the state is destroyed, and so on. Android does not track or count the number of `startService()` calls to a service, and it does not care which client sends the appropriate `stopService()` call. Only one `stopService()` command is needed to end the service, regardless of how many `startService()`methods the service received in its lifetime.

▓ Code your service logic so that the service calls `stopSelf()` itself, in effect terminating its own existence. You might do this as part of some logical culmination to the logic of your service, such as when a download has completed or an audio track has finished playback.

You are free to experiment with either approach to stopping services or just to leave the business of service cleanup to Android. Binding with services differs markedly in this area; I cover this next.

Binding to Services with bindService()

Whereas a command-driven approach of `startService()` is useful for one-time interaction with a service, at times you will want your application to have a longer-lived interaction with a service in which it sends multiple commands and receives data in response as part of the functionality you want to provide your users.

When a client binds to a service, in effect, it sets up a duplex communication channel that allows access to the service's published API through the service's `Binder` object. This `Binder` is the object returned from the `bindService()` call from the client, and it acts as the conduit for further activity. Just as with `startService()`, the client can signal to Android by using the `BIND_AUTO_CREATE` flag that it wants the service started if it is currently stopped. Unlike with the `startService()` approach, once a client releases the bind with the service, the service becomes a candidate to be shut down. I cover the shut down mechanics later in the chapter.

Caution If you attempt to bind to a service that is not already running, and you do not provide the `BIND_AUTO_CREATE` flag as part of the `bindService()` call, then the method returns `false` and no `Binder` object, which leaves you without a service to talk to. Even if you think you know the service's state, you should practice clean exception handling and always check for `bindService()` failure in these cases.

An additional flag is available to help you with non-graceful shutdown situations if the Android device is under memory pressure. The BIND_ALLOW_OOM_MANAGEMENT flag indicates that you are happy with your binding being considered noncritical, and that your application can tolerate the consequences of Android killing the service to recoup memory in out-of-memory situations. You are, in effect, signaling your willingness to sacrifice your binding for the sake of other applications.

A Binder class is provided by the Android framework, and normally you subclass this to implement whatever methods you want exposed as a form of API to your service's clients. Your imagination is pretty much the only limit here—you can have as few as one method, or as many as you deem necessary to provide your desired features.

A client's call to bindService() is an asynchronous call that includes the intent with which to identify the service, and the already-introduced optional (but usually useful) BIND_AUTO_CREATE flag. As an asynchronous method, the client making the bindService() call does not know the state of the service and this call until it interrogates the ServiceConnection object and the resulting Binder object is returned from onBind(). This is the point at which the client can start calling the Binder methods and actually interact with the functionality of the service.

Your client code is free to retain the ServiceConnection for as long as you desire. When the work with the service is ultimately finished, the unbindService() call signals that the binding to the service can be released and the ServiceConnection object and associated resources are freed. This process also means onServiceDisconnected() is eventually called, that the Binder object is no longer in scope, and that its API-like methods should no longer be invoked. If other client applications have bound to the service, and are therefore still happily using it, your call to unbindService() does not cause the service to stop. However, the last client to unbind will implicitly trigger Android to shut down the service without explicit calls or intervention from you.

Because your binding to a service is notiionally for a long time, you need to handle other lifecycle events that might affect your application. Configuration changes, such as screen rotation, are the main events to handle, and you can accommodate these by ensuring that your call to bindService() uses the application context, rather than the literal activity, so that your context survives the destroy-and-re-create process of the activity during rotation. You should also use the onRetainNonConfigurationInstance() lifecycle method to persist any state or resources you need.

Service-to-Client Communication

From the introduction to the service used in the preceding section, you can see client-to-service communication is well-covered by the command approach and the bind approach. The reverse flow, from the service to a client, is far less structured, although there are enough options to cover almost any scenario you can imagine. Let's cover the main options so you form an appreciation of what to use in various situations.

Use bindService Methods for All Communication

The first and most obvious option for service-to-client communication is to have all interaction happen via bindService() and the methods you create for clients to use. The advantage of the bind approach is that you control exactly what the client receives by the returned objects and information from your service methods, and this guarantees that the client actually gets what it asks for.

The obvious disadvantage is that any client that chooses to use the command-style approach to interacting, by firing off startService() calls, gets no such feedback mechanism for communication. This might not sound like a drawback now, but remember that you should design services to serve many different types of clients, so in fact this limitation hinders many possible users of your service.

Intents and Broadcast Receivers

Android already has a general approach for one component to signal or communicate with another component using broadcast intents and receivers. Cast you mind back to Chapter 12, and you should remember that you can trigger a broadcast intent from your code; you can do this just as easily from a service as from an activity.

This action allows you to register a BroadcastReceiver object via registerReceiver() in a client and capture a component-specific broadcast from the service, or some action imperative that you document so that the client can differentiate broadcast intents and process them accordingly.

The main drawback to this approach is that the intent must be action-orientated, rather than simply hoping for some activity to volunteer to act on a component. Additionally, in this case, you are assuming that the client activity itself is still running with its receiver and that it hasn't been paused or chosen for destruction due to other device-level events or resource constraints.

Use PendingIntent Objects

Android provides PendingIntent objects as a way of signifying an intent with an associated action that needs to be performed. In the service realm, your client uses onActivityResult() to deal with the down-stream logic once the service performs its work. The client passes the PendingIntent object to the service by adding it as an intent extra in the startService() call, and the service itself signals the client by calling the send() method on it.

The main disadvantage to this approach is the extra client code you need to interpret the variety of send() invocations that can be used, and that you need to identify exactly which one was called.

Use Messenger and Message Objects

As if `PendingIntent` objects were not enough, Android also provides the `Messenger` object to facilitate intercontext communication, such as from a service to an activity. Individual activities all have a `Handler` object that they can use to send messages to themselves, but the `Handler` is not exposed for activity-to-activity or activity-to-service interaction. A `Messenger` object can send messages to any `Handler`, and thus such objects can be used as intermediaries to bridge the gap.

To use a `Messenger` object, add it as an extra to your intent prior to service invocation. The service receives the intent as normal and can extract the `Messenger` object from the extras; when the time comes to communicate to the client, the service creates and populates a `Message` object, and then it calls the `.send()` method on the `Messenger` passing the `Message` as a parameter. Your client activity receives this via the `Handler` and its `handleMessage()` method.

The main drawbacks here are the additional steps you need to create and exchange `Messenger` and `Message` objects, and the fact that the `handleMessage()` method for your activity is processed on the main application thread, which means you want to keep message processing to a minimum, or at least hand off heavier processing to another thread you create.

Use Independent Messaging

A twist on the built-in option of `Messenger` objects is to use some external messaging or pub/sub system to deal with service-to-client communication. You might use such an approach when you don't strictly need real-time communication, but you know you will need such communication eventually.

The external messaging can leverage not just other messaging systems on the Android device, but also Internet-based messaging systems, such as Google Cloud Messaging. Google Cloud Messaging is a large topic in its own right, but Google has provided a good set of Android examples for its use; you can find these on the developer website at `https://developers.google.com/cloud-messaging/android`.

Create Callbacks and Listeners

The preceding examples of `Messenger` and `PendingIntent` objects show how easy it is to attach objects to the intent extras that are fed to a service. The principle requirement for any such object is that it is `Parcelable`; you can create your own objects that meet this criterion, such as a callback or listener of your own.

The logic follows a flow of you defining your listener objects and having the client and service coded to deploy and drop listeners as needed at specific times when communication is required. The main problem with this approach is that it is difficult to coordinate registering and retracting listeners so that neither the service nor the client is left with dangling or defunct listeners when the other party is trying to communicate. At best, this just leads to failed communication; at worst, as defunct listeners build up, you consume large amounts of memory.

Use Notifications

Although services have no direct UI themselves, there are ways to have services communicate via a client application's UI. One of these approaches involves the Notification object, which can present directly to the user. I cover notifications in depth in Chapter 23, so I will save the discussion until then.

Services in Action

Now that you are familiar with the theory and fundamentals of services and their behavior with Android, let's examine an example service and client application. There are a range of classic patterns for which services are used, such as audio playback, message delivery, management of a long-running download that doesn't need user involvement, and so on. For the purposes of having a useful but simple example, I mock up a photo-sharing service and simple client example application to demonstrate service theory in action. Remember the focus here is on engineering a service to make the theory concrete rather than rivaling Flickr with actual photo sharing.

Choosing the Service Design

The nature of our example photo sharing lends itself to the startService() model of firing off a command to "share" and not needing an ongoing to-and-fro interaction with binding. Let's devise our service from the base Service class and do the work of implementing the onStartCommand() method and the onBind() method (even though it is not used by our example client). Other subclasses provided with Android, such as IntentService, offer to cover much of the implementation for you, such as neatly calling stopService() automatically after your startService() call completes. In this case, we do not want or need some of those helpers—specifically, we want our service to live on after the startService() call so that we can later stop sharing if we want to.

The actual photos and who is sharing them are not important for the mechanics of how the service works, so I will leave those areas set out with comments. You are free to experiment and add images or other resources if you wish.

Implementing the Java Logic for Our Service

The ServiceExample implementation is relatively straightforward, covering the necessary implementation of overrides expected from the base Service class, plus our own service-specific logic for photo sharing. Listing 22-3 contains the full service implementation from the example in ch22/ClientExample.

Listing 22-3. Service Implementation for ServiceExample.java

```
package com.artifexdigital.android.clientexample;

import android.app.Service;
import android.content.Intent;
import android.os.IBinder;
import android.util.Log;
```

```java
public class ServiceExample extends Service {
    public static final String EXTRA_ALBUM="EXTRA_ALBUM";
    private boolean isShared=false;

    @Override
    public IBinder onBind(Intent intent) {
        // We need to implement onBind as a Service subclass
        // In this case we do not actually need it, so can simply return
        return(null);
    }

    @Override
    public int onStartCommand(Intent intent, int flags, int startId) {
        String album=intent.getStringExtra(EXTRA_ALBUM);
        startSharing(album);
        return(START_NOT_STICKY);
    }

    @Override
    public void onDestroy() {
        stopSharing(); }

    private void startSharing(String album) {
        if(!isShared) {
            // Simplified logic - you might have much more going on here
            Log.w(getClass().getName(), "Album successfully shared");
            isShared=true;
        }
    }

    private void stopSharing() {
        if(isShared) {
            // Simplified logic - you might have much more going on here
            Log.w(getClass().getName(), "Album sharing removed");
            isShared=false;
        }
    }

}
```

Because we are not doing any service-specific setup at service startup, we can omit extra logic in an onCreate() call and rely on the parent class to take care of this. We implement onStartCommand() so that we can take the appropriate action when the client calls startService(). Specifically, we examine the intent used to designate the service and find out the extras the ServiceExample wants—namely the name of the photo album to share. With the album name, a call is then made to the startSharing() method implemented for this specific service.

The startSharing() method is mostly commented out, as I mentioned earlier. One useful thing we can do is deal with the fact that services have no user interface by logging relevant information at various service method points. In practice, this helps you with all kinds of debugging, usage metrics, and so on. In our example, by watching the output in LogCat, you can see that the service is actually running and being used. This can be really useful to you if, for example, you forget to add the <service> element to your manifest. A lack of log output hints that the service isn't in use or even running.

Part way through this code, the onDestroy() method is implemented, and in this case, it simply calls our service's stopSharing() method. Like startSharing(), this is mostly commented out with some logging to help you confirm that your service code is working and being reached.

Even though the client example shown later in this chapter does not attempt to bind to the service, we still need to implement onBind() based on our subclassing from Service. However, we can leave this returning null in this instance. Other clients you might write could conceivably want to bind to our photo-sharing service to do fancier things, like show a photo montage, loop through the album, and so forth.

Creating an Example Client for the Service

You can just leave the service as is, but then you are left dangling with no way to actually test to see that it does what I say it does or to try out any of the modifications you might want to make. Listing 22-4 provides a simple layout for a client to drive our ServiceExample service.

Listing 22-4. The Layout for the ClientExample Application

```
<RelativeLayout xmlns:android="http://schemas.android.com/apk/res/android"
    xmlns:tools="http://schemas.android.com/tools"
    android:layout_width="match_parent"
    android:layout_height="match_parent"
    android:paddingLeft="@dimen/activity_horizontal_margin"
    android:paddingRight="@dimen/activity_horizontal_margin"
    android:paddingTop="@dimen/activity_vertical_margin"
    android:paddingBottom="@dimen/activity_vertical_margin"
    tools:context=".ClientExampleActivity">

    <Button
        android:id="@+id/startSharing"
        android:layout_width="match_parent"
        android:layout_height="wrap_content"
        android:text="Start Sharing"
        android:onClick="onClick" />

    <Button
        android:id="@+id/stopSharing"
        android:layout_width="fill_parent"
        android:layout_height="wrap_content"
        android:text="Stop Sharing"
        android:layout_below="@id/startSharing"
        android:onClick="onClick" />

</RelativeLayout>
```

This is not a particular sophisticated UI, as you will see when you test it out. The ClientExample application has just two buttons—one labeled "Start Sharing" and one labeled "Stop Sharing"—with android:id attributes of startSharing and stopSharing, respectively.

Because we are using the command-style approach to the service, the Java logic is also quite straightforward. Listing 22-5 shows the complete client logic.

Listing 22-5. Java Implementation of the Sample ClientExample Application

```
package com.artifexdigital.android.clientexample;

import android.app.Activity;
import android.content.Intent;
import android.os.Bundle;
import android.view.View;

public class ClientExampleActivity extends Activity {

    @Override
    protected void onCreate(Bundle savedInstanceState) {
        super.onCreate(savedInstanceState);
        setContentView(R.layout.activity_client_example);
    }

    public void onClick(View view) {
        switch(view.getId()) {
            case R.id.startSharing:
                startSharing(view);
                break;
            case R.id.stopSharing:
                stopSharing(view);
                break;
        }
    }

    public void startSharing(View view) {
        Intent myIntent=new Intent(this, ServiceExample.class);
        myIntent.putExtra(ServiceExample.EXTRA_ALBUM, "My Holiday Snaps");
        startService(myIntent);
    }

    public void stopSharing(View v) {
        stopService(new Intent(this, ServiceExample.class));
    }
}
```

By now the basic onCreate() method should be familiar, inflating the layout. My onClick() implementation performs the usual check for which button the user pressed and triggers either the startSharing() or stopSharing() method as needed.

The startSharing() method instantiates an intent for the service and provides a very credible album name for the particular photos we want to share. The service is called with startService() passing the intent. The stopSharing() implementation simply calls the stopService() command with a new intent of the appropriate type to match the original service call and thus targets our service correctly for shutdown.

Testing the Service in Action

I will leave running the service and watching the results to you. Don't forget to add the <service> entry to your manifest—for example,

```
<service android:name=".ServiceExample" />
```

If you do run the ClientExample application, when it triggers the calls to the ServiceExample service, you should see entries like this in LogCat.

```
...com.artifexdigital.android.clientexample.ServiceExample: Album successfully shared
...com.artifexdigital.android.clientexample.ServiceExample: Album sharing removed
```

Chapter **23**

Communicating with Notifications

One of the enduring features of all operating systems is their ability to seek your attention, calling you to action for some form of notification. Whether it is the arrival of a new email or an SMS message from a friend, a low battery warning, the confirmation of a purchase, or traffic alerts, notifications in Android are all about trying to get your attention.

Android devices have a range of ways to notify you that we explore in this chapter. The familiar tray icons that appear at the top of the Android launcher are likely familiar to you. After the examples of using dialog boxes earlier in the book, you should know all about pop-up style messages, and you might even have seen their downside—applications that get "pop-up happy" and insist on responses again and again.

Android also supports some hardware that, among other things, lends a hand on the notifications front. The vibration and haptic feedback mechanisms of a phone or tablet help you feel notifications, and phones, including ones as old as the original Dream/G1, incorporate a pulsing light in the trackwheel or a set of buttons that provide a visual clue to the user that notifications are waiting.

To make all of this work well for the user, and to make it all so it can be easily incorporated into applications by developers, it will not surprise you to learn that Android includes a complete framework as part of the SDK to help bring notifications to your applications.

Configuring Notifications

Applications have lots of ways of grabbing a user's attention when something interesting happens. But an application can also be paused, in the background, and frankly forgotten by the user when an event happens. Services do not even have a user interface through which they catch the user's eye. Applications and services also need ways to direct the user to the relevant activity in response to an event.

All of these requirements are handled in Android by the NotificationManager system service. To gain access to the NotificationManager, you need to pass the appropriate parameter to the getSystemService() method from your activity or your own service logic. In practice, this is as simple as creating an object with a call like this:

```
getSystemService(NOTIFICATION_SERVICE)
```

With the resulting NotificationManager object, you then have access to the main notification management methods. These are the typical methods with which you will normally control your notifications:

- notify(): This is the main method you would use to raise notifications according to your desired triggers and events. This takes a Notification object as a parameter, which is the main data structure that carries the payload of your notification—text, images, and so on—as well as the way or ways in which you would like to catch the user's attention.

- cancel(): To dismiss a notification, you use the cancel() method. Android is also able to cancel notification in response to certain user actions, such as swipe-to-dismiss gestures.

- cancelAll(): Use this method when you just want to get rid of all the notifications that a NotificationManager object has active.

Customizing the Notification Object

Out of the box, notifications are quite functional and include a bunch of sensible defaults to help catch the user's attention. But sometimes you want to up the ante and make your notification irresistible. The Notification object has methods to enhance and customize your notification.

> **Note**   Some of the following methods are from the original methods and data members available for the Notification object. Starting in API level 11, several of these methods—in particular the constructor—were deprecated in favor of a slightly different approach. I cover all of the original ways of configuring a notification since this allows you to understand individual configuration options one at a time. At the end of the chapter, I demonstrate how to use the newer builder option to perform all the configurations using the new approach.
>
> The good news is the older approach may be deprecated, but it is still available all the way up to and including Android version 6.0 Marshmallow.

Adding Sounds to Your Notification

Android supports the notion of default sounds for many different types of notifications, all of which can be configured by the device user. This means that you can avoid having to manually specify sounds if you do not want to go to that effort and simply tell your Notification object to use the default sound by invoking its .defaults() method as follows:

```
Notification myNotification = new Notification(...);
myNotification.defaults = Notification.DEFAULT_SOUND;
```

Where you do wish to provide your own sounds, it is as simple as providing the Uri reference to a sound file resource. This can be a sound file of your own that you have added to your raw project resources, or a Uri reference to one of the many sounds that come prepackaged with Android.

For instance, to use the Kalimba sound that ships as part of stock Android, you can source the Uri for this resource using the ContentResolver class, and assign the sound accordingly:

```
Notification myNotification = new Notificiation(...);
myNotification.sound = Uri.parse(ContentResolver.SCHEME_ANDROID_RESOURCE +
                                 "://" +
                                 getPackageName() +
                                 "/raw/kalimba");
```

One very important aspect to remember with notification sounds (and several other notification attributes we discuss shortly) is that if you assign a sound via .sound() and set .defaults() to include the flag DEFAULTS_SOUND, then the default always overrides the custom sound, regardless of the order in which you call the methods on your Notification object.

Shining a Light for Your Notification

Almost all phone and tablet-format Android devices come with a built-in LED light below the main screen. This has several uses, but the primary one is to aid in notifying users of events like notifications. You can control this LED in various ways by configuring your Notification object.

- Set the .lights() method to true, which activates the LED.

- Where color is supported, use ledARGB and your desired hex code for the RGB-based color you wish to use to have a device change the color of the LED.

- Control blinking speed and spacing using the ledOnMS and ledOffMS values, which express on and off times in milliseconds.

Whatever customization you wish to perform, you should also make sure you set the Notification.flags field to include the Notification.FLASH_SHOW_LIGHTS flag. On devices with simpler LEDs, your choice of color might be ignored and replaced with a different brightness of the fixed color the LED supports. Also, a handful of devices have color-variable LEDs, but their manufacturers haven't included the necessary support for the Notification class so that you are able to control color.

This raises a larger point that you should keep in mind. Your application can also run on devices that do not have a notification LED, such as an Android TV or an in-car system. It is best to think of your LED customization as a useful extra, rather than the only tool for gaining the user's attention.

Vibrating to Shake Things Up

If lights and sounds are not enough to get your user's attention, try shocking them into action with a little vibration. Another default flag exists to allow use of the device-wide default.

```
myNotification.defaults = Notifcation.DEFAULT_VIBRATE;
```

Note that in order for your application to be permitted to make a device vibrate, you must ask for `<uses-permission android:name="android.permission.VIBRATE" />` in your application manifest. You can also perform custom vibration via `.vibrate()`, providing a `long[]` of the duration of on/off timing for the vibration, with values in milliseconds. For example, `new long[] {1000, 500, 1000, 500, 1000}` makes your notification vibrate three times for a second each, with a half-second pause between vibrations.

Adding Icons for Notifications

So far, each of the notification customizations has aimed to catch the user's attention. Icons differ in that they attempt to provide more information to the user regarding what the notification is about once they have actually noticed it.

In addition to providing the drawables that convey more meaning to your user, you also need to provide a `contentIntent` value, `PendingIntent`, which should be raised when the user decides to touch the icon in your notification. As you saw in earlier chapters, a `PendingIntent` acts as a wrapper and a "snooze" function allowing you to ready an `Intent` to later trigger some activity, service, or what have you.

One more flourish is available when you are adding an icon and `contentIntent` to your notification. You are also allowed to add a short piece of text to include via the `tickerText` attribute. This is where you can put the most important part of the notification text, such as the name of a person sending a message in a messaging app, the subject of an email, the caption of a photo, and so on. If you want to save coding effort and you plan on including all three of the icons, `contentIntent` and `tickerText`, the `setLatestEventInfo()` method allows you to specify all three in a single call.

Icon Sizes for Old and New Android Versions

If you like the notion of adding icons to your notifications, then consider what kind of fidelity you would like your icons to have across older and newer Android versions and different screen densities.

To support all of Android's recommended notification styles and sizes, you need to provide four or more different drawables that represent your icon:

■ A 25-pixel square for all Android versions prior to 2.3 (and regardless of actual screen density on those old devices). This is placed in the `res/drawable resource` folder.

■ A 24-pixel by 38-pixel bounding box, housing a 24-pixel square icon, for use on high-density, extra-high-density, and extra-extra-high-density screens. This icon is placed in the `res/drawable-hdpi-v9`, `res/drawable-xhdpi-v9`, and `res/drawable-xxhdpi-v9` folders.

■ A 16-pixel by 25-pixel bounding box, housing a 16-pixel square icon, for use on medium-density screens. This icon is placed in the `res/drawable-mdpi` folder.

■ A 12-pixel by 19-pixel bounding box, housing a 12-pixed square icon, for use on low-density screens. This icon is placed in the `res/drawable-ldpi-v9` project folder.

More details on icon styling and use are available in the design section of the Android developer site. This includes some useful information on up-scaling and down-scaling drawables where you decide not to include one or more of the size-and-density-specific icons for your application. It is not the end of the world to omit one of these icons, but you should at least be aware of the possible poor onscreen look of your notification if you choose to skip one.

Floating Numbers for Added Information

One type of flourish on notifications you may have already seen, and have come to appreciate, is the extra floating "number" that can appear over an icon to summarize either the count of similar notifications, or unread/unresponded notifications.

The `Notification` object includes a public member named `number` that you can set directly with the number you wish to have appear in the top-right or top-left corner of the icon (depending on locale and right-to-left or left-to-right convention on the device). By default this value is not set, and in the unset state, Android simply ignores it and does not attempt to show any number as an icon overlay.

Notifications in Action

Now that you are familiar with the concepts and customizable features of notifications with Android, let's take a look at the first example application that shows a bunch of these features in action. The `NotificationExample` sample is provided in the `ch23/NotificationExample` folder.

The layout is very similar to some of the two-button test layouts you have already seen for other examples in the book. Figure 23-1 shows the layout with the two buttons: one to fire the notification, and another to clear it.

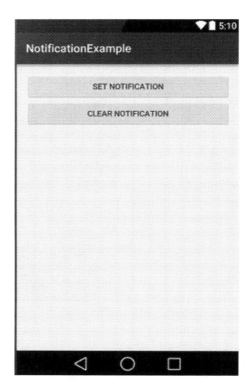

Figure 23-1. *The basic NotificationExample layout, with no notifications showing*

There are no particularly noteworthy features to the layout XML, so I will omit it to save space—feel free to browse the XML in the ch23/NotificationExample project.

Coding Notification Behavior

The code for NotificationExample, shown in Listing 23-1, is interesting.

Listing 23-1. Implementing the Code for NotificationExample

```
package com.artifexdigital.android.notificationexample;

import android.app.Activity;
import android.app.Notification;
import android.app.NotificationManager;
import android.app.PendingIntent;
import android.content.Intent;
import android.net.Uri;
import android.os.Bundle;
import android.view.View;
```

```java
public class NotificationExample extends Activity {
    private static final int NOTIFICATION_ID=12345;
    private int notifyCount = 0;
    private NotificationManager myNotifyMgr = null;

    @Override
    protected void onCreate(Bundle savedInstanceState) {
        super.onCreate(savedInstanceState);
        setContentView(R.layout.activity_notification_example);
        myNotifyMgr = (NotificationManager)getSystemService(NOTIFICATION_SERVICE);
    }

    public void onClick(View view) {
        switch(view.getId()) {
            case R.id.notify:
                raiseNotification(view);
                break;
            case R.id.clearNotify:
                dismissNotificaiton(view);
                break;
        }
    }
    public void raiseNotification(View view) {
        Notification myNotification = new Notification(
                                          R.drawable.wavinghand,
                                          "Notice This",
                                          System.currentTimeMillis());
        PendingIntent myPendingI = PendingIntent.getActivity(this, 0,
                new Intent(this, NotificationFollowon.class), 0);

        myNotification.setLatestEventInfo(this,
                                             "Title",
                                             "Notification contents",
                                             myPendingI);

        myNotification.sound = Uri.parse("android.resource://" +
                                  getPackageName() +
                                  "/" +
                                  R.raw.pop);
        myNotification.vibrate=new long[] {1000L, 500L, 1000L, 500L, 1000L};
        myNotification.number=++notifyCount;
        myNotification.flags|=Notification.FLAG_AUTO_CANCEL;

        myNotifyMgr.notify(NOTIFICATION_ID,myNotification);
    }

    public void dismissNotificaiton(View view) {
        myNotifyMgr.cancel(NOTIFICATION_ID);
    }
}
```

Although there is a reasonable amount of code here, and in the companion NotifcationFollowon class, much of it should already be familiar to you. Setting up the activity in onCreate() does the normal task of restoring or creating state and inflating the layout, in addition to the work of creating the myNotifyMgr object to bind to the system notification infrastructure. The NotificationExample class itself also sets up a ficticious ID for the notification and a counter to track how many pending notifications there are. Note that you can easily decide to have multiple different types of notifications from your application. If you decide to do this, be sure to use a different ID to distinguish each type.

Employing the onClick() method establishes the familiar pattern I use to group button-click handling together—though, again, in this example, you can just as easily have each button call the relevant raiseNotification() and dismissNotification() methods directly. It is the implementation of these methods that houses our interesting notification logic.

Within the raiseNotification() method, we perform almost all of the optional configuration and customization I described at the start of the chapter. First, we create the Notification object and assign the wavinghand.png icon and the status text to use on versions of Android that support showing status text at the time of notification.

Next, we create a PendingIntent that points at the NotificationFollowon activity. This is triggered if a user decides to click on the wavinghand.png icon in the notification drawer. The PendingIntent is then bundled with a notification title and an additional notification message using the setLatestEventInfo() method, and it is ready for deployment into the notification drawer.

Lastly, we go to town using all of the extra notification bells and whistles for the Notification object:

- .sound() is called and given the pop.mp3 sound as a resource from the raw folder.

- .vibrate() is called with a cadence of one second on, half a second off of vibration.

- .number() is called to increment the number of times the notification has been raised.

- .flags() is called to include the FLAG_AUTO_CANCEL option in the flags field.

With all of the options configured, we finally pass the Notification object and the NOTIFICATION_ID to the NotificationManager for presentation to the user.

Notifications as the User Experiences Them

Running the NotificationExample application in a virtual device provides most of the experience of notifications. Figure 23-2 shows the notification appearing in the icon bar of the home screen.

Figure 23-2. Notification triggered in top-left corner—the small waving hand icon

The little waving hand icon can be a bit hard to make out on the printed page, so definitely try running the example for yourself to see it appear in your own virtual device. Depending on the API levels supported by your AVD, you may or may not see the additional status text associated with the Notification object.

Clicking the Clear Notification button makes the icon disappear, and if you are fast enough to click it while the pop sound is still playing or a real device is still vibrating, those additional customizations also stop.

The notification stays in place throughout the lifecycle of the activity, and even after you have gone off to other applications or have returned to the launcher home screen. Try it for yourself, and you should still see the notificication icon, as in Figure 23-3.

Figure 23-3. Notification icon persists even after leaving activity

At any point after the notification has fired, the device user can access the notification drawer that collects all the notifications from all the applications on the device. They do this by grabbing the bar at the top of the screen and dragging all the way to the bottom. Figure 23-4 shows our example notification with many of the additional details we added, including the notification title and additional text.

Figure 23-4. The notifications drawer open, showing our notification

What you see in the notification drawer is heavily dependent on the release of Android you are using. The most modern Lollipop and Marshmallow approach is shown in Figure 23-4, with our icon chosen from the appropriate screen density resource or scaled from the nearest available resource packaged within the application. Our 25-by-25 pixel waving hand is far more recognizable in the notification drawer. The title and additional text are shown, along with the timestamp passed to the Notification object at creation time.

You will also notice that the number value is presented in the notification drawer of newer Android releases, instead of as an overlay on the icon in the icon bar. This change was largely driven by the tendency of the icons to become crowded and overwhelmed on phone-sized screens, so it was moved to the drawer, which made it more likely that it wouldn't be lost in the noise.

The user can click the icon to trigger the follow-on activity, or they can simply dismiss the notification—just as if they had hit the Clear Notification button on the activity home screen. In Android version 4.0 (Ice Cream Sandwich) and later, you also see the three slightly offset horizontal bars below the notifications; this is the dismiss all option. This triggers the cancelAll() method on all active NotificationManager objects, which completely clears the notification drawer.

A completely clear notification drawer looks like the depiction in Figure 23-5.

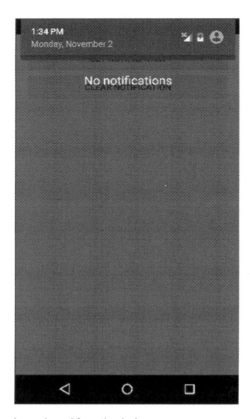

Figure 23-5. *All notifications have been cleared from the device*

Note that clearing notifications in this fashion does not necessarily clear the notification count you may have been tracking in your application. Remember, just because you have switched away from the application, doesn't mean Android has necessarily triggered onDestroy() or reaped the application for its resources.

Using the Builder Approach to Notifications

At the beginning of the chapter, I pointed out that there were newer approaches to creating your Notification objects that were introduced from API level 11 on. The main change to be aware of is the preference for using a NotificationBuilder object to handle all of the configuration and customization for your notification.

This means that the followingaspects of the original Notifcation class are flagged as deprecated, though support is still provided in the most recent Android version 6.0 Marshmallow release.

- ▓ Overloaded options for the constructor are deprecated.
- ▓ The setLatestEventInfo() method is deprecated.

The `Notification.Builder` allows you to stack method calls for all the components of the `Notification` you wish to customize. This means that in the `NotificationExample` sample application, we can replace our constructor call and our subsequent call to `setLatestEventInfo()` with the following use of the builder:

```
Notification myNotification = new Notification.Builder(context)
    .setContentTitle("Notice this")
    .setContentText("Notification content")
    .setSmallIcon(R.drawable.wavinghand)
    .setLargeIcon(R.drawable.wavinghand)
    .setContentIntent(myPendingI)
    .setWhen(System.currentTimeMillis())
    .build();
```

Note that we need to move the declaration of the `contentIntent`'s `PendingIntent` object so it falls before we use the builder so it is in scope for the `.setContentIntent()` call. In most other respects, you can see the equivalent aspects of the traditional notification constructor and other calls in the builder approach.

Other Uses and Extensions to Notifications

Notifications have enjoyed almost constant enhancement since Android was released, and I touch on more advanced uses next. There is a great deal more to the advanced features that are beyond the scope of this book, but you can read about them online at the Android developer site.

Notifications and Services

In Chapter 22, we discussed services and their traditional nature of staying in the background and being invisible to the user, while, at the same time, performing useful tasks or actions for the user. Remember that services can also be subject to Android's need to reclaim resources, and so they can be killed off when memory is heavily constrained. Although you know about the "stickiness" and out-of-memory controls for services, there is another approach to keeping services around when they otherwise might be subject to termination, and this method involves using notifications.

A service can declare that it should be considered at the priority level of foreground, which gives it the same chance of surviving as the applications that are currently in `onCreate()`/`onResume()` parts of their lifecycle. The cost to you as a developer is that you must implement a user notification that flags to the device user that your service has taken on foreground priority.

You achieve the move to foreground by calling the `startForeground()` method in your service's `onCreate()` logic. The `startForeground()` method takes a `Notification` object as a parameter, and it takes a unique ID, just as the `.notify()` method for `NotificationManager` does. You can guess what `startForeground()` does with those parameters. If you need or want to move the service to the background priority level, you call `stopForeground()` and this also uses the `cancel()` method under the hood with the relevant `NotificationManager` object to clear the related notification.

More Advanced Notification Features

Although this chapter has focused on the fundamentals of notifications, you should at least be aware of the many types of advanced notification features Google has added in recent releases. Many of these styles of notifications were tailored to suit particular derivations of Android, such as Google Glass, Android Wear, and the TV and in-car modificaitons to Android. I could fill a book that just deals with all of the nuances and possibilities of advanced notification features, but we just do not have the page count to spare.

Instead, here is an overview of some of the more interesting new-style notifications; the Android developer documentation can help you learn more.

Timeline Notifications

This is more of a formatting approach than a leap in functionality. With the introduction of Google Glass, Google created a larger notification canvas with options for much larger images. Figure 23-6 shows the classic Timeline Notification teaser.

Figure 23-6. A notification formatted for Google Glass's timeline format

Bundled Notifications

Bundled notifications take the idea of the number attribute that counts multiple notifications and turns it on its head. Instead of just presenting a count, a bundled notification presents a "top" notification and visual cues allow the user to open the bundle and see all the related notifications. Figure 23-7 shows a top-level notification for a bundled notification.

Figure 23-7. The top notification in a bundle of notifications

The key visual cue that this is a bundle is the folded corner motif in the top-right. The user can actually swipe that part of the notification to reveal all of the notifications that constitute the bundle. Figure 23-8 shows a sample of notifications in a bundle.

Figure 23-8. The notifications within a bundle

The one additional UI feature here is the subtle white bar at the bottom of the bundled notifications. The bar is divided into a number of sections equal to the number of notifications in the bundle. The highlighted part of the footer bar changes to represent which notification in the bundle the user is viewing.

Expanding Notifications

From Android version 4.1 Jelly Bean on, Google added support for expanding notifications that do not trigger an activity when the notification is clicked. Instead, expandable notifications can increase their size within the notifications drawer and show additional content as well as one or more embedded actions (I will discuss embedded actions momentarily). This allows the user to make much more use of larger screens like tablets and phablets, as well as move straight to the desired response action rather than having to navigate to the contentIntent-triggered activity and then chose an action.

Figure 23-9 shows a notification that has expanded to a much larger size, using a background image, and with two embedded actions for the user to quickly use.

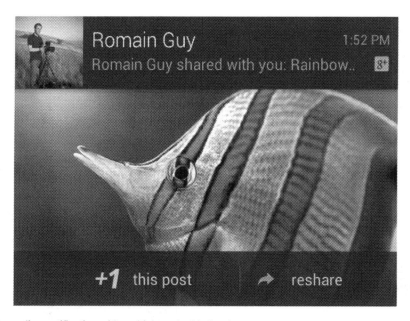

Figure 23-9. Expanding notification with multiple embedded actions

More Embedded Actions in Notifications

One particular set of new features promoted by Google across all the variants of the Android platform is the ability to add direct actions to the notification. Whereas the traditional notification can use the contentIntent member of the Notification object to trigger a specific activity, embedded actions provide more context and the abililty to label the tasks (multiple!) that can be performed. This, in effect, gives you capabilities like a mini embedded menu of actions inside the notification. Figure 23-10 shows a simple reply function surfaced within a message notification.

Figure 23-10. *Actions within a timeline notification*

Notifications Tailored for Wear

With the recent rapid growth in the wearable Android space, it will come as no surprise that specific wearable-tailored notification styles exist in Android version 4.3 KitKat and later versions. The main options available cover the aesthetics of text sizing and placement with images, as shown in Figure 23-11, plus full support for square and round screen displays translating into appropriately shaped notifications.

Figure 23-11. *Circular notifications for Android Wear*

Index

U, V

W

X

Y, Z

Get the eBook for only $5!

Why limit yourself?

Now you can take the weightless companion with you wherever you go and access your content on your PC, phone, tablet, or reader.

Since you've purchased this print book, we're happy to offer you the eBook in all 3 formats for just $5.

Convenient and fully searchable, the PDF version enables you to easily find and copy code—or perform examples by quickly toggling between instructions and applications. The MOBI format is ideal for your Kindle, while the ePUB can be utilized on a variety of mobile devices.

To learn more, go to www.apress.com/companion or contact support@apress.com.

Printed in the United States
By Bookmasters